SEXUAL ASTROLOGY

SEXUAL ASTROLOGY

MARLENE MASINI RATHGEB

AVON BOOKS ◆ NEW YORK

SEXUAL ASTROLOGY is an original publication of Avon Books. This work
has never before appeared in book form.

AVON BOOKS
A division of
The Hearst Corporation
1350 Avenue of the Americas
New York, New York 10019

Copyright © 1993 by Marlene Masini Rathgeb
Cover painting "Man's Shameful Fall" by J. Von Carolsfeld, courtsey of
Superstock
Published by arrangement with the author
Library of Congress Catalog Card Number: 92-30259
ISBN: 0-380-76888-7

Library of Congress Cataloging in Publication Data:
Rathgeb, Marlene Masini.
   Sexual astrology / Marlene Masini Rathgeb.
      p.   cm.
1. Astrology and sex.   I. Title.
BF1729.S4R38   1993
133.5'83067—dc20   92-30259
                                                              CIP

First Avon Books Trade Printing: February 1993

AVON TRADEMARK REG. U.S. PAT. OFF. AND IN OTHER COUNTRIES, MARCA
REGISTRADA, HECHO EN U.S.A.

Printed in the U.S.A.

OPM   10 9 8 7 6 5 4 3 2 1

Contents

Illuminations

*Render heavy what is light and light what is
heavy; make earth with air and air with earth;
transform fire into water and water into fire:
such is the Art.*

Hermetic Formula
Hermes Trismegistus
Ancient Egyptian Philosopher

Part 1

Sex, Sign and Psyche

Prologue

"**I**T'S A BOY!" "IT'S A GIRL!" THE MOST BASIC AND CRITICAL FACT of human identity is set in stone by this brief announcement from the attending doctor in the delivery room. With prenatal testing now a commonplace, it is often even earlier for those parents who can't wait to know the sex of their unborn child.

Belonging to one sex or the other is more fundamental to forming your "I am" than race, creed, national origin or social status. Despite the enormous changes affecting sex roles in our society, when it comes to determining who you are and how others see you, before you are black or white, American or European, have brown eyes or blue, you are a male or a female.

The primary indicator of sex is the genitalia. How they are formed and how they function carry more weight in determining sex scientifically than any other biological criterion—i.e., chromosomes, hormones, body shape or size. Though these factors play a role in the technical determination of maleness and/or femaleness, no matter how much roles are reversed or how egalitarian society eventually becomes in its treatment of men and women, anatomy really is destiny in terms of defining which sex you belong to. Beyond biology, sociology and just what kind

3

of upbringing you had, however, it is necessary to enter the conceptual/psychological realm to understand the far more complex issue of gender—i.e., what constitutes "masculinity" if not simply being a man; what is "femininity" if not merely being a biological member of the feminine sex?

As recent history has shown, being a biological male or a biological female does not, contrary to the once-popular belief of many people, automatically confer what we call "masculine" traits on men or "feminine" traits on women. These are gender characteristics and far more difficult to pin down in terms of origin or attribution. One proof of this is that in our time we have seen such dramatic shifts in sex roles that, beyond the act of conception, the process of childbirth and breast-feeding, there is virtually no "masculine" turf a woman may not tread on and no "feminine" function a man may not fulfill, or at least attempt to. Another is the fact that when we speak of an "aggressive" woman and/or a "sensitive" man, there is still the suggestion of anomaly. It just isn't "normal." Regardless of how far we have come, certain qualities and characteristics are still firmly gender-linked, and even at this point in time show few signs of becoming unglued.

As for "thinking like a man" or "thinking like a woman" (a favorite sexist subject), the jury is still out. Scientists and researchers have yet to turn up any differences between the male and female brains that are truly significant in determining abilities and attitudes. For instance, chess—one of the previously "men only" domains—has been dramatically invaded by females. Successful women architects defy the contention that men are better at thinking in three dimensions. One of the most interesting differences, however, suggests that a larger canal between the right and left halves of the brain may mean women are more able to intercommunicate between hemispheres. We also know that more women focus their language skills in the frontal lobe, while more men focus language skills in the parietal lobe, which may affect language abilities. Still, statistically speaking, even the biggest differences in male and female brain functions are not as large as the differences in male and female height, and consequently are not a major factor in explaining what makes for "maleness" and what for "femaleness."

So Why "La Difference"?

No one can deny that, despite theoretically equal access to attributes and attitudes labeled "masculine" and "feminine," there is an enormous difference in the way men and women see, react to and negotiate the world we live in. As writer P.D. James puts it, "... a visitor from Mars might immediately conclude that men and women are different species." One of the eternal questions is—and may well always be—how do men become "masculine" (attitudinally speaking) and women become "feminine"? And within these all too physically apparent categories, what accounts for the vast differences between individual men and women? Our world contains both Gloria Steinem and Zsa Zsa Gabor, Sly Stallone and Dustin Hoffman.

Most sociologists and researchers agree that the particular orientation of any specific male or female is to a large degree a matter of familial and societal conditioning. As soon as your sex is determined at birth, you start to be subjected to a whole set of gender-linked expectations and activities. Before you know if you are a boy or a girl (the difference dawns on children at about the age of three or four), your environment has had a head start, sending "masculine" or "feminine" messages to the barely yet formed human individual. Even the most enlightened parents who do their best to practice "unisex" child rearing report that gender bias creeps in anyway. Boys love anything that moves on wheels, and often "car" is the first word in their vocabulary; girls nurture whatever comes their way. However, the reverse is also true in many cases, which complicates and continues the nature/nurture debate.

Many people are convinced that male/female differences are "in the genes," and there is nothing anyone can do about it; boys will be boys and girls will be girls, with all the gender bias that connotes. Others blame gender typing on Uncle Joe, who gave Billy his first and only gun, or on Aunt Carrie, who insists her niece not be denied "girls' rights" . . . i.e., such feminine pursuits as doll play and make-believe cooking. Still others claim that, sociologically speaking, the more things change, the more they remain the same, and that signs of progress toward a more egalitarian system are merely surface changes. Children themselves, just by being the unique individuals they are, sometimes outsmart the system by coming to their own conclusions; one young woman, now a very feminine female in her twenties, spent the years between preschool and prepuberty insisting on dressing like a boy and consorting with one sole companion—a boy with whom she identified completely. When asked why she behaved as she did, she gave no complicated psychological reasons. She simply said: "I figured out very early that boys had it better."

The truth about what makes men "masculine" and women "feminine" probably exists somewhere in the tangle of all the theories. From the biological perspective, no one can deny that body size and weight, for instance, determine many differences in how men and women are perceived and how they function. Hormones rage in both sexes, and should be regarded as highly significant. But no one can say for sure.

From the viewpoint of societal conditioning, no matter how much more savvy and enlightened they have become, advertising messages literally scream stereotyped gender differences from morning to night. While both male and female "buddy" movies have caused positive comment, they are certainly not forming a wave large enough to put a dent in our classic "boy meets girl" fantasy romances. When it comes to relative femininity or masculinity, one cannot totally dismiss individual bias and personal awareness, as in the case of the prepubescent cross-dresser. Our surroundings, however subtly, put us in the "male" or the "female" box. Once inside, we find it almost impossible not to be ascribed behaviors and attitudes that are classically "masculine" or "feminine." Despite the incredible changes in our view of maleness and femaleness over the past twenty-five years, such centuries-ingrown attitudes die hard, and they are still in the death throes.

The question is not whether men and women are different from each other—they are, obviously, in countless ways and for a whole set of complex reasons. What this book seeks to explore and to illuminate is what "masculinity" and "femininity" are, apart from the biological facts, and to apply the dimension of astrology to the subject of individual gender identity—that is, both how one feels and how one acts as a member of either sex.

This book recognizes that the whole subject of sex and gender, sex roles and sexual preference, is fraught with intricate and often highly technical complications. At some point, scientists may even discover why humans—in fact, the whole mammalian class—need two sexes at all to reproduce. They tell us there are far easier and more efficient ways to produce offspring, as many lower forms of life do. We do not even really know what caused the shift to estrus, as it is called—that is, why human females are able to reproduce at virtually any time, and why the mating season is a year-round affair for human males.

For now, however—and happily for most—the two-person sex system and the human way of relating are here to stay. However, the differences between men and women—both as groups and as individuals—carry far more weight in our society than merely where they take people romantically and sexually. In a very real sense, one's degree of maleness and femaleness, one's mix of masculine and feminine characteristics, may be the most dominant factor in determining who we are as individual psychological entities, what we do with our lives and—perhaps even more important—how we relate to others, and eventually to the right partner.

Chapter 1

Astrology and Gender

THIS BOOK ADDS AN ANCIENT DIMENSION TO THE MODERN DEBATE concerning the role of nature versus nurture in the development of gender identity—a dimension that has been largely overlooked in our scientific/technological culture. That is, an individual's astrological inheritance.

The subject of astrology has passed through a number of phases since its "rediscovery" in the 1960s. Forgotten dimensions of the subject have been brought to light; scholars who would have previously dismissed the subject now find it valid for inquiry; many psychologists embrace it as an enlightening factor in understanding the human personality. Astrology has a lot to say about gender identity and individual "masculinity" and "femininity"— and its ancient/modern wisdom deserves consideration.

Masculine Signs and Feminine Signs

It usually comes as a surprise to most people, who know the signs of the zodiac mainly as lists of set-in-stone characteristics, that there is much more to the great circle of humanity the zodiac really represents. Astrology is a psy-

9

cho-philosophical system that contains dimensions virtually unknown to those who, intriguing as astrological
prediction is, confine their interest to daily horoscope
columns.

To begin to explain the "why" of the signs, it is significant that the twelve signs are grouped into six that are
designated "masculine"—Aries, Leo, Sagittarius, Gemini,
Aquarius and Libra—and six that are designated "feminine"—Taurus, Virgo, Capricorn, Cancer, Scorpio and Pisces. The mix of feminine and masculine signs the planets
are placed in, in a natal or birth horoscope, has a great
influence in determining the psychological "gender balance" of the individual.

At any given moment—for the purposes of this book,
the moment of your birth—the eight planets of the solar
system, plus the astrologically all-important Sun and
Moon, are observed from our perspective on Earth to be
placed in portions of the zodiac that correspond to specific signs. The "freeze frame" of the planetary picture in
the sky at the time of your birth is your natal horoscope
(literally "picture of the hour"). It is as individual as a fin-
gerprint and as fixed-for-life as your eye color.

For most people who are startled to learn that the signs
have gender, the first question is "Do feminine-sign men
and masculine-sign women tend to be homosexual?" No,
that's not the way it plays out. Your astrological heritage—
your natal horoscope—is not a measure of your physical
sexuality, and has no bearing on sexual preference. Astrologically speaking, gender characteristics affect psychological rather than sexual performance, and hence are
completely neutral. Any heterosexual man can be born
with a predominantly feminine horoscope, and any heterosexual woman with a predominantly masculine one.

What your astrological gender imprint does affect is
your overall personality and attitudes, your sense of gender identity, your choices about how to make your way in
the world and to organize your life. With reference to male/
female relationships, it is often the "missing piece" that

explains why we choose the people we do—and often, why the relationship works out the way it does.

Why are the signs masculine and feminine? The earliest reasons for the designations are lost in the very complex history of astrology that stretches back about five thousand years, to ancient Egypt. The Greeks made the greatest contribution to the organization of astrological knowledge and lore into a comprehensible and "neat" package, and it was probably at this time that the masculine/feminine dichotomy became one of astrology's most basic "rules." When you analyze the signs in their natural or seasonal order, you begin to get a sense of why, metaphysically, they follow naturally from each other, like the universe breathing in and out. Aries, the first sign of the zodiac, begins at the first moment of the vernal equinox. Its symbolism, highly sexual, has to do with initiating and inseminating, causing natural things to be given life, as they do in spring. Taurus, which follows it, is feminine. What Aries sows, Taurus nurtures and helps grow. Gemini, following Taurus, is masculine—a form of the "wind god" that supports whatever nature brings forth, and gives it room to grow. Cancer, the ultimate nurturer, is feminine, and brings nature to its full season in Leo, masculine.

Astrology and Androgyny

One valid way to think of the masculine signs and the feminine signs is as the two faces of humanness—opposite but equally valid ways of being in the world. Many psychologists, particularly the Jungians, as well as scholars and philosophers, believe that the ideal human being is the one who exhibits a perfect balance of male and female gender qualities.

This is the true meaning of androgyny. Rather than residing in provocative cross-dressing or blatantly publicizable behavior, androgyny is a human condition to be strived for, a state of being that transcends what we commonly think of as "masculine" or "feminine" and results in psychological wholeness. Carl Jung called the uniting of masculine and feminine qualities in the individual the "inner marriage" and regarded this as the highest level of human development.

A person's astrological heritage—or imprint—places him or her somewhere on the spectrum between ultramasculine and ultrafeminine, with the androgynous personality as the midpoint. One thing this book does is show you where you fall on that spectrum, and tells you how you can become more totally human by developing gender characteristics you may need. In effect, *Sexual Astrology* is about becoming more androgynous: hence, more human. And also more capable of developing more harmonious and rewarding relationships with the opposite sex. Psychologists like C. G. Jung and June Singer believe that no truly positive or meaningful relationship can be developed between two people until both have achieved the balance of masculine and feminine in themselves.

Astrological Signs as Sex Symbols

Astrology, rightly understood, is a symbolic language; one astrologer refers to the signs of the zodiac as the "twelve-letter alphabet." Actually, the zodiacal signs are really symbols: they stand for a whole body of meanings which add up to a single concept. A true symbol has a multitude of connotations that are really shades of one central idea or theme. An example is the American flag; what it signifies can't be summed up in a few well-chosen words, but all of its connotations belong in one basket.

Each of the masculine signs (Aries, Leo, Sagittarius, Gemini, Libra and Aquarius) stands for a specific facet of "masculinity." Each of the feminine signs (Taurus, Virgo, Capricorn, Cancer, Scorpio and Pisces) symbolizes a specific aspect of "femininity." In sum, they stand for the "ideal" human personality. It is doubtful that throughout history any such individual has ever existed. More to the point, it is highly unlikely that this book can transform any all-too-human being into the perfect personality. However, once you know your own astrological gender profile, learn which qualities it has and which it lacks, you will be in a far better position to "do the right thing" when life requires it.

Chapter 2

Sex Vs. Gender: Drawing the Line

IT TAKES SOME MIND-STRETCHING TO CONCEIVE OF THE QUALITIES of the "masculine" and the "feminine," apart from flesh-and-blood human beings of either sex. There are several ways of "thinking about the unthinkable" that are help-ful—and essential if you are to use this book to assess your own mix of masculine and feminine characteristics positively, and begin to regard gender in a neutral way.

One is the ancient Oriental concept of Yin and Yang. In this philosophical system, Yin (femaleness) and Yang (maleness) are general principles or symbolic images. Everything in the universe that can be experienced by the senses is seen as partaking of various proportions of Yin and Yang—"feminine" energy and "masculine" energy. They are like two poles of a battery—essential opposites. Yang, or masculine energy, is seen as outgoing, positive, active . . . the "plus" side of the battery. Yin, or feminine energy, is receptive, intaking, passive . . . the "negative" pole of the battery.

It is already easy to see why, in Western society, value

judgments are immediately applied to each type of energy. Yang is seen as "stronger," more "productive," belonging to men or the masculine in general. Yin, the lesser active, is naturally interpreted as feminine. As you learn more about the "masculine" and the "feminine," you will undoubtedly find yourself rethinking such words and concepts as weak/strong and active/passive, and thinking of them more as two sides of a coin.

If you look at the Yang/Yin symbol, you will see that the masculine (white) contains a dot of black, and the black (feminine) contains a dot of white. This is meant to symbolize that the two forms of energy are not only complementary; each is necessary to the existence of the other.

Yang energy is associated with light, heat, all that connotes penetration and pushing forward. In the Yin basket are all things that symbolize darkness, containing, drawing in. Does this sound a little like the sex act? Of course: but from a symbolic point of view; it is the act of creation itself.

Yang is the power to generate; Yin is the power to hold and bring forth what is generated. Yang is phallic energy; Yin is gestating, containing energy. In virtually every creation in myth and religious tradition, there is a male/female metaphor. Either a great "earth" mother mates with a powerful "sky" god, or the origin of all that is in the universe emanates from a dual-sexed being, or—as in the Judeo-Christian tradition—the creator of all things brings forth a dual creation—male and female.

These are heady concepts, especially for those of us who are caught in the techno-intellectual climate of Western society. Yet Yang and Yin exist not somewhere out in the stratosphere or deep in the minds of philosophers; they are with us in day-to-day living as components of human psychology. Though symbolically linked to one sex or the other, the components of Yin and Yang are equally available to both sexes, whether experienced in a male or a female body.

Instrumental and Instinctual

Robert Ornstein labels masculine or Yang energy as *Instrumental,* Yin or feminine energy as *Instinctual.* Here are some of the antithetical but equally valid opposites that result from this distinction.

Instrumental	*Instinctual*
Objective	Subjective
Doing	Being
Thinking	Feeling
Strength	Vulnerability
Product-oriented	Process-oriented
Autonomous	Related
Analytical	Creative
Competitive	Cooperative
Logical	Empathetic
Necessity-oriented	People-oriented
Hard	Soft
Self-seeking	Other-oriented

Putting aside any value judgments these words suggest to you, try to describe a particular human being, male or female, whom you know well. You will undoubtedly find yourself picking some from column A and some from column B—or even getting confused, because a single person can be one thing under one set of circumstances and another under a different set of circumstances. The point is that the list on the left does not automatically "belong" to men, nor the list on the right to women. These are all human possibilities available to both sexes. They are neither good nor bad (in proper proportion); they simply *are.*

A Quick Snapshot

Another productive way to think about maleness and femaleness in the abstract is as the positive and the negative of a photograph. The positive (a masculine metaphor) is sharp, clear, easy to decipher; the negative (a feminine concept) is dark, hard to read, "mysterious." Yet, without the negative, no photographic positive is possible. In other words, maleness and femaleness are as indispensable to each other as day is to night, black is to white, cold is to hot, pleasure is to pain. It is literally impossible to have the experience of one without the other. But back to the photograph: It can be overexposed (too much light) or underexposed (too much dark). Like photographs, people—males or females—can be "overexposed" to the masculine aspects of life and "underexposed" to the feminine—or vice versa.

Duality

Many philosophical and religious traditions, as well as individual writers and thinkers, lean strongly toward the notion of duality in the universe to explain the basic nature of human consciousness. The following list is excerpted from one compiled from many sources by Robert Ornstein, an important contemporary thinker on the subject of duality and the "masculine" and "feminine."

Masculine	Feminine
Day	Night
Intellectual	Sensuous
Time/history	Timelessness/eternity
Active	Receptive
Right side	Left side
Left hemisphere	Right hemisphere
Explicit	Tacit
Linear	Nonlinear
Sequential	Simultaneous
Light	Dark

Masculine	*Feminine*
Time	Space
Argument	Experience
Causal	Acausal

Chapter 3

The Topsy-Turvy Playing Field

B EFORE GOING FORWARD INTO THE SPECIFICS OF YOUR ASTRO-gender profile, it's important to look at the current status of men and women in our society and at least sum up what the "new rules" appear to be. Though it is beyond the purposes of this book to give a history of the women's movement, the reasons for the patriarchal bias of our society and the current state of male/female relationships both personally and professionally, it is important to point out a few home truths.

It is well known, not just by feminists but by many who have explored the subject, that at some point in human prehistory there was a profound shift from a female-centered world to a male-centered world. Great earth-goddess mothers were replaced by all-powerful male gods, and the position of women subtly began to shift. In more recent history we have seen two thousand years of the male-centered, Judeo-Christian tradition leave an indelible imprint on society. Equally if not more important to the male bias of society was the advent of the scientific era

and the industrial revolution. By their very nature, they
vaunted and deemed as superior the "masculine" virtues
as opposed to the "feminine." Doing, analyzing, dissecting,
producing, striving, competing became the "powers that
be." And, of course, these things had to be done by men.
Women were alloted their roles as handmaidens, house-
keepers, and mothers, and were presumed to be happy in
their "proper" place. The kind of work that men began to
do at this point in history initiated the "absent father" and
the "ever-present mother"—a family structure that is now
seen as unbalanced by people of both sexes.

The counterrevolution, socially speaking, of the past
thirty years has brought women—angry women, strong
women and just ordinary women—to a point where they
recognized changes that could be made in the system, and
proceeded to make those changes happen. What they
didn't change, however—and couldn't change—is society's continuing "masculine" bias—the assumption that
"what works" is what's best, and that "doing" is more valuable than simply "being." It was only natural that women
began to devalue their own femininity, and to long for what
they did not have—masculine prerogatives—believing
them to be "better." Most any woman who has worked in
the world of men will tell you that one must learn a whole
new vocabulary, with metaphors that have their origin
mainly in war and competitive sports. To "hit the ground
running," to "blindside," to "take a hit," to "make an end
run" are merely a sprinkling of phrases that underscore
the fact that no true dent has yet been made in society's
assumption that "men are tough" and "women are weak."

Further complicating the picture, while women worked
for what they wanted—more autonomy and respect—and
got a lot of it, men barely seemed to notice the shifting
sands under their feet. National opinion organizations like
Roper, which has been tracking attitudes over decades,
report that only now, and in a small way, are men beginning to show trends toward recognizing change, and determining to act on certain gender-linked issues. At the

same time, the more visible parts of the "men's movement" are beginning to make news. As *The Wall Street Journal* stated, "For the last 20 years the women's movement has grabbed the headlines. But while women have been rattling the gates of male privilege, men have been slipping quietly into the women's world through the back door." Phenomena such as house husbands, parental leave for either sex and a return to the "good father" role are evidence of men's changing attitudes toward gender stereotypes.

On another front is the male bonding issue, with its cult-like invoking of the "wild man" complete with energetic rituals and strong emotions. Robert Bly has touched a nerve, not just for men but for everyone, by pointing out the "missing elements" in the world we live in. The patriarchal world is a dry one, lacking in fire—the element of spirit and spontaneity—and water—the element of feeling. As we look at the astrological elements as the basis of all that the signs stand for, it will become more evident that the gender qualities labeled "feminine" are what have been repressed in our society, and the effects have been felt by both sexes, personally and professionally.

So as we begin to examine the role of your astrological inheritance in determining what kind of woman or what kind of man you are, it is wise to keep in mind that the sexes are playing on a far-from-level playing field, and one that is constantly shifting. Never before in our history have the traditional definitions of masculinity and femininity in flesh-and-blood human beings been so under siege. Never before in our culture have so many men and women felt "gender-uncertain." In fact, a root cause of the outbreak of gender-bashing by both sexes, and of the early warnings of a new and even more hostile "battle of the sexes" breaking out, is the dimly perceived truth that men and women are—or can be—more like each other than either care to admit.

In looking at your own masculinity or femininity from an astrological point of view, it is important to keep two facts of life in mind: Biology determined your sex, and therefore a whole set of built-in abilities and tendencies; the world around you is circumscribed by gender issues that will take more than a little time to sort themselves out.

Chapter 4

Air, Fire, Earth, Water:
The Elements of Masculinity
and Femininity

IF YOU ARE ONE OF THOSE PEOPLE WHO LOVE TO PLAY "WHAT'S My/Your Sign," this book is going to teach you another game: "What's Your Element?"

Each sign of the zodiac belongs to one of the four element groups established by the ancients as the four "building blocks" of the universe—the sine qua non of all that existed. Obviously, this was not literal talk, but a philosophical way of categorizing all that was known of the universe. The Greeks, and later the scholars of the Middle Ages, saw the universe as interconnected; every thing, thought or person a subset of a larger concept.

By the Middle Ages, and later the Renaissance, the four elements were already recognized for their psychological validity—a useful and startlingly accurate way of categorizing the primary nature of a human being. In medicine, the elements were critical to diagnosis and became transmuted into the four "humors"—the first form of psychosomatic medicine and a major practical use of astrology.

The feisty, restless "choleric" person subject to impatience and anxiety, and prone to stroke, heart attack and what we today would call other Type A disorders, had an overbalance of Fire in his system. The moody, sensitive, "imaginary invalid" was ruled by his emotions, and therefore a Water type. The "melancholic," subject to depressions and weighted down by necessities and the general malaise caused by "black bile," obviously had been alloted too much Earth in his horoscope. The strung-out, over-busy, nervous, talkative individual who always had to be right was clearly an Air type.

Another way of understanding what the elements meant to people at that time is to classify them as elements having "levity" (Air and Fire) and elements with "gravity" (Earth and Water). Air and Fire move outward and are "extensional"; Earth and Water have more inertia, because they concentrate at the lower level. While the outgoing Fire and Air elements have the strength of creating and spreading outward, Earth and Water have the strength and endurance to *be*.

The elements as intrinsic human qualities were reflected in literature as well. It was best said by Shakespeare in *Antony and Cleopatra:* When Marc Antony sums up the nobility of Brutus, he extols him by saying, "The elements so mixed in him that nature might stand up and say to all the world, 'This was a man.' " It may not be going too far to say that Shakespeare, whose incredible awareness of gender issues, as seen in his portraits of women such as Portia and Claudia, really meant, "This was a whole person."

The Elements Today

To regard the elements as anachronistic in our scientifically biased world is to ignore their psychological validity, their usefulness in tagging an individual's personal take on the world. Carl Jung, a friend of astrology and many other "nonlinear" pursuits, did not specifically relate his famous typology to the elements, but the resemblance is both striking and amazingly accurate.

Jung identified four necessary functions of human consciousness—the *thinking,* the *sensate,* the *feeling* and the *intuitive* processes. It is a framework that still stands at the base of all contemporary psychological typology, such as the Meyers Briggs Type Index used in the field of personnel. Each individual has one of the four psychological functions as his or her dominant mental attitude, and self-orients in one of the four ways described below.

Like the medieval doctors who saw "cholerics," "melancholics" and the like in their patients, Jung analyzed people by categorizing them as "thinking types," "intuitives," "feeling types" or "sensors." While Jung's work with typology became far more complex, and is beyond the scope of our subject here, he never deviated from the "rule of four"—or from a firm belief in inborn typology.

Sensing means we can perceive; that is to say, we know there is something there. Sensing types are always very aware of the things around them and can give accurate descriptions.

Thinking means we can determine what it is that we have perceived, with the goal of fitting it into our view of reality. For a thinking type, something has to "belong" to his view, or he can be totally baffled by it.

Feeling means we are aware of the emotions of pleasure or displeasure evoked by what we have perceived, and that it affects our actions.

Intuition is somehow "knowing"—not necessarily rationally—what is behind the apparent reality, where it came from and where it is going. Intuition is "knowing" without proof.

Function Types and Relationships

All four functions are possible to everyone, but everyone has one function that overrides the others, and also one that is difficult to make use of. Thinking types have trouble with feeling, and vice versa. Intuitives, future-oriented, find it hard to see what is really there in the here and now—which is the sensor's orientation. In typological theory, the two types which have most difficulty with each other are intuitives and sensors. However, the answer is all in knowing what and whom you are dealing with. Later on in this book, when we talk about relationships and astro-gender types, you will see more specifically how each type deals with each other—and how to take practical steps to defuse stress and to promote harmony.

Psychology Joins Astrology

Contemporary psychologically oriented astrologers—of which there are many—immediately saw Jung's four functions of consciousness as corresponding to the four elements. Though Jungian astrologers are not totally in agreement in all the correlations, there is one generally accepted breakdown, which will be used here. As each of the elements is described in terms of its psychological orientation, you will begin to see why two are traditionally "masculine" and two "feminine." Here are some catchwords to start off.

Air: Jung's Thinking Type—theoretical, detached, objective, rational, difficulty with emotional involvement, valuing of intellectual competence, desire for freedom, keep-it-light mentality, likes facts and figures. (Masculine)

Fire: Jung's Intuitive Type—self-centered, proud, high-spirited, competitive, needs space, childlike or naive, willful, tendency toward insensitivity, always ready for the new and risky, able to see future possibilities others cannot fathom. (Masculine)

> *Important note:* Carl Jung's use of the word "intuitive," and the way it is used in this book, do not imply any form of ESP. It is the ability to see patterns where others see chaos, hence the tendency to have hunches that are "right on."

Earth: Jung's Sensing Type—exists in the here and now, values the material, is persistent, patient, self-disciplined, cautious, dependable, unassertive, efficient; trusts only what can be apprehended by the senses. (Feminine)

Water: Jung's Feeling Type—subtle, deep, compassionate, compulsive, fearful, moody, imaginative, vulnerable to hurt, secretive, understanding, unselfish, imaginative and artistic. (Feminine)

If we were living in the Barbie and Ken world, there probably would be little doubt about which sex "belongs" with which type, because the mini-descriptions above contain so many of the conventional gender stereotypes we have lived with for years. However, in our time, and the fact that a person of either sex can be born under a sign of either gender, astrology types people in a much more interesting and multidimensional manner.

Stereotypes Vs. Metaphors

To enter the realm of astrology is to enter the realm of the impersonal. The qualities that are regarded as "masculine" or instrumental, such as "analytical," are ascribed to the "masculine" and not to any particular man. The qualities called "feminine" or instinctual are applied to a set of attributes that are metaphorically feminine, rather than describing any particular female.

The world of stereotype is the world of the personal. Here are a few typical stereotypes about men and women that are virtually taken for granted in specific situations.

"He gets depressed because of work pressure."
"She has PMS."

"He's firm."
"She's stubborn."

"He's careful about detail."
"She's a nitpicker."

"He isn't afraid to say what he thinks."
"She's an opinionated bitch."

"When a man wants a woman, he's a hunter."
"When a woman wants a man, she's a predator."

The list could go on and on, but the point is germaine: Gender qualities are *not* stereotypes, but much broader ways of being in the world—and are available to both sexes.

The Astrological Gender Spectrum

The gender spectrum unique to this author's point of view is that Air is the most masculine element and Water the most feminine. Fire, while masculine, has qualities that dilute its pure masculinity, and Earth, while feminine, has a certain strength that puts it close to the middle of the spectrum.

Carl Jung also recognized two types of basic orientation in people in addition to the four psychological types. They are *introversion* and *extroversion*. These words should not be interpreted as they usually are, i.e., that the extrovert is the life of the party and the introvert the wallflower loner. They are the qualities that account for Fire being the androgynous or "mixed" element and Earth the androgynous or "mixed" earth element. Fire is outer-directed: even if self-centered from a personality point of view, these people's real interests lie outside themselves rather than inside themselves. Air and Water, on the other hand, are inward-looking, relating everything to themselves. Their thoughts, if Air, and their feelings, if Water, are primary. Since the overall orientation of the "feminine" is outward toward the world of things and feelings rather than thoughts and feelings, Earth comes closer to the middle of the gender spectrum. Similarly, since Fire tends to look behind the external appearance of things and exhibit intuitive thinking, its masculine element qualities are slightly diluted.

Here's how the spectrum looks:

Masculine	Feminine
AIR FIRE	EARTH WATER

While this book defines personality types in terms of element rather than sign, it is useful to see where the specific signs fall on the gender spectrum, and to know some of the reasons that put them there.

Here are the signs in sequence from the most masculine to the most feminine. It is a sequence unique to this book, and does not follow the order of the zodiac.

Air: The Pure Masculine Element

Libra, highest-frequency masculine Air Sign: Any number of astrologers and astrology buffs will not agree about the ultramasculinity of Libra, but the same "fairness" that makes for great diplomats makes for ruthless generals and hard-boiled tacticians. Also, one has to be curious about the fact that so many Libran males, from Truman Capote to Gore Vidal to Rex Reed, are homosexual. One strong possibility is that the "masculinity" of Libra is such an overpowering influence that many men run to other men because of its empowering vibrations.

Women Librans are often portrayed as charming, attractive, well mannered and sweet-spoken. In real life they can be observed to have backbones of steel and a go-for-it mentality that cares little who falls by the wayside as they rush for success—in both work and love.

Aquarius: middle-frequency masculine Air Sign: Aquarians of both sexes are capable of great objectivity, a prime masculine gender characteristic. They gravitate toward such "masculine" pursuits as science and numbers, regarding theory as more "alive" than people. Their reputation for humanitarianism is real, but it is directed toward groups rather than individuals. People of both sexes born under this sign are more comfortable in group relationships than the one-on-one variety; intimacy is not their style, and they often march to their very own drummer.

Gemini: lowest-frequency masculine Air Sign: Like the other Air Signs—in fact, all the masculine signs—Gemini is outer- rather than inner-directed. Facts, rather than the human reality behind them, are what mainly draw their attention. They are discriminators between "this" and "that" rather than unifiers. Like all the Air Signs, they represent the masculine "logos" or Word, which is said in some religions to be the source of all in the universe.

Fire: The Masculine/Androgynous Element

Aries: highest-frequency masculine Fire Sign: Like all three Fire Signs, Aries possesses the quality of "heart" that comes from the warmth of fire. Aries, though warlike, belligerent and self-centered, is also immensely generous with both time and resources. In both sexes there is a tendency to rush to the aid of the "damsel" (of either sex) in distress. Aries is also the naivete of the novice, the eager but not always fully tuned-in adventurer with not only the ability to leap before looking, but also a childlike daring to do so.

Leo: middle-frequency masculine Fire Sign: Leo's natural assumption of the leadership and power positions places it firmly on the "masculine" side of the spectrum, and Leo's vaunting ambition is also a given. Here too, however, masculinity is tempered by a softer side which often makes natives of this sign recoil from the excesses of power.

Sagittarius: lowest-frequency masculine Fire Sign: Like all the Fire Signs, Sagittarius has the true "heart" that comes from the warmth of fire in the literal sense. Despite a great tendency to wander from home base, there is a caring quality in this sign. It is perhaps best seen in the myth of Chiron, the centaur/mentor who agreed to take on the eternal torments of Prometheus, condemned for stealing the gift of fire from the gods for man. The masculine manifestation of the quality of "intuition" is also perhaps best seen in Sagittarius, which tends to see unrelated things in discernible patterns rather than random pieces.

Earth: The Feminine/Androgynous Element

Capricorn: lowest-frequency feminine Earth Sign: Many people are surprised to hear that Capricorn is a *feminine* sign. Symbolically speaking, it is associated with ambition, durability, slowly but surely reaching to heights. These things are all true, yet because Capricorn is *Earth,* the picture is not one of forward-rushing accomplishment, but of the patience to build and make manifest. All the Earth Signs, in their femininity, are associated with matter and materializing, giving form to what the male signs have initiated. Capricorn is also what is called a *cardinal* sign; astrologically, that means it opens a season (winter); all the cardinal signs (Aries, Cancer, Libra and Capricorn) derive a certain power by their position in the seasonal round of the zodiac.

Taurus: middle-frequency feminine Earth Sign: Why is Taurus the bull feminine? The animal symbology of the zodiac developed slowly over long periods of time in various parts of the world. The bull was once "the great mother cow." Taurus is perhaps the best example of the growing, building, nurturing nature of the Earth Signs. Taureans are very adept at making things grow—all kinds of things, from children to other people's money. Taurus's true work is to establish a better quality of life for all, through determination and often just plain true grit. Taurus's femininity has a highly sensual quality to it. When the Wife of Bath in *The Canterbury Tales* explains her love life, she reveals she is a Taurus.

Virgo: highest-frequency feminine Earth Sign: Virgo's place in the gender spectrum—i.e., more "feminine" than Capricorn or Taurus—derives mainly from this sign's tendency to back people up rather than take the number one position. Virgoans of either sex are ideal "second bananas." They are efficient, quiet workers who would rather stay in the background and work their organizing magic from there. As for sexuality, the Virgin symbol really stands for the person who belongs to himself or herself before anyone else. Celibacy, frigidity or impotence has nothing to do with it.

Water: The Pure Feminine Element

Cancer: lowest-frequency feminine Water Sign: When someone wants to portray the essence of motherliness, Cancer is the sign that is usually evoked. The sign has traditionally been connected with childbirth, mothering and nurturing in all forms. When we reach this point in the gender spectrum, we begin to see—as in the Earth Signs—the kind of strength that may not be overt and aggressive, but rather holding and containing. Cancer is a bulwark and a place of refuge.

Scorpio: middle-frequency feminine Water Sign: Just as people are surprised to hear that Capricorn is feminine, they are equally surprised by Scorpio. There is good reason for the confusion; Scorpio/Hades is mythologically the male god of the underworld who abducts and rapes. But in the zodiac, Scorpio stands for the dark side of the feminine ... obsession, compulsion, extreme sexuality, the power to transform things through emotion.

Pisces: highest-frequency feminine Water Sign: In Pisces we come to the most feminine end of the gender spectrum. One of its aspects of femininity is lack of definition, no sharp edges to create distinct forms that hold their shape. The poetic, imaginative, inspirational attributes assigned to the gender are seen here at the ultimate. Pisces is not literally weak, but constantly searching for something or someone to create a feeling of wholeness. While gender-wise masculinity stands for separateness, femininity is relatedness, and Pisces is its ultimate manifestation.

From the Sword to the Soul

To sum up and simplify, the gender spectrum as seen in the zodiac runs from the ultramasculine steel sword of Aries to the nebulous but compelling spirituality of Pisces. If you have started to place yourself somewhere on the gender spectrum, you've jumped ahead, because the essence of true astrology is that one is not merely a Sun Sign or a stock list of characteristics. You are a man or a woman with a complex natal horoscope. That horoscope, with **all** its possibilities and predelictions, is best laid out for you in a one-on-one session with a trained astrologer. However, *Sexual Astrology* is not just about your Sun Sign—it is about your Moon Sign too, your subconscious, as it were. By exploring both factors, Sun and Moon, you will see that it is possible to get a pretty fair view of why a particular male performs and thinks the way he does, and why a particular female is the woman she is.

Chapter 5

Sun and Moon . . .
Day and Night

IF YOU ARE LIKE MOST PEOPLE, YOU KNOW WHAT YOUR SUN SIGN is and a fair amount about it. If you are among the more astrologically sophisticated, you know you have a Moon Sign—but may or may not know what it is or what it represents. The Sun Sign, Moon Sign and Rising Sign are the most important points in any natal horoscope because they designate three key areas of the personality, as defined by modern psychologists: Sun Sign=ego, Moon Sign=subconscious, Rising Sign=persona (how the world sees you).

In *Sexual Astrology,* your astro-gender profile is based on both your Sun Sign and your Moon Sign. (There are tables in the back of the book to give you this information.)

Sun=Ego=Consciousness

Your Sun Sign—that is, the portion of the zodiac the sun was in when you were born—is what you consciously believe you are, and why you are here. In esoteric astrology,

35

it is said to point to the life path you are meant to follow. There are many other factors in your horoscope—such as "aspects" or distances between planets—which give clues about how difficult or how easy it will be for you as you take the path. There are many astrologers who ascribe to the theory that we choose when to be born, hence choose our horoscope, and hence the destiny or karma that is ours during this lifetime. It is not necessary to agree with that theory to know that your Sun Sign is what you are meant to do, to be who you are and to go where you are meant to go.

In the psychological sense, the sun is your ego, or consciousness. That means it is a great part of "what makes you tick." The sun, its sign and its aspects to it from other planets are also said to reflect the kind of father/upbringing we had. But the profitable way to think about your Sun Sign in this book is in terms of its element—the basic factors that make it "masculine" or "feminine," and what that means to you, according to your biological sex.

The sun, which has been observed from ancient times to light the world, to make things grow, illuminates in the true sense of the word. For a variety of reasons, the sun has been considered closer to the masculine consciousness. What it means in this book is that males probably have greater access to abilities and tendencies of their Sun Sign than women—that is, men may be better able to hear the voice of their Sun Sign and respond to it. Women are closer to their Moon Sign.

Moon=Subconscious

By the same token, the soft light of the moon, which makes all things merge into a softer picture, makes them less sharp. Sometimes it startlingly and even frighteningly disappears altogether; the dark of the moon has always been a source of fear to humans. The moon has long been associated with the feminine. It is true that the moon has no light of its own, but reflects the light of the sun. You can factor in that information any way you like, but it does make an argument for women "reflecting" the will of men. By the same token, however, the moon's shimmering, mysterious presence also gives it the advantage of "knowing" hidden things. Therefore, it represents the subconscious—those drives and urges that are more difficult for most of us to bring out and examine.

It is worth mentioning that the sun/moon relationship, and in particular the changing phases of the moon, are said to be one root cause of society's fear of the feminine. While the sun rises every day and reaches its (phallic) high point at noon, the moon is more illusory and changeable. At one time, the moon was the only calendar known to man. It marked off a perfect lunar year, with thirteen months of feminine cycles, and phases that marked off time in days and seasons—for planting, for harvesting, for preparing for the dark time to come for birthing again. Though this book is not necessarily meant to represent a biased point of view vis-à-vis men and women, it is interesting to note that the fear of the number 13 has often been linked to the one-time importance of the moon over the sun, and of the feminine and its attributes over the masculine, with its equally essential but polar opposite qualities.

In psychological astrology, the sign in which the moon falls at the moment of birth indicates the underside of consciousness. It tells what we truly desire, what makes us feel comfortable and what we need to feel truly nurtured. It is not surprising, then, that in a horoscope reading, the moon is often taken to represent the real mother (as the sun is to represent the father).

Chapter 6

Your Place on the Gender Spectrum

WHETHER YOU ARE MALE OR FEMALE, IT MUST NOW BE OBVIOUS that your gender identity, when astrology is figured in, is much more complex than either your biological nature or your social conditioning can describe. Do not, therefore, be thrown off by some statements or buzz words that do not seem to apply to you. In fact, you perhaps should reflect upon it more fully, and come up with a different perspective on yourself.

In the following chapters, we will look at the sixteen astro-gender types possible with four elements, and two personality factors—the sun and the moon. First determine (from the tables in the back of the book) the element and gender of both your Sun Sign and your Moon Sign. Then start looking up people you know, and begin the fascinating game of "astro-gender-typing" as you meet and interact with people. It's a fascinating game, and can be very useful as well.

The Sixteen Astro-gender Types Are

Air Sun Sign/Air Moon Sign	Double Masculine
Fire Sun Sign/Fire Moon Sign	Double Masculine
Air Sun Sign/Fire Moon Sign	Double Masculine
Fire Sun Sign/Air Moon Sign	Double Masculine
Earth Sun Sign/Earth Moon Sign	Double Feminine
Water Sun Sign/Water Moon Sign	Double Feminine
Earth Sun Sign/Water Moon Sign	Double Feminine
Water Sun Sign/Earth Moon Sign	Double Feminine
Air Sun Sign/Earth Moon Sign	Masculine/Feminine
Air Sun Sign/Water Moon Sign	Masculine/Feminine
Fire Sun Sign/Earth Moon Sign	Masculine/Feminine
Fire Sun Sign/Water Moon Sign	Masculine/Feminine
Earth Sun Sign/Air Moon Sign	Feminine/Masculine
Earth Sun Sign/Fire Moon Sign	Feminine/Masculine
Water Sun Sign/Air Moon Sign	Feminine/Masculine
Water Sun Sign/Fire Moon Sign	Feminine/Masculine

Above the Battle of the Sexes

Before you go on to read your own astro-gender profile, it cannot be too strongly emphasized that masculine and feminine are truly separate but equal. Both in the bodily sense and—as we are discussing them here—in the metaphysical sense they are separate but necessary and equal opposites. There is no birth without death, there is no death that does not engender new life. It's as basic as that, and as imperative to both sexes' understanding of what each is dealing with as day is to night. As men and women battle over "the little stuff," the whole universe goes on in its dualistic way, creating no favorites. If you are truly to understand your astro-gender profile and gain from it, it is important that you approach the subject of masculinity/ femininity with an open mind. And a deep one. It's more than "what makes guys guys and what makes girls girls"; it's how we can relate to each other in more sensible and equally respecting ways.

If one of your goals is to establish a relationship that is impervious to the vagaries of trends and the instability of circumstance, you may gain some insight from these words from Somerset Maugham: "Love is what happens to a man and a woman when they don't know each other." Perhaps by knowing yourself, and the other, in a deeper way, you will begin to inch along the path to having a truly wonderful relationship.

In the next section you will read about the sixteen astrogender types. To refresh your memory about the Yin/Yang or feminine/masculine qualities that are metaphors for the "feminine" or the "masculine," apart from both stereotype and biology, the list on page 16 will be helpful.

The distinction that was made between *Instrumental* and *Instinctual* qualities can be translated into human terms by the classic notion that "men do, women are." However, it also implies that there is a duality in people, and that they can partake of some of the qualities of both parts of the duality. For instance, if a person is instrumental, he or she is actively involved in something, and he or she wants to do it better. Either a man or a woman can be competitive— ergo, can possess a quality from the masculine side of the ledger. Similarly, "instinctual" is the quality of cooperativeness—the opposite of competitiveness. If two people decide after a period of being competitive to be cooperative with each other, both the man and the woman are now exhibiting an aspect of the "feminine."

Part 2

The Astro-Gender Types

Chapter 7

Masculine Sun Sign/
Masculine Moon Sign

Air Sun Sign/Air Moon Sign

This section pertains to men and women whose Sun Sign and Moon Sign are both in Air Signs—Gemini, Libra, Aquarius. (They can be in different signs.)

> *"If we had some ham we could make some ham and eggs—if we had some eggs."*

The Air/Air type is probably the most theoretical in the zodiac. Those who have been brushed by them in one way or another might say Air/Air is all talk and no action. While it is true that Air types live in their heads and thrive beautifully on words, they eventually do get from A to B to C—and realize you have to go out and buy the ham and eggs before you can see the results of your idea. But first, you see, they have to lay out the whole plan, look at it from every possible angle, anticipate errors or problems—and,

most important, build up a theory that it is perfect in every
way before proceeding to the actualities of making it happen. This is potentially the perfect sign combination of the
theoretical physicist who ponders a problem for twenty
years before calling out, "Eureka." It then takes twenty
more years before the theory becomes reality.

Coping With Caring

Though Air is a masculine element, many people of this
sign tend to be introverts rather than extroverts. That is,
they look inward and judge what is "out there" only to the
extent that they are affected by it. This does not imply they
are selfish in the ordinary sense of the word; it is more a
case of being oblivious to the obvious. With both Sun Sign
and Moon Sign in Air, however, there is a certain "chilli-
ness" to this type that takes a while to break down. In most
cases, their upbringing and nurturing was built more
around what one said than what one did. Hugs and kisses
may have been sadly lacking. In fact, the physical dimension of love—whether in family, between friends or as
lovers—is often extremely threatening to the Air/Air personality. They are rarely "touchy/feely" types.

Air is the lightest element, and can be said to metaphorically live above it all. The harsh realities of the world
are interesting to Air/Air types, but mainly as subjects of
conversation. Air/Air thrives on information, and many
people with air in their horoscopes make their way into
one or another area of the communications business—
publicity, advertising, magazines, newspapers, radio and
television. It is fairly safe to say that they are never at a
loss for words. If they seem to tolerate with great ease that
which is unpleasant, the reason is their basic difficulty
with the feeling function. Thinking (Air) and feeling (Water) are functions of consciousness that cannot be carried
on at the same time.

Enter Cupid

When feeling, in the form of love and romance, shakes up the Air/Air person's world, it can be quite traumatic. In the earliest stages, the men—particularly Librans—are perhaps the most overly romantic of all the signs. The women don't do badly either. Air/Air people "do the right thing," more because they know they should than because an overwhelming feeling made them do it. Impeccably, they will bring flowers when they are appropriate, phone right on time, arrange for the extra-special surprise, cook that gourmet dinner. However, when relationships intensify, the Air/Air individual tends to back away—and stay there, unless the potential partner forces the feeling function to erupt. The best way to trap an Air/Air type is to catch that person off guard with what he or she would consider an outrageous demand—emotional or sexual. The technique may sound risky, but it is really worth a try. The Air/Air person may be the most private of all the sixteen types. There is a constant interior dialogue going on that is all but impossible to break into without the use of "force."

Once partnered, Air/Air people take it for granted that you know they love you; the romance may still be there, but you will rarely hear it in words. The deed is all. As for staying power in a relationship, though Gemini in particular gets a bad rap for flitting from one object of affection to another, a commitment made is a commitment to be honored for a great many Air/Air people. If they become fascinated with a different member of the opposite sex, you can be fairly sure it is a question of intellect over sexuality. And when the conversation gets boring, he/she will be back to you quite swiftly.

The Air/Air Man

It would seem logical that with both Sun Sign and Air Sign in the masculine element Air, the male of this ultramasculine type would be ultramacho. But the Air element thrives on logic, and knows that the road to success is paved with pleasant words and a nonthreatening manner. Once there, however, he is capable of throwing brickbats with the best of them. In his case, however, they will be based on thoughts and facts rather than on emotional innuendos. The masculinity of the Air/Air man lies in great part in his ability to analyze, plan, dissect and reach unemotional conclusions. In some ways he is the "hard man" who is often denigrated for his ability not to allow feelings to sway his logic. Air/Air men make excellent lawyers, since they are able to hold to a line of reasoning that will exonerate their client, guilty or not guilty, and then walk away to the next case. They are "cool" in the truest sense of the word.

One of the hallmarks of the Air/Air man is his ability to form his own code of ethics and live by it. John Dean, Sun in Libra, Moon in Gemini, is a classic example. As White House attorney, he initiated the process which led to the Watergate investigation and, ultimately, to President Richard Nixon's resignation. However, "being one's own man" is not necessarily a less-than-desirable trait. In the main, Air/Air men are responsible, reliable people who want life to make sense, and they will do all they can to keep it that way.

The Air/Air man is supremely organized and an excellent administrator. Many gravitate to politics. For an accurate example of this breed of Air/Air man, look no farther than Henry Kissinger—Sun in Gemini, Moon in Libra. His words can cut, like the ice-blooded creature some believe the Air/Air male really is, but his urbane manner and obvious superb control communicate that one is dealing with a reasonable man. Former Secretary of State Dean Rusk, Sun in Aquarius, Moon in Libra, who, eyeball-to-eyeball with the Russians during the Cuban missile crisis, "saw the other guy blink," also exemplifies the Air/Air man as politician.

Writing It Out

Besides the legions of Air/Air men who make their living communicating dispassionately about all sides of life, there are a number of Air/Air poets, playwrights and novelists whose works are uncompromisingly realistic about showing life's shadowy feeling side. To name a few: Truman Capote, Sun and Moon in Libra; William Burroughs, Sun in Aquarius, Moon in Libra; Berthold Brecht, Sun in Aquarius, Moon in Libra; Jean Paul Sartre, Sun in Gemini, Moon in Aquarius; Arthur Miller, Sun in Libra, Moon in Aquarius. It is possible that these ultra-thinking types coped with their feeling function through their writing, if not in their day-to-day lives.

The Lighter Side of the Air/Air Man

Sometimes the pure Air/Air thinking-type man realizes that the world is absurd, and instead of brooding about it, makes a joke of it. Some of the most superb comedians are Air/Air men, and in general, their wit has a biting edge. Groucho Marx, Sun in Libra, Moon in Gemini; and Chevy Chase, Sun in Libra, Moon in Aquarius, might be called zany types with the belief that "all the world is crazy save thee and me." Don Ameche, Sun and Moon in Gemini, has made a whole second career out of being a lovable and laughable curmudgeon.

Gender-correcting suggestions for the Air/Air man:

- The flip side of Air—thinking, which is your primary mode—is Water—feeling. Your natural style is to look at things abstractly from the outside. Try instead to "get inside them" and look at them with the emotion you are able to summon up. Your best bet as a "role model" is Scorpio, the intense "primal" Water Sign that operates "from the gut."

- Your tendency is to build castles in the air. Substitute something of Earth—literally. You would benefit greatly by taking up a hobby such as sculpting, which deals with tangible reality.

- Pick up some clues about combining your powers of analysis with a "feel" for things by reading some detective novels with some of the current crop of female sleuths, such as writer Sue Grafton's Kinsey Milhone.

- You above all male gender types should join a sensitivity training group. Whether all male or mixed male and female, these sessions are excellent for observing, taking in and eventually applying some of the values of the "feminine."

- Practice and literally begin to develop a belief in the power of the hunch. Even if something doesn't make literal sense but seems to have something, give it a go. Start small; you don't have to "bet the farm" the first time you try it.

Living With the Air/Air Man

Domestic life with Air/Air men is easier for buttoned-up-type women than the world's "lovable slobs." Air/Air men can be virtually military in their need and demand that life in the outer world be as clearly defined and well organized as it is in their own minds.

Air/Air men are not supremely flexible and are upset when their surroundings do not reflect the order that is in their minds. Partners of Air/Air men would do well to develop some strategies for dealing with this set of affairs. One way is to "keep things neat on the surface"; another is to learn to make order out of chaos in a twinkling of an eye.

The Air/Air man, with his inner sense of responsibility to make things work properly, can be tough on himself and on others—particularly children. Whatever the Air/Air man's children's signs and natural proclivities, they are expected to live up to his often rigid standards. Think *Major Dad* or Dwight Eisenhower, Sun in Libra, Moon in Libra.

The Air/Air Woman

This is the most difficult astro-gender type for women. With both the Sun and the Moon in Air Signs, the female's own innate feminine side has a hard time coping with itself. In many cases the woman does not know who she is, and has a classic case of gender misidentity.

The Beautiful Bitch Syndrome

Purely from a career point of view, her astro-inheritance of masculine gender qualities is an asset in terms of making it big. Air/Air women can make it from the mailroom to the boardroom faster than any other type. However, it is often at the expense of others because, with her astrological double dose of masculinity, her primary goals can be competition, ends justifying means and being number one. Because Air Sign women, particularly Librans, often possess a classic beauty, their straight-up-the-ladder climb to success often turns off both male and female co-workers. Even if she is literally blameless—has not taken special advantage—she often goes down in the books as having done so.

The sad thing for the Air/Air woman is that she usually knows something is wrong. It is not that she does not have relationships outside her work life; it is a matter of not being able to relax and live in a more natural, life-is-good-

for-its-own-sake manner. More than her male counterpart
(who by virtue of his conditioning regards stress as a fact
of life), the Air/Air executive female always seems on the
edge of burnout.

Who's In Charge Here?

Even the traditional woman of this astro-gender type—
housewife and mother of 2.5 children—is not immune to
the power/success syndrome. She may marry a man who
needs the backup her astro-masculinity provides for him.
Another scenario is her marrying a success- and power-
bound male, then trying to boss him around—not to mention making major household decisions on her own.
Divorce court is often the only answer, and there she will
fight like a tigress to win, even if possessions are not the
issue.

In both scenarios, and there are many others, Air/Air
women seem to have the most difficult time figuring out
what being a woman is all about and finding the balance
of masculine/feminine that could mean everything to their
own happiness. When you turn over the rock with this
astro-gender-type female, you almost always discover a
lack of warmth in her own nurturing. Nonemotional
homes, broken homes, homes where it was clear to the
growing female child that being "Mommy" was far from a
good deal. She literally had no one to beckon her into
womanhood.

When the upbringing is clearly reflected in the person,
astrologers who believe that we "choose our own parents"
have a field day. True or false, the evidence definitely
points that way with the Air/Air woman. With women, the
element and sign of the Moon are usually a dead giveaway
to how they were nurtured: Earth connotes "hands-on"
caring; Fire generally describes busy, active, warmhearted
mothering; Water, a lot of emotionalism and even hysteria.

The Sexless Sex Goddesses

Though there are doubtless many other examples, several Air/Air women leap out as "prisoners of gender." One route the Air/Air woman can take is the "fake female"— the ultrasensuous, all-desirable woman who, on the surface, appears to be close to the ideal of the sexually stereotyped sex goddess. Marilyn Monroe, Sun in Gemini, Moon in Aquarius; Lana Turner, Sun in Aquarius, Moon in Libra; Zsa Zsa Gabor, Sun in Aquarius, Moon in Libra; and Brigitte Bardot, Sun in Libra, Moon in Gemini, are—ironic as it may seem—all double masculine. Though their lives have differed vastly, they are all stamped with the same astrological imprint. And none seems to have found peace in her lifetime.

If you are an Air/Air woman, take heart; life can still be beautiful. Especially if you have or will have children, your feeling side will be stimulated. Or you can become aware of your own acting-out of the double-masculine destiny you have been dealt and compensate for it by learning from your "female siblings" in the zodiac.

Libra women in particular, who are ruled by Venus, the planet of beauty and beautiful interrelationships, can be plagued by the "beautiful woman" syndrome. Some, like Madelaine Kahn, Sun in Libra, Moon in Gemini; Shana Alexander, Sun in Libra, Moon in Gemini; and Angela Landsbury, Sun in Libra, Moon in Gemini, use their natural beauty and smarts and their masculine "zest for success" to carve out very special roles for themselves which combine the best of both worlds.

The Cutting Edge

Air is the element of "The Word," and writers are rife among both the males and the females of the Air/Air astrogender profile. Both Lillian Hellman, Sun in Gemini, Moon in Aquarius; and Colette, Sun and Moon in Aquarius, show in their works an acute awareness of the masculine/feminine duality, and the dilemma it creates for women of strength. Historian Barbara Tuchman, Sun in Aquarius, Moon in Gemini, has applied her Air Sign thinking function to a variety of topics that would daunt lesser writers.

Living With the Air/Air Woman

Air is the lightest of the four elements; metaphorically speaking, one can say the Air/Air woman has trouble keeping her feet on the ground. She is at her best in job situations, or any other milieu where there are fairly tight rules and regulations. Left on her own, she will try to create the situations she sees in her head, all nicely buttoned down. The problem is that her thinking function works nicely but is often untouched by practicality—an Earth function.

It takes a lot to get an Air/Air woman down, however, so she is rarely bothered by her "mistakes." One of the most delightful things about the Air/Air woman is her "light" temperament. Most things aren't worth arguing about, as far as she is concerned. She makes the kind of partner that can drive her husband wild because she just won't get upset—sometimes about things she should get upset about. Any appeal to her emotions is likely to go unheard; her antagonist, whoever it may be, should explain things "one, two, three."

The Air/Air woman's children will hear lullabies and night songs and most likely be told very often they have a "nice, pretty mother." They think so too, but they can't understand why she sometimes doesn't seem to be there at all. In spirit, anyway. Her mind is likely to be on the latest book she's read, the next party she's going to give and who would make the best mix of people. If you've gotten an accurate picture of the Air/Air woman, you've guessed that she will zero in on "people who know people." That's not all bad, however, because it's all in the interest of her little family group and she wants above all for them to live well.

Gender-correcting suggestions for the Air/Air woman:

- Air can be a "chilly" element, especially for women. Fire, though it is also masculine, offers ways for you to become more connected with your fellow beings. Leo, for instance, is a highly hospitable sign, and a bit "house-proud." You may be too, but you should attempt to entertain more from "the heart"—that is, giving less attention to surface matters and more to what your guests really care about.

- For all your attractiveness and spark, physical sex may in some ways be less interesting to you than you—or others—would like. "Steamy" romances before bed are not the answer, but perhaps some physical/emotional practice is—such as massage, certain types of yoga, etc. Whatever smacks of the sensuality of Earth.

- Especially if Gemini is in your Air/Air mix, you are extremely flexible and can turn on a dime. Perhaps too quickly. For your own sake, as well as the sake of your image, learn to practice the "one, two, three" technique of thinking before making decisions, lest you earn the label of a "flake."

- Though you may have intimate friends, you sometimes are more self- than other-involved. Make it a point to seek out a troubled friend and offer not only tea and sympathy, but also the very logical answers you may be able to bring to her/his situation.

- Develop your creative and feeling side through some introspective pursuits like poetry, creative writing or journal-keeping. The latter is an excellent way to get insight into what makes you tick from day to day.

Getting Sign-Specific

Air Sun Sign/Air Moon Sign

Gemini/Gemini: Least tough of all the double Air Signs. Tendency to skim the surface without probing. Positive and doing but restless, always jumping in and out of situations, including the romantic. A bit of a gossip. Must learn to concentrate, learn to like solitude.

Libra/Libra: Most aggressive when trying to put things in balance. Serene on surface, real desire for peace, aesthetics. Instinctively know how to make best impression on people. Don't forget, most valuable asset is in knowing how to make people like you, regardless.

Aquarius/Aquarius: You are a real organizer with true executive power. There is a touch of the independent, original; you are polarized toward new and different ideas. You are by turns self-sufficient and desirous of society. You do not take kindly to routine.

Gemini/Libra: You know how to combine business and pleasure to good advantage. You have a good deal of optimism, and are able to do a quick bounce back from any problem that comes your way. You love to tell stories, but sometimes they are too long. Learn to self-edit.

Gemini/Aquarius: You've got a sixth sense about people and rarely make a mistake. You easily adjust to changes, so that the passing parade never leaves you behind. In romance you may appear to be unstable because you search wide for perfection and sympathy.

Libra/Gemini: You combine the emotional balance and friendliness of Libra with the cleverness and adaptability of Gemini. You have a talent for making your inspirations practical; writing or education or travel is a possibility. Your voice can be your fortune.

Libra/Aquarius: You are likely to live in your mind more than in your senses. Your urge to be of service underlies your professional ambitions. You are quick to make adjustments and can experience sudden changes in feelings and judgment. High intelligence.

Aquarius/Gemini: Inwardly you are more mixed or determined than you appear in person. Success can depend on cultivating decisiveness, routine. You can tire easily of details and may become a job hopper. Companionship is vital to you. But only with the right partner.

Aquarius/Libra: You are an elusive character. You think you are faithful but can change partners at the drop of a hat. But you are fundamentally sincere, and really do desire a secure relationship. You understand people well, are tolerant and sympathetic with them.

Fire Sun Sign/Fire Moon Sign

This section pertains to men and women whose Sun Sign and Moon Sign are both in Fire Signs—Aries, Leo and Sagittarius. (They can be in different signs.)

"To be alive is to be burning."

There are those who believe Fire is the "favored" element because so many of its characteristics are positive rather than negative ones. The typical Fire type approaches the world full of enthusiasm and confidence, creative expression, almost inexhaustible energy and a bent for action that never stops. Fire people are warm, hospitable, gregarious and a lot of other good things many people would like to be.

However, with the Fire/Fire person there is a catch: It can be too much of a good thing. The Fire/Fire person can be so "hot" he or she is constantly argumentative and occasionally even violent. Too much fire can also lead to the kinds of illnesses that have to do with excesses; for instance, impatience and constant activity can lead to high blood pressure, strokes and heart attacks. Ebullience, a tendency to love to party and an empty-the-pockets generosity can leave dents in both the body and the bank account. People with the Fire/Fire combination would do well to learn some form of self-relaxation—preferably mental/spiritual rather than physical.

Fire's intuitive nature—the ability to conceive big ideas from a crumb of reality—can in Fire/Fire people lead to a life of high expectations and cruel disappointments. Even if the idea is a good one and, with the proper resources, could lead to lots of gain for everyone, it takes more practicality than the typical Fire/Fire person possesses. A wise word to the Fire/Fire Sign type: Hire Earth Signs to work for you, especially your accountant and your lawyer. On the positive side, Fire/Fire can come up with creative solutions to virtually impossible problems when the chips are down. They are ideal people to have in brainstorming to "crisis time" sessions.

Love and Marriage

Ardor describes Fire/Fire's feelings when they believe that love has walked in. No other combination can be as noisy, active and rambunctious in a love affair than the Fire/Fire type. The only problem is, it is likely to happen early and often. Parents of Fire/Fire children will be dealing with the crush syndrome earlier than they would like. Later on in life, the Fire/Fire person tends to say, "This is really it," when it isn't. In the section later in this book dealing with relationships, the Fire/Fire type will get some suggestions about whom to look for. However, if there ever was a sign combination that burned the candle of romance at both ends, it is this one. Marriage is to be entered into with great caution, and possibly even a prenuptial agreement. Obviously we are talking generalities, but in general, the Fire/Fire man is not one for home and hearth; however, he will be excellent with children, pouring his ardor on them. By the way, Casanova was born with Sun in Aries, Moon in Sagittarius.

It is appropriate at this introduction of the first astro-gender combination containing a Fire Sign that this is one of the elements that our society truly needs, in the meta-phorical sense. Fire, as a masculine element, moves forward with confidence. It is also a vital, spontaneous, joyous element. We live so much by facts, figures and proper functioning that we have shut out the "fire" in our world. Fire, in its astrological context, is also spirit and animation. The quote that begins this section—"to be alive is to be burning"—is true for more than just Fire/Fire types; it has to do with us all.

The Fire/Fire Man

With the Fire/Fire type man, a great deal depends on what signs the Sun and Moon are in. For instance, a double-Aries male might be so ultramacho as to be a turnoff, both to women and to other people he deals with. Marlon Brando has both Sun and Moon in Aries. Aries, like fire itself, is a good sign (they make excellent fire fighters), but it can be overbearing in large doses. The double-Leo man could be—you guessed it—insufferably vain. The double Sagittarian moves so fast you'll probably never get a chance to meet him. However, when the signs are mixed, as in most cases, there is a general profile that appears.

The power of a double dose of fearlessness, strength and a flair for the dramatic give the Fire/Fire man a longing to live life to its fullest, and to follow it wherever it takes him. There are several people who sum up this aspect of the Fire/Fire man, but perhaps the most appropriate is Winston Churchill, Sun in Sagittarius, Moon in Leo. What is interesting about Churchill's combination is that the Sagittarius Sun led him to a second and totally opposite career in painting. Dual jobs/careers/pastimes are typically Sagittarian, if not true of all the Fire Signs. Another who dared to live his life like drama is T. E. Lawrence, Sun in Leo, Moon in Sagittarius. Incidentally, Peter O'Toole, who came to stardom playing the title role in the film *Lawrence of Arabia,* has an astro-gender profile identical to Lawrence's.

Living a life that is somehow larger than life—yet often tinged with a touch of the bizarre or heroic—is a facet of the Fire/Fire man. Some models of the type are Vincent Van Gogh, Sun in Aries, Moon in Sagittarius; Tennessee Williams, Sun and Moon in Aries; Andy Warhol, Sun in Leo, Moon in Sagittarius; Francis Ford Coppola, Sun in Aries, Moon in Sagittarius; and Paul Robeson, Sun in Aries, Moon in Sagittarius.

Law and Honor

The Fire/Fire man is not always one to obey speed limits; in fact, with his desire for action, he can really push the pedal. Yet, when it comes to principles, he will go down fighting for what he believes is right. In its lowest form, that can mean literally punching out someone he believes is taking advantage of someone else; in its higher form, it can mean tossing over a job if he believes the company's way of doing business is not on the mark. At the highest level, it is likely to mean he will go to the mat for his family, his friends, his country or any point of honor he sees as important. Thomas Jefferson, Sun in Aries, Moon in Sagittarius, is a good historical example.

Living With the Fire/Fire Man

To ensure domestic harmony, a trailer camp is good; better yet a fully equipped recreational van. The Fire/Fire man tends to be oblivious to his surroundings unless they somehow encroach on his desperate need for space, literally and figuratively. In general, a haphazard, spontaneous living schedule is just fine with the Fire/Fire man—unless, particularly with Aries in his profile, he decides to pull a macho act. Fortunately, Fire-type people in general let a lot roll off their backs and know how to forget and forgive. Their zest for life and sense of humor can make the best of almost any situation, however dire it may be. The humor can be philosophical, as in the case of Mark Twain, Sun in Sagittarius, Moon in Aries; witty, like James Thurber, Sun in Sagittarius, Moon in Aries; or downright low-down, as in Dom DeLuise, Sun in Leo, Moon in Sagittarius.

The Fire/Fire man is a true intuitive. That means when he says, "I've got a hunch someone is trying to give me a surprise party," he doesn't have ESP; he just has put together some bits and pieces and, darn it, he's right. The intuitive faculty can make him be considered close to genius in business circles. He will shine in almost any part of the business, but research and development is the most suitable.

Gender-correcting suggestions for the Fire/Fire man:

- You are a living dynamo, but sometimes your timing/ efficiency is off and you "shoot yourself in the foot," losing the effectiveness of your masculine Fire energy. Observe a Virgo, or even retain a Virgo "trainer" (preferably male) to show you how to get your house in order, and keep it that way.

- As a child, you were probably the type who always took three steps at a time going up the staircase (and maybe tumbled down more than once). The sign for you to study is Capricorn, which represents feminine patience and the willingness to climb more slowly to the top, watching each footstep along the way.

- Especially if there is Aries or Sagittarius in your Sun/ Moon mix (less so with smoothy Leo), you are very likely to hurt others unintentionally with your bluntness. Develop the Water-like ability to observe what you see as wrong in another's appearance/idea, but comment on it as if it were an opportunity rather than a liability.

- Your ideas come fast and furious, and generally are of a large-scale nature. Both in your career life and your personal life, surround yourself with people who can "ground you"—either Earth pragmatists or Air logicians. They can help you get a better handle on reality.

The Fire/Fire Woman

Despite the "burning ardor" of Fire, in the Fire/Fire woman it does not necessarily display itself in sexual terms. Fire/ Fire women, despite their biology, are double masculine in their astrological heritage. Research also points to the fact that Fire women have been brought up in a household where "Daddy was king" and all his exploits were championed, though not necessarily by his wife. The Fire/Fire woman wants to make it, to see it happen, to make her mark in the outer world. Making things reality seems to be built into the "feminine," so the Fire/Fire woman has a better shot at finalizing her visions than the Fire/Fire man.

Aflame Wherever She Glows

True astrology does not ignore social factors: The Fire/Fire woman may want to be the best bowler in her bowling club, or the most ambitious and daring of her car pool: She'll drive through ice and snow to get the kids there; if the car balks, she'll fix it. A Fire/Fire-type role in the movie world was played by Faye Dunaway in *Network*. She so burned for the passion of success and notoriety that she failed miserably in her relationship with William Holden. This is a classic scenario of how a woman can be far more endowed with "masculine" qualities than her partner. Apparently "cooler" real-life Fire/Fire women who've obviously had the "engine" of Fire working for them are Ali MacGraw, Sun in Aries, Moon in Leo; Jackie Kennedy Onassis, Sun in Leo, Moon in Aries; and Flannery O'Connor, Sun in Aries, Moon in Leo.

A Double-Edged Sword

The Fire/Fire woman is in a tenuous spot—right near the center of the gender spectrum, but unaware of how to deal with it, or fix her need for feminine values. Diane Keaton visits us in *Baby Boom,* where she transmutes from a Fire/ Fire type to a Fire/Earth type—against her will, simply by the power of circumstance. For Diane Keaton's character, the answer came out of a clever script writer's bag of tricks. For real-life women, it may take a great deal of introspection and a drastic change in lifestyle to come to the

realization that they *are* women and that they should not
devalue their feminine side—because feminists in our society prod them on, or men (or women) in the business
world recognize that they are good at what they do.

Her Real Love: Doing

It is often not enough for the Fire/Fire woman to be a doer;
she must accomplish something that has an impact on the
rest of the world—even if it is her own small circle. Gloria
Steinem, Sun in Aries, Moon in Leo, is a prime example. It
is interesting to note that as she becomes older, she is
becoming aware of the life of the "feminine" that hereto-
fore went virtually unnoticed. Elizabeth Dole, Sun in Leo,
Moon in Sagittarius, clearly is a Fire/Fire woman who
seems to have bridged the gap, and allowed the feminine
to work in her life. Jane Fonda, Sun in Sagittarius, Moon in
Aries, spent a lot of her life at the barricades, and was
criticized by many. She too now seems to have found the
need for a true relationship. However, she and Ted Turner
have publicly made it known that it is also a partnership
. . . i.e., Jane will never stop her "doing." Ethel Kennedy,
Sun in Aries, Moon in Sagittarius, may be the classic example of a Fire/Fire woman who showed great strength on
both sides of the ledger.

The Fresh Kid

There is an aspect of the Fire/Fire woman that often puts
people off. Call it chutzpah, call it arrogance, call it the fact
that she is often an object of envy, by both men and
women. New York City Comptroller Elizabeth Holtzman,
Sun in Leo, Moon in Aries, is known for calling it like it is.
Joan Crawford, Sun in Aries, Moon in Sagittarius, evidently

made a career and a life out of abrasiveness. Jamie Lee Curtis, Sun in Sagittarius, Moon in Aries, whatever her off-screen personality, has played the "fresh kid" role to the hilt in such movies as *Trading Places* and *A Fish Called Wanda*. In general, the Fire/Fire woman is superfriendly, spontaneous, energetic and restless. But like that of the Fire/Fire man, her greatest personal sadness may be in the area of relationships. Her strongest weapon against the supermasculinity of her astro-gender type is to look within (not a Fire tendency) and consciously think about her "inner feminine" and see where it is *she* may be falling short in the relationship.

Living With the Fire/Fire Woman

If anyone has "women's intuition," it is the Fire/Fire woman. With both Sun and Moon in Fire, she has an uncanny way of knowing what something is going to look like before it exists. Even the expression "I see what you're talking about" indicates her ability to conjure up what is not there. Men who are heavily Fire have a certain amount of this ability too, but here the gender difference gives women the edge.

Because she sees what is not there, she often totally misses what is. Like the dust in her own home. It is not for lack of energy that Fire/Fire women keep rather casual, not-too-neat living spaces; it's just that their eyes and their minds are on what will be rather than what is.

Like the Fire/Fire man, the Fire/Fire woman regards living space as primarily useful for filling up with friends. Friends of friends. People they barely know but find interesting, etc., etc. If the hospitality is a bit slapdash, no one minds, because the Fire/Fire woman is so good at whatever she does that at least the food will be marvelous.

Fire/Fire women love children—not babies to cuddle, but adventurous, playful kids who can keep up with her high spirits. When it comes to infants, she is a competent but somewhat bored mother who might just as well work out of the house until her children are a little older. Ideal work for a Fire/Fire woman is leading a group of children in an "Outward Bound" setting or in any kind of sport.

Gender-correcting suggestions for the Fire/Fire woman:

- As you score big in the career world, you may find yourself rather lonely. You needn't get more involved than you like to develop some genuine friendships with men—particularly of the Water element. If there is Leo in your astro-gender mix, try especially hard to pull back and let others quietly make their point.

- Don't attempt to be "one of the boys" in your work situation. It could spell trouble in a number of ways, not the least of which is too much partying. Develop a friendly but slightly distant manner that makes it clear you are a "masculine" type in your work behavior, but clearly a female from a personal point of view.

- Learn to say "I'm sorry" before someone else has to point it out to you that you've gone too far. Fire is a marvelous element for fun, but sometimes can get a bit rough on others. Start to get in touch with the part of *you* that gets hurt but tends to cry all alone.

- In fact, learn that it's okay to cry when you hurt. You probably came from a home in which girls as well as boys were taught to "be tough" and that they could take it. You're all grown up now, and one of the most important tools you have to get in touch with your bruised "child within" is your own tears.

- Like your male counterpart, the Fire/Fire male, you need to realize that things don't simply "happen"; they have to be put in place with a logical and practical plan. Even if some of your stabs in the dark pay off, it doesn't mean they will forever. If necessary, hire someone to organize all your affairs, perhaps a Taurus. They are great at what they do, and also will appreciate your zany sense of humor.

Getting Sign-Specific

Fire Sun Sign/Fire Moon Sign

Aries/Aries: Independence is your outstanding trait, and you will say or do whatever you like. You are energetic and impatient, which can take you far though others may object. You are self-centered and must learn to objectify. Be more interested in others to get them interested in you.

Leo/Leo: You are ambitious and forceful and should get where you want to go. Though you are sunny on the surface, you have a hard streak and will never forget a slight. You are not introspective; the outer world is more interesting to you than your own inner world.

Sagittarius/Sagittarius: You are a reformer, believing the world should live on your principles. You are sensitive and temperamental, going to extremes of happiness and despair. You will not give in to unfairness or illogical argument. Nervous energy is your *bête noir.*

Aries/Leo: You love people, and they love you. You are adventurous, but are fixed enough to stay with one person, job, whatever. Ambition is keenly marked; you need success both for your own inner regard and for the plaudits of the world. People take you seriously.

Aries/Sagittarius: You are a seeker after "The Truth" along large lines. Because details do not concern you, you can easily fall into error. You need training! Yet you have a code of honor both for yourself and for others and can be a force for good in the world.

Leo/Aries: You are a fighter, with duty, justice and truth your banners. As an executive, you are an intelligent boss and a stern but just executive. The personal note is strong in your life, and you have to learn detachment. Then you will become a leader.

Leo/Sagittarius: You started early and will always be a few jumps ahead of yourself. You have a passion for variety and excitement. Your fire burns bright, but sometimes gets out of focus. Sometimes you get by on your greatest assets: charm, dash, enthusiasm.

Sagittarius/Aries: You are a super salesman of yourself, loving to hold the center of the stage. And you are well paid for what you give the world. You take yourself a bit too seriously, which is perhaps why others do. In love, you like variety; it suits your restlessness.

Sagittarius/Leo: You have a creative, photographic imagination. When you have the picture in mind, any goal becomes very nearly an accomplished fact. In love, you are loyal and idealistic, and constant as well. Anyone to whom you give your word has an unbreakable bond.

Air Sun Sign/Fire Moon Sign

This section pertains to both men and women whose Sun Sign is Gemini, Libra or Aquarius and whose Moon Sign is Aries, Leo, or Sagittarius.

"Rainbow round my shoulder, wings on my feet."

When you are in a funk, there is probably nothing more aggravating than others saying to you, "But you are always so cheerful!" Let's face it, just as there is nothing fixed about life, there is no consistently *anything* person. Even though, with an Air Sun Sign and a Fire Moon Sign, you are blessed with a generally happy-go-lucky outlook, you can spot a problem at twenty paces. More important, your nature is to want to act on it. As an Air Sun Sign, you are a "thinking" type, and subject to bouts of endless rumination, but your Fire Moon Sign propels you forward and gives you the enthusiasm to at least try to help.

Some may envy you because of your popularity; everyone wants to get on your dance card. Charm and a humorous, friendly outlook are characteristics you definitely possess. If your Sun Sign is Libra, you can really turn on the charm. If your Sun Sign is Gemini, your witty repartee is much appreciated. If you are an Aquarian, you can fascinate people for hours with your fund of knowledge and usually sound ideas. One deep-thinking Air/Fire type was one of the founders of atomic energy: Enrico Fermi, Sun in Libra, Moon in Aries.

However, there is a flip side to Air/Fire's ideas. Just as you appear to have an outgoing and unflappable nature, you tend to believe you have "the whole truth." This will be particularly true if the Moon is in Sagittarius. Obviously, this leads to the liability of arguments in which you take such a strong stand that you turn others off. From a professional point of view, for both men and women, this potential liability becomes an asset in the fields of law and politics. If you confine some of your "damn it, I know I'm right" thoughts to your own head, you could shine in the diplomatic corps. Putting it another way, you are something of a paradox to people. On the surface you are apparently tractable, reasonable and calm, but certain situations—the ones that touch on subconscious fears, desires, whatever—can make you immovable as an anvil in sand.

Here Comes the Judge

Especially if you are a man, and closer to the energy of
your Air Sun Sign, you are aware of your intellectual powers. With your Fire Moon Sign, honor and right have real
meaning for you. Therefore, you can be rather judgmental
about others and about causes. And, because you are verbal, literally harangue someone whose way of running his
life is not up to your rather rigorous standards. Yet your
winning ways usually win out, and it is rare for you to pout
and/or brood about matters of this type. Some take out
their discontent in public, like Jimmy Breslin, Sun in Libra,
Moon in Leo, in his column in *Newsday*.

The Air/Fire Man

Unlike the Fire/Fire man, the Air/Fire man generally waits
for his ardor to cool before making decisions in his love
life. The courting game can go on for a long time as the
Air/Fire man moves from thought process to thought process. Is there any potential here? Will this person's idea of
the ideal lifestyle jibe with mine? Is she a "good fit" into
the life I'm living now? However, the object of the Air/Fire
man's love is usually not in a position to complain about
his apparent indecisiveness because he is so romantic, in
the old-fashioned sense of the word. He will make each
date extra special with a different twist. Never mind that
it has been contrived to reveal more to him about her. It's
delightful.

Unfortunately, Air/Fire men can marry late or not at all,
because so much depends on making the right choice.
Women can begin to feel as if they are a biological speci-
men being examined for faults. Speaking of biology, the
Air/Fire man, once roused, makes a fantastic lover. The
"intuitive" function of his Fire Moon gets switched on, and
his true imagination goes to work. Some classic sex symbols of the Air/Fire variety are Alan Alda, Sun in Aquarius,

Moon in Aries; and Montgomery Clift, Sun in Libra, Moon in Sagittarius. Note that in both cases the charm is of the offhand variety.

Wits and Words

Most women find it hard to resist Air/Fire men. They are easy, breezy talkers who at least appear to be interested in you, and only you. They are incredibly quick on the verbal trigger and, because the Air function makes them information junkies, are able to see and often satirize the contemporary scene. Just a few Air/Fire men who have make their living by keeping them laughing are Bob Hope, Sun in Gemini, Moon in Sagittarius; Red Buttons, Sun in Aquarius, Moon in Aries; Jules Feiffer, Sun in Aquarius, Moon in Leo; and John Belushi, Sun in Aquarius, Moon in Leo. Sammy Cahn, Sun in Gemini, Moon in Sagittarius; and Cole Porter, Sun in Gemini, Moon in Aries, did their witty talking through lyrics.

The list of Air/Fire men who have run risks—physically or mentally—is impressive and illustrative of the male/male gender base they were working off. Charles Lindbergh, Sun in Aquarius, Moon in Sagittarius; and Evel Knievel, Sun in Libra, Moon in Leo, illustrate the male archetype as Man of Deed. James Dickey, Sun in Aquarius, Moon in Leo; James Joyce, Sun in Aquarius, Moon in Leo; and Gore Vidal, Sun in Libra, Moon in Aries, dared to break the old rules in their writing and are classic Men of the Word. And two who found the ultimate courage to passively resist are the Dalai Lama, Sun in Gemini, Moon in Leo; and Mahatma Gandhi, Sun in Libra, Moon in Leo.

Living With the Air/Fire Man

Air/Fire men tend to be picky—not only about the women they marry, but also about most anything in their living/working environment. Despite their happy exteriors, even a small thing that touches a nerve can set off an explosion. The Air/Fire man's mate quickly learns to "hide" minor transgressions and not to overreact to her husband's bluster. It's just all that fiery imagination "blown up" by air.

On the positive side, Air/Fire men make wonderful fathers. With their wide-ranging enthusiasm and clearheaded thinking, they can be most anything to a child—teacher, coach, "King of the Mountain." If there is anything that will make a child cringe from the Air/Fire father, it is his tendency to get hung up on details and "make a big deal" out of what a child considers to be a minor matter.

When one of these fire storms breaks out, those who really know the Air/Fire man know enough to get out of the way and wait until it blows over. As a result of his volatility, the Air/Fire man can easily suffer from high blood pressure. Therefore, those closest to him, in pointing out this tendency, should be very clear that it is in his best interests to learn to deal with things more coolly.

One solution: to have a "room of his own" where he can keep the many things—books, etc.—that feed his interests, and where he can go to get things back in perspective. After all, with his Air Sun Sign, reasoning things out should come easily.

Gender-correcting suggestions for the Air/Fire man:

- With Fire in your astro-gender mix—particularly in your Moon Sign—you should learn to trust and follow your intuition (hunches)—especially when they check out with the Air part of you. This is particularly true in the area of romantic partners. Don't "let a good one get away" simply because your "it must make sense." Air/Sun can't see the greater possibilities of the relationship.

- You are not always right, and you know it—yet your male/male astro-gender profile would like you to think so. With your Moon in Fire, the more androgynous male element, you should be able to lighten up and listen up to the suggestions of others, even if they run counter to what you firmly believe.

- Animals are good medicine for all-masculine types. They give love unconditionally and can bring out the feeling nature in virtually anyone. Almost any pet will do, but you might feel most comfortable with a large (but gentle) dog. They are amazing examples of how size and sex do not have to naturally breed animosity and anger.

- With or without a female partner, spend some time far away from your usual office and home grounds. In a sense, if you "get back to the earth" in the real sense, you will gain a great deal that can help relieve your often jangled nervous system. Air and Fire alone can make you feel very "wired" at times.

- Give some real attention to people who work for you—more than just "Let's get together after work." With your particular astro-gender profile, you could overlook someone who's really in trouble, either in or out of the office. Spend some quality time inquiring about how things are going, use your intuition to get at what may really be bothering someone, and use your good sense to correct the situation. If it is something beyond your control, do all you can to get the right kind of help for the person.

The Air/Fire Woman

The Air/Fire woman is a dynamo. Sometimes when people see her coming, they run for cover. If there is such a thing as an excess of ideas, she can be accused of it. The reason is that she tends to feel the "masculine" power given to her by her astrological heritage. There is no question that she can do, but she easily can do too much. In the Air/Fire woman, one of the keys is that her natural closeness to the energies of her Moon Sign—which is imaginative, creative fire—can overwhelm her own good sense.

In the field of interpersonal relationships, the Air/Fire woman is likely to find that her best audience, when in a group, is men. They feel comfortable with her assertive, aggressive ideas, and all but forget she is a woman. In more personal affairs, the Air/Fire woman can be a very lonely type because men can get tired of her constant planning, creating, laying out her strategies about how she is going to make it happen. He just wants to relax and have a good time when there is time for the leisure life. In the Air/Fire woman—as in all the double-masculine women types—there's a big thing missing that belongs to the "feminine." That is, a sense of play, a desire to do just for the sake of doing, or simply being. It is also, or has been, a mark of contemporary society. Things are changing, however, and people—even men—are beginning to say that the purpose of work is to support a pleasant leisure life.

Given the fact that our work-oriented society looks down at such simple pursuits as play for the sake of play, the Air/Fire woman finds it difficult to feel important unless she is performing, or talking about performing, in the (man's) world of making money and making things. A classic "performer" in the advertising world is Mary Wells Laurence, Sun in Gemini, Moon in Leo. And she did it before success for women became the rage. Another hardball player whose business acumen belies her outlook is Yoko Ono, Sun in Aquarius, Moon in Sagittarius.

Getting Close to Home

A great many women with double-masculine astro-gender profiles care more about the elegance and style of their living space than about the comfort and warmth of it. If she feels unsure of herself in the decorating area, she is likely to hire a professional, which takes her place even further away from her. Domestic pursuits are not her style, even though she may have the knowledge. When it comes to cooking, she is likely to go to that gourmet-cooking course her buddies told her about, but to have a hopelessly empty refrigerator.

Yes, buddies, because the double-masculine woman has a problem being intimate even with her female friends. Business talk before small talk is a general rule, and revealing her feelings to anyone runs the risk of exhibiting her vulnerability.

Beauty and the Stage

In general, the Air/Fire woman is the one who is most likely to be devastated by a broken fingernail. Beauty and grooming—what shows on the outside—are high on her list of priorities. There is a beautiful serenity of looks to Air Sign women, particularly Librans, like Catherine Deneuve, Sun in Libra, Moon in Leo. Appearances are highly important, sometimes too important.

Any number of Air/Fire women are drawn to performance careers—perhaps as a way of defusing their double-masculine astrological profile that gets applause and accolades, but is not clearly "men's work." Judy Garland, Sun in Gemini, Moon in Sagittarius; and Beverly Sills, who has the same profile, are two. It is interesting that Ms. Sills followed up her singing career with an administrative one. Oprah Winfrey, Sun in Aquarius, Moon in Sagittarius, clearly enjoys every moment in the spotlight. One Air/Fire woman who announced her intention to go on to a glorious performing career just before her life ended was Isadora Duncan, Sun in Gemini, Moon in Aries.

Living With the Air/Fire Woman

Air/Fire women who live in a family situation often "lose their edge"—that is, become a little softer and gentler than their sisters who follow a career to the exclusion of all else.

For one thing, the Air/Fire woman quickly learns that others can strike back when they are in the "safe" confines of the home. If she pushes too hard, someone else can push back even harder, and that includes her children. Regardless of their astro-gender profile, most children under ten or so operate mainly out of feeling. Because she is not herself a "feeling" type, the Air/Fire woman can be badly hurt by a child who says something that "gets her in the gut."

Another advantage of domestic life for the Air/Fire woman is that, unless she is very rich, she must "get her hands dirty." Household tasks are a marvelous remedy for "thinking" types because they are usually so rote that one doesn't think—one just does. Cooking is especially good for the Air/Fire type because it is really chemistry, and a good result depends on careful and accurate measurements.

Some Air/Fire women feel confined within the home and believe they need further stimulation. Since such an energetic type can handle a lot on her plate, she should not worry about volunteering, joining, organizing groups that will give her the latitude she needs and the feeling that she is "out in the world" right in her own backyard.

In these days of the home office, the Air/Fire woman is the ideal candidate either to conduct her own business or to job-share with someone else. Since she should be quite well organized, this way of working will not feel foreign to her.

Gender-correcting suggestions for the Air/Fire woman:

- As focused as you may be on whatever job/career/ project absorbs much of your time and energy, your

Moon in Fire—especially if it is in Aries—gives you an irrepressible instinct for play. Play—the ability to enjoy almost any pursuit for its own sake without regard for consequences—is one of the joys of Fire. Take a vacation without a briefcase, and be sure that wherever you go, there's plenty to play at. The more devil-may-care type of activities, the better.

- Even though you are not a "domestic" type in the classic sense of the word, your element combination—Air with its scientific bent and Fire with its "what-if" tendencies—is a natural for certain kinds of stereotypically "female" activities. Baking a cake from scratch—a combination of chemistry and the wonderment of watching something totally new take shape—is ideal balm for your sometimes overly hyper personality.

- There's a performing star in all of us dying to get out. Yours is especially strong. Even if you lack the talent, make sure you get the opportunity to be noticed. Local talent groups are ideal places to get to belt out your song or play the part you've always dreamed of. Stifling your urge to perform is liable to make you become overly critical of those who try "just for the heck of it," in every area of life.

- Because you are a female born into the masculine thinking sign, Air, and a masculine Fire Moon, you may sometimes go with your head rather than your heart. When confronted by a situation in which another seems to need help, offer support and "doable" suggestions rather than arid advice. Look inward and test out what you suggest on yourself; does it feel "comfortable"? Sometimes people need more TLC than tutoring.

- Take pride in your own exterior looks as well as your excellent mind. Sometimes a total makeover can do wonders for "success" in every sense.

Getting Sign-Specific

Air Sun Sign/Fire Moon Sign

Gemini/Aries: You float on air—sometimes hot air. However, you are generally bright and interested in whatever comes along, so that no one takes offense. Your curiosity level is extremely high, which pays big dividends.

Libra/Aries: You are far more considerate than the usual Aries. Its your Libra Sun Sign which makes you very much of a gentleman or a lady. You will go far with those who appreciate fine things. You will have a few of them yourself.

Aquarius/Aries: You have big ideas and with the right training you could get them off the ground. You are well organized and know how to get things done. With your Aries Moon, you can occasionally get rather feisty.

Gemini/Leo: You have a lot of class and insist that others who are around you have it too. You are a fair person and would be just as happy if all the world were too. You never let people know if you are down.

Libra/Leo: You are an artist no matter what you do, even if you simply make cookies. You have a strong head and opinions to match. Watch your words when you have it out with someone. You can really hurt even when you don't want to.

Aquarius/Leo: Your Sun and Moon are opposites in the zodiac—that is, you are a full moon person. Make the most of it and don't let "good luck" be mistaken for hard work. Aquarius is a loner, and often doesn't marry till midlife.

Gemini/Sagittarius: You are a constant traveler, if only by armchair. Your plans are high, wide and handsome, and generally pan out. Don't let your nerves get the better of you; you can handle it.

Libra/Sagittarius: You make people feel good by giving them a sense of confidence. On your own, you are not the greatest companion in the world because you can't make up your mind.

Aquarius/Sagittarius: If you don't have a scientific bent, it's not because of your Sun/Moon combination. If there's any problem, it's that you analyze everything and everybody to death. Try to take a more "holistic" approach.

Fire Sun Sign/Air Moon Sign

This section pertains to both men and woman whose Sun Sign is Aries, Leo or Sagittarius and whose Moon Sign is Gemini, Libra or Aquarius.

If the world were full of Fire/Air people, we would all have a lot more fun. Unless other factors in their natal charts prevent it, they have sunny, outgoing dispositions. They like, and actually need, to give to others and make them happy. They live in a constant state of expectancy, and their expectations are always positive. It is hard to be "down" around a Fire/Air person. They, of course, also need comforting at times, but they tend to keep their hurts to themselves.

With their Fire Sun Sign, this type sees the world as full of vast possibilities; with an Air Moon Sign, they have the power to work out a sensible—and often very profitable—plan. One person typical of this Fire/Air combination is

Walt Disney, Sun in Sagittarius, Moon in Libra. His warmth, humor and comic spirit—plus an extraordinary penchant for technology—reached out and touched people the world over. They enjoy life to the hilt, and—again thanks to the Fire Sun Sign—they see it as a vast playground. No matter how successful they are, they "just want to have fun." Could anyone be more typical than Malcolm Forbes, Sun in Leo, Moon in Gemini?

Some of their genius comes from their being what-if types. Not downer rehashes of the past like, "What if we had done so and so?" or, "What if I had said this to him?" but the kind that are creative. Their what-ifs are always future-oriented and experimental. "What if we sold this house and moved to Alaska?" "What if we try changing this recipe and turning it into something more exotic?" "What if we bought a cheaper car and could have two instead of one? We'd both get around faster."

People-focused and activity-oriented, Fire/Air people can be miserable if they fall into the wrong job or wrong career. If they are typical, however, it isn't likely to last for long. Fire/Air types are always willing to move on to the next possibility. This can be a detriment in terms of being labeled a job-hopper, but on the positive side, it shows a confidence and strength to take risks that is an astro-birthright of this combination. Notable in this area: Henry Ford, Sun in Leo, Moon in Aquarius.

From a gender point of view, the double-masculine Fire/Air combination plus the all-too-possible insensitivity of the Fire Signs, Fire/Airs have to be twice as careful not to bruise people (unintentionally, of course) as they leap and jump from one thing to another. If the quality of empathy is cultivated, it can produce people who are virtually worshipped by those who know them. An example from the magazine publishing world is Peter Diamandis, Sun in Sagittarius, Moon in Gemini. When he figured out a way to make a financial coup, he made sure all the people who had been loyal to him got in on the deal.

The Fire/Air Man

The paradox of this combination is that something can go awry and turn out men who abuse the "man power" of both their biological and their astrological heritages. There is almost a "dictator by right" syndrome, which can be seen in such examples as Fidel Castro, Sun in Leo, Moon in Libra; Eugene McCarthy, Sun in Aries, Moon in Aquarius; and Nikita Krushchev, Sun in Aries, Moon in Libra. On the lighter side, but still atypical Fire/Air types, are men like Leo Durocher, Sun in Leo, Moon in Libra—who couldn't be nice because "nice guys finish last"—and Walter Winchell, Sun in Aries, Moon in Gemini, who lashed many a reputation with his whiplike words. In men like these, it is the Moon Sign—in these cases, Air—that appears to come up from the subconscious in its chilliest form and subdue the warmth of their Fire Sun Sign.

Loving Friends

In a movie starring Lawrence Harvey and Simone Signoret, in which they are lovers, she describes their relationship as "loving friends." That is what probably most Fire/Air men want in a partner. The turbulence of emotional strife, the pettiness that comes with jealousy, the overly protective lover frighten the man with Fire/Air. Yet, because his Air Moon makes the thinking function available to him, he usually will give a relationship a chance before moving on swiftly, like his zodiacal sibling, the Fire/Fire man.

Ensuring the fact that a particular relationship can be made permanent, he has another ace up his sleeve—a kind of clownlike charm that lets him get away with almost anything. That is not to imply that all relationships with Fire/Air men require constant vigilance: You both set down the rules at the beginning, and if you follow them, all will go well. One Air/Fire type, with six children and a very mentally active wife, was once asked, How do you help your wife? His answer: "By taking care of myself." Independence and a natural bent toward handling the practical matters of life make the Fire/Air man a real boon as a husband.

"Let Me Entertain You"

There are any number of writers and entertainers born under the Fire Sun Sign/Air Moon Sign configuration, but some in particular stand out as examples of men who really love their art. They illustrate this masculine/masculine astro-gender's being in love with life: Mick Jagger, Sun in Sagittarius, Moon in Libra; Noel Coward, Sun in Sagittarius, Moon in Gemini; Tiny Tim, Sun in Aries, Moon in Libra. One whose thoughtful humor tells us he understands life, and is able to laugh in spite of it, is Woody Allen, Sun in Sagittarius, Moon in Aquarius.

Living With the Fire/Air Man

Fire blends with Air in the male to enlarge everything he does—and a lot do make it into the big time.

On a less-celebrated level lives the Fire/Air man who hasn't got a claim to fame. Even in his small circle, however, he is likely to be a standout and the type everyone wants to be part of the group at party time. He can be "a clown," in the upbeat sense of the word, or he can be a more serious type who has mastered, say, politics. His words carry weight with his friends, even if he isn't always right. There are also "turn-types" among ordinary Fire/Air men. Instead of projecting ebullience, gaiety or "smarts," they can be the kind who grouse loudly—and often obnoxiously—about the state of the world and everything in it. When this happens it's usually because the Fire/Air man isn't getting the respect he believes he deserves.

Gender-correcting suggestions for the Fire/Air man:

- Men of this astro-gender profile occasionally need "a kick in the head" to avoid the swelled-head syndrome. This is especially so if the Fire Sun Sign is Aries or Leo. This all-masculine profile in a male body can prove just a bit too much. Such men would do well to cultivate some friends (male or female) who are quiet, feeling types and learn what they can from them.

- Sports mania threatens the Fire Sun/Air Moon man. In fact, he can become an absolute bore in his incessant reciting of arcane statistics about teams, players, etc. If this is your astro-gender profile, the antidote is to bone up on subjects that most everyone is interested in—like movies, politics, etc., and have several bodies of knowledge to draw on, depending on your audience.

- Often without any intention of doing any harm, you are the type who can easily be accused of sexual harassment. First, there is your "big kidder" Fire Sun Sign, often unable to resist what you consider funny, even if others don't. In addition, your Air Moon Sign, with its logical bent, can't imagine that anyone could complain about your "fun and games." Watch it. Especially around masculine-sign women.

- You can be a great "lover"—of all that lives. You are the ideal candidate to spend some time helping others, especially deprived children. You would make a fabulous "Big Brother."

- With your ebullience and hard-driving style, you can bowl people over—either professionally or personally. One good bet is to work off some of that excess physical *and* mental energy with the right kind of exercise. Some, of course, should be sweat-provoking and competitive, or you wouldn't be happy. However,

for developing some of the softer gender characteristics within a masculine context, a physio-emotional
Oriental discipline, such as Tai Chi Chuan, with its
controlled, dancelike movements, would be ideal.

The Fire/Air Woman

Women born with this astro-gender configuration are very
often misunderstood—particularly by men. They are so
outgoing and enthusiastic, so ready for anything, even willing to stand at the bar with the boys, that they can be
considered "easy." On one-on-one dates they are so interested in what the man is interested in that he can mistake
it for interest in him. She can be in and out of relationships
with great speed, but once she has found the man she
wants, she is likely to go overboard. She so badly wants
to please people that she can make a lover feel like a gigolo
with her generosity.

Sweetheart or Buddy

Unless they consciously make an effort to look more traditionally "feminine" through clothes, makeup and hair,
these Fire/Air women often develop the "good buddy" reputation, and find themselves counseling men about their
relationships rather than having any themselves. Many of
this type have sharp tongues and no fear of speaking their
minds, even if it creates discomfort. Think of Bette Davis,
Sun in Aries, Moon in Gemini, and some of the roles she
played—particularly in *All About Eve*. It's either a coincidence or an example of perfect casting.

Fire Sun/Air Moon women, from author Jane Austen, Sun
in Sagittarius, Moon in Libra, to anthropologist Margaret
Mead, Sun in Sagittarius, Moon in Aquarius, have a built-
in feminist bent. Not so much the marching, flag-waving
variety, but more a natural assumption that they have
work to do in this world. In a sense, it has been one more

demerit, as far as men are concerned, until the rest of the world catches up with women of this astro-gender type. With the Fire Sun Sign, it can often be a crusade—for example, Anita Bryant, Sun in Aries, Moon in Libra. Considering her particular rallying cry, it is interesting to remember that she has a double-masculine astro-gender background. Ruth Buzzi, Sun in Leo, Moon in Libra, has developed a wit with a sharp edge that reveals her double-masculine Sun/Moon Sign combination.

With the forward-propelling movement of the Fire Sun Sign and the clear-thinking of the Air Moon Sign, these women can go far—all the way to the Supreme Court in the case of Sandra Day O'Connor, Sun in Aries, Moon in Aquarius. In some ways she exemplifies the fact that women are more inclined toward the particular energy of the Moon Sign. In Justice O'Connor's case, the sign is Aquarius—the most fair, humane and egalitarian of all the thinking Air Signs.

Marriage?

For all their pseudo-male posturing, particularly in the tomboy years, a great many Fire/Air women make good marriages and even learn to love (tolerate) children. Often the marriages have unusual arrangements. Connie Chung, Sun in Leo, Moon in Gemini, spent quite a while in a New York/Washington commuting marriage. Another Fire/Air type has a three-months-together, three-months-apart marriage in order to divvy up the responsibilities of two businesses in different parts of the country.

Just listen to the approval of a group of women when someone suggests a "weekends only" marriage. It is usually loud and heart-felt, whatever their astro-gender types. As more and more kinds of arrangements develop in relationships, it looks as if the Fire/Air woman was one of the first to recognize that women don't have to go arm in arm with men every day of the week or year.

Living With the Fire/Air Woman

If you love slightly wacky types who laugh at the drop of a hat, you would love living with the Fire/Air woman. Even if she turns moody, she generally can find a joke in it somewhere. Fire/Air women are usually as energetic as their Air/Fire sisters, but they also seem to enjoy their full lives a lot more. *First things first* is the Fire/Air woman's motto, and "first things" are usually the ones that are the most fun or the most interesting. With her Fire Sun Sign, the Fire/Air woman has a fairly broad perspective on her world; she knows that it contains jobs that simply must get done and chores necessary to running a household. However, she knows how to polish off the nitty-gritty stuff in short order to make room for the "juicier" things.

Her children may get nagged a little about keeping things neat, but it's mostly "pro forma," and she knows her children hear it in other households. An animal lover herself, she would let her children turn the house into a zoo if her Air Moon did not tell her "Enough."

It's pretty hard to pick a fight with a Fire/Air female. First of all, she's got a lot on her mind and regards it as a waste of time. Second, there isn't a lot that really bugs her, so if it's bugging you, she'll change it. The Fire/Air woman is hardly a saint, however; when she does get angry she pulls out all the stops (remember, she's double masculine) and can even throw things. Not really at you—just to show how frustrated (and possibly how dangerous) she really is.

Gender-correcting suggestions for the Fire/Air woman:

- Friend to all with a great desire to help others, you sometimes insist that all their problems will be solved by doing it *your* way. Learn to be a good listener but not necessarily a universal problem solver; people often know what's best for themselves.

- Before making any irrevocable decisions about whether or not you want children in your life (you may like them but regard them as "too much trouble"), do a stint as a volunteer working with little ones. You are an ideal candidate for the successful single parent, but for all your independence, you will find greater happiness with a man in your life as well.

- Especially if your Moon Sign is Aquarius, you have excellent equipment to make a great manager. Your Fire Moon will give you the likability; your employees will applaud your fairness. However, be careful not to get taken in by a hard-luck story. Check it out before you make a decision.

- Though your mind may be and probably is quite well organized, you may find it difficult to deal with the hands-on details of the world. Make sure to organize your nest and your office so you know where everything is.

- Try not to be so intellectually competitive with men— or to "boss them around" unless it is vital to your work. And even then, do it with a light touch. Women of your astro-gender profile sometimes marry late, often because they feel they do not need anyone. The real need for nurturing can come later in life, and you may well find it lonely without a mate.

Getting Sign-Specific

Fire Sun Sign/Air Moon Sign

Aries/Gemini: You are a child at heart and probably will stay that way all your life. While it gives you many charming qualities, it would be good for your overall future to deliberately develop some more mature values.

Aries/Libra: You are a true honor scout, always willing to do the best for people. However, you should develop some of your Aries "warlike" qualities too. They will come in very handy when you are trying to get your way.

Aries/Aquarius: You are an enigma—on the one hand all flash and dash, on the other a thinker and a planner. It's a good combination and should serve you well in what you do from here on out.

Leo/Gemini: Don't ever let them get you down. You have a fierce pride, but can easily be crushed. Think about ways you can toughen yourself without developing a hard shell.

Leo/Libra: Never let it be said that you are not hospitable. In fact, you may very well be house-proud to a fault. Enjoy your friends, but try to get beneath the surface and find out what everyone is all about.

Leo/Aquarius: You are a person of stature, no matter what you do. You are able to work at any level and do so with dignity and aplomb. Just don't let yourself get carried away by being overly serious.

Sagittarius/Gemini: You can get away with virtually any-thing. You have such charm, you find that others egg you on. If you can't get a job in the theater, entertain in your office. On a serious note, you've got great ideas.

Sagittarius/Libra: Don't waste your time trying to be cor-rect. Let your humanity come out and delight people with it. If you can, try to get some traveling in. It will delight your soul. And you may meet someone.

Sagittarius/Aquarius: You are in a special category of peo-ple who know how to rely on themselves. Fine, but it could be a lonely life unless you let others into it. You will find a great reception.

Chapter 8

Feminine Sun Sign/ Feminine Moon Sign

Earth Sun Sign/Earth Moon Sign

This section pertains to both men and women whose sun sign and Moon Sign are in an Earth Sign: Taurus, Virgo or Capricorn.

"It is better to have a permanent income than to be fascinating."

—OSCAR WILDE

The Earth/Earth people of our world are the ones who make it possible to live in it. That is not to say that they do not enjoy themselves or to imply that they stay away from earthly pleasures—Taurus particularly enjoys sensual pursuits. What it means is that Earth/Earth people are double-grounded; there is little they will "buy" without tangible proof of its effectiveness, be it a theory or a toaster. The "feminine" nature of the Earth Signs is some-

times misunderstood, because they are such "doers."
However, with the exception of Capricorn, they are more
likely to be "worker bees" than CEOs of major companies.
Taurus, the firm and dedicated, does wind up in high
places too, but usually has to be dragged there kicking and
screaming. Virgo is an incessant doer, but would rather
have no one notice. In a sense, Earth is "in service" to
more active elements of Fire and Air. Earth people often
"cannot be moved" and will hold a position even when
someone of the air element "proves" his or her theory
above reproach. Because Earth corresponds to the human
faculty of sensing, these people are often literally close to
the earth, enjoying gardening from tending to full-fledged
outside gardens to a mass of indoor flower pots. They are
also very sensuous, in the physical meaning. Such clichés
as "earth people are dull" are totally denied by their love
of feeling and touching—from hugging pals to passionate
sex.

Earth people have to have their reality confirmed by the
five senses in order to grasp it. But once they do, nothing
matches their reliability, industry and patience. Motiva-
tion comes from the inspiration of others who incite Earth
to action. They are often at odds with Fire people because
Fire's extreme enthusiasm and radiance make Earth types
nervous. In a sense, the other elements bring the world to
life for Earth. But once something is there, you can count
on its being preserved.

Two other characteristics that are rightly assigned to
Earth are reserve and an attachment to possessions. In
extreme form, say a double Capricorn, the reserve will take
a lot to break it down. By the same token, a double Taurus
can seem ebullient, but that may be the effect of the Rising
Sign, and what they reveal about themselves is only superficial. As for possessions, Earth people can be happy
collectors of virtually anything, or at the outer limits they
can border on being greedy. In the world of work, they can
be masters at the art of managing other people's money,
to say nothing of their own. A motto for Taurus might be

the Sufi saying, "All you truly possess is what will not be lost in a shipwreck."

The Earth/Earth Man

Solidity is the key word for the Earth/Earth man. It can be physical: Joe Louis, Sun in Taurus, Moon in Capricorn; Willie Mays, Sun in Taurus, Moon in Capricorn; and Yogi Berra, double Taurus, were all Earth/Earth men. But strength of character or tenacity to an ideal is also prominent in Earth men. Karl Marx, Sun in Taurus, Moon in Taurus; Lyndon Johnson, Sun and Moon in Virgo; and former Chief Justice Warren Berger, Sun in Virgo, Moon in Capricorn, are merely a few examples of the persistence and practical judgment of Earth/Earth men. For sheer perseverance and the kind of strength shown by very few, there can be no better example than Stephen Hawking, Sun in Capricorn, Moon in Virgo, the brilliant British astrophysicist who thinks, writes and lectures despite almost total disability.

Earth's Secret Sexiness

The Earth/Earth combination is not always an easy one for men to live with. Some withdraw and live out lives of good character and prudent habits, and suppress their natural maleness. A lot of them never marry. However, the sensuousness of Earth, once it is lighted by someone's Fire or moved by a Water Sign, can surpass that of many other men in the zodiac. Living in the world of the senses, they are truly "there" when making love; living with the naturalness of Earth, they take to it as an important matter of course. Some sex symbols of Earth/Earth are Sean Connery, Sun and Moon in Virgo; and Jack Nicholson, Sun and

Moon in Taurus; they typify the slumbrous lustiness of Earth/Earth men. Jimmy Stewart, Moon in Taurus, Sun in Capricorn, has the "aw, shucks" variety, but it is there. Brian De Palma, director of *Dressed to Kill,* Sun in Virgo, Moon in Capricorn, is no stranger to sex either. Sensory pleasures of other sorts also attract the double-Earth man to a life career: Food critic Craig Claiborne, Sun in Virgo, Moon in Taurus, is one example.

Loving the Earth/Earth Man

Along in the package of sensuousness comes sensitivity in the Earth/Earth man. We have now stepped over the edge, astrologically speaking, into the realm of the "feminine." The Earth/Earth man may be totally unaware of it, but beneath the outside of that bemuscled or well-taken-care-of body (Virgo) is a layer of "soft stuff" that takes him away from the insensitivity of the all Fire or Air man. It makes him an understanding, though very exacting, boss and the kind of father who, once you have proved you will stick with the rules, makes it all up with a trip to the most popular soda-and-burger shop. If there are times the Earth/Earth male seems so "wimpy" his partner wants to scream, it is because he may be suppressing his natural maleness and overusing the aspects of the "feminine" he has been given by astrology.

Living With the Earth/Earth Man

The standards of the Earth/Earth man are quite high in wanting to live well—both in the material and ordered senses. Aristotle Onassis, Sun in Capricorn, Moon in Virgo, stood out as an example of the Earth-type man whose visible possessions must shout, "I can afford it," but there are many others in the world. Along with show, the Earth/ Earth man wants "a clean, well-ordered place." No matter how high or humble his home, it must be well organized. The double-Taurus man might be a slight exception, because he will prefer the outdoors (but what a perfect campsite it must be). Double-Earth men and any other astro-gender combination can easily turn into "Odd Couple" situations. Perhaps in this age of role reversal, nitpicking men who want things "just so" will put their backs into the work it requires as well.

Another problem some find with the double-Earth male is the fact that he finds it virtually impossible to imagine what he cannot see. Earth people may be builders, but rarely architects. When a big-picture type meets an Earth person, they might as well be speaking in different languages. Yet when it comes to getting it exactly right, you would be wise to put your money on the Earth person.

The Earth/Earth man can be as good a mother as any woman in the zodiac. Earth is a feminine element, but not soft and cushy like Water, the other feminine element. Earth can cover and be protective, but Earth can also freeze and provide another kind of bulwark. In general, Earth men like the same things children do—things that taste and feel good. That puts them on the same track from the beginning. Earth cares about the basics, and the basics are what children need. Earth can be soft—or it can be hard, just as children need both types of caring for. Though Taurus can be a little lax, Earth in general expects and gets good behavior.

Gender-correcting suggestions for the Earth/Earth man:

- One manifestation of earth is rock. You, with both Sun and Moon Signs in Earth Signs, can seem positively unbending at times. Your stolid stance could take you far in business—yet it might simply be taken for stubbornness. In interpersonal relationships it is all too easily interpreted as an "I don't care" attitude, with no room for tenderness toward your partner. A productive meditation for you would be that of water washing over the rocks and gradually eroding what can be a harsh attitude.

- Patience is a virtue, but not if carried too far. Particularly in a manager, it can be taken for weakness if you seem to put up with more than is appropriate from an employee. Assert yourself in your quiet way, and use your "feminine" to communicate to the employee that you are both in this thing together.

- If you share living space with a less sensory type, male or female—i.e., less sensitive to the environment you share—try to keep friction at a minimum by reserving some space of your own, which you can keep as you want it. Many Earth men in particular are bothered by clutter—unless it's their own.

- Don't allow yourself to become an indoors type; you belong where the sun shines, or at least where there is fresh air. If you are not the type to make yourself do it on your own, join a group—for biking, hiking or any type of outdoors activity you can do on a regular basis. If you have even a patch of earth, cultivate it with flowers or plants and tend them as your "children."

- Enjoy what you earn and what you own, whatever its value. Earth men in particular are "nesters" in the sense that they want to build as much security as possible for their families. It is a trait to be praised, but not when it is carried to an extreme.

The Earth/Earth Woman

The Earth/Earth woman, if married and true to type, could be called "Mrs. Goodwife," and there are still a lot them around today. Everything she does is done in an orderly, efficient manner. One never plays while there is still work to be done. On the outside she can look a little "chilly" or sharp-edged, but that is just a front. She is the type who will do anything for anybody in need or distress at any time.

Among younger women today you will find the double-Earth woman doing a superb job so quietly you can hardly hear it. Double-Capricorn women are the exception; because they are so eager to fatten their paychecks, they will make it known what a great job they are doing.

Above and Beyond the Call

Duty is the watchword of the Earth/Earth woman, and if employers ever begin to use astrology as a measure of who is good for what they will learn that lower-level positions with heavy responsibility *can* be filled and keep someone happy. The Earth/Earth type is supremely right for the role. Now, as for creative director, an employer would be wise to look to other element combinations.

She Has a Secret Too

When Mrs.—or Ms.—takes to her bed (or his), she too can be a sexual partner par excellence. On the outside the double-Earth woman can appear modest and standoffish, although her natural sensuousness will always come to the fore. But there's a hitch. She's got to meet her match—not necessarily in the sexual arena, but in the world at large. The Earth/Earth woman does not commit herself to anyone until he has been tried, and been true to her idea of what a "real man" should be. With some double-Earth women, their sexiness shines through: Cher, Sun in Taurus, Moon in Capricorn; Michelle Pfeiffer, Sun in Taurus, Moon in Virgo; and Candace Bergen, Sun in Taurus, Moon in Virgo, are excellent examples. In her role as Murphy Brown, the last of this trio is a wonderful archetype of the androgynous female—she who is all there sexually, and an excellent administrator as well.

The Boss

Though the majority of Earth/Earth women would rather not find themselves in the social or political limelight, when they do, they shine. The late Ella Grasso, Sun in Taurus, Moon in Virgo, governor of Connecticut, had the hard head necessary for the job, but compassion and feeling for others as well. Especially when the Moon is in Virgo, the Earth/Earth woman has a need to be of service. The Moon reflects both what we need and what makes us feel useful. Coretta Scott King, Sun in Taurus, Moon in Virgo, exemplifies Earth/Earth at its best.

Though most Earth/Earth women appear to have both feet firmly on the ground, there are exceptions—but also explanations. Shirley MacLaine, Sun in Taurus, Moon in Virgo, demonstrates this by being natural and comfortable in her role (which is real life) as a mystic: Her books read as if she has really been there and observed with her own eyes. She is not self-defensive about her position, just very determined.

Wits to the Wise

Earth women—Earth people in general—can seem to take life very seriously. That's because the Earth/Earth combination is more conscious of reality than any other in the zodiac. But what can you do about reality except laugh? Life is that way because life is that way. The Earth/Earth combination has turned out some wonderful comediennes who know what's what, and how to make you laugh about it. One is Carol Burnett, Sun in Taurus, Moon in Virgo. Her down-to-earth style and no-frills roles have made millions of people (even Earth/Earth types) roll in the aisles. Joanne Worley, Sun in Virgo, Moon in Capricorn, set a new style for comediennes in the ahead-of-its-time *Laugh-In*.

Where Does She Fit

The Earth/Earth woman may find the most difficulty in adjusting to the new roles our changing society has cast women into. Because she is an extreme traditionalist—and very rigid to boot—she may find herself truly torn between nurturing and rearing a family and going out into the workplace. Even if she would like to have it all (which she generally doesn't), she is likely to try so hard to do home and work so perfectly that she gets no enjoyment out of life at all. The ideal prescription for this kind of woman is to have a third occupation—some kind of interest or hobby that takes her away from both home and job. The perfect hobby would be working with her hands and creating something useful—pottery, weaving, sewing. Her traditionalism and natural bent to hide her light under a bushel mean that she is swimming upstream in our new world where women are forced to put themselves forward; but it can be managed. Here is a case of a woman born in a woman's sign—yet smack in the middle of the gender spectrum. In a sense, she has the capacity to move toward psychological androgyny by developing some of the higher masculine traits.

Living With the Earth/Earth Woman

Living with the Earth/Earth woman can be a joy and a delight—or it can be a source of constant irritation. It depends on how the specific Earth/Earth woman lives out her astro-gender profile. Double-Earth women, Virgo in particular, are perfectionists, and so concerned about being "right" that they drive themselves mad. It doesn't matter what the subject is (it could be anything from making dinner to hosting a local charity ball); the Earth woman has a pervasive sense that something will go wrong. To her credit, whatever happens, she blames herself, not others.

However, living with such anxiety is anxiety-provoking, and you will get caught up in the syndrome of worry, worry, worry. The one sign that hides it well is Taurus, who always seems upbeat. However, let something go wrong and even Taurus will go into a funk. There's only one way to deal with a double-Earth person who is anxious about something: Stay away until it's over; then give lavish praise.

When the double-Earth woman is good, she's so good everyone wants some of her time. Though it makes her feel good to be wanted and needed, overcommitment can also lead to anxiety. However, when all is said and done, what she wants is to be seen as "good"—and when the praise comes her way, it's all worth it.

Gender-correcting suggestions for the Earth/Earth woman:

- Though many Earth Sun Sign/Earth Moon Sign women have a built-in barrier against stress and tension (they are tough!), most will need to have an escape route to maintain their bodily and sexual femininity. If you feel you haven't time in your busy schedule for a regular out-of-home regime, try self-massage. Better yet, get your partner involved.

- A double-Earth astro-profile (i.e., Earth Sun Sign, Earth Moon Sign) puts you near the middle of the gender spectrum, with true psychological androgyny at your fingertips. Don't spoil it by tipping the balance toward the superficial "feminine." In other words, don't get hung up on a spotless house, ideal children, the "perfect in every way" syndrome. If you find yourself doing so, deliberately relax one of your self-imposed regimes, and learn to live with it.

- Emotionally strong as you are, you may insist that everyone around you maintain a thumbs-up attitude at all times. (Virgo is the exception here.) For most people, it simply isn't possible—especially for children. Make sure you allow for their fears and discontents, which may seem like little ones, but can grow into absolute "monsters" if ignored or laughed away.

• Earth women, especially Taureans, can easily get caught up in the "if I like it, I'll have it" syndrome. This goes not only for food, but for alcohol as well. And occasionally sex. The area of excess is one where you must consciously call on the masculine capacity for the "competitive"—and vow to beat yourself at your own game.

• One of your "secrets" is the fact that you shy away from risk-taking, in every area. In some, like the financial, that is a virtue all could learn from. However, particularly in raising children, you will have a lot more fun if you learn to love the roller coaster or its equivalent at the theme park. Safety first is great, but all-out fun can be even better.

Getting Sign-Specific

Earth Sun Sign/Earth Moon Sign

Taurus/Taurus: A stubborn child, you become a reasonable adult with great determination, which gives you power over people. Your respect for authority is based on the desire to become the authority yourself. You are not unscrupulous, but hardheaded and loyal.

Virgo/Virgo: You are dominated by your intellectual interests, loyal and sentimental rather than romantic. You can be extremely critical when your sense of good taste is offended. You are conventional; an innate dislike of offending society keeps you on course in this regard.

Capricorn/Capricorn: Your ambition is powerful and self-control almost a fetish. Inherently self-centered, you desire the power of personal wealth. You are a realist, first, last and always; the ideal to you is only a means to an end. You will reach the summit at midlife.

Taurus/Virgo. You have charm, poise, balance and common sense. Though your executive qualities are not well marked, you are always in some way provided for. An inclination to relax and go to sleep intellectually is marked. A little adversity should wake you up.

Taurus/Capricorn: Security is of the greatest importance to you, but a sweet and gracious nature conceals your pride. You believe in fair dealing and practice it. You know how to gauge the public temperament, and that could be your way to success. You like to control.

Virgo/Taurus: If you worry, it is out of your own nervousness. This is an excellent combination. You have to work yourself out of your moods as best you can. You are aloof and shy, and must open up to enjoy personal relationships. You base your judgments on your emotions.

Virgo/Capricorn: You are quietly magnetic, restrained even when you are most eager. Your passions tend to be of the mind rather than the flesh. Success comes through devotion to duty rather than flash. You are meticulous about not hurting other people, or causing them to be hurt.

Capricorn/Taurus: You have a flair for knowing what "the crowd" wants, and a canny way of never seeming to rise above it. Your drive is not strong, however, and when things do not go well, you have a tendency to hide. You have a strong sense of duty and honor.

Capricorn/Virgo: You are impressive, but it covers up your timidity, and you are better at taking orders from someone else. You are both high-strung and highly organized. You are an intellectual and social snob.

Water Sun Sign/Water Moon Sign

This section pertains to both men and women whose Sun Sign is in Cancer, Scorpio or Pisces and whose Moon Sign is in Cancer, Scorpio or Pisces. (Sun and Moon can be in different signs.)

"I am interested only in the basement of the human being."

—FREUD

When astrologers say, "Water is the feeling element," people often respond by saying, "But I have feelings too." That is true: All signs have feelings and all people do as well. The difference with the Water element is that great emotionality and vulnerability are the keynotes from which all other things emanate. Some books call the Water element weak or unstable; however, Water people have tremendous power by virtue of the intensity of their feelings. Water, as the most feminine of all the elements, is the most receptive of all. Double-Water-Sign people almost seem to understand what you are thinking by some kind of ESP. It is really their great ability to put themselves in someone else's place. When Water people are described as unstable and/or moody, the cause is their great ability (which they may not even recognize) to adopt the behavior of others. For instance, Pisces is the sign of the actor. Not all Pisceans may make their living on the stage, and those who do so are not necessarily Pisceans; but there is a quality of "acting" that is part of the Water scenario. The drives and motivations of Water people are buried so deeply in their unconscious minds that they can develop irrational fears, hypersensitivity and strong reactions to people and places. Though they may be very adept at tapping into the subconscious of others, their own can be a deep, dark secret to themselves.

Taking Shape

Another reason people of other elements think Water people have no "real self" is that the element Water, like its counterpart in reality, has no shape of its own, and conforms to any given shape. This is not weakness, this is plasticity, and makes Water people very valuable in positions where flexibility is mandatory. Water people crave solitude, quietness and peace—perhaps because of the constant inner roiling of their emotions.

Love Is All There Is

There is no more deeply compassionate element than Water. The capacity for bringing people together and understanding their needs is considerable. The empathy for those who suffer is extraordinary. Sometimes this works itself out as an all-embracing love for all creation; but sometimes it is focused on only one person, and then becomes possessiveness or obsession. The deepest desire of Water people is to help others; psychologically translated, that means they need protection, and act it out by protecting others. The irrepressible collectors of sick puppies and abandoned cats will almost always show an abundance of Water in their horoscopes. So love and relatedness, which fall under the aegis of the "feminine," are two of the hallmarks of the double-Water person, as are many of the other values of the "feminine," like nurturing and wanting to help. Cancer, the first Water Sign, is perhaps the most moderate, as well as the most self-propelled. Cancers mother others, and tend to gather in what responsibilities they can get their hands on. That is one of the reasons that they perform well in business, gathering in responsibilities as they go along.

Gaining Consciousness

The real work of the Water person is to understand himself or herself, and to do this in an individualistic and independent way. Many Water people gain independence and wisdom as they age; some do it so well they become real saviors of others. In the meantime, many—usually Pisceans—often hang on to others almost literally "for dear life."

The Water/Water Man

Being at the extreme feminine pole of the gender spectrum presents both problems and opportunities for men. Their extreme compassion often drives them into fields where they can help others—in a major way. Both Jonas Salk, Sun in Scorpio, Moon in Pisces (discoverer of the polio vaccine), and Dr. Christian Barnard, Sun in Scorpio, Moon in Cancer (heart transplant pioneer), exemplify the Water/Water male who has not only coped in this world, but has made it a better place to live in. The whole world of the arts is the Water/Water male's realm: from poet William Blake to artists Andrew Wyeth, Sun and Moon in Cancer; Michelangelo (double Pisces); Rembrandt, Sun in Cancer, Moon in Scorpio; Claude Monet, Sun in Scorpio, Moon in Pisces; to photographer Robert Mappelthorpe, Sun in Scorpio, Moon in Pisces. Robin Williams and Harrison Ford, both double Cancers, have had, ironically and perhaps coincidentally, film roles that typify the Water/Water male.

The Downside

Is every Water/Water male a saint? Hardly, and all too many times he is quite the opposite. In searching for love, God or whatever it is that will make the Water/Water male feel he has achieved his dream, he is tempted all the way by addiction. This applies most often to Pisces, but the other signs are at risk too. It may be alcohol, drugs or even a self-help group, but whatever it is, he will not just take a moderate amount, he will take too much. There are other potential problems as well, such as addictions to people which the Water/Water male can have, particularly the double-Pisces male. Those who move to the top in spite of their double-Water horoscope—and there are not a few—often attribute their success to either workaholism or pure instinct . . . a Water hallmark.

Another potential pitfall for Water/Water males is sex. The emotions are so powerful and, for the most part, the double-Water man is so attractive that he may find himself in the "love trap" too often, then find it hard to extricate himself.

Getting the Job Done

While many a Water/Water male does quite well in the area of getting and spending, business is not their ideal milieu. In our "solar" world that values the characteristics of the "masculine" virtually to the exclusion of the feminine, the Water/Water man can wander into any number of pitfalls. One is by being so overly suspicious of his working mates that he imagines conspiracies and cabals around every corner. Scorpio in particular can become so enmeshed in office politics that the job suffers for it. Another potential problem for the double-Water male (Cancer especially) is to regard everyone—team workers as well as subordinates—as a candidate for mothering, thus setting up situations that are inappropriate in the workplace.

The Dark Side of the Feminine

It is not only that Water/Water males have not had the actual experience of childbearing that makes them strangers to the feminine. In almost every tradition, the "feminine" includes death as well as birth, both destruction and renewal. In the Indian tradition the gods of birth and death are one. The feminine is all of nature, which also dies and renews itself. Thoughts of our own mortality are frightening, and it is probably the Water/Water male who buries them most deeply "in the basement of the human mind." Hades is often linked to Scorpio, despite its being a feminine sign in astrology. The prejudice many people have, particularly against Scorpio, may spring from this myth. In astrological truth, Scorpio is Water—but intense Water, like the pressure of it against a dam. If the metaphorical dam breaks, many people around the particular Scorpio can be hurt. For a man or a woman, having Scorpio as a Moon Sign is a double-edged sword. It pushes one toward achievement, but is particularly upsetting to the emotions.

Living With the Water/Water Man

At close quarters, in his own domestic environment, the Water/Water man is likely to go through periods of quiet. His partner, if sensitive, may realize that some obsession or other has taken him away for a while. It is the rare Water/Water type who will want to talk about it. Even for him, a "feeling" type, anything that touches on the emotions is difficult to talk about.

In his "up" times, however, he can be a real character— one who can entertain, spin tales, tell outrageous stories. All the Water Signs have a "touch of the poet" in them— Pisces the most. It takes a lot to get Scorpio going, but then you are likely to hear of some fascinating adventures you never knew before.

Water, like Earth, makes available the "feminine" qualities to men. Double-Water men—especially Cancer—take to fathering quite naturally, and add a mothering dimension to it. With the possible exception of Scorpio, who can be tough and keep control, Water fathers are pushovers for their children, and both sides love it. For most Water men it is even a kind of "therapy" that helps them recover from the day-to-day "masculine" work world they (secretly) find a drag.

"Comfort" is the key word for the double-Water man as far as his environment is concerned. Plump pillows, deep chairs, an eat-in kitchen are requirements. However, one reason may be that such things do not constantly have to be in the neatest of states—because he isn't either.

Gender-correcting suggestions for the Water/Water man:

- No matter what your job or profession, or how successful you are, there's a deep, quiet part of you that would like to work silently in the background, observing and absorbing what goes on around you. For a man to be a feeling type puts him toward the "feminine" end of the gender spectrum, and he can put it to fantastic advantage by virtually "feeling" what is going on, and acting on it as he sees it played.

- A large component of feeling (for anyone) is pain; you feel it particularly acutely. With your masculine conditioning not to talk it out and/or cry it out, your pain could become overwhelming, and lead to some sort of addiction—from alcoholism to workaholism. If you sense the beginnings of a problem, immediately turn for help.

- Many men with both Water Sun and Water Moon find some form of the arts the way to self-expression and wholeness—and it almost "chooses" them rather than the other way around. You may be of ordinary talent, but your perceptions of the world around you—or indeed your own feeling life—could be your route to understanding the "feminine" in a masculine context.

- Some men of double-feminine signs refuse to acknowledge their greater sensitivity, and can rage against it by becoming overly macho. In effect, they can exacerbate "the battle of the sexes" by treating women in demeaning ways—then chalking up their reactions to oversensitivity. Develop some good female friends, preferably those most likely subject to this kind of behavior, and discuss their feelings with them.

• Learn to take it with grace when your less sensitive male cohorts dish it out. You can play the game with the best of them. In fact, sports—especially team and/ or contact sports—are good for both your spirit of camaraderie and your occasionally overwrought feelings.

The Water/Water Woman

Water/Water women may wish just as much to run from the dark side of the feminine, and that is perhaps where the brickbats of "overly emotional" spring from when there is a personality component upon which a job depends. So, in a sense, at this pole of the gender spectrum men's problems are not that different from women's problems, even if society may not see it that way. The Water/ Water male might make an ideal, if insufferably sloppy, "house husband" and be considered "strange"—but he will be accepted. The Water/Water female can be accused of becoming a drain on everyone around her—including her children. She is so needy of love and tolerance that the slightest rebuke, even if given in a friendly manner, can seem like a death blow.

A Woman Without a Man

As the song says, "There's nothing worse in this universe than a woman without a man." Water/Water women, unless there are several steadying aspects in their horoscopes, can excel as sex objects, but fail miserably in just plain life. Grace Kelly, Sun in Scorpio, Moon in Pisces; Elizabeth Taylor, Sun in Pisces, Moon in Scorpio; and Jennifer

Jones, double Pisces, exemplify the breed, but you'll find such women in every walk of life, hanging on to some male's arm. It is almost as though the women's movement left them behind, or they never comprehended it at all.

The Real Feminine

When you enter the realm of the feminine, you inevitably encounter sorrow. The myth of Demeter and her daughter Persephone says much about the mother/daughter connection and the sorrows that can attend it. Persephone wandered away from her mother and was picking a flower when Hades, god of the underworld, broke through and carried her away to be his consort. Demeter wandered the world for years sorrowing for her lost daughter, and finally struck a bargain with Hades to let Persephone live half of the year underground and half on earth with her mother. One real-life Water/Water woman who lost a child and chronicled it in writing is Anne Morrow Lindbergh, a double Cancer. Another double Cancer who is not afraid of the subject has written about death and the dying with great empathy. That is Elisabeth Kübler-Ross, also a double Cancer. A preoccupation with death particularly haunts the Water woman, and suicides abound. Poet Anne Sexton, Sun in Scorpio, Moon in Cancer, and columnist/TV celebrity Dorothy Kilgallen, a double Cancer, are two who found the "gravity" of water too much to bear.

Sing Hallelujah

Feelings are not necessarily bad feelings. Joy is a feeling, and one we should all try to inject more of into our lives. Four Water/Water women who choose to shout out their feelings are Marion Anderson, Sun in Pisces, Moon in Scorpio; Lena Horne, Sun in Cancer, Moon in Scorpio; Liza Minnelli, Sun in Pisces, Moon in Cancer; and Dinah Shore, Sun in Pisces, Moon in Cancer. By putting their feelings to music, they have also managed to avoid the worst fate of the double-Water female, lack of independence in making their way in the world.

The Golden Mean

Even though having a Water Sun Sign and a Water Moon puts you out at the limits of the feminine end of the gender spectrum, there are many, many women who cope marvelously—and know how to talk to the world in a feeling way. A personal candidate for the ideal Water/Water woman might be Jane Pauley, Sun in Scorpio, Moon in Cancer. She is sensitive yet strong, caring, but also crisp if need be. Another Water/Water female who managed a unique way to get out of the Water/Water woman's trap is Erma Bombeck, double Cancer. She just thinks it's all hilarious, and so does Phyllis Diller, also a double Cancer.

Living With the Water/Water Woman

For all the accusations of overemotionalism of the double-Water Woman, there is a very positive side. She is able to create an atmosphere of serenity that benefits everyone around her. Think of the contrast of storm at sea with the calmest water you've ever seen. Living with the Water/Water woman means developing adaptability to a number of "climates," including the calm and serene.

One of the secrets of the Water/Water woman's emotional life is that she really wants to love everybody, and wants everybody to love her. When she feels she is in that state, life is blissful—for her and everybody else.

If she is typical, the Water/Water woman will want her home to be done in soft pastels—and that does not work at cross-purposes with her tendency to let children "play loose." Because she does not believe in "bad children," she treats hers with equanimity—plus a lot of hugs and kisses. Children are one place she can lavish her feelings without being considered in excess.

Gender-correcting suggestions for the Water/Water woman:

- If you suspect you fall into the category of Water Sun Sign/Water Moon Sign women who would fall apart without an opposite number (male or female) to rely on, start reading books by and about women who not only lived a solo life, but loved it that way. That does not mean *you* have to, but it will give you some ideas about the great feminine strengths you carry around in you by virtue of your sex and your astrological heritage.

- If there is any truth in the proposition that men are better at dealing with cold, hard facts than women, those of your astro-gender profile may have something to do with it. It is not that you are incapable of seeing or grasping "the real thing" when it is right there in front of you; the problem is that you filter everything through your feelings first. Make a conscious effort to correct this.

- You are the ideal candidate for volunteer work—the kind that puts you in touch with people who have serious physical or emotional problems. Particularly in the latter case, your feeling nature should be able to pick up clues about a person's inner psyche, and be of real help to the professionals who deal with them. Important point: If you get into it, stick with it. You sometimes can be less than reliable about carrying out commitments.

- Try deliberately to be less self-conscious about your image. You tend to be insecure enough to believe you are loved because you always look, if not perfect, then close to it. Try a supermarket run without makeup for starters.

- Water/Water women, their children quickly learn, can often be easily manipulated by tears and fears. Start to stiffen your back and not give in to your kids at the first whimper. Instead, start to do some real rough-and-tumble kind of play; kids bend, but they rarely break—even though they can do a real job on *your* tender heart.

Getting Sign-Specific

Water Sun Sign/Water Moon Sign

Cancer/Cancer: You are sensitive and self-protective. Because of real or imagined hurts, you are suspicious of many people. You are artistic, and might find your most congenial work there. In business, your taciturn nature can make you a shrewd trader and bring you success.

Scorpio/Scorpio: Your creative force is terrific. You are capable of extremes of loyalty, from ardent love to fierce hate. If unchecked, you can become a sensationalist who could make many lives unhappy. Yet you have tremendous self-control and look down on those who don't.

Pisces/Pisces: You need to keep a firm grip on reality, and to live as conventionally as possible. You are an unusual person and really quite wound up in yourself. You must also surround yourself with people in order not to become lonely: You are so introspective that it is a danger.

Cancer/Scorpio: You are lavish in your affections, but not especially faithful. You have a self-protective ruthlessness, although you don't like to hurt people; you are not cruel. Your personality attracts attention, and people like to show you around; you have a strong magnetism.

Cancer/Pisces: You are so agreeable, pleasant and affable it's hard to know where you stand. You are suspicious of others and don't take many into your confidence, but play your hunches yourself, much to your advantage. Learn to be a little less secretive, a little more open.

Scorpio/Cancer: You don't go out of your way for people, but let them come to you. You are strongly opinionated, although logic is not as important to you as winning your point. Your emotions are very powerful and your wits are keen. You believe in hunches, as you may often experience them.

Scorpio/Pisces: You have an instinct for the right thing, which could make you hypercritical. In addition to being somewhat of a recluse, you may have fits of despair. Turn them to creative imagination; after all, you have the creative edge to really do something.

Pisces/Cancer: You really are a shy person, and your forcefulness is the product of rigid discipline. You are sensitive and alert to the opinions of those around you, but also moody and temperamental. You are courteous, considerate and genuinely charitable.

Pisces/Scorpio: You have an extraordinary sense of humor, being able to see the humorous, the ridiculous and the pathetic in anything. Fundamentally, you are sad and can even be depressed, even when you are clowning. You like to lead a private life, with your imagination.

Earth Sun Sign/Water Moon Sign

This section pertains to men and women who have Sun Sign Taurus, Virgo or Capricorn, and Moon Sign Cancer, Scorpio or Pisces.

"Dead solid perfect"

If you are not familiar with the phrase "dead solid perfect," borrowed from golfing, you might interpret it as a negative. Far from it. The Earth/Water person is "dead solid perfect" because he or she may be one of the most well-balanced types all along the astro-gender spectrum. It is here that you most often find caring, sensitive men (not that you don't find them elsewhere) and women who are comfortable with their psycho-physical selves and traditional female roles.

With an Earth Sun Sign, this type appears to be cautious and even aloof. But the presence of the Water Moon makes them surprisingly spontaneous and ready and willing to jump in and take charge if a situation warrants it. Socially, both sexes of this astro-gender combination may seem to stand back and simply observe what others are doing. There is a method to their madness, however, because once they've got the situation down pat, they can join in any group and jump right into the conversation.

They are especially skillful with their hands, and are happiest when they can "fix things." They often don't even need to follow directions and are highly time- and energy-efficient.

The Earth/Water Male

This is the best of the double-feminine combinations for a man. With an Earth Sun Sign, he is by nature a producer and can jump into the manager's seat at almost any time. In fact, this is the man who can take over at a moment's notice and appear to have been in the role already. He is almost a human computer who takes in volumes of information and can call upon singularly useful skills—example par excellence, Harry Truman, Sun in Taurus, Moon in Scorpio.

Earth is the least "feminine" of all the feminine signs,

giving the Earth/Water male a powerful presence. He is the classic strong, silent type who, when you get to know him, really has a lot to say. Earth men—particularly Taurus and Virgo—have a male-skewed tenderness and empathy that can turn up in many different forms. Cleveland Amory, Sun in Virgo, Moon in Pisces, is exemplary in both his love of animals and his hands-on approach to improving the quality of life for them. Famed pediatrician Benjamin Spock, Sun in Taurus, Moon in Cancer, was perhaps the best example of the breed because both his Sun Sign and his Moon Sign are the most caring in the zodiac. He too shows the perseverance and endurance in doing what he believes is his mission.

There is a highly attractive sexuality about the Earth/Water male. With his emotional Water Moon and his superb sensory equipment given him by his Earth Sun Sign, he is an excellent lover—and rarely a leaver. Anthony Quinn, Sun in Taurus, Moon in Cancer; and Robert Duval, Sun in Capricorn, Moon in Cancer, exude much of the kind of sensuality this type possesses. Michael Jackson, Sun in Virgo, Moon in Pisces, is somewhat of an anomaly born with this astro-gender combination. It is possible that he feels the "feminine" of his Sun and Moon very acutely, and it causes him a kind of gender confusion. Elvis Presley, Sun in Capricorn, Moon in Pisces, used his sexuality brilliantly well in terms of his career, but he too may have felt the vibes of this combination and not been comfortable with it.

Earth people are builders by nature, and it can be virtually anything from a brilliant career to an artistic life to a spiritually dedicated one. Stanley Marcus, the phenomenal retail maven, has Sun in Taurus, Moon in Scorpio. When Scorpio is in the Earth/Water mix, there can be an awesome business ability. Architect I. M. Pei, Sun in Taurus, Moon in Cancer, is a literal builder par excellence. Martin Luther King, with the strongest of the Earth Sun Signs, Capricorn, and the most spiritual of the Water Moon Signs, Pisces, brilliantly illustrated how forceful and dedicated this astro-gender combination can be in men. Writer Christopher Isherwood, Sun in Virgo, Moon in Pisces, is another who turned to the spiritual life—one of the influences of the "feminine" in its archetypal form.

Not all Earth/Water males are wholly comfortable with their inherited astro-gender profile. Some turn to the arts, like dancer Alvin Ailey, Sun in Capricorn, Moon in Cancer. Some lead lives of great power, like J. Edgar Hoover, Sun in Capricorn, Moon in Pisces, but are anomalous in the sexual arena.

As a life mate, the Earth/Water male is a wonderful partner. He has a sense of whimsy and fun that springs from his Water Moon. Because he appears so distant, people can be astonished when he's the first one in when someone suggests a moonlight swim.

Living With the Earth/Water Man

The "ordinary" Earth/Water man would probably be startled to hear he is a double-feminine type, astrologically speaking. He isn't particularly introspective and lives a fairly ordinary life—at least by his own standards. Typically, he is more than moderately successful in both his business and his home life—tolerant, kind, admired by all for his quiet yet firm ways. At least that's the way it's supposed to be for this astro-gender profile. Not all men will live up to it, but the potential is there.

His earthiness gives him a solid base to work off, yet with the immediacy and "this is it" practicality of Earth. Water adds the element of feeling *and,* because the Sun Sign is also feminine, guarantees that it is true feeling, and not mere sentimentality.

He is a live-and-let-live type—unless someone or something gets in the way of how he thinks things should be. Then you can see the firmness and determination of Earth at work at its best. He can quietly but without equivocation let his point of view be known. He is particularly good with shrill women—able to understand their point of view, yet able to bring the situation under control.

The Earth/Water male will take a great interest in the landscaping of his home, constantly improving it and making sure it is the best it can be. For most, being close to the earth is a kind of therapy, though they would not call it that or believe that's what it is. The Earth/Water male will simply tell you that working around the grounds of his house makes him "feel good."

Gender-correcting suggestions for the Earth/Water man:

- Appreciate the fact that you could be the "new man" if you understand how your feminine astro-profile can work itself out both in the world of work and in your personal life. The strongest combination is Capricorn Sun/Cancer Moon, and if this is yours, you can easily go far. You are an ideal manager of people with your earthy (sensate) understanding of their real problems and your Cancerian concern with its element of cautiousness about not becoming overly sentimental.

- Unless your Moon is in Pisces (in which case you may have an irrepressible sense of humor), you should make it a point to surround yourself with upbeat, even carefree people to counter your tendency to see things overly seriously and/or literally.

- Never forget that until further notice it's still a man's business world. If your Sun Sign is Virgo, particularly, you may have similar troubles breaking through the "glass ceiling" as a woman. You must assert yourself—sometimes in ways that are not entirely to your liking—and even appear at least to be hanging on to old values as you move forward.

- Watch for a tendency—particularly if you are a Taurus Sun Sign with Moon in Scorpio or Pisces—to do things to excess: eating, drinking, even talking, and—not least—sexual pursuits. With your earthy Sun Sign nature and Water Moon, some things simply feel too good to resist.

• Though Capricorn and Virgo Sun people can be quite careful and conscientious about physical exercise, Water Moon men can have a tendency to slough off and "veg out" a lot. Try to stick to an exercise regime that you enjoy and make it part of the easily structured and balanced life you are capable of living.

The Earth/Water Woman

Perhaps one reason you don't find too many Earth/Water women among the famous is that they are so comfortable doing what they are doing that they see no reason to go for the brass ring. As Earth Signs, they would do brilliantly in the kind of work that requires persistence and a sense of purpose—managing, analyzing, correcting others' mistakes. Taurus women are notoriously good at managing money. Oveta Culp Hobby (First Commander of the Women's Army Corps and first Secretary of Health, Education and Welfare in the U.S.), Sun in Capricorn, Moon in Cancer, is a terrific example of the kind of career Earth/Water women excel in.

It is not a put-down of the Earth/Water woman to say that she probably rarely has a sense of being put down. Comfortable, competent, with a built-in sense of self-esteem, she is unlikely to do much rallying for women's causes—except, and it's a big *except,* the woman's right to choose when it comes to abortion. She is such a natural mother that it would never occur to her that a woman should have a baby she does not want, and might not care for as the Earth/Water woman does for her children.

Earth/Water women, despite the strength of their Earth Sign, tend to be pushovers for their children, however. Not in the way of allowing them privileges beyond the range of their age group, but more in catering to their desire for "good things to eat" and their wish to be as messy and rumble-tumble as they like. It is a particular burden for the Virgo woman, who desires order above all things, but she will put up with mess if her children find themselves happy in that kind of play. She will be the first, also, to start demanding at an early age that they pick up after themselves.

The Earth/Water combination for a woman can cause a terrific pull between her desire to be a housewife and her practical sense of having a wage-earning job so she can contribute to the family's discretionary income. Because her Water Moon Sign gives her a great amount of imagination, she is likely to come up with some ingenious scheme where she can have the best of both worlds. Job-sharing was probably the inspiration of an Earth/Water female.

As a wife and homemaker, she is likely to be quite traditional, taking great joy in family celebrations, and even dreaming up reasons for having them. Even if she does work outside the home, she will manage to keep close ties with other female neighbors and friends, and participate in community activities. The Earth/Water female is the one who will sit in the back at the local school board or PTA meeting, and then come up with a startling question or solution.

Like the male of this particular species, the Earth/Water woman will have a highly sensual nature. Because of her Earth facade, however, it will not be blatantly obvious. Think of Audrey Hepburn, Sun in Taurus, Moon in Pisces; or Sandy Dennis, Sun in Taurus, Moon in Scorpio.

Physically, this is a strong combination for women, in the literal sense. She is the type who can excel at athletics without losing an ounce of her womanliness. Olga Korbut, Sun in Taurus, Moon in Pisces, is a good example.

If the Earth/Water woman has the misfortune to marry a man with a violent streak, she is all too likely to put up with it for too long. Eventually, however, she will stand on her own strong legs, say "Enough" and end the situation.

Living With the Earth/Water Woman

If you yourself do not keep a shipshape home, you might be intimidated by the Earth/Water female's living quarters. She doesn't make a "thing" out of it, however, because it comes so naturally to her. You might be surprised at having dishes whisked away so quickly and the kitchen clean before dinner is served. In a sense, the Earth/Water woman is the "German Hausfrau," but without the stiffness.

As a partner, the Earth/Water woman will more than pull her weight, especially as she works both in the home and out. She can relieve her mate of any number of "male tasks" because she is quite able to figure it out herself, and get it done without fuss and bother. She will be willing to "go along with the program" for the most part, although if she objects to something her husband has "ordained," you will see just how strong-willed Earth women are.

Meals and mealtimes are almost sacred to the typical Earth/Water woman—and that is where she may run into trouble with her children as they grow and have more and more out-of-house activities. She sees the family table as a place where busy people meet for at least a while. Her "feeling component" (Water Moon) recognizes, if not even consciously, that family meals are something people carry memories of indefinitely.

Gender-correcting suggestions for the Earth/Water woman:

- In the best-case scenario, you are "all woman." Astrologically speaking, that means you are extraordinarily able to deal with the world around you in all its complexity without falling apart. The strongest of the combinations is Capricorn Sun/Cancer Moon. However, especially in the case of Virgo Sun and Pisces Moon, your stability is not so great and you may become a "nervous wreck" under stress. It is not necessary. Try to summon up the strengths that are particular to "the female" and you will come through. You are a creature of the "lower"—i.e., more elemental—elements. Exercise and the outdoors are your milieu.

- Politics are ideal for certain Earth/Water women. There is a toughness that is also gentle, and an ability to "read the crowd" by virtue of your feeling Water Moon. For less aggressive types, you still can lead the pack as head of the car pool, organizer of the day-care center—or an excellent manager of people in any business you choose.

- In real life, earth and water make mud; that can be the case symbolically in astrology as well. Earth/Water women, capable and caring as they are, can tend to slip into comfortable ruts and literally have to be hauled out by more frivolous people. Make sure some of your buddies—or the man/men in your life—can give you a real sense of fun—and adventure. You needn't try bungie-jumping it may just be a matter of seeing the wackiest, most offbeat movie in town.

- Earth—particularly Taurus—and Water—particularly Pisces—are a wonderfully musical combination. And a powerful prescription for several aspects of your life. Children will love to hear you sing, even if it isn't bel canto, and you can, if you apply your sensate skills, even learn a simple instrument. The reasons are not entirely frivolous; music—playing or listening—can help to take you out of the Earth mode, and put you in a much more intuitive frame of mind.

Getting Sign-Specific

Earth Sun Sign/Water Moon Sign

Taurus/Cancer: You are, whatever your sex, a true earth mother. Your greatest delight is taking care of things and making them grow. The mix of earth and water is a fertile one, so you should have great ideas too. Childbirth is your big moment.

Taurus/Scorpio: You are the toughest Taurus of the lot, but remember that Scorpio is a Water Sign, and that does take the edge off it. One of the fields you would be outstanding in is banking and finance.

Taurus/Pisces: You might be rather shy, but underneath you have a marvelous sense of humor and a healthy appetite for all good things. You will go far because of your quiet ways and the fact that people like you.

Virgo/Cancer: You can be the sweetest of people, or a horrendous harridan. A lot depends on mood. You have to take care not to be taken over by your emotions. They can lead you astray.

Virgo/Scorpio: Don't let it be said that you bear a grudge against the world. Make yourself feel up even when you're down. Virgo takes a lot of criticism, but it isn't all deserved. And Scorpio is similarly maligned.

Virgo/Pisces: You can be the loveliest, softest person in the zodiac. But if you forget yourself, you can make people uncomfortable and upset. Try to use your Pisces Moon to take you on wonderful flights of fancy.

Capricorn/Cancer: You are truly stately. You carry yourself proudly in the world, and at the same time you have a true feeling for others. Particularly others who need help. Try once in a while to get down to others' levels. You can be intimidating.

Capricorn/Scorpio: You are one of the people who seems to have an advantage. But a lot of your "strength" is on the outside. You are really a very feeling person who wants to do what must be done without hurting a soul.

Capricorn/Pisces: You wear a disguise, the Capricorn disguise that covers up your jittery Pisces Moon. It operates on pure feeling, but you can make it stronger by daring yourself to do things. . . . It can be as simple as going to a party.

Water Sun Sign/Earth Moon Sign

"Enjoy when you can, endure when you must."

—GOETHE

With this Sun/Moon combination we come to the last of
the double-masculine and double-feminine astro-gender
types. As the Water element and the Earth element are
compatible between people, so are they when found as the
Sun/Moon combination in an individual. Unless there are
major aspects in the natal horoscope that can cause conflict, they are generally serene people who do not seem to
be out to conquer the world. Yet many of them are highly
successful. They are the ones who early on realize that by
nature they are so quiet that there is a necessity to make
some noise in order to become visible. As an overriding
tendency, this type has very little need to control others,
but an exceptionally high ability to take in what is around
them, and to be in touch with themselves as well.

With the Sun in a Water Sign, they have excellent "re-
ceptors," and are able to pick up the small nuances that
others miss. This Water ability linked to a "doing" Earth
Moon often makes them remarkable mimics. Even those
without this entertaining ability have a wonderful sense of
humor. Dr. Seuss was one, with a Pisces Sun Sign and an
Earth Moon Sign.

The Water/Earth Man

Of all the types, it is this combination that produces the
true nurturing male. As a father, he is so comfortable
switching roles with his wife that in many households the

father becomes the parent the children see as the one to
go to for solace, for treats and for good, practical sense
about how to get something done. This is the father who
builds model ships with his sons and plays softball with
his daughters. For kids of both sexes, he will take them
out on a starry night to marvel at the expanse of the universe, as well as at the sight of specific stars and planets.
Perhaps Bill Cosby has become a national symbol for the
good, if harried, father, partly because of his astro-gender
profile: Sun in Cancer, Moon in Virgo.

The Water/Earth male is a romantic—both in terms of
his own pursuits and as a swain to his wife or lover. At
love's first blush, he will "fall in love with love." Once
mated, because being loved and cared for is so important
to them, Water/Earth men are some of the most devoted,
loyal, cherishing and caring in the zodiac. Women who
want stability, certainty and caring in marriage—but not
a high need for excitement—would do well to look for a
Water/Earth male for a husband.

Professionally, the Water/Earth man can very often be
found in the helping professions, for which he is eminently
well suited. Doing good is as important to many Water/
Earth men as doing well. Prince Charles, well known as a
champion of humanitarian causes, has Sun Sign Scorpio,
Moon Sign Taurus.

While many men with this profile tend to "hide" themselves rather than reach out for fame and fortune, the Water Sun Sign has a charismatic effect when it is "turned
on." Politics can be attractive to the Water/Earth man. To
illustrate how the signs have an effect on the element combination, you need look no farther than Bobby and Ted
Kennedy. Bobby had Sun Sign Scorpio, Moon in Capricorn,
while Ted has Sun in Pisces, Moon in Virgo. To fully appreciate the differences, you might refer back to the cap-
sule profiles of the signs earlier in this book. Our first
president, George Washington, was a Water/Earth man, Pi-
sces/Capricorn. The charismatic character of this astro-
gender profile can also be seen in Billy Graham, Sun in

Scorpio, the "strongest" Water Sign, and Moon in Taurus, "the sign which will not be moved."

Inevitably, the list of artists, actors and other artistic people with this astro-gender profile is long and impressive. To name a few: Richard Burton, Sun in Scorpio, Moon in Virgo; Robert De Niro, with the same sign combination; writers Brendan Behan, Pisces/Taurus, and John Berryman, Scorpio/Capricorn; artists from Leonardo da Vinci, Taurus/Pisces, to Rubens, Cancer/Capricorn, to Andrew Wyeth, Cancer/Capricorn.

Living With the Water/Earth Man

At his best, the Water/Earth male is quietly effective. At his worst, he can earn the title "wimp." The latter becomes true when a particular male refuses to "hear" the messages of his Earth Moon. Earth, though "feminine," adds backbone to almost any astro-gender profile. The Water/Earth male who takes advantage of his "feminine strength" can often get the better of a double-masculine male. Earth is strong, and Water is subtle—an almost unbeatable combination from office to sports field.

Some Water/Earth males become "security blankets" for the whole family, from children through wife. He is the true "nurturer"—the person who makes others grow and flourish to eventually be on their own. No matter how much of a "nice guy" he is, he knows his children have to be on their own one day, and his wife must learn to cope without him. If he marries a hard-driving wife, she might find him overly sentimental and even "weak." That impression will be dispelled the first time he gets passionate about some matter or another and decides to do something about it. His "feeling" Water Sun Sign will get solid backup from his Earth Moon, and nothing can stop him.

Comfort is the watchword for this astro-gender combination. Actually, the Water/Earth male might not even notice what color the furniture is—only that it "feels good."

If his wife is an impeccable housekeeper, the situation might provide fodder for arguments from time to time.

Gender-correcting suggestions for the Water/Earth man:

- Your feeling function is a double-edged sword in business. While it makes you sensitive to the feelings of others, it also can make you manipulative in using what you "pick up" against someone you would like to better. Try to summon up some analytical ability to see that it could blow up in your face.

- You can be the ultranurturing father, but you can also tend to harbor hurt feelings against children who may not appear to return your affection. Keep remembering that kids are kids—and take a look at your own children's astro-gender profiles and how they relate to yours. You may find some clashing, especially with a child with Fire or Air in his/her horoscope. You may also find something to learn.

- Not all Water/Earth men prefer the "softer" things of life, but many do. Make sure you include in your own regimen, as well as in your "quality time" with your children, some physical exercise and some rough-and-tumble play. You'll all benefit. Even consider some kind of activity like "Outward Bound," where real physical courage can be developed.

- While some or many of your friends—particularly male—may consider astrology "frivolous" or simply outside the male frame of reference, you can learn a lot by observing them in relation to their astro-gender profiles. The Fire man—particularly Sun Sign Aries or Sagittarius—can be living out the macho role to the hilt. Consider your own psychological strengths in relation to theirs, and see where your "feminine" Water and Earth make you a more balanced person.

- You sometimes tend to take too long making decisions. There are times when it's better to shoot for the moon than to let the occasion go by. Your Earth Moon can make you hesitate out of natural caution. Your Water Sun may make you shy away from competition with other types, especially the Fire Signs. You have what it takes; use it.

The Water/Earth Woman

The women of this astro-gender combination are, to use a very apt cliché, the "Jewish mothers" of the zodiac. They are so eager to serve others that they often forget their own needs. Then, one scenario is that they feel they have been put upon, another is that they want the same loving and caring back from someone—mate, child or friend—who may not be able to give it.

Even more than their Earth/Water zodiac siblings, Water/Earth women are less likely to go "into the trenches" and fight it out in the career arena. Many do well at—what else—jobs in the helping professions. This is an excellent combination for a psychologist or a psychiatrist—once she gets her own problems out of the way. As far as jobs and career are concerned, she generally bows to her husband. For instance, if she has an excellent job which she loves, and her husband is offered a promotion/relocation, she will drop her job and pick up and go quite happily.

Peace and serenity are among their highest priorities, and they will go the whole way and more to see that these are maintained in their homes. Again, like their Earth/Water zodiac pals, they may marry abusive men, and take the abuse longer than they should. Women with Water as a Sun Sign do a lot of crying, but unless they have a very strong—or masculine—Moon Sign, they will take little action against others.

In contrast to their highly developed sense of duty toward all that smacks of a want or a need of someone in their households, they are eager for time to "stop and

smell the roses," both for themselves and for those they
care about (who may even be the letter carrier in the
neighborhood). Women of this combination are also the
"grandmothers of the world." What they call "retirement"
others might call taking full care of their children's
children.

Water is a highly feeling element, and women with a Wa-
ter/Earth combination may even have a touch of hypo-
chondria. Every pain and twinge is felt so easily that they
very often take to their beds. But not without guilt, an emotion that is essential to them. All feelings are their territory, and it is amusing that Ann Landers and Abby Van
Buren—the "sob sisters"—have a Cancer Sun and a
Taurus Moon.

The charisma of the Water Sun Sign works its wonders
for women too—and much more naturally. Wouldn't you
be able to guess that three of the most powerful actresses
have this astro-gender profile? There is no way Meryl
Streep, Cancer Sun/Taurus Moon; and Katharine Hepburn,
Scorpio Sun, Virgo Moon; and Anna Magnani, Pisces/Tau-
rus, could give less than a passionate performance.

"From the heart" songwriters and singers emotionally
appeal to audiences: Linda Ronstadt, Cancer/Virgo; Carly
Simon, Cancer/Capricorn; and Helen Reddy, Scorpio/
Capricorn, share a Water Sun Sign/Earth Moon Sign astro-
gender profile. It is a supple, physically strong combination as well, shared by Twyla Tharp, Cancer/Virgo, and
Billie Jean King, Scorpio Sun, Virgo Moon.

**Note: You will find the sign of Virgo prominent in the
charts of many who have mastered an art, craft or skill.
It is the hallmark of the perfectionist.**

At the head of this chapter there is a saying by Goethe,
"Enjoy when you can, endure when you must." It could
have been written specifically of Rose Kennedy, Sun in
Cancer, Moon in Virgo.

Living With the Water/Earth Woman

If it can be said that a woman's home is her castle, it can be said of the typical Water/Earth female. Home and everything related to it take top priority—even if she works outside the home. She is a natural mother, and probably can describe the experience of childbirth with real feeling. Her Earth Moon is the "engine" that drives her to get tasks done; otherwise, she might spend a lot of time on make-work projects, the telephone or simply daydreaming.

Some Water/Earth women without families become a kind of "office mother" (regardless of age) who is the one who remembers birthdays and does something about them, arranges showers, makes sure everyone feels like part of the "family." When Water/Earth women don't marry, this is often an effective substitute for them to get out their nurturing feelings.

The children of a married Water/Earth woman can easily feel suffocated by "over-mothering"—especially if they are in independent signs. The Water/Earth woman will feel she is missing something if she doesn't know everything that went on at school, at a friend's house, etc. Along with the "Jewish mother" syndrome goes food—a lot of it. For the Water/Earth woman more than any other in the zodiac, food is love, and she can misuse it if she isn't careful.

Gender-correcting suggestions for the Water/Earth woman:

- Make a strict list of "dos" and "don'ts" for your children—and make them stick. Do not make structured behavior contingent on "goodies" of any sort. Your children will survive better with loving discipline than a slapdash schedule. Your good-sense Earth Moon should tell you that.

- Water/Earth women make excellent personnel people. If you are not yet enmeshed in a career, consider this one. Your Water Sun Sign gives you the ability to pick up a great deal about people from what may appear to be small talk; your practical Earth Moon can tell you where—or if—this person would fit into the organization. Don't be afraid to go for the top spot either—Cancer Sun Sign or Scorpio Sun Sign women particularly.

• Though you can read others easily, you are sometimes a tough one to figure—especially Cancer and Scorpio Sun Sign people. This can be a great success skill if you know when and how to use it. Instead of reacting immediately, you can take in information and process it quite easily. Others need not know what your immediate reaction is, which gives you time to do some wheeling and dealing.

• Like your gender sibling, the Earth/Water woman, you are highly tactile and sensitive to both sybaritic pleasures and the pleasure of creating something with your hands. Nerves, no matter what one's astro-gender profile, can become a problem. In fact, for women with a Water Sun Sign, they can become troublesome. Try to develop some pursuit that totally absorbs you in color, texture, feel; in design, plan and construction. It can be anything from needlework to metalwork, but it should involve some "natural" material.

• To pick up your spirits when they sag (Water and Earth being the "heavy" elements), you can go one of two routes. The first is to play directly to your pleasure-loving body, via massage or a top-to-toe makeover. The other is to give your personality a breath of fresh air by exercising your mind. There are, of course, many adult courses that are fascinating, but in your case a better choice might be a reading group where you combine getting your own handle on a good book with discussions that can really turn you on.

Getting Sign-Specific

Water Sun Sign/Earth Moon Sign

Cancer/Taurus: You are a sweet soul who would like it if all the world were the same way. Cancer, however, has some push—so don't feel you have to take a backseat. Taurus too can be very staunch when necessary.

Cancer/Virgo: You tend to be a bit nervous. One good way to keep nerves under control for you is swimming or water exercises. In your private life, leave some room for simple "doing nothing." It will have a tonic effect on you.

Cancer/Capricorn: You can be a bit of a prude about some things. Relax and live and let live. You are a workhorse but should not overdo. For companions, choose people from the Fire and Air groups.

Scorpio/Taurus: You have a will of iron, and everyone around you will know it sooner or later. If you can give in occasionally, it would be very good for you. People harden up emotionally when they are always in the driver's seat.

Scorpio/Virgo: Temper, temper. You won't get anywhere by constantly being in a bad mood. Scorpio, more than any sign, needs to relax. You have a fine analytical mind and should put it to use where it will help people.

Scorpio/Capricorn: You are truly tough to deal with, but you make a great leader in whatever field you choose. To get people to warm up to you, try using that famous sardonic Scorpio sense of humor. A Capricorn Moon makes you more approachable.

Pisces/Taurus: You have the soul of a poet, if not the talent. You can make almost anyone forget his troubles with your brand of comforting. Be careful that Taurus doesn't get "drowned" by Pisces emotion.

Pisces/Virgo: You have a couple of problems in the relationship area. You probably would do anything, including die, to hold on to the person you love and serve. Try to stiffen up your backbone and live alone for a while. It would do you good.

Pisces/Capricorn: You are the kind of person who can make things happen quietly. You do have pride, but you prefer a calm lifestyle and quiet pleasures. Your Capricorn Moon is excellent ballast for your Pisces Sun.

Chapter 9

Masculine Sun Sign/
Feminine Moon Sign

In the foregoing section you read the astro-profiles for people whose Sun Sign and Moon Sign are in the same gender—either masculine or feminine.

In this section you will read about people with mixed-gender profiles—Sun Sign masculine, Moon Sign feminine, or the reverse. Whether male or female by sex, these people tend to have a more complex nature. The reason is that the elements are not only from different genders, they are also "opposite" in the facet of human consciousness they represent, or at least "incompatible."

For instance, Fire is intuition—the ability to live in the future, the inability to believe in and admit the realities of the world as it really is. The Fire element's opposite function is the sensory, corresponding to Earth. Earth, unlike Fire, believes what it can comprehend with the five senses, and is superb at making sense of the physical world. When the two elements combine there obviously is friction—but, just as it can cause personality problems, it can be enormously productive.

When it comes to Fire, masculine intuition, and Water, feminine feeling, you can almost illustrate the incompatibility pseudo-chemically. Fire is one of the higher, above-the-surface-of-the-earth elements; Water is "heavy" and "deep." Yet, once again, people with both Fire and Water in their Sun/Moon combination can be the "colorful characters" of the world, as you will see in the "real people" rundowns included in each category.

Similarly, the most masculine element, Air, is out of synch with both Earth and Water. However individuals with these elements in combination can rise above the gender conflict and even add new insights to our changing world of sex roles.

Fire Sun Sign/Earth Moon Sign

"Bite off more than you can chew, then chew it. Plan more than you can do, then do it."

With the Fire/Earth combination of Sun and Moon Signs, we enter the area of astro-gender types who should have a leg up on same-gender Sun and Moon Sign combinations. Their astrological heritage has given them the advantage of at least having greater access to attributes and attitudes of both the "masculine" and the "feminine."

People born with the Sun in a masculine sign and the Moon in a feminine sign seem to face any challenge not only with determination to overcome it, but also with the kind of glee that comes from frankly enjoying a new way to overcome things. Improvisation is their forte and change is their chosen way of life. They hate uninspired routine and have little regard for pecking orders that don't seem to work. They are entrepreneurial at heart, and their broad understanding—which comes from the Fire Sun Sign—makes them value freedom from restrictions. Obviously Fire/Earth people exist at all levels of society and come from a wide diversity of backgrounds, but when you see someone fighting the odds and winning, you probably are seeing a Fire/Earth type at work. A classic example is

"Stormin' Norman" Schwarzkopf, Sun in Leo, Moon in Capricorn.

Anyone who has worked for a Fire/Earth boss can tell you about Fire/Earth's no-training style. Since they can do it themselves, they are most likely to say to a new recruit, "There's your new job, go do it. And by the way, your predecessor made off with all the files." To a Fire/Earth person, such a challenge is a joy and a delight: "Who cares how it was done before? Here's the way I'm going to do it." For others, working for a tireless and constantly on-the-go boss can be quite enervating. But he or she is not going to change, so the answer probably is to change jobs.

The Fire/Earth Man

This type is not likely to settle down with a partner early in life. For one thing, he is usually too busy getting his one-a-minute ideas off the ground. This is true particularly if the Sun Sign is Sagittarius. Just as the Fire/Earth person is in constant pursuit of the new idea or theoretical challenge, he is constantly (with one eye) on the alert for the right partner. He somehow knows in his heart that there are only certain types who could put up with his slapdash and often screwy lifestyle, so he is more likely to choose someone who will not hold him down. Nevertheless, because he is so creative and adaptive, he must be certain that his partner can also keep up with him intellectually. Since rules mean little to the Fire/Earth type in other aspects of his life, they are not likely to mean much in a permanent liaison. There are many happily married Fire/Earth men, but you will find that their mates are highly unusual as well. If you wonder whether or not your Fire/Earth man can really make a go of what he talks about, remember the accomplishments of financier J. P. Morgan, Aries/Virgo.

As is true with Fire Sun Sign people, you will find the Fire Sun Sign/Earth Moon Sign has honor, and is honest. One example: Magic Johnson, Sun in Leo, Moon in Capricorn.

And innovative: Norman Lear's Sun in Leo, Moon in Virgo made him capable of virtually turning what America sees on television. Arnold Schwarzenegger, Sun in Leo, Moon in Capricorn, is constantly surprising us, and undoubtedly will continue to do so for some time to come. Arthur C. Clarke, famed for his futuristic writing, has Sun in Sagittarius, Moon in Capricorn. It is no surprise to find that rock artist Frank Zappa has the same Sun/Moon combination.

Comparing the way Arnold Schwarzenegger lives out his Fire/Earth profile and Dustin Hoffman, Sun in Leo, Moon in Virgo, does his is illustrative in the sense that both exhibit "strength" in everything they do, yet their individual styles are so different. The Earth Moon (feminine) is a grounding factor to the Fire Sun—and both factors play a role. It is probably the reason that both men, so different, are able to play such sensitive roles so convincingly. As for fighting against the odds, there is no better role model than Sammy Davis, Jr., Sun in Sagittarius, Moon in Virgo.

Humor—often slapstick or just plain corny—is another route Water/Earth men take. Bert Lahr, Leo/Taurus, and Fatty Arbuckle, Aries/Taurus, were both true to type. David Letterman, Aries/Capricorn, probably wouldn't be sorry to hear himself called the contemporary king of this kind of comedy.

Living With the Fire/Earth Man

The typical Fire/Earth man may not strike you as particularly unusual on first meeting, but you will soon discover that you like being in his company. One reason is that he is so upbeat, and, unless life has recently dealt him a heavy blow, so positive about things in general. Those who live with him might tell a slightly different story, however. One version: "He makes jokes out of everything"; another: "He can't sit still"; a third, "He gets so aggressive in arguments." All probably true. The Fire/Earth man is operating out of a powerful combination of elements, and it would be amazing if he didn't make some waves.

With the visualizing power of Fire and the hands-on, get-it-done ability of Earth, the Fire/Earth man may constantly be making changes on his home turf, some of which can be unsettling to others. However, when Fire/Earth says, "I'll get it done," it is something you can count on. The other things come along with it.

As for Fire/Earth's temper: Fire gives a positive outlook, but it can scorch at times as well. Those who know the Fire/Earth man have seen him do his slow burn—usually when someone isn't moving fast enough—and witnessed the mini-eruption that comes after. The good part is that the air is cleared very quickly.

Gender-correcting suggestions for the Fire/Earth man:

- Some Fire Sun Sign/Earth Moon Sign men get side-tracked into an all-work, no-play mode. The ardent desire of the masculine Sun to "make it happen" is overly influenced by the "don't stop for a minute" message of the feminine Moon; this is particularly true if the Moon is in Virgo or Capricorn. Remind yourself that yes, man's work is sometimes done, and he is entitled to "goof off." If you are a Leo, you will know this instinctively.

- If your Fire Sun Sign (particularly Aries) gets too "hot," it can dry up the natural feminine moistness of your Earth Moon. In these cases you can get a lot of temper, temper, temper! and/or a tendency to exhibit the all-too-possible insensitivity of Fire to the feelings of other people. If you find yourself getting disgusted with the "ordinary" people of the world, remind yourself that one of the most valuable potential virtues of Earth is humility.

- You can be one of the world's greatest overpromisers—particularly to women. The point is that at the time you are "laying it on," you are not lying, but not self-correcting your fiery enthusiasm with the practical bent of your Earth Moon. Learn to say, "Perhaps," "Maybe," or "It could be possible," instead of "I'm sure of it" all the time.

- Fire is a highly spirited element; Earth for the most part is not (especially Virgo). One thing that means for Fire Sun/Earth Moon men is the possibility of dramatic mood swings. You may be the type of boss whose secretary everyone checks with each morning to say, "How is he today?" Learn to level out.

- Even more than men with Air in their Sun/Moon astroprofiles, you may be one of the most highly competitive types in the zodiac. Not just in business, but in sports or verbal battles as well. Your Fire Sun's enthusiasm tells you you *will* win; your Earth Moon's tenacity tells you you must win (especially if it is in Capricorn). Take most of life's little battles more lightly; save your strength for the big ones.

The Fire/Earth Woman

Women with this element combination are often admired by their female peers and are intimidating to men. It is no wonder. This combination of Fire/Earth in women could be called the "Amazon" of ancient mythology. Ironically, it is one of the most potentially androgynous of the element combinations. It's just that people like Madonna, Sun Leo, Moon Virgo; Maria Callas, Sun Sagittarius, Moon Virgo; and Tina Turner, Sun Sagittarius, Moon Capricorn, come on so strong that many women would like to have their strength and most men are scared of it. What's interesting about women of the Fire/Earth profile is that they are exhibiting the energy of their Fire Sun Sign and the "feminine" strength of the Earth Moon Sign—plus its sen-

sual, sexy "feminine" style. Some people have called Fire/
Earth women "steamrollers with heart."

There is no doubt that the Fire Sun Sign makes them
willful (Madonna; Diana Ross, Aries Sun, Taurus Moon; Lu-
cille Ball, Leo/Capricorn), but they generally have their will
carried forward—which is a lot more than you can say
about many men with different astro-profiles.

Fire Sun Sign/Earth Moon Sign women—like the men—
play out their lives at many different levels, but they are
very often the ones who get things done. And the ones who
tread where women have never gone before. Geraldine
Ferraro has Sun Sign Leo, Moon Sign Taurus. What is interesting about this particular combination of signs is that
both Leo and Taurus are what are called "fixed" signs—
meaning it takes an awful lot to bring them down. A different but equal kind of strength was shown by Betty Ford,
Sun in Aries, Moon in Taurus. Like the men of the Fire/
Earth element combination, women born with it show little
regard for precedent, and see no reason why they should
not go their own way, even against obstacles.

For the same reason, women with this Fire/Earth astro-
gender profile are quite hard to live with. Some, the ones
who would be horrified by living a single life, often choose
much weaker men, then come to not respect them. Others
marry men with very different goals from their own, but
who are equally dedicated. In these situations it's very
much a case of a "you go your way, I'll go mine" relationship, but with the right guidelines laid down up front, it
works. Any number of women with this combination
choose (perhaps after many relationship disappointments) not to have a permanent partner at all. This is
particularly true of Sagittarian women. With an "androgynous" masculine Fire Sign and their feminine Moon Sign,
there is often a kind of confusion about gender identity—
not sexually, but more "Where do I fit in this world?" And
it is true that our world still values more highly the stereotype of "real women," which is rarely their style.

Fire/Earth women pursue a broad spectrum of careers—

and sometimes will even have two, "a little something on the side." They are daring (Amelia Earhart, Sun in Leo, Moon in Virgo), they are dashing (Diana Ross, Sun in Aries, Moon in Taurus), they are durable (Ann Miller, Sun Aries, Moon Virgo). One who seems to have taken her astro-profile and turned it to her very own uses is Julia Child, Sun in Leo, Moon in Virgo. Her slapdash cooking style and habit of throwing the rules away when they don't work are virtually a portrait of a Fire/Earth woman doing her thing. And it isn't a coincidence that she has built virtually an empire out of the very thing she liked most to do.

Fire/Earth people do have potentially serious faults, however. One is not paying attention to detail. The women often avoid it better because they can "hear" the practical messages of their Earth Moon Sign better than men can. One way around this problem is to do what many Fire/Earth people do: Take a job where you are in the start-up phase of a project, where your ability to see new possibilities and unheard-of connections is of great value. Then leave the details to "the other guys."

Living With the Fire/Earth Woman

Since Fire/Earth is so (unconsciously) androgynous, many women of this astro-gender profile have very different, almost eccentric living styles. Wherever and however they live is unique to their personality. This is one reason that Fire/Earth women who do marry or choose to live with a partner can run into problems when they do not want to do things the "right" way, but their way. Fire/Earth women are often highly unusual people, and often go to some pains to disguise it. However, their problem is impatience, and it will eventually come out when the Fire/Earth woman is frustrated by someone slower and less "together."

Their energy level is high, and many who follow their own beat find the nine-to-five daily regime is not for them. For the woman as for the man, Fire/Earth is the most potentially successful of all the astro-profiles. Partly because of the androgynous quality, and partly because Fire and Earth are the "best" elements for doing in this world. As a consequence, Fire/Earth women are a lot more versatile than more traditional feminine types; though housework is not their first love, they can do it quickly and efficiently, and cooking and entertaining come under the category of "fun" rather than obligation.

Gender-correcting suggestions for the Fire/Earth woman:

- Those Fire/Earth women who try too hard to listen to the "just do it" message of their masculine Fire Sun Signs by taking the "hard line" of their practical Earth Moons (particularly Virgo and Capricorn) can become real sticklers—more on the job than at home. Trying to mask the "masculine" easy-come, easy-go message of their Sun Signs, they demand perfection from all— and can get respect from few.

- Fire/Earth women at their best can be whirling dervishes of activity with a definite method to their madness. However, their natural love of life (Fire Sun) and know-how and can-do (Earth Moon) can be overpowering to gentler souls. No matter how easy something is for *you* to accomplish, let them see you sweat occasionally.

- Fire/Earth women are among those who may hesitate about having children, lest it interfere with their career and worldly pursuits. However, it happens to be one of the best "mothering" combinations in the zodiac—the Fire Sun granting fun and freedom to be, the Earth Moon dealing almost naturally with children's physical needs. Don't close your mind off to the possibility.

- Try to be a better team player. As is true for your masculine counterpart, winning—or getting the most praise—may be too important to you. Look at your contributions from the point of view of the whole group, and rejoice for everyone.

- Earthiness (your feminine Moon) means a lot more than being a practical, do-it-all taskmaster. It means you have more ability than many to enjoy life's sensual delights. Do not deny them to yourself, but don't let your Fire Sun send you overboard. Weight can be a problem, particularly with a Sagittarius Sun and/or Taurus Moon (in which case you can become virtually a female Falstaff).

Getting Sign-Specific

Fire Sun Sign/Water Moon Sign

Aries/Taurus: You are tactful and forceful, and hence get away with whatever you want. You are a strong and implacable fighter and give no quarter. Yet you are too set on your goals to worry about revenge. Your attitude toward pleasure is take it or leave it alone.

Aries/Virgo: You have a fine critical and analytical mind. Success comes through attention to details. You expect to do your best and never want to stop learning. You are a bit of a puritan and have little use for human frailty and weakness. You are easily forgiven.

Aries/Capricorn: You have definite ideas about where you are going and how to get there; your manner of expression is forceful without being offensive. You seem always to know the right thing to say at the right time. Powerful people will always be there to help you.

Leo/Taurus: No one is ever in doubt about where you stand. Though you are liable to errors in judgment, you are just as sure when you are wrong as when you're right. Your integrity will rarely be questioned, nor will your power over people. You see things in the large.

Leo/Virgo: You have a large streak of timidity under your aggressive exterior, which is likely to mask an inferiority complex. If you allow your good taste to come out, you can win people over to you through your charm. Your independence, however, can make you enemies.

Leo/Capricorn: This is one of the most powerful Sun/Moon polarities. You know what you want and see that no one gets in your way. You spoil yourself, making demands of the world. Your great strength is unswerving purpose and the energy necessary to accomplish your ends.

Sagittarius/Taurus: You are genial, idealistic and romantic. Though you are practical, you will do best in an artistic or creative career. In love you make a wonderful partner, idealistic, impulsive, loyal and devoted. You put a high premium on education, constantly studying.

Sagittarius/Virgo: You are a realist without being hard-boiled, a romanticist without being impractical. You are a diplomat and can win people over to your side by your charm, which is the unconscious and calm variety. There is nothing petty or small about you.

Sagittarius/Capricorn: You know how to appeal to groups of people. You have leadership qualities, but you are likely to jump to conclusions. You have a righteous anger that makes you feared by those who would cross you. You take yourself seriously; so do others.

Fire Sun Sign/Water Moon Sign

This section applies to men and women who have either Aries, Leo or Sagittarius as a Sun Sign and Cancer, Scorpio or Pisces as a Moon Sign.

> *"The principal thing in this world is to keep one's soul aloft."*
>
> —GUSTAVE FLAUBERT

Fire/Water People

If you think literally about the elements, the most logical interaction between these two is that water puts fire out. However, as a Sun Sign/Moon Sign combination, the Fire Sun tends to heat up the Water Moon and produce people who are, in a sense, colorful characters. To start by naming a few: Eddie Murphy, Sun in Aries, moon in Scorpio, and *Playboy* magazine's Hugh Hefner, Sun in Aries, Moon in Cancer. In addition to many other eccentricities, Hefner has a zoo license, and keeps animals, mainly tropical birds, at his mansion in Los Angeles. In Murphy, we see the antic, wild and wacky side of the Aries Sun Sign working with the powerfully willful Scorpio Moon Sign.

While Fire/Water people color our world with their uniqueness, they also bless it with an upbeat, always-willing-to-help nature, and an attachment to important values. Among the men, one might cite the late United Nations president Dag Hammarskjöld, Sun in Leo, Moon in Cancer; among the women, Bella Abzug, Sun in Leo, Moon in Scorpio. The former, in addition to his diplomatic duties, was a writer who expressed a very personal code of ethics. Of the latter, one can surely see that Abzug's Aries Fire is surely not extinguished by her Scorpio Moon, but only burns the brighter—and more vitriolic in service to her cause.

There is tremendous empathy in the Fire/Water combination, and many Fire/Water persons have reached out to help not only themselves but a whole group of disadvantaged people. Most we don't hear of; one we have is the farm labor leader Cesar Chavez, Sun in Aries, Moon in Pisces. On a day-to-day level, it gives Fire/Water people great pleasure to give pleasure to others. And with their active imaginations, they are very good at figuring out just the right thing for just the right problem.

The Fire/Water Man

Here we meet the male of our species with a powerful masculine Sun Sign and a very feminine, passionate Moon Sign. And, sexually speaking, that is what you can expect. Before you get to that point, however, you may have spent quite a while being courted in a highly unusual manner and then, suddenly, a date is set. Warren Beatty, Sun in Aries, Moon in Scorpio, is an excellent example of the breed. For whatever reason, Fire/Water men tend to run in packs, and have undying loyalty to their pals. Frank Sinatra, Sun in Sagittarius, Moon in Pisces, seems to pass that test. So realize that, if trouble strikes, he is more likely to go off and help a buddy instead of you. This loyalty, at least among ordinary people, however, can prove to be a failing. For instance, a Fire/Water boss may so protect one of his favorites among those he manages that both lose out in the end. Yet it is an endearing trait, and women who are loved by a Fire/Water man may often feel that they have met the metaphorical knight on a white charger. On a day-to-day basis, the Fire/Water man may not be the most buttoned-up person to live with, but whatever his transgressions, his humor will generally make up for it all. Men of this type are given to whimsy with a message, like "Peanuts" creator Charles Schulz, Sun in Sagittarius, Moon in Pisces. (Whenever Pisces is part of a male's astro-gender profile, he may not always be constant, but you will always be amused.)

Among the other Fire/Water people of the zodiac who amuse with an intent to educate (or get a serious message across) are humorous sociological columnist Russell Baker, Sun in Leo, Moon in Cancer; and Charlie Chaplin, Sun in Aries, Moon in Cancer. Another who is multital-ented, and outrageously good as a comic actor, is Dudley Moore, Sun in Aries, Moon in Scorpio.

A highly developed imagination and the power to pro-duce with it are other marks of the Fire/Water person. Steven Spielberg, Sun in Sagittarius, Moon in Pisces, does it on film; two who did it with poetry are William Blake, Sun in Sagittarius, Moon in Cancer; and Baudelaire, Sun in Aries, Moon in Cancer. One of the most amazing displays of the ability of the Fire/Water person to put a whole body of information into an imaginative format is famed "Myth Man" Joseph Campbell, Sun in Aries, Moon in Cancer. Note that in a number of these cases the Moon is in the sign of Cancer. Cancer is the poet and the romantic's Moon. When ordinary men try to deny its strong ability to turn feelings and impressions into stated language, they really have a hard time.

Living With the Fire/Water Man

It is on the day-to-day level that you see the volatility of the Fire/Water man. Though he is in general gentle and humorous, he can be thrown out of control by certain sit-uations that engage his Water Moon. He is likely to have a colorful imagination, and that applies to his own and his family's lives. With the Water Moon, he is particularly tuned in to the women around him, from wife to daughters. With teenagers, he is likely to be highly suspicious of their activities and be a bit of a harridan about dating hours and curfews. When he is operating out of the energy of his Fire

Sun, he is more "rational" than when the feminine Water Moon roils things up.

No matter how hard he works, the Fire/Water man wants to play at the same rate—and he often, at whatever age, has a "gang" or a group he likes to play with. The partners of the Fire/Water man may have to set down some rules about what can go on where and when. With his feminine Water Moon, his friends are truly important to him—it's a lot more than a case of "boys' night out"—or in. If his wife is sensitive to this, she will go out of her way to accommodate the Fire/Water man, one of the more caring and loyal in the zodiac.

Gender-correcting suggestions for the Fire/Water man:

- Don't be intimidated by the "technical brat pack"— i.e., those computer whizzes who seem to have learned it in the cradle. Chances are most of them have a good bit of Air (logic) and/or Earth (hands-on) in their horoscopes. Your contribution, with your Fire Sun, is to show them where things fit in the big picture, and where it's all going; your Water Moon can "feel out" the conclusions. If you can't get the details, don't sweat it. You're the real leader of the pack.

- When Fire (your Sun) heats up Water (your Moon), the result can be a blast of steam—or hot air. Carefully cultivate an analytical attitude you can bring into play when disagreements occur. You have the ability to hang back, if you wish, and not jump into a line of reasoning (arguing) that is ineffective—and even embarrassing. Use your "feeling" Moon to assess people's real agendas before you get into any fray.

- Women find you have a natural charisma—perhaps they feel "in synch" with your Water Moon and find your occasionally abrasive Fire Sun sexy. If, particularly in office situations, women come on to you, use the gregariousness of Fire to keep things in a group, or get to know the person with the friendliness of Fire first. If it's right, you'll know, and the passionate Water side of you can come into play.

- Almost no one can feel more stuck in the wrong job situation than a Fire/Water male. His Fire makes him antsy and even unpleasant; his Water Moon can make him ultramoody. Don't hesitate to say "So long" if you are sure the spot is not for you.

- Although by its nature Fire tends to make people move around a lot and even be considered "hyper," you may be one of those Fire/Water types who falls prey to the calmness (potential sloth) of a Water Moon. Even on days when your Moon tells you that you don't "feel" like it and would really rather read a novel, get out there and run like the Fire type you are.

The Fire/Water Woman

Though the Fire/Water woman is a very close sister to the Fire/Earth woman, in that they both have male Sun Signs and female Moon Signs, the Fire/Water woman is generally a lot softer—but less sure of where she fits on the gender spectrum. Writer Zelda Fitzgerald, wife of F. Scott Fitzgerald, Sun in Leo, Moon in Cancer, is one who succumbed to the painful pull toward doing (Fire) and feeling (Water). One who worked it out in *her* own way was "Madame" Polly Adler, Sun in Aries, Moon in Scorpio (sex), whose house was definitely not a home.

Among the exceptions to the "softer" rule are Bella Abzug, already cited, and writers Erica Jong, Sun in Aries, Moon in Cancer, and Marguerite Duras, also Aries/Cancer. These last two women go right to the heart of the gender conflict, in plain words. With Jong, the words are barbed but funny; with Duras, they are sadder but, in the opinion of some, also wiser. And singer Aretha Franklin, also Aries/Cancer, is truly their soul sister.

There are any number of achieving women who appear to handle the Fire/Water astro-gender profile with ease and grace—making their mark but not shouting out a revolutionary message. Linda Ellerbee, Sun in Leo, Moon in Cancer; Julie Christie, Aries/Scorpio; and Chris Evert, Sun in Sagittarius, Moon in Scorpio, seem to exude a friendly femininity while getting what they want in a "man's world."

One potential trap for the Fire/Water woman, when caught between a rock and a hard place, is to lose touch with her thinking ability and become all feeling (Water) and imagination (Fire). It is this kind of female that men are constantly referring to as if they represent all of femininity. The Fire/Water woman who wants to succeed—in business and/or in her love life—must learn to cope with this tendency.

On the positive side, she can enliven men in a way that the seeresses of old used to do. She can virtually be a muse to a man who wants to express his emotions in writing; she can enter the life of an arid Air/Earth type and make him see it in color for the first time.

Perhaps the quintessence of the Fire/Water woman is poet Emily Dickinson, Sun in Sagittarius, Moon in Scorpio. Virtually isolated in a remote New England house, she managed to describe the world not just of the senses, but of the feelings, and she understood how the whole world works emotionally. In a time when women were background people, her Sagittarius Sun Sign allowed her to pursue a course of action, at least with her mind.

Living With the Fire/Water Woman

There's a lot of potential charm for a woman with this combination. Her Fire Sun is generally upbeat and outgoing; her Water Moon takes any edge off the Fire, and gives a gently humorous outlook. Yet, just as she must avoid swinging between the extremes of Fire and Water, she must also guard against their clashing. When Fire heats Water, you get steam, and a potentially dangerous explosion.

Though she has the Water "feeling" Moon, and theoretically should be an ultraloving mother, her impatience sometimes gets the better of her when her children act up. When that happens, she yells (Fire people are loud) and completely confuses the children, who remember her singing lullabies last night. The one who suffers most by the confusion is the Fire/Water woman herself. Whichever side she swings to, she feels guilt from the other.

Fire/Water women should make it a point to keep themselves "in balance" via exercise. In addition to the traditional gym situations, there are certain Oriental disciplines which are specifically designed to promote inner serenity and harmony of mind and body.

Most Fire/Water women choose to work outside the home, and that is appropriate for the Fire Sun. However, those who choose not to, or are unable to exercise their skills in the workplace, must also find some meaningful way to feel "accomplished." With her lively imagination, the Fire/Water woman is most likely to find her own way and just the right "sideline."

Gender-correcting suggestions for the Fire/Water woman:

- With your built-in feminine nature, when your Fire Sun and Water Moon heat each other up, you can become the classic spitfire. In your personal relationships, people may learn that you really don't mean it, or can (like your closest male) learn to "turn it off." However, in business it can be a real drawback, and only work against women in general. When things get you riled, smile sweetly and try to defend your argument rationally.

- With your combination of "passionate elements," you are a natural target for sexual harassment of a variety of types. For one thing, you probably tend to be friendly to one and all—and someone can misinterpret your meaning. Second, there is a natural sexiness about women with Water in their horoscopes. No harm in looking great, but you would do well to play down overly sexy clothes and makeup.

- Even with your outgoing Fire Sun, if your Water Moon combines with your female nature in a certain way, some of you are likely to be the "quiet one in the corner." In fact, it could make you totally miserable. You needn't put on a show to let people know your power to entertain and amuse; a few funny anecdotes can get around, and suddenly you'll be the one with the "wit like a whip."

- If you choose to become a mother, choose also to curb your sometimes excitable, irritable nature. Nothing is more threatening to a child than inconsistency in a close caregiver. Of course, there will be times you will want to scream—and probably will—but follow it with hugs and/or the distracting games you play so well. With your Water Moon, your feeling nature is so strong that often your overreactions are from fear that something or someone may harm your child.

- If there is anything your Fire Sun can help you do, it is to compete with the men in your work world. If there is anything your Water Moon can do to make sure it works the way you want it to, it is to help you do it with grace—even under pressure.

Getting Sign-Specific

Fire Sun Sign/Water Moon Sign

Aries/Cancer: Your intellectual powers are strong and you have an intuitive handle on people and things. You are self-centered rather than selfish. Though you wouldn't deliberately hurt anyone, you do without knowing you are doing so. You are colorful and dramatic.

Aries/Scorpio: You have a passion for living that gives you inner drive and energy. You rarely get down, because of a combination of faith in yourself and a belief in your luck. You are so competent no one will give you sympathy, but that is perfectly all right with you.

Aries/Pisces: You worry a lot, though people don't always know it. Many of your troubles are self-created; solitude is a good prescription. You tend to like odd people, which further complicates your life. You have a true gift for language and should use it.

Leo/Cancer: You are intense and have great common sense. You have a sense of humor that prevents you from getting too "heavy" about your self-centeredness. You have a real feeling for other people and try your best to understand them and help them.

Leo/Scorpio: You know yourself well enough to try to keep yourself from bursting out into anger, hate or any of the other "animalistic" emotions. You are possessive, and though you prefer to travel alone, you are capable of getting people to give you their undying loyalty.

Leo/Pisces: You know when to stay and when to go, and your timing brings you success. You take care of the people who are dependent on you, which earns their devotion. Your expansive spirit is likely to seek more than one person in love, but you cannot be called fickle.

Sagittarius/Cancer: When you are thinking clearly you can see through anything or anyone. No task is too hard for you when you've set your mind on it. Be careful, however, not to waste your energies on the impossible. Be willing to see things through to the end.

Sagittarius/Scorpio: You know what you want and some-how or other get it. You believe in live-and-let-live and are always willing to listen to someone who wants your ear. You are a great companion, laughing easily and being able to see the ridiculous behind the real.

Sagittarius/Pisces: Broad generalities are what count with you. You are not practical. You are impressionable and romantic, and can be preyed on by people who want some-thing from you. You are free of meanness, incapable of holding a grudge, yet you put up with people's foibles.

Air Sun Sign/Earth Moon Sign

"Politic, cautious and meticulous."
—SHAKESPEARE

The elements Air and Earth, while very different in their overall consciousness, have an important commonality. One (Air) is capable of thinking through a situation; the other (Earth) sees things as they really are—literally. As a result, Air/Earth people are regarded as, and generally are, people who can come in, fairly quietly take charge and straighten out the mess that intuitive Fire or emotional Water people have made.

Every management consultant firm should be sure to have at least one Air/Earth person on its employee list. The Earth Moon is almost always a guarantee that the per-son is organized (most so in Virgo) and practical. The Air Sun Sign gives him/her the logic—and the political savvy—to solve tempests without making waves.

In the Air/Earth combination, we come to the current organizational/managerial style of American business. It was the man in the gray flannel suit; now his clothes are different, but the "personality" hasn't changed. One of the key elements is that this combination is task- rather than relationship-driven; though most companies would deny it, the bottom line is more important than personal issues. While there are many other performance styles in individuals born with this configuration, one classic Air/Earth type is Lee Iacocca, Sun in Libra, Moon in Taurus. There has been and continues to be a change in the more people-oriented management style, but progress is slow. One irony of the women's movement is that instead of bringing "feminine" (relational) values into the business world, many women—particularly the highly placed—picked up the old way of doing things.

Both Air and Earth are opposed to the two elements that are lacking in most people's lifestyles, and in the country at large. Fire has enthusiasm, spontaneity and passion for whatever it undertakes. Water values relationships, and is able to judge situations by bringing in the feeling values. We are beginning to see change, but the "organization man"—or woman—is still the ideal most people look up to.

One of the values that has been missing, and is a "feminine" value, is visibly coming to the fore. That is, the value of pure play—play for its own sake. Advertising campaigns, magazine articles and marketing journals are beginning to get the concept, and a national poll by Roper reveals that there was a sudden jump in the early nineties to a greater percentage of people saying they work in order to be able to enjoy more leisure and "play" time. In play, you see Fire and Water in great abundance.

The Air/Earth Man

Air/Earth people are usually regarded as "smart." Whether or not they did well at school (which they probably did), there is a sophisticated, knowledgeable side of them that brings many an Air/Earth man to politics. The list is quite long, starting with Machiavelli, Sun Taurus, Moon Aquarius. Whatever your politics or your preferences, you can count among Air/Earth men Ronald Reagan, Aquarius/Taurus; Abraham Lincoln, Aquarius/Capricorn; George Bush, Gemini/Taurus; John Kennedy, Gemini/ Virgo; and Jesse Jackson, Libra/Taurus. Though his Moon Sign is not clear, FDR was an Aquarius too. On the fringes you'll find Oliver North, Libra/Capricorn, and Jimmy Hoffa, Aquarius/Taurus. Even Bob Dylan, Gemini/Taurus, writes songs with "political" messages.

What has this got to say about the style of "man in the street" Air/Earth men? They will be charming (particularly if the Sun is in Libra), they will be witty, they will be able to charm the birds out of the trees, so to speak. However, even with the "feminine" Earth Moon, you'll find a tough streak somewhere. This is the ideal man for the woman (and there are still many) who wants a man to take charge and run both their lives. Along with that territory comes the fact that any business or community political project will come before you.

However, with the Earth Moon, these men can be quite sensual, if you can get them to stop thinking and just feel. Even in his sexual life there will be a kind of order and schedule; one way to break the pattern is to surprise him. Be warned beforehand that this Air/Earth man can never be embarrassed or humiliated, so be cautious. He is.

Living With the Air/Earth Man

Chances are you won't be living with him unless you yourself are bright, witty, quick on the trigger, able to handle a very full plate. If it doesn't sound very romantic, that is because the Air/Earth man is able to keep his fantasies (if he has them) securely locked in his head. In fact, he prides himself on being a realist, even a cynic. In some cases this is a cover-up for the unfamiliar feminine vibes coming from his Earth Moon.

If he has anything to say about it, the house will be sparely decorated—literally "no frills." The Air/Earth man, even more than the Air/Air man, has an almost military mentality. If he uses it too much on his family, the relationship won't last. However, if the family comes to regard it as a running joke, they may learn to live with it.

Physical strength and sports competence are likely to be high on his agenda. However, when it comes to Little League and other parent/children sports events, he probably will not be in evidence. This is not a nurturing type, even though he may not have a mean bone in his body. If he carves out a logical place for himself as "head of the family," and everyone agrees with it, all should go well.

Because he is in tune with the general tenor of our society, the Air/Earth man is likely to have a ruling passion— money. Not so much making it, although he will do well at that too, but at saving it, manipulating it, making it go as far as possible. Some of this astro-gender type can accurately be called "cheap." Others may simply make a game out of things like coupons and "two-fers." If it does not become an obsession, the family may really benefit from it.

Gender-correcting suggestions for the Air/Earth man:

- You can easily get a bad rap for always thinking, thinking, thinking and doing, doing, doing—and not seeming to have any fun. It is ironic, because Air is the naturally verbally wittiest element in the zodiac. Become more open and share your thoughts with others; you may have the funniest thing anyone has thought of saying about the Xerox or fax machine with a mind of its own.

- Though a Gemini Sun Sign can make you more flexible, for the most part you Air Sun, Earth Moon people want things done their way, in their time. You do not leave much room for imagination—either your own or that of other people. You can practice by deliberately deviating from routine, by doing something in a whole new way, by laughing at yourself if you find that your rigidness is noticed by others.

- Air/Earth men tend to "live in their heads." As capable as they are of doing, thinking often overtakes it. This is as true of the businessman as the householder. One way to make things a reality is to take on projects around your home—at first, ones where you can see immediate results of what you have imagined. There is no better formula for a fretful, thoughtful type than working with your hands.

- Even if "creativity" means to you anything from kids' paper constructions to museum-quality art, you should get a handle on what it really is. Take a leaf from the Fire types, who often create ideas virtually out of thin air (your element). The way to do it is to imagine something that no one has thought of yet; you don't necessarily have to make it or do it, but it will show you that you don't have to be an artist to be creative.

- Though the Air Sun Signs, particularly Gemini and Libra, can make highly romantic gestures and are known for soft lights and sweet music, they often find the real thing disorienting. Use the nitty-gritty elements of your feminine Earth Moon to get you on track, and take the real action from there.

The Air/Earth Woman

Air Sun Sign, Earth Moon Sign women are able to make out like bandits in today's business world. Most companies value them highly for being organized, logical, practical. At the lower levels on the job ladder, it works out better than it does at the career level. Air/Earth women are every bit as ambitious as their male counterparts, and can even have an edge on them from a productivity point of view. The tougher types are generally not admired by either sex, personally speaking. But higher-ups are often mesmerized by the Air/Earth woman's problem-solver thinking and programs. In their drive to the top, they may not make too many friends, but they will make money.

Lest this type sound too hard, there is a bright side to the Air/Earth combination in women. While their male counterparts can be "get-organized" tyrants in their own homes and with their own children, the women of this type are able to utilize the softening aspects of their Earth Moon. They can be exceptionally patient with children, and provide a bulwark for them against the woes of the outside world. Mia Farrow, Aquarius/Capricorn, exemplifies the offbeat quality of Air (particularly Aquarius) with the sturdiness of the "Earth mother" combined.

Air/Earth women tend to value themselves, and some prominent ones were in the vanguard of the women's movement including Germaine Greer, Aquarius/Taurus. Many Air (communications)/Earth women have a lot to say, especially in down-to-earth, practical ways. Joyce Brothers, Libra/Capricorn, and Virginia Johnson, Aquarius/Virgo (of Masters and Johnson), are typical of this breed, and illustrate the pragmatism of both sexes with this Sun Sign/Moon Sign combination.

Air/Earth women can be sharp-tongued and even shrill (Margaret Thatcher, Libra/Virgo; Ayn Rand, Aquarius/Capricorn) or caustic and very funny (Joan Rivers, Aquarius/Taurus, and Carrie Fisher, Libra/Taurus). They show the strength of the masculine Air Sign. One who does it physically is Martina Navratilova, Libra/Capricorn.

In general, Air/Earth women are better able to negotiate the dry coolness of this element combination, but they have to be constantly alert not to fall into the trap of the "man's world," with all that that connotes.

Living With the Air/Earth Woman

The place the Air/Earth woman has most fans is right under her own roof. In business or local community groups she is likely to give the impression that she knows it all and can be tough about having things go her way. This may or may not be true. Some Air/Earth women are just so "into" whatever they are doing, they concentrate on the issue as if it were mortal combat. They may really not be as hard-nosed as they seem—just serious.

This is a serious combination, and the Air/Earth woman may even suffer from depression from time to time. Her motto is "So much to be done, so little time to do it."

The good part is that her Earth Moon softens up her attitude toward children. Playing with them, which she will sometimes find time to do, is the best "medicine" for her blue days. Another literal interpretation of the elements uses earth itself as a panacea for the Air/Earth woman. Working in a garden, no matter how small, will put her in touch with true earth, and provide her with a link with the real world. One of her problems is that she lives too much in her head, and not in the rough-and-tumble real world.

In order to be comfortable the Air/Earth woman must be "doing." With her logical Air Sun, taking a course in money and investment—or, even better, pure mathematics—would give her good, clear mind something noncompetitive to work on.

Gender-correcting suggestions for the Air/Earth woman:

- If, as is highly likely, you don't seem to be able to find/hold the kind of male in your life you would like, the singles' column is not the answer. What may be is to evaluate what you are really looking for—someone as career-savvy, hard-working and ambitious as you who is also sensitive and emotional. Perhaps you would do better to look for the latter "feminine" values in a man, and tell yourself you can do the big earning. A support group of women also looking for the "perfect man" might help.

- If you are partnered, with or without children, try to "switch off" your outside concerns, like work, before going home to your family. The combination of Air Sun and Earth Moon in a woman who does well in business can be a rather "dry" combination. Let your family enjoy the playful, earthier you.

- You should be well organized; if you are not, it's possible a Taurus Moon gives you the "easies" and lets you let up on yourself occasionally. However, even then, you must be more tolerant with others who are not so buttoned up about exactly what goes where and what happens when.

- For pure pleasure, try doing a "Julia Child" bit—that is, master a dish or a group of dishes that are highly complex and where you can show off your perfectionist style. With an Air Sun Sign, particularly Gemini or Libra, you probably love to entertain. With an Earth Moon Sign, you like to get and give pleasure with tangible things. Remember, cooking really is chemistry, and should appeal to the analytical part of you while giving you the pleasure of a nurturing pursuit.

- You need interpersonal stimulation—lots of it, and with both sexes—to bring out the best of your double-gender astro-profile. No matter how busy your schedule or how remote your living arrangements, you must make a point to join groups. They can range from the arts to politics, but any one you join should offer you both the chance to match wits and to do hands-on work as well.

Getting-Sign Specific

Air Sun Sign/Earth Moon Sign

Gemini/Taurus: You are extremely popular. Your cleverness attracts people and your Taurus stability makes them stay. You make a good manager, with persistence that is surprising to those who don't know you well. You see through people, but are tolerant of them.

Gemini/Virgo: You have a tendency to feel misunderstood or unappreciated. You have a hard time settling down into or doing a job. You start things with great enthusiasm, and then drop them—including friendships. You are quick and adaptable, great for success.

Gemini/Capricorn: You look "easy," but underneath, you are all determination. You are intensely ambitious. Though good, you are somewhat cold. You are sensitive to others but can overlook it. You are capable of the utmost in diplomacy when it is called for.

Libra/Taurus: You have to believe completely in whatever you involve yourself in. You know how to put yourself across so that people like you. You have charm, independence and a liberal dose of sentimental feelings. You need affection and are willing to give it in return.

Libra/Virgo: You are not particularly warm, but you are extremely self-sufficient. You can argue reasonably, then go ahead and do just as you please. You are able to say what is bothering you without holding a grudge. However, you are surprised when others get angry.

Libra/Capricorn: You know what you want and you know how to go about getting it. Others sometimes see you as "above the crowd" and cannot get to like you until you come down to their level. You have a tendency to let your nerves get the better of you, and act impulsively.

Aquarius/Taurus: You would make an excellent executive, but you really don't want to be one. You are not interested in gaining control over other people. Personal development is what interests you, and your motto could easily be "Live and let live." And other people don't mind.

Aquarius/Virgo: You are capable of keeping your emotions under wraps and reasoning things out. Yet your emotions are bound up with your thinking process and you feel that those who love you must agree with you. You are expressive in either writing or speech.

Aquarius/Capricorn: You are a law-and-order type with a strong sense of honor. You combine humanitarianism with a strong sense of the facts. You have imagination and an honesty of purpose. You can remain unspoiled even if you make it to the top.

Air Sun Sign/Water Moon Sign

"A tender heart is the cross I bear."
                                        —DON MARQUIS

This is one of the more difficult of the Sun/Moon combinations for both sexes to negotiate. Some—or most—of the men ignore the feminine Moon and fall into deep depressions or dark moods when that "feminine" Moon is trying to tell them something. The women, hair and makeup perfect on the outside, can hurt like crazy from ignored emotional needs and feelings.

A highly successful young female advertising executive was brought up short when asked her birth information. When she was told by an astrologer that she would never be comfortable being tough with her staff, she gasped, "But that's my biggest problem in business."

The Air/Water Man

Ironically, men with this combination, if they would delve into their natures with or without professional help, have the potential of becoming the "man of steel with soul." The ultramasculine "thinking" Air Sun Sign has the potential to make them capable of being logical and detached, to step back from any problem and see it clearly. Because they are also precise, they will see it from all angles. Then their Water Moon Sign should make them capable of seeing how the project relates to people, and to think about it in "feeling terms." Far too many men of this combination get caught in the trap of "all work, no play" and/or "all brains, but no heart."

One who has not only avoided the trap but actually made a career out of combining thinking and feeling is Bill Moyers, Sun in Gemini, Moon in Pisces. His "world of ideas," metaphorically speaking, is as long on capturing the feelings of a people or a situation as it is on transmitting fascinating information. Paul Simon, Libra/Cancer, makes music that is at once lively and entertaining, and appealing to the more universal emotions. Al Capp, Libra/Pisces, worked it out via humor in the comic strip "Li'l Abner." Those in an age group old enough to remember the ongoing saga will recall that Capp was able to bring cartoon characters to life with all their feelings and emotions.

To some it may be startling to hear that General Douglas MacArthur, Aquarius/Cancer, is an Air/Water person. But if you think about it in astrological terms, it makes some sense. The Cancer Moon, particularly, is known not only for its feeling qualities, but also for tenacity. MacArthur was a fantastic strategist and "steely" warrior by virtue of his Air Sun; but the grip of his Cancer Moon turned his actions into passions.

Mario Cuomo, Sun in Gemini, Moon in Scorpio, is an enigma to many, but astrology may explain some things about him. The Gemini Sun can be indecisive and fickle, but more important is the Scorpio Moon, which gives him tremendous emotional depth and an acute sense of when to use it to his best advantage.

Air/Water men seem to range all over the career field, but outrageousness and adventure would appear to have driven many. Science fiction writer Jules Verne, Aquarius/Scorpio; Norman Mailer, Aquarius/Cancer; Oral Roberts, Aquarius/Cancer; John Wayne, Gemini/Scorpio; and Babe Ruth, Aquarius/Cancer, have all left a unique, and often perverse, trail behind them. Though still young, Dan Quayle, Aquarius/Cancer, surely has a mixed bag of role models to follow.

Air/Water men have all the right astrological equipment to be marvelous at the romantic. Air gives them the ideas and the graceful words to express them; the Water Moon should make all their gestures come from the heart. However, women who involve themselves with this type should be cautious about taking sworn statements seriously. The Air/Water man is not a charlatan; he simply sometimes means what he says at that moment, and no other. One who obviously meant whatever he said to Joanne Woodward is Paul Newman, Aquarius/Pisces. It is interesting to note that she is a Pisces/Gemini—the exact reverse of Newman's element combination.

Any woman who has a partner or lover who is an Air/Water astrological combination probably knows about his "bitchy" moods. And that is exactly what they are. His "inner feminine"—which he can't get out via talking, crying or simply feeling emotion—he usually takes out on the one nearest him at the time. This is the "moody guy" whose secretary warns people away on "bad days."

Living With the Air/Water Man

Because he looks at life from both sides—the masculine and the feminine—the Air/Water man has great potential to incorporate different values into his life and become a very "rich" person. However, the society we live in doesn't make that easy to do. With feminine values repressed on all sides, what's a simple guy to do with these feelings he has? In some cases the pressure may be great enough for the man to go into therapy—where he will find out, surprisingly enough, that everyone has feelings. The question is what to do with them. He might get into a men's consciousness group too, which is another excellent place to learn about feelings.

However, he will most likely still run smack into the "no-feeling zone" if he works in a typically masculine-dominated office. He doesn't have to harass women to belong "to the group"; but he would most likely be considered quite strange if he approached a woman to talk about feelings.

Because the Air/Water man can be overcome by misunderstood feelings and go into a downer, this is another of the astro-gender types who should have a room of his own to retreat to. It would benefit everyone.

Gender-correcting suggestions for the Air/Water man:

- With the lightest element, Air, as your Sun Sign, and the heaviest element, Water, influencing your Moon, you are a walking conflict of interests. In fact, it may become noticeable in terms of inconsistent behavior patterns and/or extreme "ups" and "downs." Especially if you are an Aquarian, you may get a reputation for being a bit on the erratic side. As a member of the male sex born into the analytical male "thinking" element, you should be able to draw up your own agenda for using your emotional side smartly, and coming off as Mr. Calm.

- Some of you, particularly Gemini and Libran Sun Signs, could walk away with the "charm" award any day of the week. However, since your Water Moon signals an intensity you may not totally intend, you could give people the wrong idea. When the time is right to keep it light, be sure you do.

- Make good use of your arbitrating skills. Your logic will let you understand what everyone is saying; your feeling Water Moon will give you clues about what each side *really* wants. You should then be able to serve hidden agendas as well as spoken ones, and at least make everyone come out a little more comfortable.

- Be sure not to cut off the feminine part of you that is your Moon. Many Air/Water men are good at doing that. One way to avoid this: Spend as much time with your children as possible. Let them—both girls *and* boys—know that it's okay to have a good cry, scream with frustration, find some movies too sad to watch, temporarily "hate" their sibling. Also make sure they know how to keep control when necessary.

- No matter how hard you try, you will from time to time feel the "dark side" of your Water Moon (particularly if it is Scorpio). You know you can, with subtle logic, manipulate both people and situations to your advantage. If it gets too rough, however, you may be the loser in the long run. If you get stuck obsessing over such an issue, hard, almost mindless exercise is the answer. Sweat it out.

The Air/Water Woman

Air/Water women can go any number of ways, but they are usually quite successful at it. With their feminine Moon, and their ability to access it more easily than men, they can also outdistance men at what they do. One prime example of an Air/Water woman who has made an indelible mark is Helen Gurley Brown, Sun Aquarius/Moon Scorpio.

She literally created the "Cosmopolitan Girl" and the magazine the Cosmo girls read has been a phenomenal business success, in good times and bad. Anyone who has heard her speak or seen her interviewed on television must be awed by the rather soft-voiced woman who comes on like a dynamo and has no problems discussing sexuality—anyone's. The women's movement helped, but Helen Gurley Brown deserves a lot of the credit for making "good sex" okay for women as well as men. Incidentally, the so-called "Happy Hooker" has Sun in Gemini/Moon in Scorpio, in the same element combination.

The ability to communicate—in writing or any other way—is a prime attribute of the Air element. Air/Water women are superb at communicating and getting to the heart of things at gut level. They themselves have a lot of guts. Two who can be cited are Barbara Walters, Libra/Pisces, and Rona Barrett, Libra/Cancer. The ability to draw out people's emotions (particularly those of men) and talk about them in public is a rare gift, but when it works, it works.

A number of onscreen beauties have this element combination, and in some cases it gave them a not-so-subtle sexiness. Think about Rita Hayworth, Libra/Pisces; Colleen Dewhurst, Gemini/Pisces; and Tallulah Bankhead, Aquarius/Scorpio. Mimicking her own astrological profile onscreen was a highly successful venture for Julie Andrews, Sun Libra, Moon Scorpio, in the film *Victor Victoria.* Both as a man and as a woman, she was charming, dashing, audacious—and beautiful. It would be interesting for any Air/Fire woman to see that film to learn more about her element combination. It is a good one with lots of potential for success.

Speaking of success, the Air/Water combination in women can be even more driving in business than Air/Earth. As with General MacArthur, the Water Moon can turn ambitions into passions. As someone said about an Air/Fire woman she knows in business, "That one really goes for the throat, doesn't she?" Since most people even-

tually do marry (even if they are marrying later), the Air/
Water woman should not cut herself off from her feminine
roots by deciding babies are not for her. She would make
the best of mothers with her "caring/feeling" Moon, and
would carry on a business career at the same time with
great ease.

Living With the Air/Water Woman

Living with the Air/Water woman can play itself out in several different scenarios. With the woman who has "sorted
herself out" and understands the very diverse aspects of
herself, it can be ideal. If her Air Sun works as it should,
she will be fair, and able to see all points of view; her Water
Moon will make her a tender and compassionate person.
However, there is another possibility. And that is that the
Air/Water woman is operating from two poles . . . Air, the
most masculine, and Water, the most feminine. In this case
there will rarely be a serene atmosphere, as she goes from
hard-driving (career) person to weepy, moody, discon-
tented housewife. With her clear-thinking, clear-talking Air
Sun Sign, she should be able to articulate her unhappiness,
and put it away. However, the emotional power of the Water Moon is such that she often doesn't know what the
problem is—until later.

In the middle is the average Air/Water woman who can
resonate to both Sun and Moon, when it is appropriate.
She's pleasant to be around, but not overly sweet. She can
organize things, but not be above asking for help. As far
as her children are concerned, she is consistent in her
treatment of them—except for occasional outbursts
brought on by their unhappiness. The Air/Water woman's
true *bête noir* is other people's misery. In some way, deep
down, she feels she is responsible for it.

She tends to rely on the men around her to deal with
the "mechanical" tasks of the household. It is not a feminine ploy, but more a kind of "fear" of anything that can

break. Once again, the fear seems to come from the notion that she is responsible.

Gender-correcting suggestions for the Air/Water woman:

- Give in to the feminine promptings of your Moon Sign when the time and place are appropriate. No matter what the specifics of your looks are, you "own" a special kind of glamour, as do most women with Sun or Moon in Water. You can be particularly good at "keeping them guessing" by a charming but nonconclusive manner, if you choose. This can be a particular asset in business/social situations and needn't be labeled sexist because it is available to both men and women with Water in their astro-profile.

- When you focus on a problem, try to do it from two levels: the levelheaded, no-nonsense approach of your Air Sun Sign, and the emotional, feeling level of your Moon Sign. As a female, you should be able to do it—and, when the fates of people are involved, earn for yourself the title "The Great Arbitrator."

- When it come to complementing your astro-profile— for business or romantic success—you would do well to seek out people who have Fire or Earth dominant in their horoscopes. The Fire people will combine with your Water Moon in dramatic ways; the Earth people will keep you in touch with day-to-day reality, like making sure the car gets a checkup.

- You could get a reputation for being unpredictable— specifically, for maintaining a calm exterior, then suddenly bursting into a "bad mood" that can verge on hysteria. This is all too common for those of you Air Sun Sign women who like the feeling of being "in control" of themselves that logical Air gives. However, meanwhile, your Water Moon—particularly if in Cancer or Scorpio—can be fulminating with sometimes irrational rage, and suddenly break forth. Always check yourself when you find yourself saying, "Why am I staying so calm in this situation?"

- Life isn't always fair, though the Air person would like to think it is. Never hesitate to speak up—with feeling—if you sense you are being taken advantage of or not getting your due.

Getting Sign-Specific

Air Sun Sign/Water Moon Sign

Gemini/Cancer: You have what it takes for literary achievement or other intellectual pursuits. However, your problems can be nerves—an inability to concentrate. You should make a strong effort. You have strong convictions about what you believe and no one can sway you.

Gemini/Scorpio: You are sensitive to the impressions you receive from other people and your power over others is both your strength and your weakness. Though you have a streak of brilliance, you tend to be attracted by the "lost" people of the world who can bring you down.

Gemini/Pisces: You have a quick, perceptive mind when you can keep it from wandering. You spend a lot of time getting your emotions in a place where they can't be hurt—which sometimes means you get overly defensive and overly talkative. You crave understanding.

Libra/Cancer: You are as adaptable as a chameleon. You have a habit of guessing where the other person is going, and fitting your opinion to his. Peaceful and tactful, you will avoid arguments if you can. But if your personal rights are interfered with, you will fight for them.

Libra/Scorpio: You are on the side of change, progress and "the new." You are an enthusiast in everything—loves, hates, business arguments, politics. You don't like to hurt people's feelings, but will risk that rather than compromise the truth as you see it.

Libra/Pisces: An air of mystery hangs about you which increases people's interest in you. You are both reserved and shy, which is an inner poise that gives you a particular charm. You gain your knowledge from observation, and are intuitive rather than intellectual.

Aquarius/Cancer: You are restless, and your susceptibility to outside influences makes you highly changeable. You combine the originality and independence of Aquarius with the feeling sensitivity of Cancer for a gracious and considerate nature.

Aquarius/Scorpio: You are a dynamic and positive combination of the Sun and Moon. Your intensity makes you noticed by others, particularly superiors, and you should do very well in life. For the sake of your health, learn to let go and relax from time to time.

Aquarius/Pisces: Both independent and imaginative, you are interested in detail, method and order. There is a highly sentimental side to your nature, which increases your interest in the romantic. You benefit most from avoiding allowing things to drift.

Chapter 10

Feminine Sun Sign/ Masculine Moon Sign

IF THE SUN, AS IS THE USUAL BELIEF IN ASTROLOGY, REPRESENTS the aggressive, outgoing "masculine" principle, then having a feminine Sun Sign is—for men—a blessing in disguise. It lends them a softening of focus without detracting from their strength. For women, having a masculine Moon Sign—the Moon energy being easier for them to access— and a feminine Sun could be the best of all possible worlds for both sexes, bringing her closer to the androgynous ideal.

Earth Sun Sign/Fire Moon Sign

"Firmness is that admirable quality in ourselves that is detestable stubbornness in others."

—ANON.

People of both sexes born with this Sun/Moon combination often exhibit what might be called "quiet strength"; with some people it becomes more flamboyant and might be called "ornery stubbornness." In day-to-day life, people with this astro-gender profile can do very well in virtually any kind of business or enterprise. Because the feminine Sun does not automatically announce their presence with fanfare, it may take a while before their value and contributions are recognized; but once they are, these people become VIPs in the sense that it is virtually impossible to knock them off their pedestals, and higher-ups find themselves depending on these "Rocks of Gibraltar."

Because the strength of the masculine Moon in unconscious (though less so in women), it operates quietly, lending weight and credibility to the overall personality and performance. It can just as easily, however, turn into an almost irrational stubbornness in some. When it does, they are either savvy enough to recognize their shortcomings and correct them—or they find themselves left out in the cold by their co-workers who find them rigid and even fanatical. When the two factors of Earth and Fire operate well together (as we saw in Fire Sun Sign/Earth Moon Sign), it is generally, however, a felicitous combination. Fire is the element that reaches out and grasps for the new; Earth is the element that gives the "reality test" to everything it perceives.

The Earth/Fire Man

To understand the Earth/Fire man in some of his manifestations, it is important to know that poet Robert Bly—author of the men's movement and proponent of the "wild man," an aspect of maleness he believes has been suppressed—has Sun in Capricorn, Moon in Leo. What Bly is trying to stimulate in men is almost a "feminine"—i.e., feeling and touching—style of relating to each other, and a personal renewal through the "fire" of rite and ritual. While in the early days of any movement there is a tendency to excess, Bly's formula could be characterized as pushing men out of their airtight boxes into the living, breathing androgyny. One Earth/Fire man who, though in his very own arena, exemplified the kind of fiery energy and passionate caring Bly is talking about was composer/conductor Leonard Bernstein, Sun in Virgo, Moon in Aries.

In a way, Bernstein might be called "best of the breed," but there are others who illustrate Bly's "wild man" concept in its other manifestations. One has a manic or at least offbeat sense of humor: George Burns, Sun Capricorn/Moon Aries; Sid Caesar, Virgo/Aries; and Charles Addams, Capricorn/Leo, all must be counted among the "wilder" humorists of our time. Among the "wilder" political characters were Huey Long, Virgo/Aries, and Earl Long, Virgo/Sagittarius. Whatever their politics, their styles were among the more colorful that we have seen in this century. If part of the "wild man" profile is interpreted as warlike—but in search of a cause—it can be seen in Malcolm X, Sun Taurus/Moon Aries, and Moshe Dayan, Sun Taurus/Moon Leo. Throughout this book you may have noticed that when the signs of Taurus and/or Leo appear in a profile, they indicate 1) tenacity and 2) courage. It was not for nothing that Richard the Lion-hearted was so named.

An ability to see and make comprehensible in words and pictures the darker side of life, much of it belonging to the "feminine," is found in Arthur Koestler, anti-Communist writer (Virgo/Sagittarius); Stephen King, horror novelist (Virgo/Sagittarius); William Golding, author of Lord of the Flies (Virgo/Leo); and Salvador Dali, never-to-be-forgotten Surrealist artist (Taurus/Aries).

There is a definite lyrical side to this astro-gender combination for men, perhaps the "passionate" side of the Fire Moon urging on the feminine Sun. To name a few of the music makers born with this Sun/Moon profile: David Bowie, Capricorn/Sagittarius; Bobby Short, Virgo/Aries; Cab Calloway, Capricorn/Leo; Stevie Wonder, Taurus/Aries; Lorenz Hart, Taurus/Leo; and Bing Crosby, Taurus/Sagittarius.

Good as a combination as Earth/Fire can be in turning out fascinating men with real heart, there are a number of exceptions that prove illuminating. Howard Hughes, Sun

Capricorn, Moon Sagittarius, became overpowered by his obsessive fears and anxieties; Arthur Godfrey, Virgo/Sagittarius, had an offscreen interpersonal reputation that was far from sterling; and Al Capone, Capricorn/Aries, is not in the record books for his humane achievements.

It is important to remember that, while this book does not deal with the individual signs as such, there are indeed great differences. For instance, Virgo is as notoriously difficult for a man to live with as a Sun Sign as Aries is for women.

Living With the Earth/Fire Man

With the combination of Earth, the androgynous feminine element, and Fire, the androgynous masculine element, you have the possibility of a most unusual kind of man, at least in this society. He will be tough without being judgmental; he will be able to focus both on the here and now and on the results of his efforts to come; he will be work-minded and results-oriented, yet with a sense of play.

Earth and Fire, though their functions of "sensing" and "intuiting" are opposite, can work well within the individual. When they don't, however, you can have the kind of man nobody really likes to be around. For instance, notions (Fire) become hardened (Earth) and there is a tendency to be ultrasure of oneself. Or you can have a man whose good sense (Earth Sun) is overpowered by the impetuousness of his Fire Moon.

He will make a good father, if true to type. The Fire Moon lends him a spirit of play and adventure; his Earth Sun gives him a nurturing quality. You will see this come into play if a child hurts himself while playing. The Earth/Fire man will know it hurts and that it's all right to cry about it. In the kitchen he will be inventive, and have no problem either fending for himself or cooking for the family.

Gender-correcting suggestions for the Earth/Fire man:

- With your Fire Moon—particularly Sagittarius—taking you to faraway and exotic places when your Earth Sun keeps your nose to the grindstone right here, you could become frustrated and/or depressed without even knowing why. It is important to find an outlet for your sometimes suppressed sense of adventure. You needn't climb Mount Everest; buy a small boat and "dream" in your element.

- This is an excellent combination for men in the work world. Your Earth Sun makes you somewhat of a perfectionist, but your Fire Moon can never be satisfied. There's always something more difficult to do, something more visionary to be accomplished. Don't squelch the visionary part of you by censoring it with your Earth Sun. Always take the chance, examine the risk before you decide against it.

- You have what it takes to be an excellent father—most likely the type who makes or builds things around the house with his children, and does roughhouse and sports things outside. Sure, you know you love your children, but do they? Sometimes words speak as loud as or louder than actions. Put your feelings into words once in a while.

- In the years of "the hunt" your Fire Moon could make you fall in love twice a week. Fire does not immediately always sees things as they really are. Let your Earth Sun Sign check the person out by getting some good, hard information about her attitudes, habits, etc.—the things that really count in the long run.

- Especially if your Sun is in Capricorn, or even in Virgo, you may have a tendency to be a bit tyrannical, at home or at the office. Fire is a lot "easier" than Earth in that it allows for change and flexibility. If you find that you are building up a reputation for being "hard as a rock," consciously get in touch with that part of you that really likes fun, and can get bored without "play" of some sort. Oddly enough, it's your masculine Fire side, but some would say the most important element of the four both for sociability and success.

The Earth/Fire Woman

If you had to pick three women for whom "never give up" might be engraved on their birth certificates, Barbra Streisand, Queen Elizabeth and Martha Graham would not be bad choices. Interesting that the three have in common a Taurus Sun Sign and a Leo Moon Sign. As has been mentioned before, Taurus and Leo have as an overarching characteristic the virtue of tenacity. It can be carried too far, however, as many who have worked with or for Barbra Streisand can supposedly testify. Also, it is doubtful that, barring illness, Queen Elizabeth will step aside for her son/king-in-waiting any time soon.

In addition to tenacity, however, the women cited above have made tremendous artistic and political contributions to our/their world. The Earth Sun/Fire Moon woman is less aggressive than her Fire Sun/Earth Moon sister; they are rivals for productivity and ability to take control. Strong as they are, there is a kind of "softness" often lacking in the Fire/Earth women, and a greater ability to relate to men, in both their personal and their professional lives. Once again, it is a case of "the right gender in the right place." With their masculine Moons, they are able to comprehend the drive of the "masculine" but not necessarily to use it in a way that makes them a poor imitation of the real thing. With the feminine Sun, once they contact its power, they can take a power position without abusing it. Yes, that is the ideal, and not always the reality, as you will see from some other examples of the Earth/Fire women.

This combination seems to turn out superb stage and screen performers who are consistent in performance in their offscreen lives. Anne Bancroft, Sun in Virgo, Moon in Sagittarius; Faye Dunaway, Capricorn/Leo; Dolly Parton, Capricorn/Leo; and Glenda Jackson, Taurus/Sagittarius, are but a few examples. Because of the strength of this combination, one might make the inference that it was the source of Marlene Dietrich's longevity (Capricorn/Leo) and Patricia Neal's incredible survival and comeback.

Wit and sweetness with an edge characterize some of the women born with this astro-gender profile: Two who exemplify it are Lily Tomlin, Virgo/Aries, and the late Country-Western singer Patsy Cline, Virgo/Sagittarius. Perhaps more than coincidence accounts for the fact that two of this century's most cogent and effective writers on the subject of "the feminine" have Earth/Fire profiles: Simone de Beauvoir, Capricorn/Aries, and Kate Millet, Virgo/Sagittarius. In women, Earth/Fire gives the ability to present the real story accurately, but with great passion.

Perhaps it is because the words of Earth/Fire women carry weight that Martha Mitchell was able to virtually shake the foundations of the capital with hers during the Watergate scandals. Virgo/Leo is a powerful and stinging combination.

Perhaps the best illustration of what a powerhouse of a combination Earth/Fire can be, but yet leave the Earth/Fire woman loved by many, is Eva Peron, Sun in Taurus, Moon in Sagittarius. The secret may lie in the subtle sexiness of Taurus, which is legendary in both men and women.

Living With the Earth/Fire Woman

The down-to-earth Earth/Fire woman is a match for her more celebrated sisters. She is tenacious and won't let go of something once she's envisioned it with her Fire Moon, then grasped it with her Earth Sun. If one makes allowances for errors in judgment, that means that sometimes she's got the wrong thing in hand.

No problem, however. This is the kind of woman who can laugh at herself and see the joke in the situation. Earth and Fire, most of the time, are a jolly combination. These women have enormous reserves of energy and a comic spirit that makes anything—even hard work—a lark, for themselves and others. The real dilemma for the Earth/ Fire woman is whether or not to work outside the home (if she has the choice). She adores children and makes the ideal "nanny"/companion/playmate. However, her great drive can make her feel that she is "wasting her time." In business, she invariably does well and definitely has management ability. Whichever way she goes, she loses something, and her good sense tells her so.

If other conditions are met—start-up money, for instance—she is the perfect candidate to start up her own business. People with their own businesses work harder than anyone, but she's got the stuff. She's also got Fire— charm and salesmanship—and Earth—common sense and an eye for detail.

Gender-correcting suggestions for the Earth/Fire woman:

- Chances are you are admired by many, both for your ability to get things done and for your generally sunny disposition (slightly less so if the Moon is in Aries) and sense of fun. However, nobody's perfect; the problem is you may begin to think you are. The Capricorn/Leo combination may be most prone to pride, but the danger exists for all combinations.

- Most Earth Sign people, men and women, are quite serious about improving things, if not on a grandiose scale. They generally pick some aspect of their world and work on it—relentlessly. This can be a bore, especially to a lighthearted Air or Fire partner. It is at this point that you should consciously use your Fire Moon to relax, have fun and even risk taking your feet off the ground. Not everything you do has to have a practical outcome.

- Earth/Fire women in business may be an employer's dream, but they can be a work-mate's nightmare. If Earth takes over, there can be a priggishness that is highly unpleasant. If Fire dominates, there may be a tendency to want all of the credit and none of the effort. Try to think of your career life the way you do about your home. The best it can be under the circumstances, but the joint effort of a number of people. Competition belongs on the tennis court.

- Even without meaning to, you may attract the kind of men who want to hang on and be taken care of. If this happens, make it clear from day one that this is a partnership, not a charity for the infirm. As a matter of fact, you might try a little leaning yourself. It could help in the mutual understanding of the problem.

- You are a highly sensual/sexual being. Earth Sign women, and to a great degree the men too, derive great pleasure from all kinds of sensory experiences. In addition to sex, which goes without saying, you, with your "fantasy" Fire Moon, should take every possible advantage for indulging yourself physically. (Not with food, however; that's a problem for Earth women.) Make a luxurious bath a nightly routine, join a stretch-and-dance class, have a professional massage when you can. If you can, do the ultimate and visit a spa.

Getting Sign-Specific

Earth Sun Sign/Fire Moon Sign

Taurus/Aries: You have a powerful personality. You can be ruthless in getting what you want, though not everybody knows it. You are so sure of yourself you may lord it over others. Put your energy into becoming successful, and let other people live their own way.

Taurus/Leo: If you can relax a certain stiffness of approach, you can be extremely popular. You tend to take a dislike to certain people and that's that. Relax and you'll have more friends. And when you have a friend, your loyalty knows no bounds. You really are not proud.

Taurus/Sagittarius: You like to know the right people. High principles and a keen moral sense are fine, but you use them against others. On top of that you tend to be a gossip. Use your qualities of fair-mindedness and imagination as logically as you do in debate.

Virgo/Aries: You are not really self-confident; there is lot of timidity in you. Act first and talk about it later, for best results. In love, there may be a streak of hardness. Become more interested in other people's feelings to better your love life.

Virgo/Leo: You always fulfill your obligations. In fact, what you do is not always recognized as it should be in the outer world. Do not resign yourself to being misunderstood and frustrated; take every opportunity that comes along to show what you really are made of.

Virgo/Sagittarius: Dash, enthusiasm, optimism and directness are your aces in the hole. You can generalize without losing sight of details. You can think fast and swiftly change your views, which is a sturdy weapon to have in business or in any pursuit you follow.

Capricorn/Aries: You can't be bought, but you can find a way around a situation that is acceptable to everyone. Your mind is always working and you are tense and highstrung. You should learn moderation in work, in opinions, in forcefulness. In other words, cool down.

Capricorn/Leo: Yours is a strong personality and you have the ability to make friends among powerful people. You believe in yourself and translate that belief to others. Your machinelike precision could be warmed up to your great advantage. Add to your prestige by love.

Capricorn/Sagittarius: Wit, fluency and ambition carry you far. You have a keen sense of values and the ability to make your opinions felt. In love, you look for the intellectual rather than the romantic. When you find the right one, however, you can quickly switch sides.

Earth Sun Sign/Air Moon Sign

"Don't take the bull by the horns, take him by the tail, then you can let go when you want to."

—JOSH BILLINGS

People born with the Earth Sun Sign/Air Moon Sign astrogender profile should be a natural fit with Western society. Earth is the element that believes only in the here and now; Air is the element that can deal best (or only) with ideas that follow logically from one thing to the next. Only linear thinking makes sense to Air; Earth can't even dream of "pie in the sky."

In effect, our society lives by the above ideals. Breakthrough thinking, when it comes, finds resistance—because the Earth element cannot imagine what it will look like, and because Air is afraid that the consequences might not be "logical." The word "radical" is meant to denigrate any person or group that strays too far from the norm, or that proposes something that is different from the status quo.

As a result, Earth Sun/Air Moon people of both sexes are probably more comfortable with themselves and with others of their type than any other combination in the zodiac.

They can be quite solid citizens with values everyone approves of, and can have lives that, while they will experience as many ups and downs as any other, are not seriously perturbed by what they see as society's aberrations. Unless they threaten to encroach on Earth/Air territory.

As the sensing element, Earth stands for an innate understanding of how the material world works, and how you get from here to there. Generally, Earth Sign people are fairly self-disciplined in the sense that they know about persisting until a goal is reached.

People of the Air element have the ability to detach themselves from the immediate experience of daily life, enabling them to gain objectivity, perspective and a rational approach to everything they do. Since people of the Air element don't feel the need to get heavily involved with other people's worries or emotions, they are quite able to work successfully with a broad range of types. One of the reasons the Air Signs are considered the most "social" is that they can objectively listen to other people's thoughts, regardless of whether or not they agree with them.

If it all sounds very dull, it is only because we are talking about Earth in contrast to the other "feminine" element, Water—which is all about feeling and emotions—and contrasting Air with the other "masculine" element, Fire—which is future- rather than now-oriented, highly passionate and "burning" to get things done.

The Earth/Air Man

The pragmatism and nonemotional quality of this combination of elements have made it the ideal one for political thinkers and policy makers, not to mention ordinary politicians. According to the record, Machiavelli (author of *The Prince*) had Sun in Taurus, Moon in Aquarius. In more modern times, Woodrow Wilson was Capricorn/Aquarius, and Richard Nixon is Capricorn/Aquarius as well. Ho Chi Minh was a Taurus/Gemini combination.

The ability to see problems clearly and try to solve them nonjudgmentally may be what gave Freud, Taurus/Gemini, his extraordinary powers—and his reputation as the father of the modern science of psychiatry. However, it is interesting to note that his pupil, and later enemy, Carl Jung, had a Leo Sun Sign, and wanted to go beyond the tenets of Freud's theory, which Earth/Air Freud considered set in stone.

"Cool," in all its connotations, describes a number of the men born with the Earth/Air combination. Both "cool" and light on their feet are Muhammed Ali, Capricorn/Aquarius; Fred Astaire, Taurus/Gemini; and Ray Bolger, Capricorn/Libra. Air, in the literal sense, makes Air, the element, light—and sometimes even capricious. No matter how intense his interviews became, Edward R. Murrow, Taurus/Aquarius, could always "dance" a subject superbly, and never was at a loss for a quick comeback. Among comedians, none is "cooler" than Bob Newhart, Virgo/Libra, or George Carlin, Taurus/Libra.

Getting sign-specific, the anomaly among the Air Signs is Aquarius, because, though the interest may just be theoretical, this is a sign that thinks big and is always open to the new (if it seems to make sense). It is also quirky. Which may explain why Orson Welles, Taurus/Aquarius, was a bigger thinker than even David O. Selznick, Taurus/Gemini.

Where you find Libra in the mix, you find sexiness, style and grace. The first two are certainly apt for Humphrey Bogart, Capricorn/Libra, and Henry Fonda, Taurus/Libra, and there are few matches for the grace under pressure of Jack Nicklaus on the links.

Living With the Earth/Air Man

The Earth/Air man is a rule follower; if you agree with him, you might call him Mr. Right; if you don't, you could call him a number of other things, like "blockhead." He is so under the influence of logical Air and practical Earth that anything new and original is almost frightening to him.

Even in his own home he becomes so used to having things a certain way that any other way is "threatening." How does he deal with the "threatening"/unfamiliar? One way, say in the case of furniture, is to move things back the way they were. He is happiest when things are the way they were. However, since we're talking about a man with a mate, this is not always a solution that brings good relations. He should be introduced to any idea of change slowly, be made to see why it makes sense/is an improvement. Earth/Air men sometimes have trouble with their neighbors when they make changes; however, unless it is a violation of a code, there's not much he can do about it but accept.

If the Earth/Air man has a job to which he commutes every day, making the same trains or leaving and arriving at the same time, he will be content. However, since he is quite smart in both theoretical and hands-on situations, he is likely to move up the ladder—even to another office. Since his sense of company spirit is probably quite high, he will accept it with good grace, even if he also regrets that his routine is disrupted.

In sum, he is a familiar type in our familiar world. Though he may not be overly exciting, he always tries to do the "right" thing, and most of the time he does.

Gender-correcting suggestions for the Earth/Air man:

- With your combination of elements, you are likely to be what is called conservative. Far beyond what political party you belong to, this can be an overriding part of your personality, making you suspicious of anything new, and even cynical about it. For your own sake, and for those around you, develop your Air Moon to stimulate your curiosity and your sense of humor about the world, even if it doesn't meet your standards.

- Air and Earth can be a parched combination. With the dryness of logic and the "it must make sense" approach of Earth combined, you could be an automaton with employees. To remind yourself of Earth's moist, nurturing quality and the constant changes we see in nature, keep a bank of green plants in your office and tend them yourself.

- You have a great opportunity to be an exemplar of the best of the "masculine" and the "feminine" qualities. Earth can be tough but it can be tender too. Air can operate in specific situations virtually without emotion—but is the most people-to-people element of all, wanting to know all about them. You would be great at local politics or any cause designed to improve the infrastructure or environment.

- People with the two genders active in their astroprofile can feel the pull between them from time to time. For instance, your Earth Sun Sign may make you want to take the family routine apart and put it back together your way. When you need peace and relief from what you see as imperfection, do the kind of reading that appeals to Air, your Moon Sign: biography, history, popular science—anything basically nonemotional that will soothe your outbreak of the "inappropriate feminine." Reserve a quiet, neat retreat to do your reading in.

- Partly because you are not in awe of the "feminine," and partly because having someone keep things shipshape is a given for you, you may take your mate for granted. Leave room for surprises now and then—particularly the kind some might consider "sexist" . . . i.e., dinner out, fragrance or lingerie, jewelry.

The Earth/Air Woman

A woman with an Earth Sun Sign and an Air Moon Sign is likely to be regarded by her friends and associates as the one to go to when you've got a problem that involves one of the "heavier" emotions—jealousy, anger, fear or—especially in office situations—being in love with the "wrong guy." Earth/Air women appear to, and generally do, have "a good head on their shoulders." For some, it is a compliment; others find it sad that they are not considered more exciting. However, whatever the scenario, the Earth/Air woman will be able to listen dispassionately to the problem, then offer good, solid advice.

As with the men who are Earth Sun/Air Moon, this profile does come in many shapes and sizes, however—depending a lot on the particular signs involved. The Aquarius Moon brings out the quirkiness in Earth women. Diane Keaton, Sun Capricorn/Moon Aquarius, has played herself in too many roles to count. Another actress with the same Sun/Moon profile, but a very different life, was Marion Davies. In her, the outrageousness of the Aquarius Moon took a completely different form, but it surely wasn't run-of-the-mill.

One very interesting manifestation of an Earth/Air woman with Moon in Aquarius was Planned Parenthood founder Margaret Sanger (Virgo Sun sign). Surely the issue she took on—birth control—was of the most mundane nature to some, but a life-and-death matter to many women. It would be fair to say that her Virgo Sun gave her her subject (Virgo has much to do with female sexuality), but it was her Aquarius Moon that was able to see the far-ahead ramifications of the situation, and bring some new thinking to it.

With Taurus as a Sun Sign and Libra as a Moon Sign, Israel's Golda Meir made a forceful leader, but one with the grace not to ruffle too many feathers. More typical Libra Moon Sign types are Judy Collins and Ella Fitzgerald, both with the musical Sun Sign, Taurus. The style and grace of the Libra Moon in combination with the meticulous Virgo Sun has no better illustration than Agatha Christie. Her intricate plots wind and unwind so naturally that you don't even see the hard work that goes into one of her mysteries.

Earth Sun Sign/Air Moon Sign women do have an androgynous quality—or at least access to it. In terms of the world we live in, one thing this means is that they are reality-driven. Take Gypsy Rose Lee, Capricorn Sun, Gemini Moon. She knew what she needed and she knew how to get it. As for Nixon's secretary, Rosemary Woods, who shares the same Sun/Moon profile, one can only say that if she did what some think she did, it was clearly a case of doing what had to be done.

Living With the Earth/Air Woman

With her Earth Sun and Air Moon, this woman strikes an interesting balance between female and male. Her Earth Sun gives her the "stronger" feminine element; her Air Moon gives her the more masculine of the two masculine elements.

Though her looks may belie it, she is like a finely tuned, high-power engine. Unlike the Earth/Air male, she is able to deal with change better, and can get in touch with the "growth" qualities of Earth. She will be relatively calm, saving her strength for real crises. She will be the one friends will call on to listen to problems. Though she does not have Water, the feeling element, in her profile, she can assess emotional issues and give good advice about where to take things. In a sense, she is the ideal therapist.

Her children may find her a little matter-of-fact, but they probably will be the cleanest, best-fed kids on the block. Appearances mean a lot to the Earth/Air woman, and she will gladly put herself out for them. Though she generally does not have the "me-first" mentality, she really should work outside the home. It would give her the balance she needs in her own life.

Gender-correcting suggestions for the Earth/Air woman:

- Ultracapable as you are with your "hands-on" Earth Sun Sign and your keen Air Sign Moon, you may be passed over in the workplace when promotions are being handed out. Astrological reason: You lack the flamboyance of Water and/or Fire in your horoscope—an element that makes people stand out and be memorable. Solution: Read up on Fire and Water and act your heart out.

- For your own pleasure, and to compensate for your elemental lack, make sure you include Fire and Water people in your social circle. (It may simply "happen," because people tend to gravitate toward the elements they lack.) For the best of all worlds, make someone who is predominantly Fire or Water your lifetime partner. He can provide the fun and sense of joy; you'll know when to put the brakes on.

- You are an ideal combination for the kind of woman who makes the perfect home for her husband and children. Your Earthiness will provide the perfect launching pad for their activities; your Air Moon will help *you* keep perspective on what you are doing, and—not so incidentally—contribute mightily to the family financial affairs. If this is an option for you, don't be made to feel like a second-class citizen by your friends who work in the outside world.

- Earth Sun Sign people generally find it easy to get close to people—simply by being there for them when they need it and listening quietly. With your Air Sign Moon, you have a double whammy because you are able to make rational suggestions instead of simply suggesting wrathful revenges. Do not underestimate this capacity when you are looking for work or thinking about changing careers.

- With your combination of elements, it is possible you lack imagination and the capacity to "see the big picture." Do not disdain those who do, or "pick their dreams apart" before they can be assessed on the large scale. It's important to remember that each of us has his or her own strengths.

Getting Sign-Specific

Earth Sun Sign/Air Moon Sign

Taurus/Gemini: You will travel far and wide, but not feel you are getting anywhere without proper education. You also must wrestle with a tendency to be critical toward others. First you love them, then you hate them. Take a steadier course, starting with caution.

Taurus/Libra: You are an optimist and nothing can keep you down for long. You take advantage of things as you find them; you have no wish to bend the world to your will. You are a good storyteller, but your tales can get too convoluted and long. Learn to self-edit.

Taurus/Aquarius: You smile on the outside, but have a hard inner core that people are amazed at. You are independent, a self-starter; you haven't a trace of an inferiority complex. You understand people well, including yourself, and they are attracted to you in great numbers.

Virgo/Gemini: Figuring things out analytically is your strength. However, you are likely to neglect the emotional part of your life, which erupts and causes you trouble. You are impressionable but somewhat cold in response. You should take advantage of every opportunity.

Virgo/Libra: You manage to organize your life to exclude those who bore you; you are somewhat of a snob. You are able to take care of yourself in your own quiet way. You like to live as you please and are able to do so; sometimes it can be a "secret life" that draws you.

Virgo/Aquarius: You are a detached sort of person, even capable of hurting others by abruptly breaking ties. If you are cold, however, you are also capable of helping others when they need it, then going your own way again. You have a reasonably scientifically accurate mind.

Capricorn/Gemini: Glibness comes easily to you; in fact, you don't even have to develop your powers to the highest, though that would be a shame. Your cleverness is not shallow, because you are really a serious person. Yet you delight in doing the unexpected, the devilish.

Capricorn/Libra: You are something of a fighter and must overcome touchiness. You have an imaginative viewpoint and must learn to explain yourself to others. You are extremely sociable and like to have people around, yet it is difficult for you to warm up to them quickly.

Capricorn/Aquarius: You believe in the status quo, wanting to do all the "right" things. You are calm and intelligent and stable. You won't go out of your way for people you consider dull and profitless; your tactfulness breaks down in the face of stupidity.

Water Sun Sign/Air Moon Sign

When for either sex the Sun Sign is in Water—feeling—and the Moon in a masculine sign, either Fire—spirit and animation—or Air—thinking and logic—the "natural order" is disturbed, but makes for mainly quite positive results. In both astro-gender combinations, there is a tendency to "make waves," sometimes of a soft, subtle and sexy nature, sometimes of tidal-wave proportions.

"To find your own way is to follow your own bliss."

—JOSEPH CAMPBELL

The Water/Air Man

In this particular astro-gender combination, Sun in Water/ Moon in Air, the two elements are at opposite ends of Jung's function types. Theoretically, no one can feel and think—both perfectly legitimate human modes of consciousness—at the same time. The people who come to public attention with this astro-gender combination lead a broad variety of lifestyles and operate in almost totally unrelated ways. Yet there is a common denominator—a uniquely personal way of dealing with the dichotomy in their astro-gender combination. That it is personal is no surprise. Water is, in all its effects, the most personal of all the elements. It is at home with emotion, in one-on-one relationships, in "womanly" kinds of dealings.

In real-life situations, what is the underlying connection among ballet dancer Rudolph Nureyev, Chopin, actor Michael Caine, lawyer Roy Cohen, melodramatic screen "bad man" Peter Lorre and perennial laughing TV host Ed McMahon, all of whom share the Sun Sign Pisces/Moon Sign Libra? First, the Pisces Sun Sign puts them at the extreme feminine end of the zodiac gender spectrum, setting up from birth a self-consciousness about identity—plus the Piscean need for drama and emotion in life. Second, the Libra Moon, while its at-bottom desire is to be pleasing to all and disturb none, looks for the beautiful and desirable *on its own terms*. That is, within the nature of the particular human being. Each of these individuals took a highly individual route—but all can be said to be "extremists and survivors." Michael Caine thrives on films that do not follow the normal "boy meets girl" pattern, and uses his sexy charm in films like *Dressed to Kill* and *Educating Rita.* Peter Lorre literally created himself by the roles he played in films like *Casablanca* and *The Maltese Falcon.* Is Water/Air Sly Stallone Rocky, or did Rocky "create" Stallone? People might have chuckled at Ed McMahon, but he laughed right back, and enjoyed himself every step of the way. Roy Cohn gained notoriety for his unique lawyerly style. Nureyev and Chopin are more "pure Pisceans" for whom dance and music became their total lives.

Two Sun Scorpio/Moon Aquarius people who showed the greater strength of the Scorpio Sun and the more outrageous "I think, therefore I am" qualities of the Aquarius Moon were John Erlichman, one of "the President's men" during the Nixon administration, and Dylan Thomas, the broad-thinking Welsh writer. A Scorpio Sun man with the lightest Air Gemini Moon, Ed Koch, showed us that serious mayoring could be combined with a virtually manic personal style.

A third kind of Water/Air man appears with a Cancer Sun. William Zeckendorf, humanitarian real estate tycoon, had a quick-thinking, take-the-current-when-it-serves Gemini Moon. Mel Brooks takes the "mothering" Cancer Sun into a zany world of his own creation via his Aquarius Moon. And why does Sylvester Stallone belong among Water/Air men? His individualistic Cancer/Libra astro-gender profile imprints him as an original; if Rocky hadn't created Sly Stallone, Sly would have invented him, if only to make an "earth mother" out of a male Cancer.

Living With the Water/Air Man

The Water/Air man can be a real enigma—especially for those he lives with. As a Water man, he is a feeling type with his Sun in the most feminine element. Some of his comments are shocking because they reveal a source of knowledge not generally available to his sex, and he's willing to talk about it. At the same time, he can cut to the bone with comments that point out the reality and logic of things. When you experience both sides of him, they don't seem to fit.

His life is rather idiosyncratic too, in terms of the variety of things that strike his fancy, from music to cars to sports to household pursuits. He is likely to like cooking, a mix, perhaps of influences from his Water Sun (cooking to make people happy) and his Air Moon (cooking as a fascinating chemistry experiment).

In spite of his double-sided nature, which can be very apparent, the Water/Air man tends to be a rather mellow type, content with simple things and few demands. In business, he will be successful at something that combines creativity and numbers, perhaps marketing. He will not particularly like holding to a firm schedule, but somehow he will. However, in many ways his life is more important to him than his work.

He likes young people more than very small children, though babies are fine for cuddling. In general, the Water/Air man is an interesting example of the male/female mix and a good candidate for androgeny.

Gender-correcting suggestions for the Water/Air man:

- Some men with this astro-gender profile have such a hard time with their bent for feeling that they deny it altogether and/or turn it into a tendency to "rage at the world and everyone in it." Surely feeling—genuine emotion—is one of the most difficult human functions to deal with. When you feel a "fit" coming on, apply the logic of your Air Moon to deal with the situation in a constructive way.

- Water Sun Sign men are often irresistible to women, perhaps because women sense they understand what the "feminine" is (even if it is superficial knowledge).

You are capable of strategizing (Air Moon) to get the woman you want. Make sure your motives are genuine and that you are playing it straight. You could hurt others in the process.

• Despite the "lightness" of your Air Moon, you could be subject to virtually inexplicable "downs." The prescription is twofold: First, take up exercise of a graceful yet demanding nature (some form of dance or martial arts discipline); second, make it a point to get together with people who enjoy your sometimes sarcastic wit and who can "give it right back to you."

• Strike a blow for "men's rights" by not being afraid to show/express/be interested in emotion. If you have children, they are a natural to practice on. Another technique is to break out of the "man-talk" role at work. Show that you know life is not all facts and figures and sports statistics. Begin to ask other men how they feel about certain things, and don't be afraid to comment if you see they are upset.

• Simply for fun, or to soothe your own jangled feelings, chess is an ideal game. Your Air Moon can "compute" logically and quickly; your Water Sun can put a subtle spin on your moves and keep you from telegraphing your intentions.

The Water/Air Woman

With Water/Air women, it seems to be the presence of an Aquarian Moon that makes for the more breakaway types. It might be fitting to mention at this point that the Sun Sign—main control tower for both sexes, in spite of feminine closeness to the Moon—is in the main "comfortable" and "safe" for a woman when it is in Water.

Some women who have leaped out as more than the norm are Diahann Carroll, Cancer Sun/Aquarius Moon;

Princess Diana, also Cancer/Aquarius; stage legend Gertrude Lawrence; feminist writer Margaret Atwood (*The Handmaid's Tale*); photographer Dianne Arbus, Pisces/Aquarius; and female sexologist Mary Calderone, Cancer/Aquarius. Though there may not be general agreement on the point, it would appear that all these women have "done their thing" not only quietly, but virtually effortlessly. They seem to have the capacity—more difficult than for the Water/Air man—to make feeling and thinking work in an on/off mode rather than on a collision course. Princess Diana, of course, has led a life of such bright-light publicity that many would make her out to be a villain. But in many ways the real difficulty could be the interaction of her own and her husband's astro-gender profiles. (Read the chapter on relationships for more information.)

Scorpio/Gemini also seems to be a felicitous combination for women in the Water/Air astro-gender group. Whatever their particular talent, they have honed it well, and just "kept on marching" to their particular drummer. Goldie Hawn, Bo Derek, Bonnie Raitt and Kaye Ballard are all astro-sisters, not only by their astro-gender type, but also by the sign combination of their Suns and Moons. Perhaps it is the Gemini Moon that gives them all a light touch, and the Scorpio Sun that is the engine behind their success.

A perhaps too-pat example of how the most feminine Pisces, when it is the Sun Sign, and Libra, the most masculine male sign, when it is in the position of the Moon, can almost undo each other is Elizabeth Barrett Browning. Despite the popular romantic quality of her poetry, life—her own psyche—did not treat her kindly.

Two Water/Air women who lives ended in tragedy, despite the outstanding bravery of both, each in her own way, were Indira Gandhi, India's Prime Minister (Scorpio/Libra), and Sylvia Plath, also Scorpio/Libra. With Gandhi, it was an assassin's bullet that ended her strong career; with Plath, it was the final act in a life that included a brave fight against depressive illness.

Living With the Water/Air Woman

While the Water/Air man may be a mellow type, his female counterpart is more of a brooder. Water Sun Sign women have a tendency to moodiness, at least some of the time. When she does vent her cool, sometimes cruel logic on others, it can come as an icy blast. Her intention is not to hurt, but her ability to see things as they are sometimes frustrates her.

She is generally not a dynamo of physical energy, and her living quarters will reflect it. She is the type who would rather sit and dream and imagine, and, if she can, put it into poetry. Actually, she has the tools to be a quite competent poet—Water supplying the concepts and fantasies, Air providing the framework and structure.

Water/Air women are, naturally, found in business, but it is generally far from where they want to be. Aside from writing, the theater, any of the music arts, and painting are all Water/Air women's careers. In a way, there is something old-fashioned about this astro-gender type. In a world where women push forward toward success on the job, the Water/Air female is in general perfectly content to stay around the home and children. However, she will not be content if her children take up too much of her time. Feeling type that she is, she has a cutoff point beyond which she needs her own time and solitude.

Gender-correcting suggestions for the Water/Air woman:

- With your Water Sun Sign at the feminine pole of the gender spectrum and your Air Moon at the masculine end, you have tremendous potential to develop an androgynous personality—almost by force. When your Air Moon makes you react "dryly" and even unfeelingly, your Water Sun Sign can self-correct by bringing emotion to the situation. By the same token, if you go overboard emotionally, your Air Moon can keep you from "drowning" in feeling.

- The "feminine" part of you likes things warm and cozy—and even a little messy if it suits your purposes. The Air Moon, however, calls for order, as may your spouse. Be sure to reserve a room or space, no matter how small, where you can go to "be yourself," keep the things you value, even cry all alone if you feel like it.

- With children, you tend to be a "kiss and slap" mother (not a bad thing to be, by the way). At least your children know where they stand with you, even if you seem to have moods that come out of nowhere. Children can be lightly disciplined if they know they have your love—and with your Water Sun, they will be sure of that.

- If you don't have a creative hobby, start one—preferably the type that demands some precision too. With your complex astro-gender makeup, you must have at least one or two "escape routes" from your occasionally conflicted nature. The ideal would be to take up an instrument, from which you can derive pleasure musically, and which also demands complete concentration.

- You are a good candidate to lead a women's support group. You have the capacity to listen dispassionately (Air Moon), then apply true emotion (Water Sun) to your suggestions and guidance. Even if you are not trained as a counselor, there are plenty of groups looking for both help and leadership.

Getting Sign-Specific

Water Sun Sign/Air Moon Sign

Cancer/Gemini: You feel the world around you with more sensitivity than may be good for you. You are trusting, eager, anxious to please; you tell your plans before they are ready. You can cultivate reserve and become more sure of yourself internally and less sensitive.

Cancer/Libra: You don't give a great deal of yourself, being a touch introverted. You are afraid of our own emotions, afraid of being hurt, of being fooled. If this happens, you become highly self-protective. You will stabilize and mature when you are in a place of your own.

Cancer/Aquarius: You combine the emotional sensitivity with the friendliness of Aquarius. Your personal warmth and sincerity impress many, attracting good will in both business and personal life. You like to make a good impression, so you are careful in what you say and how you do it.

Scorpio/Gemini: You give the appearance of great decision and determination, but often you are really wavering. You might miss opportunities through not being able to make up your mind. A quality of reserve lends charm to your vocal and voluble manner of expression.

Scorpio/Libra: You have a certain naivete that is jolted when you discover not everyone is as direct as you. Your self-confidence amounts almost to pride, but it rarely becomes offensive. In love, you are tolerant of others and sensitive to their every need.

Scorpio/Aquarius: You are a powerful and independent thinker. You do not believe in intolerance, so you manage to cover up your reactions to other people's thoughts. You like flattery and, if in business, are probably an executive surrounded by "yes men (or women)."

Pisces/Gemini: You yield when you should be firm and stand your ground when you should give way. This is the result of a fundamental lack of self-confidence. Learn not to talk until your mind is made up, because what comes out of your mouth may be new to your ears.

Pisces/Libra: You are strongly sensual; everything you touch gets a bit of romantic and idealistic glamour. Appeal to the emotions, rather than to the intellect, should be your aim. You are more an intuitive type than an intellectual; try to bring the parts together.

Pisces/Aquarius: You like to do things for people in a big way. And would do well to go into public life as the devoted public servant. You are emotionally ardent and sincere, with a real sympathy for the people you love. Your moods can be dark.

Water Sun Sign/Fire Moon Sign

Here the energy between the feminine Sun Sign and the masculine Moon Sign is more compatible because, as we have noted before, Fire is a more androgynous masculine element than Air.

When Water and Fire combine, the overarching atmosphere they create is "passion unbound." Passion, of course, comes in many forms. When it is sexual, we can say the Water element is in control; when it is of a different nature, Fire is the cause.

Fire is in many ways the most interesting element. In the astrological world just as in the real world, Fire can both destroy and heal; it can both warm things up and burn things to devastation and death. When it combines with Water—again, both metaphorically and actually—its destructive powers are negated. Astrologically speaking, combined with Water, Fire is at a psychological advantage for turning out people who color our world in a positive way.

"I tried in my time to be a philosopher; but I don't know how, cheerfulness was always breaking in."

—OLIVER EDWARDS

The Water/Fire Man

Whoever wrote "Send in the Clowns" could have had the Water/Fire man in mind. Look at this list of hilarious, zany, outrageous, lovable men who are, when all is said and done, some of the most wonderful "clowns" in our society: Milton Berle (Cancer/Sagittarius), Jerry Lewis (Pisces/Aries), Carl Reiner (Pisces/Sagittarius), Jackie Gleason (Pisces/Sagittarius), Zero Mostel (Pisces/Leo) and the *Today* show's Willard Scott (Pisces/Sagittarius). The prevalence of Sagittarius as a Moon Sign in these witty and wise individuals brings out the fascinating dual nature of this quite philosophical sign. If it is comedy Sagittarius brings to the party, it is of the cosmic type—that is, it is truly funny in how it comments on mankind and its foibles in general.

Sagittarius—indeed, Water/Fire in general—also happens to turn up in the astro-gender profiles of a number of religious thinkers and practitioners. Not specifically a religious type, but known not only for his spectacular scientific brain but also for his cosmic/religious thinking ("God doesn't play dice with the universe"), was Albert Einstein, Pisces/Sagittarius. Other religious "standards" in the Water/Fire group are St. Augustine and Martin Luther, both Scorpio/Aries.

Colorful characters of all pursuits turn up in this last and perhaps most interesting astro-gender group. Writers: John Updike (Pisces/Leo), Tom Wolfe (Pisces/Leo), W. H. Auden (Pisces/Leo), Kurt Vonnegut (Scorpio/Leo) and Howard Fast (Scorpio/Leo). Actors: Burt Lancaster (Scorpio/Sagittarius), Rex Harrison (Pisces/Aries), Rock Hudson (Scorpio/Sagittarius) and Richard Dreyfus (Scorpio/

Aries). Musicians: Lawrence Welk (Pisces/Leo) and James Taylor (Pisces/Aries). Regardless of one's individual opinion of anyone in this astro-ragbag, you've got to admit that each brought to what he did some special quality that makes people talk—one way or another.

Rebels with a cause, empire builders, military men and just plain brilliant businessmen whose names are virtually household words turn up in this strong astro-gender profile too: consumer crusader Ralph Nader (Pisces/Leo); Frank Borman, astronaut and former CEO of Eastern Airlines (Pisces/Sagittarius); Mikhail Gorbachev (Pisces/Leo); and Rupert Murdoch (Pisces/Sagittarius). And, the most colorful Frenchman of them all, Charles de Gaulle (Scorpio/Aries—both, by the way, signs of war).

There is a darker, or some would simply say anomalous, side to the Water/Fire male. In this group fall "Commie-chaser" Senator Joseph McCarthy (Scorpio/Sagittarius), pornographer Larry Flynt (Scorpio/Leo) and heavyweight champion and alleged rapist Mike Tyson (Cancer/Sagittarius). Yet the overall theory holds: Whatever these Water/Fire men did, they are and will be remembered as people who broke the rules and made a lot of noise doing it.

Living With the Water/Fire Man

Most Water/Fire men come under the heading of those who can get away with anything because they are charming and amusing. In combination with the Fire Moon, the Water Sun bubbles and perks with all kinds of ideas and insights. The Fire Moon itself gives the personality a depth and breadth that can almost be called "mythic."

Now what about the ordinary guy? Same deal, except perhaps at a lower frequency. But can you live with this man? That's a matter of personal taste, but a lot of people choose to. What they give up when he is around is serenity, silence and quiet time. What they gain is a companion whom they can quote, someone who constantly surprises them and an upbeat type who can see the bright side of almost anything.

There are exceptions to the rule, however, and there are times when the Water/Fire man can get lost in a "storm" of feeling. It is generally not on his own behalf, however, but someone else's, or a general principle. The Water/Fire man is what you call a "stand-up guy," and is an excellent example for his children. He tries to do the right thing, and will expect it of them. He gains their respect by being such a "good guy" that they want to follow his lead.

Gender-correcting suggestions for the Water/Fire man:

- When these dramatic elements combine (particularly in a man), they can produce an ultra-attractive person. Not necessarily physically, but with an aura that others find mesmerizing. Of course, not every man of this combination exhibits this quality, but enough do to make it mentionable. Unfortunately, there is not always the quality of soundness as well, and those who would follow this man anywhere may get lost in the process.

- Even those of this combination who do not do it professionally can be natural actors. It is an excellent combination for a salesman of virtually anything—or anyone who makes a living convincing others of their point of view. Caution: Don't take it too far, and keep it honest. Reserve real acting for the stage.

- In the Water/Fire man, there is generally a love of risk, danger and excitement. Though you may be only an armchair competitor, you get way into it. If you actually play competitive sports, you can be a real winner. The reason: You have a passion that's hard to beat. In team sports you easily may have a tendency to play too hard to win, or to take the outcome too seriously. In other words, you can be a sore loser.

- With the feminine and the masculine so blended in you, you probably are or could be "super-Dad." Not the demanding kind of father who insists that his kids be "the best," but a fun-loving, roughneck companion who probably has a great sense of humor and can tell a great story. If you are holding yourself back because you think you should be a more traditional father, you are denying yourself and your children great pleasure.

- When you've got something to say—particularly about yourself—you would do well to check yourself and hold yourself back. Your natural passion/enthusiasm will make you want to "tell all," but that is not always wise, especially in the business arena. If you are burning with things to say about what it's like to be you, and be a man, join a men's group and you'll have plenty of opportunity.

The Water/Fire Woman

You want to meet a strong and sexy woman? Look for one with this astro-gender profile. She won't be perfect, but she'll light up your life in a way other women can't. There is something in the Water/Fire combination for women as well as for men that makes them virtually unforgettable.

Among the positive comments you will hear about the Water/Fire woman are likely to be brickbats like "What a bitch"; "Who does she think she is?"; "Why does she think she's so great?" Though the comments could come from a male who does business with her, they are most likely to come from other women.

You will also be able to say the same thing about her that is the general opinion of the Water/Fire male: "She's an original, but I wouldn't like to go up against her." Yet this is a slightly better astro-gender profile for a man than for a woman. Some women might be called "cold fish" because they let the fire go out, and come across as both bland and slightly depressed. Others listen to the prompt-

ings of their Fire Moon too literally and "raise hell," becoming the harridans of the zodiac. Unless a Water/Fire
boss is well balanced, it's not a lot of fun working for her
when she is on a rampage.

One favorite example of what the Water Sun and Fire
Moon can help a woman produce is Barbara Cartland (Can-
cer/Aries), the British romantic novelist. She is both pro-
lific and consistent in bringing out the kind of romantic
novels that women eat up. Her books burn with passion,
but she also knows just when to turn on the waterworks.

Another classic case of Water Sun/Fire Moon is Nancy
Reagan (Cancer/Aries). Her intensely mothering Cancer
Moon made her treat her husband more like a child who
needed protecting than the president of a huge country.
Yet her rash, sometimes rude Aries Moon made her run
things at the White House with an iron hand, and also gave
her the guts to go to covert means to attain her goals—
once again, her husband's safety and success. As person-
alities, other presidents' wives come and go; Nancy will be
a legend for a long time into the future.

Perhaps the dean of all Water/Fire women was writer
Anais Nin, who lived in Paris during the 1920s and '30s.
Her lifestyle, her circle of literary friends, her frank love of
her own sexuality, her daring to write open personal dia-
ries at the time she did, are all qualities of the Pisces/
Sagittarius woman.

Throughout this book you may have noticed that the
combination of Pisces and Sagittarius produces the most
unusual and interesting people, men or women. Both are
extremist signs, willing to go to any length for their art,
their lifestyle, what they believe in. Ironically, both also
have great wit and a virtually cosmic sense of humor.
When they laugh, the world laughs with them.

It's not for nothing that in the Water/Fire astro-gender
profile you find the names of women stars and musical
types who headed for success, got it and know how to stay
there. Among them are Jodie Foster (Scorpio/Leo), Sally
Field (Scorpio/Aries), Linda Evans (Scorpio/Aries), Lauren

Hutton (Scorpio/Sagittarius), Carly Simon (Cancer/Leo) and Mahalia Jackson (Scorpio/Sagittarius).

The prevalence of Scorpio as the Water Sun Sign in this group underscores the strength of this feminine sign, in men or in women. It is tenacious, focused and generally determined not to give up once a goal is decided upon. A much softer but infinitely sexy Water/Fire superstar was Jean Harlow (Pisces/Aries). Her Pisces Sun gave her an unforgettable aura of sexuality, but not necessarily the drive her Scorpio and Cancer sisters have. Gloria Vanderbilt (Pisces/Leo) has made her mark, but with less panache than other Water/Fire Sign women.

From earlier eras, Pearl Buck (Cancer/Leo), one of America's first highly recognized novelists, and George Sand (Cancer/Aries) are excellent examples of the ability of the Water/Fire woman to fight the odds and win.

Living With the Water/Fire Woman

The female of this astro-gender type has a flair for the dramatic. Those who live with her quickly learn that whatever the issue, it is not half as bad a she makes it sound. Though she has a Fire Moon, her Water Sun can easily extinguish it, and she can become a frightened, nervous wreck.

The remedy: Get her to turn her passionate interest to something that ideally helps others. In emergency situations involving someone who is hurt, she literally becomes another person—brave, sturdy, sure of what to do and what not to do. If the EMS doesn't have a place for her, she would be an ideal hospital aide—especially in the emergency room.

In a nine-to-five job she will quickly learn that dramatics are frowned upon—particularly by male managers. However, she can turn her emotion into enthusiasm and a sureness that she will get ahead in business. Whatever happens, her demeanor will earn her points.

When all is said and done, she is really too volatile for

office life, unless it is something quite different from the norm. A highly creative atmosphere like an advertising agency would be ideal. And out of that volatility often come very good ideas. What she needs is someone to sort them and figure out how they can be applied.

Her home will reflect her love of drama, but she can go overboard and make it just too offbeat. This astro-gender type is another who would benefit greatly from a room where she can retreat to "when the world doesn't understand her."

Gender-correcting suggestions for the Water/Fire woman:

- With the combination of a Water Sun and a Fire Moon, you are likely to have more than your share of bad moments—i.e., generalized anxiety and even depression. The Water Sun imagines, the Fire Moon magnifies. One excellent resource for warding off or ending such moods is a large bank of "up" people you can call on to do things with. Particularly active things like tennis. It's difficult to keep your mind on your worries when your eye is on the ball.

- Unless you are an unusual Water/Fire female, your life is not totally buttoned up. For one thing, it's boring; for another, keeping all the kinks out wastes a lot of time you could be doing other things with. For domestic harmony—or for your own good if you are single—at least try to know where everything is, and when which payment is due to whom. A chaotic life ends up being more trouble than it is worth.

- With children, you are likely to be the classic stage mother. There's so much in you that wants to perform that you will pass it on to the next generation, whether they want it or not. Better that you yourself join an amateur theatrical group, or any performing group—even the church choir.

- While Fire Sun Sign women tend to let their tempers pop at will, you, with your Water Sun and Fire Moon, are more likely to do a slow boil. The problem is that by the time you "blow," you can do real harm to others' feelings. When you feel anger building up at someone or at a situation, gradually comment on how you feel so that others begin to get the picture.

- You've got the kind of charisma that can lead a group forward if you can get your act together. In business you are a great cheerleader, and that would be recognized in addition to your other skills. What you need is a shot of "Earth"; perhaps you could hire an Earth Sign assistant.

Getting Sign-Specific

Water Sun Sign/Fire Moon Sign

Cancer/Aries: You have a quick mind and a remarkable memory; you are popular and respected. In love, you are ardent but suspicious; you do not want your feelings to be hurt. Because you are so sensitive, you can play "detective" when you think something is being put over on you.

Cancer/Leo: You go along with the crowd, not letting them know how superindependent you are. You put on a happy face, but when someone crosses you, you simply walk away. In love, you are loyal but not constant. You tolerate the foibles of the world, including your own.

Cancer/Sagittarius: You have a forceful manner of speech, and despite your diplomacy, people know where you stand. You are very sensitive and easily hurt, but you forgive and don't hold grudges. You are able to organize your life long-term, and stick to the plan.

Scorpio/Aries: You are the center of your world. Your ambition is definite and highly personal. You are passionate in love, but not an easy person to be in love with. You are demanding, exacting and vain, and require the ultimate in devotion. There is an underlying cold streak.

Scorpio/Leo: You have a strong, positive personality, great stability of purpose. Despite these many good things, the danger of your nature comes from emotions. You can take up all your energy daydreaming. You have a realistic approach to matters of sex, and you expect loyalty.

Scorpio/Sagittarius: You are idealistic, somewhat aloof from life. You are affectionate, loyal and sincere, almost to a fault. You like nice things, but won't buy them at the price of your honor. You want nothing better than that men should live in peace.

Pisces/Aries: Your self-respect is tremendous, and working hand in hand with your independence of spirit, carries you along in the world. There is something solid and substantial about you that other people respect. You are a bit quarrelsome, and need peace and calm.

Pisces/Leo: If you fail, it is because of a fundamental lack of willingness to engage in competition. When you are not in a mood or a dejected state, you are excellent company with a lively sense of humor. You need affection, sympathy, love and understanding.

Pisces/Sagittarius: A certain spiritual quality is attached to everything you do. You are a highly expansive person and may try to spread your energies too far. You have tremendous confidence in yourself and your mission—no matter how large or how small.

Part 3

Relationships and the Astro-Gender Types

THE BURNING QUESTION, ASKED OF ALL ASTROLOGERS, IS "WHO would I get along with best?" There are two problems with the question that make the answer(s) less than simple. First, the usual reason for wanting to know is heterosexual and romantic, rather than a broader frame of reference; second, there are any number of reasonably valid astrological ways of rating relationships, but none of them is perfect.

The most exhaustive, and usually most accurate, is synastry, which literally means "stars together." For this method it is imperative to know both persons' complete birth information—i.e., not only date and year of birth, but also place and reasonably precise time as well. When an astrologer has this information, he or she then does a complicated analysis, which includes relating the positions of all ten planets in one chart to all ten in the other. Synastry is based very much on "aspects"—that is, the mathematical distances on a 360-degree circle from a planet in one chart to a planet in another. It usually provides a reasonably accurate picture of what the relationship will be like, but unless both charts are progressed into the future, the eventual outcome is still elusive.

Synastry is beyond most people—not astrologers, but the individuals who want to know their fate—because it is difficult enough to get accurate and precise birth information for one person, let alone two.

Astro-Gender Relationships

Especially in our time, the one-on-one, two-sex romantic relationship is pretty limited territory. With homosexual and bisexual relationships both commonplace and accepted, the spectrum is incomplete without this dimension. Also, with most women now enjoying participation in much fuller lives than before, there are many other kinds of relationships that must be covered: those with bosses, with child-care professionals, with intimate friends who impact their lives more importantly than before and also, of course, with co-workers and business acquaintances.

The advantage of the astro-gender system is that it is basic—elementary, if you will. Before complications of aspects between planets, and the particular signs the planets fall in, the astro-gender system goes straight to the heart of the issue: Do two people's astro-gender profiles—i.e., element combinations—mix well, or is there an underlying difficulty that more sophisticated forms of rating relationships will miss?

For the relationship rating system that follows, the four mixes of Sun and Moon Sign genders—masculine/masculine, feminine/feminine, masculine/feminine and feminine/masculine—are analyzed for both males and females with both males and females of the same or a different astro-gender mix. The relationship descriptions are broad-scale in the sense that they can be interpreted from the romantic all the way to the most mundane.

If there is a specific individual with whom closer involvement may or may not be a lifetime situation, it is highly recommended that you seek out the services of someone well versed in one-on-one synastry. The analyses here are valid, and work on an overall basis, but they cannot replace the information available in a full chart reading.

Relationships—1
The Masculine Sun Sign/
Masculine Moon Sign Man

With another masculine/masculine man:

Personal: On any level there is too much masculine energy here to avoid pride-of-place issues, if not all-out conflict. If you do pair off, you both should study up on issues of the "feminine" and try to incorporate them into your lives. It can be as simple as caring for a baby or attending a group on gender issues.

Business: Unless you become self-aware, you will have constant run-ins based on whose idea is better and who should get the gold star. The boss is key to how this one works itself out. Most executives do not like in-fighting among their employees. Clean up your act to save your job.

With a masculine/masculine woman:

Personal: You are each other's sexual and astro-gender counterpart; that means that despite gender differences, you will find lots to like about each other. Particularly with Fire, you probably both will enjoy sports—participatory and events. With Air, your interests will probably run more toward the artistic and intellectual. She could be a best buddy—even more fun than the masculine/masculine male. As for sex, it would be dynamic, but probably would

214 Marlene Masini Rathgeb

not last very long. You and she would find it an exhausting competition.

With a feminine/feminine man:

Personal: You will admire this person for his serenity and artistic interests. However, before anything gets going, boredom will set in for you. Somehow or other he doesn't have enough get-up-and-go. In order for this to work, you would have to change some of your habits and so would he.
Business: In business you would find yourself giving the all-female man bad marks for his lackadaisical attitude. He regards himself as having attained "inner peace," but you see it as a lack of a "winning attitude." Whatever your opinion, it is best to keep your thoughts to yourself.

With a feminine/feminine woman:

Personal: At first you may be taken with her softness and aura of glamour. And that could start something. However, once she has you, she'll never let you go; she is a clinger and a hanger-on. With your desire to roam, it is an unlikely combination. The only way it might work is if she has a strong desire to stay home and run a house and children.
Business: You may find yourself amazed at how the female/female is treated in business. Eventually you will find yourself raging with jealousy at what she gets away with; the boss is likely to treat her like a china doll and give her treats (good accounts) to boot. Your best bet is just to keep plugging away with your brash style. You may even find she stays away from you.

With a masculine/feminine man:

Personal: You may not know why, but you may find yourself drawn to this person. He has something you don't—a touch of the feminine. When you talk you may find him very wise about people and what makes them tick.

Business: You admire him for the buttoned-up way he works plus a "soft spot" for other people. When other types—like you—are about to go round the bend with frustration, the masculine/feminine male is getting into position to zero in on the problem, which is obviously arising from feelings.

With a masculine/feminine woman:

Personal: You may go head-to-head with this person because you both have masculine egos. You may be appalled at her toughness and her bravado. She is not even fun. You will probably find yourself walking away from this one.

Business: This will be a Mexican standoff. You will be very impressed by her work style and the results it gets, but you will not be able to get beyond what you see as her toughness. It would be advantageous to sit in on some meetings with her to observe how she does what she does.

With a feminine/masculine man:

Personal: This person might just become your best buddy. With his feminine Sun and your masculine one, there is a nice balance. Yet the two of you share a masculine Moon. Certain kinds of activities will bring out the harmony between you—one, literally, is music. If you can, make it a point to jam. Also, another "artistic" hobby you could enjoy in common is photography.

Business: The feminine/masculine male is closer to the center of the androgeny scale than you. In a way, you are a couple of odd fellows, but it works. You have a way of jamming yourself through doors in hopes of making a killing; he will insinuate himself into a situation instead. And do better. Oddly enough, you do not mind, but watch closely and learn your lessons.

With a feminine/masculine woman:

Personal: You do not appear to understand the feminine/masculine woman. She baffles you with her soft outer shell and hard inner shell. For a while it might interest you with its quirkiness, but before long you will be both confused and confounded. Sexually it works quite well, but there is not enough "glue" to hold you together.

Business: As a co-worker, the feminine/masculine female strikes the right note. She is generally not loud or "one of the boys." As a consequence you find her pleasant to have around. You are also fascinated by her subtle business ideas. You say, "I couldn't think of that!" Yes, you could, if you had some of the feminine in your astro-gender profile. You also can learn.

Relationships—2
The Masculine Sun Sign/
Masculine Moon Sign Woman

With the masculine/masculine woman:

Personal: In spite of what you have in common, any interaction between you two will be spoiled by a competitive spirit. Even as just good buddies, your double-masculine profiles would all but prohibit intimacy. When it comes to sex, you will each want the man the other has—not because he's so great, but because you're both so jealous.

Business: In business you will compete as well, but since you both are theoretically going toward the same goal, there will be more between you. You can make a game out of "who's got the best idea" and "who's going to get the bonus." Strangely enough, women in business who have mainly masculine profiles tend to form their own little "clubs"—but with more serious business in mind than the opposite sex.

With the masculine/masculine man:

Personal: This could be the battle of the titans or the most glorious love affair. With all that masculine energy to show off to each other, sexually it could be outstanding. If it goes the other way, one or the other could get the urge to literally punch the other out. Masculine energy without any feminine to "refine" it can get out of bounds.

Business: When masculine/masculine men meet masculine/masculine women in the workplace, a mutual admiration society is often formed. Whether or not it is true that women work harder and smarter, many men perceive it so, and admire it. Women, on the other hand, have not had time to develop the "slap on the back" technique that men use to such advantage. Under these conditions friendliness at least is virtually guaranteed.

With the feminine/feminine woman:

Personal: In this case, opposites do not necessarily attract. The feminine/feminine woman will be labeled a wimp by the masculine/masculine female. On the flip side, the feminine/feminine woman will find the masculine/masculine rough, coarse and loud. The question is whether or not they can find any use for each other. The masculine/masculine woman will immediately place her at the bottom of the ladder where cleanup is prime. The feminine/feminine woman will have greater trouble coming up with a place for her counterpart.

Business: It is a case of who will be more outraged—the feminine/feminine woman or the double-masculine woman. The latter will see the calm demeanor of the feminine/feminine female and say, "But that's not the way we act anymore." The double-feminine female will be embarrassed by the free and easy ways and language of her counterpart.

With the feminine/feminine man:

Personal: The masculine/masculine female may be at-tracted—fatally—to the feminine/feminine man. Some-thing tells her he's got what she wants in herself. However, as a romantic/sexual relationship, it will eventually fall apart because, though she loves his soft and loving ways, she doesn't respect them. While it lasts, however, she will be in seventh heaven.

Business: The double-masculine female would walk all over the feminine/feminine man—if she didn't feel so sorry for him. He is in a world that just doesn't match with his astro-gender profile, and she may see him "getting it" from other males in the office environment. So, easy as it might be for her to take away all his cookies, she will refrain—and look for think-alike business partners elsewhere.

With the masculine/feminine woman:

Personal: She is like you yet not like you. However, you could be a good balance for each other. You both share a masculine Sun, but you could learn from her feminine Moon. Your relationship would have its ups and downs—her downer moods and your occasional macho displays. The best thing for you to try is to be a sounding board for each other. Your differences might bring out new insights for both of you.

Business: As co-workers or partners, you could mutually run a very productive and efficient business. Yes, there would be times you would be working at cross-purposes—especially when the masculine/feminine female wants to be lenient, with a client, say, and you are loaded for bear. But for the most part, it works well.

With the masculine/feminine man:

Personal: You, the masculine/masculine female, are wary of many relationships. You find men either too abrasive or too weak. Here's an astro-gender type that, without major problems, could be the man of your dreams. He has that active, energetic Sun Sign you admire, and he has another dimension too—a feminine Moon. He will be able to pick up on your thoughts, and even tell you why you feel the way you do. With his masculine Sun, however, there's little chance of the affair getting too mushy for you.

Business: The masculine/feminine man matches your work energy, yet you might not see eye to eye. You look more at the face of things, while he digs down to see what else is there. This may annoy you or make you feel inadequate. He, on the other hand, may find your business ways a little slapdash. You are better as silent partners than as co-workers.

With the feminine/masculine woman:

Personal: You will most likely be fascinated by the range of her interests and her tendency to gossip about small things. If you can find some sports/hobbies, etc., in common, the relationship will serve an important need for you. It will show you the "feminine" as it operates as a Sun Sign ...i.e., as the "engine" that drives the personality.

Business: She will give you a run for your money because she wants to win. If you two become overly competitive, it could ruin a possibly mutually rewarding relationship. She will listen to your problems and give you some insightful answers; you can give her tips about strategic moves she can make toward her own ends.

With the feminine/masculine man:

Personal: You will be amazed at how much you have in common. He is a mild-mannered type with a dynamic will that moves him forward. When you are in "female" mode, you and he could make it romantically. However, when you are acting out your astro-gender type, he will be turned off. But still will remain a good friend.

Business: Regardless of what you think of his business style, he will be a "star"—and you might not like it. You can learn from him and smooth out your own more-than-occasionally abrasive style.

Relationships—3
The Feminine Sun Sign/
Feminine Moon Sign Man

With the masculine/masculine man:

Personal: You could be the best of friends, even more. Your astro-gender profile is at one extreme; his is at the other. Yet, as a couple, you fall near the middle of the astro-gender spectrum. You will rarely be bored, since the masculine/masculine male has so many facets to him; on the other side, you can literally change him into a much more aware, softer person,
Business: Since most business discourages intimacy, it is unlikely you would get close enough to enjoy the benefits mentioned above. You are likely to find the masculine/masculine male crude, loud and overly ambitious; he is likely to find you a bit of a wimp. Not much interchange here.

With the masculine/masculine woman:

Personal: You will probably find her delightful—animated, energetic, talkative, worldly. If you can give back to her some of the many things you have to give, this could be an excellent match, romantically speaking. For marriage, you would have to be very sure you are willing to hold up your end of the bargain.

Business: Here too you would find the masculine/masculine woman a boon companion. Watch your step, however, if you want her to keep liking you back. If necessary, put on a show of "going for the brass ring" with energy and enthusiasm. She might not respect you in an office situation where you seem bored and lethargic.

With the feminine/feminine man:

Personal: You share one of the most unusual astro-gender types in the zodiac. Many males with this profile end up creating a very unique lifestyle—private and personal, with few good friends. If this kind of life appeals to you, you've got a soul mate. If not, you might at least have a like-minded friend.

Business: Many female/female men gravitate toward the arts. There you could share many experiences. However, if you both end up in a less compatible career, you will find yourself sharing headaches and getting into bad moods that poison the air around you. Take care not to pick up on each other's "downs."

With the feminine/feminine woman:

Personal: You would make a very interesting couple with definite ideas about how to live well and how to raise children. If both are "strong" with the better qualities of the feminine, it could be a model family. This is definitely a case where Father will be as involved as Mother in child care and the passing on of values. If, however, each is "weak," you will drive each other crazy—she by hanging on, you by being passive.

Business: Chances are you would ignore each other, not finding enough there to get hold of. In mainstream business the female/female man tends to sit back and see what happens rather than putting his back into the job. The feminine/feminine woman is prone to looking for someone to help her, and you don't seem the type.

With the masculine/feminine man:

Personal: Together you are better than apart. His masculine Sun compensates for your lack of the masculine; your feminine Moons complement each other. The pattern makes it possible for you to enjoy so many things together—and to understand them in a feeling way. This is the kind of relationship that can start very young and last for a lifetime, regardless of where you go or meet again.

Business: You are bound to be a little jealous of the masculine/feminine man. First, around the office he is so "ordinary," so "one of the boys." You would like to have those easy ways with your compatriots, but it is more difficult for you. Suggestion: Get to know the masculine/feminine male well . . . follow him around if necessary. It could do a lot for your astro-gender profile.

With the masculine/feminine woman:

Personal: She will probably be more attracted to you than you are to her—at the beginning. Her feminine Moon responds to your feminine profile, and she sees you as a soft, gentle person, yet with all the masculine attributes. You may regard her as a hanger-on, but eventually will see where she is coming from. As a marriage mix, this is very good for you.

Business: The masculine/feminine woman is just about perfect for you to work with in business. Her masculine Sun zeroes in on the most pertinent facts; her feminine Moon brings insight to complicated situations. You understand them too, and can use help in fixing on what the root of the problem really is, and her Sun helps you.

With the feminine/masculine man:

Personal: This could be a "best buddy" situation in which each of you finds something to admire greatly in the other.

For instance, in you, it could be your sense of humor. In him, you could like him for his get-up-and-go. You should have a lot of things in common—for instance, a form of the arts, perhaps the movies. You will rarely square off, but he will take a protective attitude toward you.

Business: When there is a sense of urgency, things take a different turn. The feminine/masculine man will go into action and put his mind where his business is. You will take more time to analyze the situation. Each of you will end up annoying the other. This is one of those relationships to keep far away from the work world.

With the feminine/masculine woman:

Personal: The question is not will you like her, but will she like you? For your part, you will relate to her feminine Sun; for her part, she will relate to a man with a double-feminine astro-gender profile. Not that it sticks out all over, but it will eventually become obvious. The feminine/masculine female may picture herself holding up the roof as the rain is coming in, once she gets to know you. It's not that you are lazy; it's that you like life to be peaceful all the time.

Business: In an office situation, you will stand out as quite attractive compared with more macho types. The feminine/masculine woman could get interested. And you could make use of the situation by getting her, a fairly passive type, to do all kinds of work for you. This works for a while, but remember, the lady has a masculine Moon, and could get fed up with "helping."

Relationships—4
The Feminine Sun Sign/
Feminine Moon Sign Woman

With the masculine/masculine woman:

Personal: She doesn't intimidate you because, regardless
of astro-gender profile, you share the same sex. She may
fascinate you and amuse you with her tomboyish ways,
and you may pick up some tricks for dealing with the
world. In fact, you two could be a mutual admiration society on the basis that opposites attract, and become the
best of friends.

Business: If you go head-to-head with the all-masculine
woman in a business situation, you are likely to lose out.
One of the things she can do is make noise. Number one,
that embarrasses you; number two, she can outshout you
any day of the week. While you would probably prefer a
quiet, one-on-one conversation, that is not likely what
you'll get. Keep it strictly friendly, and don't cross over
into each other's territory.

With the masculine/masculine man:

Personal: There is an outside chance that you will find the
all-masculine man exciting and attractive. More likely,
however, you will find him a bit of a boor. Exceptions could
be Gemini and Libra. One thing that may appeal to you is
his protective stance; part of the masculine ethic is taking
care of women like you. Though that might make you comfortable for a while, in the long run you would find it
suffocating.

Business: Depending on how well you have altered your
situations, he is aware of the "feminine" and knows you
are a very feminine creature. This is one of those office
situations that could grow into something more. Don't
push it, however.

With the feminine/feminine woman:

Personal: You are both "ultrafemales," though one of you may have Earth (stronger) and one Water (less strong) in your astro-gender profiles. That means you understand each other, even if you don't necessarily like each other. Regardless of what you do (stay home, work), there is a softness about you—even if Capricorn is in the mix. If on no other level, you will enjoy discussing mutual friends and "straightening their lives out for them."

Business: If you work with another feminine/feminine woman, you may see your own characteristics reflected in her. One may be a tendency to panic when the pressure is on. On the other hand, the feminine feminine woman can appear serene while she is having internal hysterics. The all-female female can work very hard and keep her eye on the ball.

With the feminine/feminine man:

Personal: It's a toss-up who wins the prize for being more uncomfortable in our "masculine" world—you or he. However, as a couple, you can bolster each other's confidence and make each other feel at least pseudo-masculine, in the sense of being outgoing and sturdy.

Business: Chances are that in any work environment there will be all variations of an astro-gender profile. In this kind of place, if you notice the feminine/feminine male, it will be as a kind of "character," perhaps with an excellent sense of humor. When you gauge him against the other males, you realize you like him, but that he doesn't seem to have what it takes to make it big. He may become a friend to go to cultural events with.

With the masculine/feminine woman

Personal: You two should get along very well because you both have strengths that many women do not have. You

can be buddy/buddy and at the same time have a lot of
fun together. However, if those two feminine moons clash,
there could be all-out war.

Business: When you two are in the office, you make a serious and heavyweight pair. There is no jealousy because
you are so well matched that there is no reason for it.
However, if one or the other of you goes pulling ahead,
there may be some bad feelings. No envy, just the fear of
one of you being in a different place than the other.

With the masculine/feminine man:

Personal: You are bound to be fascinated by the mascu-
line/feminine man. He seems to have everything you want,
including a sentimental streak like yours. If he is typical,
you will find yourself being wined and dined and talked to
about the finer things in life. Don't make a decision before
he does, however.

Business: You may find yourself a little shy working with
this man. He is so nose-to-the-grindstone that you may feel
like a butterfly. One way to handle the situation is to find
yourself a juicy project of your own that you can apply
your ESP/feeling to and come up with a solution. In the
meantime, your serious gentleman will find out that you
are a genius.

With the feminine/masculine woman:

Personal: It depends on where you individually are coming
from to assess how this will work. If you both are grown-
up, "mature" women, you probably will enjoy each other
very much. The feminine/masculine female is a lot like you
in that her Sun Sign—the "engine" of the chart—is feminine. You should find lots of activities to do together, many
of them in the home and with children.

Business: You two would find each other rather quickly in
a business situation. The "masculine" work world can be

quite confusing with its set of "masculine" rules. You and the feminine/masculine woman can help each other see the real meaning behind the sometimes meaningless way of doing things. She, with her masculine Moon, should be able to tap into things and get more information.

With the feminine/masculine man:

Personal: He may just be the man who strikes the best note with you. With his feminine Sun, he's on your side; yet his masculine Moon creates the proper distance to keep things interesting. You would respond to his ways; he would admire your femininity. From a casual affair to a permanent relationship, this should work quite well.

Business: The all-feminine woman is most mystified by and occasionally put off by the masculine world we *all* live in. The feminine/masculine male—especially if his sun is in Taurus or Cancer—can show you the way through the labyrinth. However, don't expect him to literally do your work for you. He is quite self-sufficient and would expect you to be too. In addition, he maintains a sense of humor about what goes on in the workplace, and that can work wonders.

Relationships—5
The Masculine Sun Sign/
Feminine Moon Sign Man

With the masculine/masculine man:

Personal: You have just the right stuff to pull the masculine/masculine man off his horse. With your feminine Moon Sign, you have a powerful implement to defuse the male/

male's occasional combativeness. While at first he may resent your attempts at making him look inside, eventually you two could be the best of friends.

Business: You have the upper hand, no matter what position the masculine/masculine man holds. He is so fixed on competing and winning that he is bound to miss the subtleties that are the real key to the situation. If necessary, wait it out, and you will see that business come your way.

With the masculine/masculine woman:

Personal: This could be a Katharine Hepburn/Spencer Tracy scenario. The double-masculine lady acts out her maleness while you, the masculine/feminine male, find it all very amusing. The double-masculine woman is all "go," without much reflection. Your feminine Moon gives you insight into the action. You could end up being the best of friends, or even take it further. It's a good mix.

Business: This lady is usually most "on" in situations where she perceives herself to be the focus of attention. If this is the case in an office situation with you, you are not likely to be charmed. In fact, your masculine/feminine nature might be offended enough to tell her what you really think.

With the feminine/feminine man:

Personal: Many feminine/feminine men feel quite different from their counterparts with a masculine Sun or Moon. And therefore a bit "out of it." With your feminine Moon, you could easily understand the feminine/feminine male— and you both could learn from each other. You probably would come closest together in conversation, or in going to various cultural events. Your feminine Moon longs for what is beautiful.

Business: Depending on the nature of the mutual work you perform, you could find the feminine/feminine man brilliant—or a nuisance. You would rarely fight, but your patience could be sorely tried. As could his. The problem is that your masculine Sun lets you zero in on the work problem, while it takes him a lot longer to get there. Choose a different work buddy.

With the feminine/feminine woman:

Personal: For the most part, feminine/feminine women—particularly with Water Signs—are the most malleable of creatures. Your masculine Sun may want someone a little sturdier and feistier. If you do get together, keep things on a romantic level—as you can do with your feminine Moon. If she proves out under these circumstances, you might go further,
Business: Just as the masculine/masculine female turns you off in business, her polar opposite may as well. Another possibility, however, is that you will find yourself taking the role of mentor, which you may find irresistible. She may be a sterling student too.

With the masculine/feminine man:

Personal: Well balanced as you are, so is he—at least from an astro-gender point of view, Of course, there may be differences—you could have a Fire Sun, he could have a Water Moon. But the same rules apply. With your two masculine Suns, you are likely to be competitive in the sports sense. Depending on who wins, and whose feminine Moon is bruised, there could be trouble. But in general, you are bound to see life from the same side.
Business: Here, too, competitiveness is likely to get in the way of a beautiful friendship. However, without the physical nature of sports to dispel the problem, you could end up really going at it. If it happens, make a pact to exercise after you work.

With the masculine/feminine woman:

Personal: Your counterpart on the female side can look as if she can take care of herself—and she probably can. However, she can also startle you by a burst of emotionalism when, as far as you are concerned, none is called for. Your feminine Moon can get you in the form of a bad mood—but rarely a "storm." The masculine/feminine woman could be very good for you in helping you deal with your own kind of emotionalism.

Business: This combination works well in business. She is a self-starter, but needs occasional prodding. You will come out the better of the two, though she will outdo you in all those details that make a good business better.

With the feminine/masculine man:

Personal: In theory, you complement each other, and therefore should have a serene relationship. On the contrary, you constantly battle over who is right and what is the right thing to do. One way to avoid such troubles is to agree to talk them out—really talk them out. With your feminine Moon and his feminine Sun Sign, you should be able to come at things not head-on, but in a more roundabout way, to talk about your feelings rather than simply the issue itself.

Business: In the work environment you two operate smoothly and effectively. What's at issue in your personal lives is not at issue here. You make a superb team in going after a new client or new business. You smooth-talking ways complement each other beautifully.

With the feminine/masculine woman:

Personal: If you are looking for a romantic/marriage partner, you should have to look no farther than the feminine/masculine woman. It would be a "traditional" match, since you hold the power of the masculine in your Sun. However, since women have strengthened their sense of self, it would be a much more well-balanced pairing. She would also understand some things about you that are still murky to you.

Business: Your mistake could be in treating this woman like an underling. But since you are theoretically "enlightened" by your feminine Moon, you will not do that. Instead, make her a confidante and discuss all your problems with her. Chances are you will get a lot more good advice than from any of the men in the group.

Relationships—6
The Masculine Sun Sign/
Feminine Moon Sign Woman

With the masculine/masculine woman:

Personal: There isn't much more to say about the masculine/masculine woman than that she seems to be everyone at once, and not too gracefully, either. You can outdo her in the grace department any day. You may regard each other as "specimens," but it is a far cry from a close and intimate relationship.

Business: If, as is still usually the case, you outrank any woman in your workplace, you've got the perfect opportunity to put the masculine/masculine woman to work— and see how she performs. You may discover that a lot of her energy is expended on unnecessary things. Then you'll have your chance to speak.

With the masculine/masculine man:

Personal: He is likely to notice you and make an egregious pass. After all, the "glamour" of your feminine Moon Sign shines through. For your part, especially if he has Air Signs, he is much too "dry" for you. If he is Fire, he could be overbearing. If, however, he has made an effort to understand the "feminine," it could be interesting.

Business: The masculine/masculine is unlikely to find you at all threatening when work and money are the issues. That means you can silently observe his modus operandi, put the techniques to work and most likely come out on top.

With the feminine/feminine woman:

Personal: If she's an Earth type, you'll enjoy her sturdiness and ability to do tough things well, but without an edge. If she's Water, you'll love to talk about feelings and where they come from. Either way, though it may not be a lifetime romance, there will be mutual sharing and admiration.

Business: Don't underestimate the strength of a feminine/feminine woman. If you do, and don't give her the attention she needs, you will find just how willful she can be. That is, assuming you are the one she needs information from. If you aren't, she won't bother you. She can find out on her own.

With the feminine/feminine man:

Personal: Your feminine Moon Sign gives you an immediate kinship with the feminine/feminine male. Whether it is Water or Earth, the feminine element lends a softness to your way of being, and gives you an edge in understanding feelings and the immediacy of the senses. You two might become hiking buddies or spend weekends in the open air. Your degree of intimacy depends on the individuals involved.

Business: You two may find yourself vying for "most consulted." People sometimes come to you just to chat, but give a business reason for it. Since you two are right on the same track, you probably will find yourselves using similar techniques. Some other masculine males might be jealous.

With the masculine/feminine woman:

Personal: If there were ever two act-alikes, it is you. You are like a couple of kids, constantly laughing at each other's antics. However, sooner or later your Suns and Moons will get into conflict and a bonfire of the jealousies will break out. Hopefully, you two will come to an agreement before things get out of hand.

Business: There is one thing to be said for two people having the same Sun and Moon: There is always hope that you will get to know yourself better and that you will reach a better understanding of what makes each of you tick.

With the masculine/feminine man:

Personal: You and the masculine/feminine man could get very comfortable together. With complementary Suns and Moons, communication will just flow between you. If there is a sticking point, it will be with the masculine/feminine male who gets hung up on small points. If you can get through to him about becoming more malleable, both of you will enjoy life more.

Business: It could be a fascinating competition—who does better in the office and out of it? You both have virtues, and, to go by the Sun, one has the masculine and one the feminine. For backslapping good times, the masculine/feminine should do better. For "stroking" and making people feel good, the prize should go to the feminine/masculine. Both of you do well with peers.

With the feminine/masculine man:

Personal: The fact that your Suns and Moons are in opposite genders has an expansive effect on both of you, and that could mean anything from a booming friendship to a lovely romance. The things you like, you like a lot; the things that turn you off do so mutually. This is a good relationship to keep an eye on.

Business: It's not all moonlight and roses when the workplace is involved. After all, you do have a masculine Sun, and that makes you want to be in the driver's seat. And your opposite number's feminine Sun Sign won't make it any easier for you. Advice: Confine this relationship to courtship.

With the feminine/masculine woman:

Personal: Regardless of the difference in gender of your signs, you two are true soul mates. If you can agree about the smaller things of the world, you can have a blissful time enjoying/discussing the grander.

Business: You two would probably be cited for paying less attention to work than each other. Though you both have the will and the way to work—hard—you find each other more interesting than work's grubby details. Try to divide the day so that you devote some of it totally to work—and some to your friendship.

Relationships—7
The Feminine Sun Sign/
Masculine Moon Sign Man

With the masculine/masculine man:

Personal: There is an underlying hostility between you two. The feminine Sun Sign man finds the double masculine man to be insensitive and boorish. The masculine/

masculine male finds the feminine/masculine male soft and a bit womanish. This will never fly.

Business: Things go a lot better under the office roof. The feminine/masculine man looks up to the masculine/masculine male for his go-for-it mentality and daring. The double masculine man envies the feminine/masculine male for his subtlety and his canny way of getting what he wants.

With the masculine/masculine woman:

Personal: If you want to see a show, watch the feminine/masculine man with the masculine/masculine woman. She won't give an inch; he will keep trying to wind her around his little finger. If one or the other gives in, the masculine/masculine woman will be embarrassed. The feminine/masculine man will wonder why he tried so hard.

Business: It would be difficult for the feminine/masculine man to complain about the performance of the double masculine woman—at least in terms of results. However, he can and will make a lot of noise about her own noisy and cutting ways.

With the feminine/feminine man:

Personal: You two are not as far apart as you seem. In fact, you are brothers under the skin. You may even talk about things with each other that you would not like others to hear. Go ahead, develop this friendship.

Business: You may discover that your ideas click like crazy and that you even decide to go into business together. You both like to dream on a wing and a prayer, and should have happy landings.

With the feminine/feminine woman:

Personal: In spite of your feminine sun signs, you will find it difficult to discover anything in common. The lady has

a way of making trouble from the start. She is also prone
to disasters—or at least what *she* considers disasters.
Business: In business it is a slightly different story. You
perceive very quickly that the lady can tell a tale in dramatic fashion, and that it helps business. You still do not
want to have her on your team at all times, however.

With the masculine/feminine man:

Personal: You could form a beautiful friendship. Your masculine Moon and his feminine one mesh beautifully and
each can learn a lot from the other. In addition, your
senses of humor get along swimmingly.
Business: Just as you make a great pair in your personal
lives, you can be sure that no matter what business you
go into, it will thrive because you two are so very
compatible.

With the masculine/feminine woman:

Personal: There is hardly a twosome that can become as
close as you. There are a number of reasons for this, but
the main one is that each of you "crosses over" with each
other's gender, and thereby each one adds a missing element to the other's life. Your conversations should be
marvelous.
Business: There is an edge in business that may make your
relationship less than blissful. Neither of you is lazy, but
hard work can never take the place of "clouds in your
coffee."

With the feminine/masculine man:

Personal: You are a couple of strange ducks. One minute
you're each other's best friend, the next you are feuding.
It makes sense to blame it on the Moon—the competitive,
masculine Moon. It takes a while before a man can learn

to live with his Moon, whether masculine or feminine. However, there is light at the end of the tunnel for both of you.

Business: The same applies to the two of you in business. It will take some growing up and maturing before you can really work together.

With the feminine/masculine woman:

Personal: If there were not the possibility of it developing further, you two might be "kissing cousins." It isn't a question of your not knowing what makes the world go 'round—and when the time comes, you'll both be ready.

Business: This is a good bet for work. You trust each other and want to see each other do well. In fact, you might form a kind of cottage industry where the "goods" come from nature.

Relationships—8
The Feminine Sun Sign/
Masculine Moon Sign Woman

With the masculine/masculine woman:

Personal: She would make a great role model for you— even if she occasionally goes overboard in the masculine direction. Observe the way she pushes ahead and doesn't let anyone get in her way. It isn't always graceful, but it usually works. You can take from it what you need and leave the rest behind.

Business: Though you may not find it a very pretty sight, you can learn from the masculine/masculine woman in business. Because hers is a pseudo-macho modus operandi, it can become a caricature of a well-controlled man in business. It doesn't "fit," but you can see where the broad strokes are and learn from them.

With the masculine/masculine man:

Personal: Some people find the masculine/masculine man "adorable." You, with your feminine Sun Sign, might be one of these. But you might use the word "quaint." The masculine/masculine male strikes most people, if he is typical, as a throwback. However, you may feel it worthwhile to try to "pull him along the gender path" by teaching him how to feel.

Business: The masculine/masculine man may find you quite attractive with your feminine Sun and the gutsiness of your masculine Moon. If he comes on, maintain your dignity and try to get to know him better. If he balks, it wasn't worth the experience anyway.

With the feminine/feminine woman:

Personal: You could be of great help to the feminine/feminine woman by telling her that until men and women get the message that business and lifestyles are changing for real, she will be swimming upstream. She will listen to you because of the way your masculine Moon "charges" your Sun and makes you more independent.

Business: There's really no contest in the business environment. The feminine/feminine woman will take a back seat to almost anyone. You can begin her "gender education" by pointing out certain specifics of behavior among both men and women. She will gradually raise her voice and her expectations.

With the feminine/feminine man:

Personal: You could form a very rewarding friendship, if not more than that. You can help him find the grounding in the feminine; he can help you control your sometimes hotheaded masculine Moon. Together you should enjoy many things in life, with the emphasis on the here-and-now of whatever is beautiful.

Business: You may be simply amazed at what this pulls off and comes up with. And you should observe. He has a kind of subtlety that doesn't exactly amount to chicanery, but his charm makes up for the rest. It is not always the best manifestation of the feminine, but it will give you a better idea of what it can be.

With the masculine/feminine woman:

Personal: You are a match made in gender heaven. Not that you need exclude men entirely, but that you will find each other right on target in what you want to talk about, what your dreams are, etc. The fact that your Sun Signs and Moon Signs are opposite genders is a plus. It gives the two of you a broader perspective about what being a female in today's world means.

Business: You two are a "dream team" when it comes to operating in business. However, for the sake of the job and the company, you should spread yourself around, i.e., don't strategize so much together that others lose out on the value of your balanced brain.

With the masculine/feminine man:

Personal: You will be attracted to each other for several good gender reasons. Your feminine Sun Sign objectifies what he feels from his own mood; thus you can clarify it. His masculine Sun Sign lets you in on the meaning of masculine gender. Underneath the surface both your Moons are listening to each other. This could be a sane love match.

Business: There may be too much going on here to allow for concentration on work. In the microcosm of the workplace you two could keep on pointing out behavior and language, and relating it to gender. Better find two different places and keep work separate.

With the feminine/masculine woman:

Personal: Here's another duo who can become fast friends. You are both balanced somewhere near the center of the gender scale. If you two have different Suns (Earth and Water), you will be able to have even more mutual insights into what the feminine is. You should read your astrogender profiles and see what you can glean from them.

Business: You are two likely candidates to do some "underground" work at your place of business. It wouldn't take much to get a group of gender-minded people together—both male and female—and talk about the subject for a real-life point of view. Uninitiated males might be vocal at times, but then, they are learning too.

With the feminine/masculine man:

Personal: You, despite your sexual differences, find a lot to talk about. In fact, there is hardly a time you are not talking. That's the feminine sun sign leading you to a cozy and comfy place in each other's hearts. Before you get too close, however, be sure to examine where he is coming from. It's possible there is one—or maybe more—other female waiting to get her hands on him.

Business: Don't get the idea that if this person is in charge, that he really is the boss. He would like to give that impression by making emotional noises and "scaring the troops." You are one woman who cannot be fooled and will call his bluff every time. Sooner or later, though, you will see eye to eye and he will thank you for your help.

Appendices

Your Sun Sign

Aries: March 22–April 21

Taurus: April 22–May 20

Gemini: May 21–June 21

Cancer: June 22–July 21

Leo: July 22–August 22

Virgo: August 23–September 22

Libra: September 23–October 22

Scorpio: October 23–November 22

Sagittarius: November 23–December 21

Capricorn: December 22–January 20

Aquarius: January 21–February 19

Pisces: February 20–March 21

How to Use the Moon Charts in this Book

Every month the Moon makes a complete circle of the zodiac, going through all twelve signs. At the moment of your birth it was in one of them. In addition to your Sun Sign, your Moon Sign is the most important factor in your overall horoscope—and the one most difficult to ascertain because it moves so quickly, changing signs every two to two and a half days.

To find what sign the moon was in when you were born, use the following charts, which are arranged by year and month. Turn to the year and month of your birth, then find the specific day. If there is only one sign in the "box" (indicated by the abbreviations listed below), that sign is your Moon Sign. If there are two signs, you must ascertain the time of your birth to find out which of the two signs you were born under. You will note there is a clock time (Eastern Standard) in the box. That is the time the Moon passed from one sign to the following sign. If your birthtime is before the time indicated, your Moon Sign is the one shown in the upper left hand corner; if your time of birth was after the clock time shown, your Moon Sign is the one in the upper right-hand corner in your birth date "box." If you have difficulty ascertaining the time of your birth, you may be able to get it from the Bureau of Vital Statistics in most states.

Abbreviations of the twelve signs of the zodiac as you will find them in the charts.

A = ARIES, **T** = TAURUS, **G** = GEMINI, **C** = CANCER, **L** = LEO, **V** = VIRGO, **LI** = LIBRA, **S** = SCORPIO, **SG** = SAGITTARIUS, **CP** = CAPRICORN, **AQ** = AQUARIUS, **P** = PISCES.

1920

```
           1     2     3     4     5     6     7     8     9     10    11    12    13    14    15
      T    T  G G   G  C C   C  L L   L  V V   V     V LiLi   Li S S    S
Jan  5:13p       5:19p       5:31p       7:46p             1:50a       11:58a

     G  C C   C  L L   L  V V   V LiLi   Li  S S    S     S Sg Sg   Sg Cp Cp
Feb  2:54a       3:33a       6:19a      11:21a       8:14p       8:25a       9:14p

     C    L L   L  V V   V LiLi   Li   S S    S Sg Sg   Sg    Sg Cp Cp   Cp    Cp Aq
Mar 12:33p       3:41p       8:54p       5:11a       4:36p             5:25a       4:58p

     V    V LiLi   Li S S    S     S Sg Sg   Sg Cp Cp   Cp    Cp Aq Aq   Aq P P
Apr  6:00a       1:35p      12:42a       1:25p             1:31a      10:49a

     Li   S S    S     S Sg Sg   Sg Cp Cp   Cp    Cp Aq Aq   Aq P P    P    P A A
May  8:38        8:00a       8:39        9:09a       7:32p       2:22a

     Sg   Sg    Sg Cp Cp   Cp Aq Aq   Aq    Aq P P    P    A A    A T T    T G G
Jn   3:05a       3:38        2:42a      10:56a       3:34p       4:57p

     Cp   Cp Aq Aq   Aq    Aq P P    P    A A    A T T    T     T G G   G C C
Jly  9:31p       8:37a       5:38       11:44p       2:39a       3:03a

     Aq P P    P    P A A    A    A T T    T G G   G C C    C L L    L V V
Aug  2:18p      11:09p       5:56a      10:14a      12:11p      12:42p       1:28p

     A    A T T    T G G   G C C    C L L    L V V    V     V LiLi   Li S
Sep 11:19a       3:57p       7:04p       9:02p      10:55p       2:12a       8:20a

     T G G   G     G C C    C L L    L V V    V LiLi   Li S S    S     S Sg
Oct  9:32p      12:29a       3:14a       6:23a      10:45a       5:14p       2:31a

     C    C L L    L V V    V LiLi   Li    Li S S    S S Sg   Sg Cp Cp
Nov  8:38       12:04p       5:25p      12:51a      10:27a      10:03p

     L V V    V LiLi   Li    Li S S    S Sg Sg   Sg Cp Cp   Cp Aq Aq   Aq
Dec  5:45p      10:51p       6:51a       5:10p       5:00a       5:39
```

1921

```
           1     2     3     4     5     6     7     8     9     10    11    12    13    14    15
     L    L S S    S Sg Sg   Sg    Sg Cp Cp   Cp Aq Aq   Aq    Aq P P    P A A
Jan 12:28p       7:24p      11:10a      11:50p      12:10p      11:14p

     S Sg Sg   Sg Cp Cp   Cp    Cp Aq Aq   Aq P P    P    P A A    A T T    T G
Feb  5:04a       5:14p       5:59a       6:04p       4:51a       1:44p       8:04p

     Sg   Sg Cp Cp   Cp Aq Aq   Aq    Aq P P    P A A    A T T    T     T G
Mar 12:04a      12:46p      12:44a      10:58a       7:15p       1:26a

     Cp Aq Aq   Aq    Aq P P    P A A    A    A T T    T G G   G C C    C L
Apr  8:22p       8:28a       6:31p       1:59a       7:16a      10:59a       1:48p

     Aq P P    P    P A A    A T T    T G G   G C C    C L L    L V V
May  4:46p       3:13a      10:31a       2:51p       5:19p       7:17p       9:52p

     A    A T T    T     T G G   G C C    C L L    L V V    V L L    L S
Jn   8:03p      12:16a       1:46a       2:19a       3:42        7:10a      12:22p

     T    T G G   G C C    C L L    L V V    V L L    L S S    S S Sg
Jly 10:22a      11:55a      11:34a      11:27a       1:30p       6:43p       3:06a

     C    C L L    L V V    V L L    L S S    S     S Sg Sg   Sg Cp Cp   Cp
Aug 10:11a       9:19p       9:53p       1:35a       9:00a       7:30p

     L V V    V L L    L S S    S Sg Sg   Sg    Sg Cp Cp   Cp Aq Aq   Aq    Aq P
Sep  8:07a       8:06a      10:25a       4:22p       1:59a       2:01p       2:39a

     L    L S S    S     S Sg Sg   Sg Cp Cp   Cp Aq Aq   Aq    Aq P P    P A A
Oct  8:38p       6:38p       1:24a       9:46a       7:13p       9:51a       9:34p

     S Sg Sg   Sg Cp Cp   Cp    Cp Aq Aq   Aq P P    P    P A A    A T T    T G
Nov 11:09a       6:38p       5:18a       5:51p       5:52a       3:19p       9:40p

     Sg Cp Cp   Cp Aq Aq   Aq    Aq P P    P A A    A    A T T    T G G   G C
Dec  3:33a       1:42p       2:04a       2:36p      12:45a       7:08a      10:11a
```

1922

```
           1     2     3     4     5     6     7     8     9     10    11    12    13    14    15
     Aq   Aq P P    P A A    A    A T T    T G G   G C C    C L L    L V
Jan  9:45a      10:42p       9:58a       8:26p       6:47p       9:21p       9:13p

     P A A    A T T    T     T G G   G C C    C L L    L V V    V LiLi
Feb  5:36a       5:42p       2:41a       7:30a       8:40a       7:58a       7:35a

     A    A T T    T     T G G   G C C    C L L    L V V    V LiLi   Li S
Mar 11:51p       9:48a       4:18a       7:10p       7:23p       6:44p       7:15p

     T G G   G C C    C    C L L    L V V    V LiLi   Li S S    S Sg Sg
Apr  3:29p      10:46p       3:12a       5:09a       5:36a       6:07a       8:26a

     G C C    C L L    L V V    V LiLi   Li S S    S Sg Sg   Sg    Sg Cp Cp
May  4:12a       9:05a      12:19p       2:22p       4:01p       6:33p      11:27p

     L V V    V LiLi   Li S S    S     S Sg Sg   Sg Cp Cp   Cp Aq Aq   Aq    Aq P
Jn   5:48p       8:44p      11:43p       3:19a       8:31a       4:26p       3:26a

     V LiLi   Li    Li S S    S Sg Sg   Sg Cp Cp   Cp    Cp Aq Aq   Aq P P    P A A
Jly  2:05a       2:05a      10:06a       4:13p      12:28a      11:17a      11:59p

     S    S Sg Sg   Sg Cp Cp   Cp    Cp Aq Aq   Aq    Aq P P    P    P A A    A T T    T
Aug  3:36p      10:23p       7:19a       6:23p       7:06a       7:57p

     Cp   Cp Aq Aq   Aq    Aq P P    P A A    A    A T T    T G G   G C C
Sep  1:13p      12:42a       1:29p       2:24a       1:50p      10:12p

     Aq   Aq P P    P A A    A    A T T    T G G   G     G C C    C L L
Oct  6:41a       7:36p       8:20a       7:44p       4:52a      11:01a

     P A A    A T T    T     T G G   G C C    C L L    L V V    V     V Li
Nov  2:04a       2:39p       1:33a      10:23a       5:05p       9:36       12:01a

     T    T T G G   G C C    C L L    L     L V V    V LiLi   Li S S
Dec  8:34a       4:33p      10:32p       3:09a       6:40a       9:14a
```

Grid 1

16	17	18	19	20	21	22	23	24	25	26	27	28	29	30	31
S	Sg Sg 12:44a	SG Cp 1:33p	Cp	Cp Aq Aq 12:39		Aq P P 9:34a		P A A 4:32p		A T T 9:43p		T	T	G G 1:04a	
Cp	CP Aq Aq 8:20a	Aq 4:38	Aq P P		P A A 11:13p		A A T T 3:05a		T G G 6:42a		G C C 9:41a				
Aq	Aq 1:24a	Aq P P		P A A 6:43a		A T T 9:58a		T G G 3:26p		G C C 3:02p		C L L 6:21p		L V V 10:40p	
P A A 4:29p		A T T 7:08p		T G G 8:15p		G C C 9:23p		C L L 11:50p		L 4:22a	V V		V Li Li 11:19		
A T T 5:35a		T G G 6:13a		G C C 6:01a		C L L V V 6:50a 10:12p		V 4:51p		V Li Li	Li 2:33a		Li S S	S Sg 2:21p	
G C C 4:27p		C L L 4:02p		L V V 5:45p		V Li Li 11:07p		Li 8:20a		Li S S 8:15p		S Sg Sg	Sg 9:06a	Sg Cp	
C L L 2:23a		L V V 3:14a		V Li Li 7:03a		Li S S 3:04p		S 2:32a		S Sg Sg 3:22p		Sg Cp Cp	Cp Aq Aq 3:36p		
V Li Li 4:29p		Li S S 11:14p		S 9:46a		S Sg Sg 10:22p		Sg Cp Cp 10:36a		Cp Aq Aq 8:55p		Aq P P	P 5:03p	P A	
S 5:58p		S Sg Sg	Sg	Sg Cp Cp 6:09a		Cp Aq Aq 6:33p		Aq 4:57a		Aq P P 12:34p		P A A 5:49p		A T T	
Sg 2:17p		Sg Cp Cp	Cp	Cp Aq Aq 2:52a		Aq P P 1:56p		P A A 9:52p		A 2:33a	A T T 4:59a		T G G	G C 6:35p	
Cp Aq Aq 10:46a		Aq P P 10:37p		P 7:45a		P A A 1:01p		A T T 2:59p		T G G 3:12p		G C C 3:33p		C L L	
Aq P P 6:03a		P A A 4:29p		A T T 11:21p		T 2:14a		T G G 2:13a		G C C 1:17a		C L L 1:39a		L V V	V Li 9:47a

Grid 2

16	17	18	19	20	21	22	23	24	25	26	27	28	29	30	31
A	A T T 7:40a	T G G 12:22p		G C C 1:35p		C L L 12:45p		L V V 12:05p		V L L 7:41a		L S S 7:26p		S	
G	G C C 10:57a	C L L 11:34p		L V V 11:21p		V L L 12:22a		L S S 4:29a		S Sg 12:36p					
G	G C C 6:36a	C L L 7:52a		L V V 9:08a		V L L 10:50a		L S S 7:35p		S Sg Sg 9:35p		Sg	Sg Cp Cp 7:58p		
L	L V V 4:21p	V L L 7:25p		L S S 11:55p		S 6:45a		S Sg Sg 4:28p		Sg Cp Cp	Cp 4:26a	Cp Aq Aq			
V	V L L 1:47a	L S S 7:22a		S Sg Sg 2:54p		Sg 12:35a		Sg Cp Cp 12:18p		Cp Aq Aq	Aq 12:50a	Aq P P	P A 12:04p		
S	S Sg Sg 9:06p	Sg Cp Cp 7:34a		Cp 7:24p		Cp Aq Aq		Aq 8:04a		Aq P P 8:02p		P A A	A T 5:13a		
Sg	Sg Cp Cp 1:44p	Cp 1:44a		Cp Aq Aq 2:23p		Aq P P	P 2:41a		P A A 12:57p		A T T 7:37p		T G G	G C 10:17p	
Cp Aq Aq 7:42a		Aq P P 8:20p		P 8:30a		P A A 7:07p		A T T 2:57a		T 7:18a	T G G 8:31a		G C C		C L L	
P	P A A 2:29p	A 12:40a		A T T 8:41a		T G G 2:05p		G C C 4:56p		C L L 6:02p		L V V 6:41p		V L	
A	A T T 7:08a	T G G 2:20p		G C C 7:32p		C L L 11:06p		L 1:40a		L V V 3:49		V L L 6:34a		L S S	
G	G 1:41a	G C C 4:32a		C L L 7:17a		L V V 10:32a		V L L 2:38p		L S S 8:03p		S Sg Sg	Sg		
C	C L L 11:41a	L V V 1:03p		V L L 3:53p		L S S 8:33p		S 3:02a		S Sg Sg 3:02a		Sg Cp Cp	Cp Aq Aq 9:32p		

Grid 3

16	17	18	19	20	21	22	23	24	25	26	27	28	29	30	31
V	V Li Li 10:23p	Li 2:03a		Li S S 8:34a		S Sg Sg 5:29p		Sg Cp Cp 4:17a		Cp 4:34p	Cp Aq Aq		Aq P P	P	
Li S S 9:24a		S Sg Sg 2:33p		Sg Cp Cp 11:06p		Cp 10:13a		Cp Aq Aq 10:45p		Aq P P 11:41a		P	P A		
S	S Sg Sg 10:36p	Sg Cp Cp 5:42a		Cp Aq Aq 4:18p		Aq 4:56a		Aq P P 5:49p		P A A 5:36a		A	A T T		
Sg Cp Cp 2:03p		Cp Aq Aq 11:29p		Aq 11:44a		Aq P P 12:37a		P 12:07a		P A A	A T T		G G	G	
Cp Aq Aq 7:46a		Aq P P 7:21p		P 7:13a		P A A 7:46p		A T T 4:28a		T 10:26a	T G G 2:34p		G C C		C L L
P	P A A 4:12p	A 4:08a		A T T 1:01p		T G G 6:27p		G C C 9:28p		C L L 11:37p		L V V		V	
A	A T T 12:27a	T G G 10:09p		G 3:55a		G C C 6:27a		C L L 7:22a		L V V 7:09a		V Li Li 11:00a		Li S S	
T G G 6:43a		G C C 1:39a		C L L 4:45p		L V V 5:16p		V Li Li 5:06p		Li S S 6:02p		S Sg Sg 9:27p		Sg 11:00a	Sg Cp
C	C L L 2:47a	L V V 4:06a		V Li Li 3:44a		Li S S 3:28a		S Sg Sg 5:12a		Sg Cp Cp 10:17a		Cp Aq Aq 7:03p				
L V V 2:03p		V Li Li 2:43p		Li S S 2:27p		S Sg Sg 3:07p		Sg Cp Cp 6:34p		Cp 2:01a	Cp Aq Aq 1:06p		Aq P P	P	
Li 12:59a		Li S S 1:52a		S Sg Sg 3:20a		Sg Cp Cp 10:37p		Cp Aq Aq 8:40p		Aq P P 9:21a		P 10:00p	P A A	A T	
S Sg Sg 11:28a		Sg Cp Cp 2:36p		Cp Aq Aq 8:10p		Aq 5:14a		Aq P P 5:23p		P A A 6:13a		A T T 5:02p		T G G	

1923

	1	2	3	4	5	6	7	8	9	10	11	12	13	14	15
Jan	G 12:39a	G	C C 5:34a	C	L L 8:59a	L	V V 11:59a	V	Li Li 3:05p	Li	S S 6:34p	S	Sg Sg 10:57p	Sg	Sg Cp Cp
Feb	L 5:12p	L	V V 6:38p	V	Li Li 8:37p	Li	S S	S	S Sg Sg 12:00a	Sg Cp 5:06a	Cp	Cp Aq Aq 12:19p	Aq	Aq P 9:44p
Mar	L 3:41a	L	V V 4:01a	V	Li Li 4:17a	Li	S S 6:06a	S	S Sg Sg 10:35a	Sg Cp 6:02p	Cp	Cp Aq Aq	Aq	Aq P 4:06a
Apr	Li 2:26p	Li	S S 2:35p	S	Sg Sg 5:20p	Sg	Sg Cp Cp 11:50p	Cp Aq Aq	Aq	Aq P P 9:51a	P	P A A 10:09p	A	A
May	S 1:00a	S	Sg Sg 2:16a	Sg Cp Cp 7:05a	Cp Aq Aq 4:00p	Aq P P	P	P 4:13a	P A A	A 5:13p	A T T	T	T
Jn	Cp 4:05p	Cp Aq Aq 11:44p	Aq P P	P 11:03a	P A A	A 11:56p	A T T	T	T 12:03p	T G G	G 10:09p	G C C
Jly	Aq 8:28a	Aq P P 6:51p	P A A	A 7:25a	A T T 7:37p	T G G	G 5:33a	G C C	C L L 12:53p
Aug	P A A 3:12a	A T T 3:22p	T	T G G 3:47a	G C C 2:07p	C L L 9:19p	L	L V V 1:43a	V Li 4:27a
Sep	T 11:50a	T G G 10:58p	G C C	C 6:56a	C L L 11:16a	L V V 1:02p	V	V Li Li 1:47p	Li S S 3:04p	S Sg
Oct	G 7:00a	G C C 4:14p	C L L 9:40p	L V V 11:35p	V	V Li Li 11:25p	Li S S 11:09p	S	S Sg Sg	Sg	Sg Cp 12:44a
Nov	L 7:07a	L L 10:23a	L V V 10:37a	V Li Li 9:37a	Li S S 9:38a	S	S Sg Sg 12:41p	Sg Cp Cp 7:47p	Cp Aq Aq	Aq P
Dec	V 7:24a	V Li Li 9:14p	Li S S 8:57p	S Sg Sg 8:32p	Sg Cp Cp 10:11p	Cp Aq Aq	Aq	Aq P P 3:37a	P A 1:09p

1924

	1	2	3	4	5	6	7	8	9	10	11	12	13	14	15
Jan	Li 5:22a	S S 6:48a	S Sg 7:22a	Sg Cp Cp	Cp	Cp Aq Aq 8:55a	Aq P P 1:15p	P A A 9:23p	A	A T T 8:49a
Feb	Sg Cp Cp 4:03a	Cp Aq Aq 6:43p	Aq P P 11:13p	P	P A A 6:37a	A T T 5:10p	T	T G G 5:35a	G C 5:33p
Mar	Cp 2:12a	Cp Aq Aq 7:45a	Aq P P 3:27p	P A A	A 1:36a	A T T 1:44p	T G G	G 2:07a	G C C
Apr	P 10:46p	P A A 9:12a	A	A T T 9:13p	T G G 9:53a	G C C 9:15p	C	C L L	L	L V 5:21a
May	A 3:37p	A T T 10:27p	T	T G G 3:48a	G C C 4:31a	C	C L L 4:30a	L V V 1:56p	V Li Li 7:28p
Jn	T G G 9:48a	G C C 10:27p	C	C L L 10:29a	L V V 8:40p	V	V Li Li 3:40a	Li S S 6:57a	S Sg 7:17a
Jly	G C C 4:28a	C L L 4:11a	L	L V V 2:15a	V Li Li 9:54a	Li S S 2:35p	S	S Sg Sg 4:31p	Sg Cp 4:49p
Aug	L 8:05a	L V V 3:19p	V Li Li 8:24p	Li S S 11:31p	S Sg Sg	Sg 1:20a	Sg Cp Cp 2:52a	Cp Aq Aq 5:29a	Aq P
Sep	Li 1:54a	Li	Li S S 5:00a	S Sg Sg 7:41a	Sg Cp Cp 10:33a	Cp Aq Aq 2:17p	Aq	Aq P P 7:42p	P A A
Oct	S 10:54a	S Sg Sg 1:03p	Sg Cp Cp 4:20p	Cp Aq Aq 9:07p	Aq P P	P 3:31a	P A A 11:51a	A T T	T G 10:23p
Nov	Cp 9:54p	Cp Aq Aq 2:35a	Aq P P 9:40a	P A A 6:44p	A T T 5:35a	T G G 5:57p	G C C
Dec	Aq 8:39a	Aq P P 3:12p	P A A 12:34a	A	A T T 11:53a	T G G 12:21a	G	G C C 1:13p	C L L

1925

	1	2	3	4	5	6	7	8	9	10	11	12	13	14	15
Jan	A 6:31a	A	A T T 5:53p	T G G 6:33a	G	G C C 7:14p	C L L 6:55a	L	L V V 4:32p	V Li
Feb	T 12:33a	T G G 1:11p	G C C 1:49a	C	C L L 1:00p	L V V 10:06p	V Li Li 4:54a	Li	Li S S
Mar	T G G 8:27a	G C C 8:38p	C	C L L 9:22a	L V V 8:24p	V	V Li Li 4:43a	Li S S 10:37a	S Sg 2:51p
Apr	C 5:32p	C L L 4:54a	L	L V V 1:03p	V Li Li 6:04p	Li S S 9:05p	S Sg Sg 11:32p	Sg Cp Cp	Cp
May	L 1:37p	L V V 10:25p	V	V Li 3:21a	Li 5:27a	Li S S 6:30a	S Sg Sg 8:09a	Sg Cp Cp 11:24a	Cp Aq Aq	Aq P
Jn	V 7:30a	V Li Li 1:20p	Li S S 3:33p	S Sg Sg 3:45p	Sg Cp Cp 3:54p	Cp Aq Aq 5:41p	Aq P P 10:04p	P A A	A
Jly	S 1:54a	S	S Sg Sg 3:33p	Sg Cp Cp 2:24a	Cp Aq Aq 1:50a	Aq P P 2:07a	P A A 4:54a	A T T 11:06a	T G 8:38p
Aug	Sg Cp Cp 12:46a	Cp Aq Aq 12:41a	Aq P P 12:24p	P A A 1:48p	A T T 6:25p	T	T G G 2:58a	G C C 2:39p
Sep	Aq P P 11:03p	P 12:03a	P A A 3:29a	A T T 10:40a	T G G 9:35p	G C C 8:30a	C	C L L	L V 10:56p
Oct	P A A 10:06a	A T T 1:21p	T G G 7:35p	G	G C C 5:33a	C L L 6:09p	L	L V V 6:44a	V Li 4:57p
Nov	T 4:45a	T G G 2:07p	G C C 2:16a	C	C L L 3:06p	L V V 1:51a	V	V Li Li 9:05a	Li S S
Dec	G C C 10:19a	C	C L L 10:13a	L V V 11:13p	V	V Li Li 10:51a	Li S S 7:04p	S Sg Sg 11:22p	Sg

```
 16    17      18      19    20      21      22    23      24      25      26    27      28      29      30      31
```

Block 1

```
 16      17           18         19    20           21         22    23           24           25
Cp     Cp Aq Aq     Aq P P      P     P A A        A T T      T     T G G        G C C        C L
       5:06a        1:58p             1:38a        2:33p            2:06a        10:18a       2:56p

P      P            P A A       A T T      T     T G G        G C C        C     C L
       9:20a        10:15p            10:30a       7:57p            1:29a

P      P A A        A           A T T      T G G        G     G C C        C L L        L V V        V Li
       4:06p        5:00a             5:33p   4:05a            11:12a       2:35p        3:06p

A T T        T G G        G     G C C        C L L        L V V        V     V Li Li     Li S
11:07a       11:33p            10:27a       6:51p        11:55p             1:48a        1:33a

T G G        G C C        C     C L L        L V V        V P Li       Li S S       S Sg Sg      Sg Cp
5:27a        4:03p             12:40a       6:54a        10:24a       11:23a       11:36a       12:28p

C      C L L        L V V       V Li Li      Li S S       S Sg Sg      Sg Cp Cp     Cp     Cp Aq
       6:12a        12:22p      4:44p        7:21p        8:47p        10:20p              1:45a

L V V        V Li Li      Li    Li S S       S Sg Sg      Sg Cp Cp     Cp Aq Aq     Aq P P       P
6:10p        10:05p            1:08a        3:43a        6:33a        10:43a       5:24p

Li     Li S S       S Sg Sg      Sg Cp Cp     Cp Aq Aq     Aq    Aq P P       P A A        A T T
       6:38a        9:12a        12:50p       6:03p              1:26a        11:15a       11:12p

Sg     Sg Cp Cp     Cp Aq Aq     Aq    Aq P P       P A A        A T T        T G G
       6:14p        11:54p             8:03p        6:24p        6:23a        7:06p

Cp     Cp Aq Aq     Aq P P       P     P A A        A T T        T     T G G        G C C        C L
       5:30a        1:44p              12:34a       12:48p             1:29a        1:39p        11:59p

P      P A A        A T T        T     T G G        G C C        C     C L L        L V
       6:25a        6:53p              7:32a        7:28p              6:01a        2:17p

A      A            A T T        T G G        G     G C C        C L L        L V V        V     V Li Li
1:22a               2:03p        1:39a             11:39a       7:51p             1:50a
```

Block 2

```
 16      17      18      19    20           21         22    23           24           25      26
T G G        G     G C C        C L L        L     L V V        V Li Li      Li S S       S Sg Sg
9:28p        9:05a             6:33p              1:48a        7:14a        11:06a       1:52p

C      C            C L L        L V V        V Li Li      Li S S       S Sg Sg      Sg Cp Cp
3:08a               9:45a        1:57p        4:47p        7:16p        10:13p

C L L        L V V        V Li Li      Li    Li S S       S Sg Sg      Sg Cp Cp     Cp Aq Aq     Aq P
12:30p       7:27p        11:00a             10:07a       1:30a        3:38a        7:47a        2:14p

V      V Li Li      Li S S       S Sg Sg      Sg Cp Cp     Cp Aq Aq     Aq P P       P A
9:26a        10:24a       10:05a       10:34a       1:31p        7:39p        4:40a

Li S S       S Sg Sg      Sg Cp Cp     Cp Aq Aq     Aq    Aq P P       P A A        A T T        T
9:10p        8:34p        7:49p        9:05p              1:51a        10:37a       9:23p

Sg     Sg Cp Cp     Cp Aq Aq     Aq P P       P A A        A     A T T        T G G        G
       6:29a        6:42a        9:53a        4:57p              3:28a        3:51a

Cp Aq Aq     Aq P P       P     P A A        A T T        T G G        G     G C C        C L L
5:12p        7:31p              1:14a        10:37a       10:37p             11:11a       10:38p

P      P A A        A T T        T     T G G        G C C        C     C L L        L V V        V Li
10:33a       6:54p              6:15a        6:48p              6:19a        3:18p        9:37p

A T T        T G G        G     G C C        C L L        L     L V V        V Li Li      Li S
3:40a        2:25p             2:54a        2:52p              12:05a       5:56a        9:00a

G      G C C        C L L        L     L V V        V Li Li      Li S S       S Sg Sg      Sg Cp
       10:48a       11:21p             9:32a        3:48p        6:26p        7:03p        7:39p

C      C L L        L V V        V     V Li Li      Li S S       S Sg Sg      Sg Cp Cp     Cp Aq
6:51a        6:11p              1:50a        5:17a        5:30a        4:57a        5:26a

L      L V V        V Li Li      Li S S       S Sg Sg      Sg Cp Cp     Cp Aq Aq     Aq P P       P A
1:06a        10:14a       3:24p        4:55p        4:18p        3:42p        5:07p        9:58p
```

Block 3

```
 16      17      18      19    20           21         22    23           24           25      26
Li     Li S S       S     S Sg Sg      Sg Cp Cp     Cp Aq Aq     Aq P P       P A A        A T T
       11:10p       2:33a        3:22a        3:09a        3:47a        6:59a        1:59p

S Sg Sg      Sg Cp Cp     Cp Aq Aq     Aq P P       P A A        A T T        T
9:27a        12:02a       1:21p        2:37p        5:22p        11:05p

Sg     Sg Cp Cp     Cp Aq Aq     Aq P P       P     P A A        A T T        T G G        G C
       6:07p        8:51p        11:34p             3:05a        8:35a        5:08p        4:43a

Cp Aq Aq     Aq P P       P A A        A T T        T     T G G        G C C        C     C L
2:08a        6:03a        10:45a       5:00p              1:34a        12:46p              1:36a

P      P A A        A T T        T     T G G        G C C        C     C L L        L V V
4:35p        11:42p             8:51a        8:08p              8:58a        9:35p

A T T        T G G        G     G C C        C L L        L     L V V        V Li Li      Li S
5:16a        2:58p             2:37a        3:31p              4:21a        3:14p        10:31p

G      G C C        C L L        L     L V V        V Li Li      Li    Li S S       S Sg Sg
       8:33a        9:32p             10:17a       9:29p              5:56a        10:55a

C      C L L        L V V        V     V Li Li      Li S S       S Sg Sg      Sg Cp Cp     Cp Aq Aq
3:41a        4:12p              3:05a        11:44a       5:50p        9:19p        10:41p

V      V            V Li Li      Li S S       S Sg Sg      Sg    Sg Cp Cp     Cp Aq Aq     Aq P P
9:18a               5:18p        11:17p       3:36a              6:29a        8:19a

Li     Li           Li S S       S Sg Sg      Sg Cp Cp     Cp Aq Aq     Aq    Aq P P       P A A        A T T
12:12a              5:11a        8:57a        12:12p       3:14p              6:24p        10:30p

S Sg Sg      Sg Cp Cp     Cp Aq Aq     Aq P P       P     P A A        A T T        T G G
1:12p        3:38p        5:48p        8:38p              12:32a       5:46a        12:51p

Sg Cp Cp     Cp Aq Aq     Aq P P       P A A        A T T        T G G        G     G C C        C L
12:50a       1:36a        2:52a        5:58a        11:26a       7:19p             5:27a        5:27p
```

1926

	1	2	3	4	5	6	7	8	9	10	11	12	13	14	15
Jan	L	L	L	V V	V	Li	Li	Li	Li	S S	S	Sg Sg	Sg	Cp Cp	Cp Aq Aq
		6:26a		6:44p		4:18a			10:01a		12:08p		12:07p		
Feb	V	V Li Li		Li S S		S	Sg	Sg		Sg Cp	Cp	Cp Aq Aq		Aq P P	P A A
	1:10a		11:38a		7:02p		10:48p		11:37p		10:57p		10:49p		
Mar	V	Li Li		Li S S		S	Sg	Sg		Sg Cp Cp	Cp	Aq P P		P A A	
	7:03a		5:28p		1:39a		7:07a		9:39a		10:03a		9:52a		
Apr	S	S Sg	Sg		Sg Cp Cp	Cp	Aq Aq		Aq P P		P A A		A T T		T G
	7:08a		1:04p		5:00p		7:04p		8:03p		9:32p				1:22a
May	Sg Cp Cp		Cp Aq Aq		Aq		Aq P P		P A A		A T T		T G G		G C C
	6:32p		10:31p			1:32a		3:55a		6:33a		10:47a		5:53p	
Jn	Aq		Aq P P		P A A		A T T		T G G		G		G C C		C L L	L
	6:53a		9:46a			1:29p		6:43p			2:16a		12:30p		
Jly	P A A		A T T		T		T G G		G C C		C L L	L		L V V	V Li
	3:15p		6:59p		12:58a		9:17a		7:51p				8:08a		8:52p
Aug	T		T G G		G C C		C		C L L		L V V	V		V Li Li	Li S S
	6:25a		3:09p			2:13a		2:39p				3:26a		3:17p	
Sep	C		C C		C L L		L V V		V Li Li		Li S S		S	S Sg Sg	Sg Cp
	8:01a		8:40p			9:23a		9:15p			7:21a			2:36p
Oct	L	L		L V V		V Li Li		Li S S		S Sg Sg		Sg Cp Cp		Cp Aq
		2:49a		3:28p		2:58a		12:53p		8:46p				2:01a
Nov	V Li Li		Li	Li S S		S Sg Sg		Sg		Sg Cp Cp	Cp Aq Aq		Aq P P		P A
	10:22p		9:37a		6:51p		2:10a		7:42a		11:21a		1:28p	
Dec	Li S S		S	S Sg Sg		Sg Cp Cp		Cp Aq Aq		Aq P P		P A A		A T T
	5:39p		2:31a		8:52a		1:21p		4:44p		7:33p		10:23p	

1927

	1	2	3	4	5	6	7	8	9	10	11	12	13	14	15
Jan	Sg	Sg Cp Cp		Cp Aq Aq		Aq P P		P		P A A		A T T		T G G	G C
	5:51p		9:10p		11:06p			1:00a		3:56a		8:31a		3:00p
Feb	Cp Aq Aq		Aq P P		P A A		A T T		T G G		G C C		C	C L L
	7:22a		8:07a		8:20a		9:51a		1:56p		8:51p			6:12a
Mar	Aq		Aq P P		P A A		A T T		T G G	G		G C C		C L L	L V
	7:06p		6:19p		6:07p		8:30p			2:31a		11:52a		11:23p
Apr	P A A		A T T		T G G		G C C		C L L	L		L V V	V Li Li
	5:30a		4:37a		5:26a		9:43a		6:00p		5:19a		5:54p	
May	T		T G G		G C C		C		C L L		L V V	V		V Li Li	Li S S
	3:53p		6:52p			1:40a		12:04p			12:27a		12:52p	
Jn	G C C		C L L		L V V		V	V Li Li		Li S S		S	S Sg Sg	Sg
	4:51a		10:38a		7:56p			7:50a		8:16p			7:16a		3:51p
Jly	L	L		L V V		V Li Li		Li	Li S S		S Sg Sg		Sg	Sg Cp Cp	Cp Aq
		4:28a		3:48p		4:17a		3:36p			12:05a		5:31a
Aug	V Li Li		Li	Li S S		S	S Sg Sg		Sg Cp Cp		Cp Aq Aq		Aq P P	P A
	11:44p		12:16p		12:13a		9:22a		2:45p		5:04p		5:57p
Sep	S	S		S Sg Sg		Sg Cp Cp		Cp		Cp Aq Aq		Aq P P		P A A	A T T
	8:10a		6:28p			12:48a		3:15a		3:18a		3:04a		
Oct	Sg	Sg		Sg Cp Cp		Cp Aq Aq		Aq P P		P A A		A T T		T G G	G C
	2:12a		10:06a		1:49p		2:14p		1:18p		1:13p		3:51p
Nov	Cp Aq Aq		Aq P P		P		P A A		A T T		T G G		G C C		C L L
	5:26p		10:55p		12:53a		12:37a		12:04a		1:17a		5:49a	
Dec	Aq P P		P A A		A T T		T G G		G C C		C L L		L V V	V
	5:36a		9:20a		10:46a		11:11a		12:12p		3:33p		10:26p

1928

	1	2	3	4	5	6	7	8	9	10	11	12	13	14	15
Jan	A T T		T G G		G C C		C		C L L		L V V	V Li Li		Li	Li S
	6:15p		8:20p		10:28p			1:53a		7:54a		5:18p		5:27a
Feb	G	G C C		C L L		L S S		S	S Li Li		Li S S		S	S Sg Sg
	6:22a		10:53a		5:10p		2:04a		1:42			2:32		
Mar	C	C L L		L	L V V		V Li Li		Li S S		S	S Sg Sg	Sg Cp Cp
	5:39p		12:52a		10:05a		9:31p			10:24a		10:32p	
Apr	L V V		V Li Li		Li	Li S S		S Sg Sg		Sg	Sg Cp	Cp	Cp Aq Aq	Aq P
	6:54a		4:47p		4:28a		5:20p		5:56a		4:06p		10:18p
May	Li	Li	Li S S		S Sg Sg		Sg	Sg Cp Cp		Cp Aq Aq		Aq	Aq P P	P A
	10:38a		11:32p		12:05p		10:57p			6:37a		10:29a
Jn	S	S Sg Sg		Sg Cp Cp		Cp	Cp A Aq		Aq P P		P A A		A T T	T G
	5:38a		6:00p			4:40a		12:53p		6:13p		8:46p		9:24
Jly	Sg	Sg Cp Cp		Cp Aq Aq		Aq P		P	P A A		A T T		T G G	G C
	12:27a		10:32a		6:23p			12:03a		3:49a		6:00a		7:36a
Aug	Aq	Aq	Aq P P		P A A		A T T		T G G		G C C		C L L	L V
		12:34a		5:33		9:18p		12:22p		3:03p		5:57p		10:08p
Sep	P A A		A T T		T G G		G C C		C	C L L		L V V	V Li Li
	12:26p		3:07p		5:43p		8:51p		12:50a		6:02a		1:13p	
Oct	T	T		T	T G G		G C C		C L L		L V V	V Li Li		Li	Li S S
	12:10a			2:22a		6:18a		12:14p		8:15p			6:29a	
Nov	G C C		C L L		L	L V		V	V Li Li		Li S S		S	S Sg Sg	Sg Cp
	9:41a		12:15p		5:42p			2:06a		12:54p			1:20a		2:25p
Dec	L	L		L V V		V Li Li		Li S S		S	S Sg Sg		Sg Cp Cp	Cp	Cp Aq
		12:18a		7:53a		6:46p			7:29a		8:26p			8:35a

```
      16    17    18    19    20    21    22    23    24    25    26    27    28    29    30    31
Aq    P  P     P  A  A     A  T  T     T     T  G  G     G  C  C     C  L  L     L     L  V  V
11:49a   1:05p        5:16p             12:56a   11:31a   11:52p                 12:49p

A     A  T  T     T  G  G     G  C  C     C     C  L  L     L  V  V     V
1:10p    7:22a        5:28p        6:00a              6:59p

A  T  T     T  G  G     G     G  C  C     C  L  L     L     L  V  V     V Li Li     Li     Li S
11:08a   3:43p           12:31a   12:36p        1:36a            1:26p              12:17a

G     G  C  C     C  L  L     L     L  V  V     V Li Li     Li     Li S S     S Sg Sg
8:55a    8:07p              8:59a    8:52p           6:19a          1:18p

C     C  L  L     L  V  V     V     V Li Li     Li S S     S Sg Sg     Sg Cp Cp     Cp Aq
4:21a    7:54a        5:04a          2:41p        9:14p             1:24a            4:19a

L  V  V     V Li Li     Li S S     S     S Sg Sg     Sg Cp Cp     Cp Aq Aq     Aq  P P
12:49a   1:18p       11:39p     6:35a          10:17a         12:01p         1:14p

Li    Li     Li S S     S Sg Sg     Sg Cp Cp     Cp Aq Aq     Aq  P P     P  A A     A     A T
8:07a          8:28p        9:48p          9:46p          10:14p               12:48a

S     S Sg Sg     Sg Cp Cp     Cp Aq Aq     Aq  P P     P  A A     A  T T     T  G G     G C
12:38a   6:23a        8:30a          8:14a          7:30a    8:25a      12:41p     8:49p

Cp    Cp Aq Aq     Aq  P P     P  A A     A  T T     T  G G     G C C     C  L
6:23p    7:07p          6:20p     6:13p      8:51p      8:51p        3:36a        2:11p

Aq    Aq  P P     P  A A     A  T T     T  G G     G C C     C  L L     L     L  V V
4:29a    4:56a          5:02a     6:50a      12:10p    9:31p              9:43a

A     A T T     T  G G     G C C     C     C L L     L  V V     V     V Li Li
2:54p    5:11p        9:55p              6:11a     5:36p        6:14a

T     T G G     G C C     C  LL     L     L  V V     V Li Li     Li     Li S S     S Sg
2:00a    7:20a        3:18p              2:03a     2:31p          2:28a           11:49a
```

```
      16    17    18    19    20    21    22    23    24    25    26    27    28    29    30    31
C     C  L L     L     L  V V     V Li Li     Li     Li S S     S Sg Sg     Sg     Sg Cp
11:32p   10:10a        10:27p           10:54a     9:20p                4:11a

L  V V     V     V Li Li     Li S S     S     S Sg Sg     Sg Cp Cp     Cp Aq
5:16p    5:31a          6:09p       5:34a          1:54p       6:13p

V     V     V Li Li     Li     Li S S     S Sg Sg     Sg Cp Cp     Cp     Cp Aq Aq     Aq  P P
11:40a      12:21a          12:06p     9:38p         3:38a         5:52a

Li    Li S S     S Sg Sg     Sg     Sg Cp Cp     Cp Aq Aq     Aq  P P     P  A A     A  T
6:20a    5:49p          3:35a          10:42a     2:36p        3:43p        3:29p

S     S Sg Sg     Sg Cp Cp     Cp Aq Aq     Aq  P P     P  A A     A     A T T     T  G G
11:57p   9:11a         4:15p          9:01p      11:37p          12:51a       2:03a

Cp    Cp Aq Aq     Aq     Aq  P P     P  A A     A  T T     T  G G     G C C     C  L
10:04p   2:25a             5:29a      7:54a      10:27a       2:04p       7:49p

Aq    Aq  P P     P  A A     A  T T     T  G G     G C C     C     C L L     L  V V
8:43a    10:58a       1:24p      4:47p      9:31p      4:01a        10:43p

A     A T T     T  G G     G     G C C     C L L     L  V V     V     V Li Li     Li S
7:12p    10:09p        3:20a          10:40a     7:56p          7:02a        7:36p

T  G G     G C C     C L L     L     L  V V     V Li Li     Li     Li S S     S Sg
4:30a    8:50a     4:14p          2:02a      1:31p          2:06a        2:54p

C     C     C L L     L  V V     V Li Li     Li     Li S S     S Sg Sg     Sg     Sg Cp Cp
10:08a       7:44a      7:28p          8:08a          8:48a        8:22a

L  V V     V     V Li Li     Li S S     S     S Sg Sg     Sg Cp Cp     Cp Aq Aq     Aq
2:15p    1:41a          2:27p       2:53a          2:00p       11:06p

V Li Li     Li S S     S     S Sg Sg     Sg Cp Cp     Cp     Cp Aq Aq     Aq  P P     P  A A
8:55a    9:31p       9:59a          8:37p          4:54a        11:00a       3:18p
```

```
      16    17    18    19    20    21    22    23    24    25    26    27    28    29    30    31
S     S Sg Sg     Sg     Sg Cp Cp     Cp Aq Aq     Aq  P P     P  A A     A T T     T     T G
6:06p    4:49p           12:27p     5:24p      8:48p        11:43p             2:47a

Sg Cp Cp     Cp Aq Aq     Aq     Aq  P P     P  A A     A  T T     T  G G     G C
1:53a    9:46a             2:05a      4:09       5:42       8:08a      12:05p

Cp    Cp Aq Aq     Aq  P P     P  A A     A  T T     T  G G     G C C     C L L     L
7:31a    12:19p       1:53p      2:06a      2:56p      5:42p      11:05a

P     P     P  A A     A  T T     T  G G     G C C     C L L     L  V V     V Li
12:39a       12:36a       12:10      1:15a      5:12a      12:29p        10:36p

A     A T T     T  G G     G C C     C L L     L     L  V V     V     V Li Li     Li S S
11:25a   10:57a       10:58a     1:18p      7:07p          4:37a        4:41p

G     G C C     C L L     L     L  V V     V Li Li     Li S S     S     S Sg Sg
9:35p    11:03p       3:28p          11:44a     11:17p         12:13p

C     C L L     L  V V     V Li Li     Li     Li S S     S Sg Sg     Sg     Sg Cp Cp     Cp Aq
9:06a    12:54p       8:03p          6:48a          7:34p        7:47a          5:33p

V     V     V Li Li     Li S S     S     S Sg Sg     Sg Cp Cp     Cp     Cp Aq Aq     Aq  P P
4:54a    2:58p          3:29a          3:58p          1:56a        8:30a

Li S S     S     S Sg Sg     Sg     Sg Cp Cp     Cp Aq Aq     Aq  P P     P  A A     A  T
11:05p   11:23a          12:15a     11:00a     6:01p        9:31p        10:00p

S Sg Sg     Sg     Sg Cp Cp     Cp Aq Aq     Aq     Aq  P P     P     A     A T T     T G
6:44p    7:50a          7:33p          3:49a      8:04a        9:16a        9:11a

Cp    Cp     Cp Aq Aq     Aq  P P     P  A A     A  T T     T  G G     G C C     C  L
2:39a    12:18p       6:14p      8:30p      8:23p      7:44p      8:29p

Aq    Aq  P P     P     P  A A     A  T T     T  G G     G C C     C L L     L  V V
6:49p    2:14a          6:25a      7:40a      7:17a      7:07a      9:13a
```

1929

Month	Columns 1–15 (signs)	Times
Jan	V Li Li Li S S S Sg Sg Sg Sg Cp Cp Cp Aq Aq Aq Aq P P	3:09p · 1:10a · 1:50p · 2:51a · 2:32p · 12:21a
Feb	S S Sg Sg Sg Sg Cp Cp Cp Aq Aq Aq Aq P P P P A A T T	8:59p · 10:00a · 9:34p · 6:43a · 1:41p · 7:02p
Mar	S S Sg Sg Sg Cp Cp Cp Cp Aq Aq Aq Aq P P P A A A A T T	5:03a · 5:55p · 5:44a · 2:44p · 8:51p · 1:05a
Apr	Sg Cp Cp Cp Aq Aq Aq Aq P P P P A A A T T T G G G C C	2:03a · 2:18p · 11:52p · 5:58a · 9:17a · 11:13a · 1:05p
May	Aq Aq Aq P P P P A A A T T T G G G C C C L L L	8:51a · 3:51p · 7:18p · 8:22p · 8:44p · 10:03p
Jn	P P A A A T T T G G G C C C L L L V V V Li Li	12:58a · 5:34a · 6:57a · 6:35a · 6:25a · 8:20a · 1:39p
Jly	A T T T G G G C C C L L L V V V Li Li Li Li S S	2:32p · 5:14p · 5:21p · 4:37p · 5:10p · 8:54p · 4:45a
Aug	G G C C C L L L V V V Li Li Li S S S Sg Sg Sg Sg Cp	3:15a · 3:11a · 3:23a · 5:56a · 12:22p · 10:45p · 11:21a
Sep	L L V V V Li Li Li S S S Sg Sg Sg Cp Cp Cp Cp Aq Aq	1:27p · 3:51p · 9:21p · 6:39a · 6:45p · 7:17a
Oct	V V Li Li L S S S Sg Sg Sg Sg Cp Cp Cp Aq Aq Aq Aq P P	1:10a · 6:40a · 3:19p · 2:49a · 3:25p · 2:40a
Nov	S S Sg Sg Sg Sg Cp Cp Cp Aq Aq Aq Aq P P P A A A A T	11:47p · 10:57a · 11:33p · 11:30a · 8:43p · 2:19a
Dec	Sg Sg Cp Cp Cp Cp Aq Aq Aq P P P P A A A T T T G G	6:25p · 6:58a · 7:27p · 5:57a · 12:50p · 3:49p

1930

Month	Columns 1–15 (signs)	Times
Jan	Cp Aq Aq Aq Aq P P P A A A T T T T G G G C C C L	1:30p · 2:04a · 1:27a · 9:58p · 2:47a · 3:34a · 2:37a
Feb	P P A A A A T T T G G G C C C L L L V V V Li	7:23p · 4:48a · 11:07a · 1:54p · 2:00p · 1:15p · 1:52p
Mar	P P A A A T T T G G G C C C L L L V V V V Li	1:08a · 10:18a · 5:16p · 9:34p · 11:25p · 11:54p · 12:44a
Apr	T T G G G C C C L L L V V V Li Li Li S S S Sg	10:42p · 3:11a · 6:09a · 8:11a · 10:17a · 1:46p · 7:50p
May	G G C C C L L L V V V Li Li Li S S S S Sg Sg Sg Cp	8:54a · 11:32a · 2:11p · 5:30p · 10:07p · 4:39a · 1:40p
Jn	L L V V V Li Li Li S S S Sg Sg Sg Cp Cp Cp Cp Aq Aq	7:37p · 11:05p · 4:31a · 11:57a · 9:21p · 8:39a
Jly	V V Li Li Li S S S Sg Sg Sg Sg Cp Cp Cp Aq Aq Aq Aq P P	4:48a · 9:57a · 5:50p · 3:50a · 3:23p · 3:57a
Aug	S S Sg Sg Sg Sg Cp Cp Cp Aq Aq Aq Aq P P P A A A A T	11:25p · 9:35a · 9:27p · 10:03a · 10:32p · 9:37a
Sep	Sg Cp Cp Cp Cp Aq Aq Aq P P P P A A A T T T T G G	3:36p · 3:28a · 4:08p · 4:21a · 3:18p · 12:00a
Oct	Cp Aq Aq Aq P P P P A A A T T T T G G G C C C L	10:10a · 10:48p · 10:51a · 9:14p · 5:29a · 11:29a · 3:19p
Nov	P P A A A A T T T G G G C C C L L L V V V	6:35p · 4:37a · 11:58a · 5:05p · 8:45p · 11:41p
Dec	A A T T T G G G G C C C L L L V V V Li Li Li S	1:31p · 8:32p · 12:31a · 2:53a · 5:04a · 8:05a · 12:20p

1931

Month	Columns 1–15 (signs)	Times
Jan	T G G G C C C L L L V V V Li Li Li S S S Sg Sg Sg	6:34a · 10:20a · 11:32a · 12:07p · 1:49p · 5:41p · 11:51p
Feb	C L L L V V V Li Li Li S S S Sg Sg Sg Cp Cp Cp Cp Aq	10:24p · 9:57p · 9:55p · 12:06a · 5:22a · 1:40p · 12:15a
Mar	C L L L V V V Li Li Li S S S Sg Sg Sg Cp Cp Cp Cp Aq Aq	9:24a · 9:21a · 8:33a · 9:03a · 12:32p · 7:39p · 6:04a
Apr	V Li Li Li S S S Sg Sg Sg Sg Cp Cp Cp Aq Aq Aq Aq P P P A	7:49p · 7:51p · 9:53p · 3:22a · 12:43p · 12:49a · 1:48p
May	Li S S S Sg Sg Sg Cp Cp Cp Aq Aq Aq Aq P P P A A A A T	6:26a · 8:14a · 12:37p · 8:37p · 8:02a · 8:57p · 8:54a
Jn	Sg Cp Cp Cp Cp Aq Aq Aq P P P P A A A T T T T G G	10:08p · 5:24a · 4:01p · 4:44a · 4:54p · 2:21a
Jly	Cp Aq Aq Aq Aq P P P A A A A T T T G G G C C C L	1:57p · 12:10a · 12:40p · 1:13a · 11:13a · 5:30p · 8:41p
Aug	P P A A A A T T T G G G G C C C L L L V V	8:10p · 9:05a · 8:01p · 3:09 · 6:31a · 7:25p
Sep	A T T T T G G G C C C L L L V V V Li Li Li S S	3:59p · 3:43a · 12:13p · 4:47p · 6:04p · 5:43p · 5:41p
Oct	G G G C C C C L L L V V V Li Li Li S S S Sg Sg	10:03a · 7:37p · 1:48a · 4:34a · 4:50a · 4:19a · 4:52a
Nov	C C L L L V V V Li Li Li Li S S S Sg Sg Sg Cp Cp Cp Aq Aq	8:38a · 1:07p · 3:02p · 3:21p · 3:39p · 5:53p · 11:42p
Dec	L V V V Li Li Li Li S S S Sg Sg Sg Cp Cp Cp Aq Aq Aq P P	7:17p · 10:44p · 12:43a · 2:04a · 4:18a · 9:11a · 5:51p

```
      16    17    18    19    20    21    22    23    24    25    26    27    28    29    30    31

P     A A   A T T   T G G   G C C   C L L   L V V   V     V Li Li   Li S
8:07a   1:37p   4:43p   5:52p   6:17   7:47p   12:19a   8:57a

T G G   G   G C C   C L L   L V V   V Li Li   Li S S
11:02p   1:45a   3:41a   5:59a   10:15a   5:54p

T G G   G C C   C L L   L V V   V Li Li   Li   Li S S   S Sg  Sg   Sg
4:23a   7:24a   10:27a   2:05p   7:12p   2:50a   1:26p

C L L   L V V   V   V Li Li   Li S S   S Sg  Sg   Sg   Sg Cp  Cp   Cp Aq
3:51p   8:06p   2:14a   10:36a   9:16p   9:43a   10:19p

L V V   V Li Li   Li S S   S   S Sg  Sg   Sg Cp  Cp   Cp   Cp Aq  Aq   Aq P P
1:34a   7:53a   4:54p   4:04a   4:34p   5:17a   4:37p

Li S S   S   S Sg  Sg   Sg Cp  Cp   Cp   Cp Aq  Aq   A P P   P   P A A
10:33p   10:03a   10:45p   11:24a   10:59a   8:21a

S Sg  Sg   Sg   Sg Cp  Cp   Cp Aq  Aq   Aq   Aq P P   P A A   A T T   T   T G
4:00p   4:48a   5:20p   4:39a   2:13p   9:25p   1:43a

Cp   Cp Aq  Aq   Aq   Aq P P   P A A   A   A T T   T G G   G C C   C L
11:50p   10:46a   7:47p   2:55a   8:03a   11:04a   12:57p

Aq P P   P   P A A   A T T   T G G   G C C   C L L   L V V
6:07p   2:30a   8:45a   1:25p   4:52p   7:28p   8:52p

P A A   A T T   T G G   G C C   C   C L L   L V V   V Li Li   Li S
11:02a   4:29a   7:54p   10:24p   12:55a   4:09a   8:39a   3:02a

T   T G G   G C C   C L L   L V V   V Li Li   Li S S   S Sg
4:53a   5:53a   6:58a   9:32a   2:23p   9:40p   7:08a

G C C   C L L   L V V   V Li Li   Li   Li S S   S Sg  Sg   Sg Cp  Cp
4:05p   3:35p   4:22p   8:03p   3:12a   1:12p   12:56a
```

```
      16    17    18    19    20    21    22    23    24    25    26    27    28    29    30    31

L     L V V   V Li Li   Li S S   S Sg  Sg   Sg   Sg Cp  Cp   Cp Aq  Aq   Aq   Aq P
1:58a   3:46a   9:26a   6:56p   6:53a   7:33p   7:59a

Li   Li S S   S   S Sg  Sg   Sg Cp  Cp   Cp   Cp Aq  Aq   Aq P P
5:45p   1:50a   1:13p   1:57a   2:13p

Li   Li S S   S Sg  Sg   Sg Cp  Cp   Cp   Cp Aq  Aq   Aq P P   P   P A A   A T
3:47a   10:25a   8:41p   9:05a   9:23a   8:00a   4:20p

Sg   Sg   Sg Cp  Cp   Cp Aq  Aq   Aq   Aq P P   P A A   A   A T T   T G
5:08a   4:59p   5:23a   4:09p   12:07a   5:26a

Cp   Cp   Cp Aq  Aq   Aq P P   P   P A A   A T T   T G G   G C C   C L
1:04a   1:34p   12:55a   9:15a   2:06p   4:26p   5:45p

Ap P P   P   P A A   A T T   T G G   G G C C   C L L   L V
9:12p   9:14a   6:35p   11:59p   1:57a   2:06a   2:29a

P A A   A   A T T   T G G   G C C   C L L   L V V   V Li Li   Li S
4:26p   2:53a   9:38a   12:21p   12:19p   11:35a   12:19p   4:08p

T   T G G   G C C   C L L   L V V   V Li Li   Li   Li S S   S Sg  Sg
5:46p   10:01p   10:57p   10:14p   9:59p   12:12a   6:05a

G C C   C L L   L V V   V Li Li   Li S S   S Sg  Sg   Sg Cp  Cp   Cp
5:42a   8:18a   8:45a   8:44a   10:08a   2:36p   10:49p

L   L V V   V Li Li   Li S S   S   S Sg  Sg   Sg Cp  Cp   Cp Aq  Aq   Aq   Aq P
5:26p   6:43p   8:33p   12:25a   7:27a   5:54p   6:23a

V Li Li   Li S S   S Sg  Sg   Sg Cp  Cp   Cp   Cp Aq  Aq   Aq P P   P   P A
2:27a   5:37a   10:01a   1:40p   2:24a   2:33p   3:06a

S   S Sg  Sg   Sg   Sg Cp  Cp   Cp Aq  Aq   Aq P P   P   P A A   A T T   T
5:55p   1:12a   10:44a   10:36a   11:29a   10:51a
```

```
      16    17    18    19    20    21    22    23    24    25    26    27    28    29    30    31

Sg Cp  Cp   Cp Aq  Aq   Aq   Aq P P   P A A   A T T   T   T G G   G C C
8:02a   6:04p   5:55a   6:55p   7:10p   4:17p   9:09p

Aq   Aq P P   P   P A A   A T T   T   T G G   G C C
12:24p   1:21a   1:53p   12:12a   6:47a

Aq P P   P   P A A   A T T   T   T G G   G C C   C L L   L V V
6:27p   7:24a   7:44p   6:19a   2:03p   6:29p   7:58p

A   A   A T T   T G G   G C C   C   C L L   L V V   V Li Li
1:50a   11:55a   7:42p   1:03a   4:09a   5:35a

T   T G G   G C C   C L L   L V V   V Li Li   Li S S   S   S Sg  Sg
6:26p   1:25a   6:27a   10:07a   12:51p   3:08p   5:48p

G C C   C L L   L V V   V Li Li   Li S S   S   S Sg  Sg   Sg Cp  Cp
8:38a   12:36p   3:32p   6:23p   9:35p   1:27a   6:35a

L   L V V   V   V Li Li   Li S S   S Sg  Sg   Sg Cp  Cp   Cp Aq  Aq   Aq   Aq P
10:22p   12:07a   2:57a   7:19a   1:23p   9:25p   7:46a

V Li Li   Li S S   S Sg  Sg   Sg Cp  Cp   Cp   Cp Aq  Aq   Aq P P   P   P A A
7:45a   9:11a   12:48p   6:58p   3:38a   2:28p   2:57a

S Sg  Sg   Sg   Sg Cp  Cp   Cp Aq  Aq   Aq P P   P   P A A   A T T   T
7:40p   12:49a   9:18a   8:29p   9:09a   10:07p

Sg Cp  Cp   Cp Aq  Aq   Aq   Aq P P   P A A   A   A T T   T G G   G   G C
8:19a   3:40p   2:33a   3:21p   4:12a   3:47p   1:26a

Aq   Aq P P   P A A   A   A T T   T G G   G   G C C   C L L
9:33a   10:09p   10:59a   10:11p   7:09a   2:05p

P   P A A   A T T   T   T G G   G C C   C L L   L   L V V   V Li
5:50a   6:45p   5:59a   2:21p   8:16p   12:40a   4:17a
```

1932

	1	2	3	4	5	6	7	8	9	10	11	12	13	14	15
Jan	Li	Li	S S	S Sg	Sg	Sg Cp	Cp	Cp Aq	Aq	Aq	Aq P	P	P A	A	A
	7:24a		10:16a	1:37p		6:44p					2:50a		2:07p		
Feb	Sg	Sg Cp	Cp	Cp.	Cp Aq	Aq	Aq P	P	P A	A	A	A T	T	T G	G
	8:39p			2:49a		11:15a		10:17a			11:05a			11:27p	
Mar	Sg Cp	Cp	Cp Aq	Aq	Aq P	P	P	P A	A	A T	T	T	T G	G	G C
	2:07a		9:00a		6:19p		5:35a		6:20p			7:03a			5:46p
Apr	Aq	Aq P	P	P A	A	A	A T	T	T G	G	G	G C	C	C L	L
	12:05a		11:52			12:44a		1:27p			12:47a		9:22a		
May	P A	A	A	A T	T	T G	G	G	G C	C	C L	L	L V	V	V
	5:46p			1:32a		6:46a		7:20p		6:34a		3:46p		10:13p	
Jn	T	T	T G	G	G C	C	C.L L	L	L	L V	V	V Li Li	Li S	S
	1:32a		12:21p		9:14p		4:06a			8:41a		11:00a		
Jly	G	G C	C	C	C L	L	L V	V	V Li	Li S	S	S Sg	Sg	Sg Cp
	7:07p		3:18a		9:33a		2:12p			5:28p		7:38p		9:36p
Aug	C L	L	L V	V	V Li Li	Li S	S	S	S Sg	Sg	Sg Cp	Cp	Cp Aq	Aq
	10:57a		4:15p		7:56p		10:49p		1:32a		4:38a		8:54a	
Sep	V	V Li Li	Li S	S	S Sg	Sg	Sg Cp	Cp	Cp Aq	Aq	Aq P	P	P A
	3:32a		5:06a		12:00p		10:12a		3:16p		10:31p		8:01a
Oct	Li S	S	S Sg	Sg	Sg Cp	Cp	Cp Aq	Aq	Aq	Aq P	P	P A	A	A	A T
	1:44p		2:02p		4:00p		8:44p		4:27a		2:36p			2:24a
Nov	Sg Cp	Cp	Cp Aq	Aq	Aq P	P	P A	A.	A	A T	T	T G	G	G
	11:55p		3:06a		10:07a		8:25p		8:34a		9:13a		
Dec	Cp Aq	Aq	Aq P	P	P	P A	A	A T	T	T	T G	G	G C	C	C
	11:47a		5:08p			2:35a		2:42p		3:26a		3:28p		

1933

	1	2	3	4	5	6	7	8	9	10	11	12	13	14	15
Jan	P	P A	A	A T	T	T	T G	G	G C	C	C	C L	L	L V	V
	10:14a		9:37p			10:19a		10:16p			8:26a		4:41p	
Feb	A T	T	T G	G	G	G C	C	C L	L	L V	V	V	V Li Li	Li S
	5:40a		6:05p		6:13a		4:16p		11:42p			4:59a		8:46a
Mar	T	T	T G	G	G C	C	C	C L	L	L V	V	V Li Li	Li S	S
		2:18a		2:43p		1:17a		8:41a		1:02p		3:27p	
Apr	G C	C	C	C L	L	L V	V	V Li Li	Li	Li S	S	S Sg	Sg	Sg Cp
	10:50p		10:16a		6:33p		10:59p		12:32a		12:52a		1:54a
May	C L	L	L	L V	V	V Li Li	Li S	S	S Sg	Sg	Sg Cp	Cp	Cp Aq	Aq
	6:06a			3:40a		9:16a		11:06a		10:43a		10:16a		11:47a
Jn	V	V Li Li	Li S	S	S Sg	Sg	Sg Cp	Cp	Cp Aq	Aq	Aq P	P	P A
	6:14p		9:24p		9:32p		8:33p		8:42p		11:51p		6:51a
Jly	Li	Li S	S	S Sg	Sg	Sg Cp	Cp	Cp Aq	Aq	Aq P	P	P A	A	A T	T
	5:56a		7:32a		7:15a		7:05a		9:02a		2:32p			11:50p
Aug	Sg	Sg Cp	Cp	Cp Aq	Aq	Aq P	P	P A	A	A	A T	T	T G	G	G
	4:40p		5:22p		7:11p		11:42p			7:45a		6:57p		
Sep	Cp Aq	Aq	Aq P	P	P A	A	A T	T	T	T G	G	G C	C	C L
	2:00a		4:44a		9:15a		4:36p			3:01a		3:25p		3:30a
Oct	P	P A	A	A	A T	T	T G	G	G C	C	C	C L	L	L V	V
	5:51p			1:19a		11:19a		11:29p			12:01p		10:24p	
Nov	A T	T	T G	G	G	G C	C	C L	L	L	L V	V	V Li Li	Li S
	8:53a		7:02p		7:05a		7:58p		7:24a		3:11p		6:52p	
Dec	T G	G	G C	C	C	C L L	L V	V	V	V Li Li	Li S	S	S Sg
	1:45a		1:53p			2:49a		2:59p		12:17a		5:26a		6:49a

1934

	1	2	3	4	5	6	7	8	9	10	11	12	13	14	15
Jan	C	C L L	L V V	V	V Li Li	Li	Li S S	S Sg	Sg	Sg Cp Cp	Cp Aq
	8:56a		9:08p		7:20a		2:11p		5:17p		5:37p		4:56p
Feb	L	L V V	V Li Li	Li S S	S	S Sg	Sg Cp Cp	Cp Aq	Aq	Aq P P
	3:01a		1:00p		8:30p		1:14a		3:23a		3:57a		4:28a
Mar	V	V Li Li	Li S S	S Sg	Sg Cp Cp	Cp Aq	Aq	Aq P P	P A
	7:02p		1:59a		6:58a		10:22a		12:36p		2:25p		5:00p
Apr	Li S	S	S Sg Sg	Sg Cp Cp	Cp Aq Aq	Aq P P	P	P A A	A T T
	8:35a		12:37p		3:45p		6:43p		9:52p		1:40a		6:56a
May	Sg	Sg Cp Cp	Cp	Cp Aq Aq	Aq P P	P A A	A T T	T G G	G
	9:53p			12:06a		3:26a		8:09a		2:24p		10:38p	
Jn	Cp Aq Aq	Aq P P	P A A	A T T	T	T G G	G C C	C	C L
	6:55a		9:07a		1:32p		8:17p		5:14a		4:14p		4:53a
Jly	P	P A A	A	A T T	T G G	G C C	C	C L L	L	L V
	7:39p			1:47a		10:55a		10:20p		11:07a		12:07a
Aug	A T T	T G G	G	G C C	C L L	L	L V V	V Li Li	Li S
	8:25a		4:49p		4:13a		5:08p		5:59a		5:32p	
Sep	G	G C C	C L L	L	L V V	V Li Li	Li	Li S S	S Sg Sg
	10:40a		11:32p		12:16p		11:23p			8:19a		3:03p
Oct	C	C L L	L V V	V	V Li Li	Li S S	S Sg Sg	Sg	Sg Cp Cp
	6:44a		7:31p		6:20a		2:31p		8:32p			1:04a
Nov	L V V	V Li Li	Li S S	S	S Sg Sg	Sg Cp Cp	Cp Aq Aq	Aq P P
	3:36a		2:41p		10:32p		3:33a		6:56a		9:52a		12:56p
Dec	Li	Li	Li S S	S Sg Sg	Sg Cp Cp	Cp Aq Aq	Aq P P	P A A	A
		8:05a		12:53p		3:09p		4:34p		6:31p		9:52p	

Table 1

16	17	18	19	20	21	22	23	24	25	26	27	28	29	30	31

A TT — T GG — G CC — C — C LL — L VV — V LiLi — Li SS — S Sg
3:02a   2:47a   11:22p   4:39a   7:47a   10:07a   12:43p   4:07p

G — G CC — C LL — L VV — V LiLi — Li SS — S Sg Sg — Sg
9:02a   2:49p   5:25p   6:22p   7:20p   9:39p

C C — C LL — L VV — V LiLi — Li SS — S Sg Sg — Sg Cp Cp — Cp Aq Aq
12:56a   4:18a   4:56a   4:35a   5:07a   8:08a   2:31p

L VV — V LiLi — Li SS — S Sg Sg — Sg Cp Cp — Cp Aq Aq — Aq — Aq P P
2:22p   4:00p   3:33p   2:57p   4:15p   9:05p   5:55a

V LiLi — Li SS — S Sg Sg — Sg Cp Cp — Cp Aq Aq — Aq P P — P — P A A — A T
1:32a   2:15a   1:48a   2:13a   5:31a   12:58p   12:09a   1:05p

S Sg Sg — Sg Cp Cp — Cp Aq Aq — Aq P P — P — P A A — A TT — T T G
11:55a   12:31p   3:12p   9:26p   7:34a   8:08p   8:35a

Cp — Cp Aq Aq — Aq P P — P A A — A — A TT — T GG — G — G CC
12:45a   6:34   3:52p   3:54a   4:26p   3:07a

Aq P P — P — P A A — A TT — T — T GG — G CC — C LL — L — L V
3:14p   12:18p   11:58a   12:33a   11:50a   8:03p   12:58a

A — A TT — T — T GG — G CC — C — C LL — L VV — V LiLi
7:34p   8:14a   8:13p   5:32a   11:07a   1:22p

T — T GG — G — G CC — C LL — L VV — V — V LiLi — Li SS Sg Sg
3:03p   3:26a   1:57p   9:03p   12:16a   12:31a 11:40p

G CC — C LL — L — L VV — V LiLi — Li SS — S Sg Sg — Sg Cp Cp
9:32a   8:35p   5:08a   10:00a   11:38a   10:58a   10:16a

C LL — L VV — V LiLi — Li SS — S Sg Sg — Sg Cp Cp — Cp Aq Aq — Aq — Aq P
2:13a   11:09   5:31p   8:53p   9:42p   9:31p   10:23p   2:17a

Table 2

16	17	18	19	20	21	22	23	24	25	26	27	28	29	30	31

V LiLi — Li — Li SS — S Sg Sg — Sg Cp Cp — Cp Aq Aq — Aq P P — P A A — A
11:02p   3:24a   5:54a   7:18a   8:57a   12:32p   7:21p

S — S Sg Sg — Sg Cp Cp — Cp Aq Aq — Aq P P — P — P A A — A T
11:42a   2:23p   5:29p   9:57p   4:43a   2:21p

S Sg Sg — Sg Cp Cp — Cp Aq Aq — Aq — Aq P P — P A A — A TT — T — T GG
5:18p   7:47p   11:40p   5:16a   12:50p   10:32p   10:14a

Cp — Cp Aq Aq — Aq P P — P A A — A — A TT — T GG — G — G CC
5:00a   10:55a   7:14p   5:31a   5:18p   5:58a

Aq P P — P — P A A — A TT — T GG — G — G CC — C — C LL — L V
4:34p   12:46a   11:27a   11:32p   12:12p   12:33a   11:05a

A — A TT — T — T GG — G CC — C — C LL — L VV — V — V Li
5:12p   5:06a   6:07p   6:17a   5:01p   1:10

T — T GG — G — G CC — C LL — L VV — V — V LiLi — Li SS — S Sg
11:44a   12:24a   12:18p   10:35p   6:44a   12:20p   3:26p

G CC — C LL — L — L VV — V LiLi — Li SS — S Sg Sg — Sg Cp Cp — Cp
7:32a   7:23p   5:07a   12:29p   5:44p   9:21p   11:52p

L — L VV — V LiLi — Li SS — S — S Sg Sg — Sg Cp Cp — Cp Aq Aq — Aq P
1:12p   7:51p   11:59p   2:49a   5:23a   8:27   12:27p

V — V LiLi — Li SS — S Sg Sg — Sg Cp Cp — Cp Aq Aq — Aq P P — P A A
5:07a   8:27   9:54a   11:14a   1:49p   6:17p   12:41a

S — S Sg Sg — Sg Cp Cp — Cp Aq Aq — Aq P P — P — P A A — A TT — T
7:35p   7:24p   8:21p   11:51p   6:13a   3:04p

Sg — Sg Cp Cp — Cp Aq Aq — Aq P P — P A A — A TT — T — T GG — G CC
6:08a   5:38a   5:34p   12:17p   0:40p   7:43a   8:07p

Table 3

16	17	18	19	20	21	22	23	24	25	26	27	28	29	30	31

Aq — Aq P P — P A A — A — A TT — T GG — G — G CC — C LL — L
5:17p   8:28p   3:26a   1:54p   2:24a   3:11

P A A — A TT — T GG — G — G CC — C LL — L — L V
6:39a   12:04p   9:17p   9:23a   10:13p   9:46a

A — A TT — T — T GG — G CC — C — C LL — L SS — S — S Li
9:46p   6:52a   5:13p   6:03a   5:44p   2:37a

T GG — G — G CC — C LL — L — L VV — V LiLi — Li SS — S Sg
2:41p   1:26a   2:10p   2:20a   11:32a   5:07p   8:02p

G CC — C LL — L — L VV — V LiLi — Li — Li SS — S Sg Sg — Sg Cp Cp
9:17a   9:54p   10:35a   8:43p   2:52a   5:28a   6:12a

L — L VV — V — V LiLi — Li SS — S — S Sg Sg — Sg Cp Cp — Cp Aq Aq — Aq P
5:51p   4:59a   12:25p   3:49p   4:24p   4:02p   4:28p

V — V LiLi — Li SS — S — S Sg Sg — Sg Cp Cp — Cp Aq Aq — Aq P P — P A A
11:47a   8:31p   1:28a   3:04a   2:43a   2:20a   3:46a

Li SS — S Sg Sg — Sg Cp Cp — Cp Aq Aq — Aq P P — P A A — A TT — T GG
2:51a   9:11a   12:27p   1:18p   1:08p   1:44p   4:55p   11:56p

Sg Cp Cp — Cp Aq Aq — Aq P P — P — P A A — A TT — T GG — G CC
7:35p   10:07p   11:14p   12:13a   2:47a   8:34a   6:14p

Cp Aq Aq — Aq P P — P A A — A TT — T GG — G — G CC — C LL — L
4:32a   7:10a   9:28a   12:34p   5:58p   2:46a   2:43p

P A A — A TT — T — T GG — G CC — C LL — L — L VV — V Li
4:26p   8:47p   2:47a   11:25a   10:54a   11:52a   11:39p

A TT — T GG — G CC — C — C LL — L VV — V — V LiLi — Li S
2:56a   9:58a   7:11p   6:37a   7:32p   7:59a   5:41p

1935

	1	2	3	4	5	6	7	8	9	10	11	12	13	14	15

Jan: S Sg Sg Sg Sg Cp Cp Cp Aq Aq Aq P P P A A A T T T G G
11:27p 1:44a 2:04a 2:17a 4:03a 8:25a 3:43p

Feb: Cp Cp Aq Aq Aq P P P A A A T T T G G G C C C L
1:26p 12:46p 12:49p 3:22p 9:35p 7:24a 7:35p

Mar: Cp Cp Aq Aq Aq P P A A A T T T G G G C C C C L
12:16a 12:13a 11:41p 12:43a 5:12a 1:52p 1:48a

Apr: P P A A A T T T G G G C C C C L L L V V V
10:31a 11:18a 2:36p 9:46p 8:52a 9:47p

May: A T T T T G G G C C C L L L L V V V Li Li Li
9:09p 12:26a 6:50a 4:55p 5:26a 5:48p

Jn: G G C C C C L L L V V V V Li Li Li S S S Sg Sg
3:44p 1:19a 1:26p 1:59a 12:35p 7:57p

Jly: C C L L L V V V V Li Li Li S S S S Sg Sg Sg Cp Cp
7:13a 9:08p 9:52a 9:14p 5:27a 10:03a

Aug: L V V V Li Li Li Li S S S Sg Sg Sg Cp Aq Aq Aq P P
4:06a 4:54p 4:57a 2:24p 8:10p 10:24p 10:18p

Sep: Li Li S S S Sg Sg Sg Sg Cp Cp Cp Aq Aq Aq P P P A A A T
11:22a 9:48p 5:08a 8:44a 9:15a 8:21a 8:10a

Oct: S S Sg Sg Sg Cp Cp Cp Aq Aq Aq P P P A A A T T T G G
3:40a 12:02p 5:20p 7:26p 7:20p 6:53p 8:14p

Nov: Cp Cp Aq Aq Aq Aq P P P A A A T T T G G G C C C L
11:38p 3:20a 4:54a 5:59a 6:52a 10:56a 6:51p

Dec: Aq Aq P P P A A A T T T G G G C C C C L L L V
9:02a 11:52a 2:02p 4:37p 8:54p 4:07a 2:33p

1936

	1	2	3	4	5	6	7	8	9	10	11	12	13	14	15

Jan: A A T T T T G G G C C C L L L V V V V Li Li
8:11p 12:04a 5:29a 1:02p 11:05p 11:10a

Feb: T G G G C C C L L L L V V V Li Li Li Li S S S Sg
5:38a 11:58a 8:26p 6:48a 6:46p 7:24a 6:56p

Mar: G C C C C L L L V V V V Li Li Li S S S S Sg Sg
5:26p 2:20a 1:18p 1:27a 2:03p 2:06a

Apr: L L V V V V Li Li Li S S S S Sg Sg Sg Cp Cp Cp Cp Aq
7:07p 7:31a 8:05p 8:03a 6:23p 1:49a

May: V V Li Li Li Li S S S Sg Sg Sg Cp Cp Cp Cp Aq Aq Aq P P
1:43p 2:16a 1:54p 11:56p 7:47a 12:53p

Jn: Li S S S Sg Sg Sg Sg Cp Cp Cp Aq Aq Aq P P P A A A T T
9:13a 8:37p 6:02a 1:17p 6:26p 9:47p 11:48p

Jly: S Sg Sg Sg Cp Cp Cp Aq Aq Aq Aq P P P A A A T T T G G
4:27a 1:34p 7:56p 12:10a 3:10a 5:46a 8:38a

Aug: Cp Cp Aq Aq Aq P P P A A A T T T G G C C C C C L
4:25a 7:36a 9:21a 11:12a 2:12p 6:52p 1:20a

Sep: P P A A A T T T G G G C C C L L L V V V
5:43p 6:04p 7:55p 12:16a 7:13a 4:20p

Oct: A A T T T G G G C C C L L L V V V Li Li Li S
3:25a 3:37a 6:28a 12:45p 10:01p 9:19a 9:47p

Nov: G G C C C L L L L V V V Li Li Li Li S S S Sg Sg
3:00p 7:37p 4:00a 3:15p 3:52a 4:34p

Dec: C C L L L V V V Li Li Li Li S S S Sg Sg Sg Sg Cp Cp
4:34a 11:31a 9:55p 10:28a 11:07p 10:25a

1937

	1	2	3	4	5	6	7	8	9	10	11	12	13	14	15

Jan: V V V Li Li Li S S S S Sg Sg Sg Cp Cp Cp Cp Aq Aq Aq P
5:56a 5:59p 6:42a 5:50p 2:23a 8:28a

Feb: Li Li S S S Sg Sg Sg Sg Cp Cp Cp Aq Aq Aq P P P A A A T
2:11a 2:58p 2:32a 10:57p 4:07p 7:11p 9:35p

Mar: S Sg Sg Sg Cp Cp Cp Cp Aq Aq Aq P P P P A A A T T T G
10:23 11:08p 11:20a 8:29p 1:48a 3:59a 4:55a

Apr: Cp Cp Aq Aq Aq Aq P P P A A A T T T G G G C C C L
7:13a 11:45a 2:25p 2:39p 2:36p 4:07p

May: Aq Aq P P P A A A A T T T G G G C C C L L L V
1:05p 8:51p 12:43a 1:29a 12:57a 1:03a 3:30a

Jn: P A A A T T T T G G G C C C L L L L V V V
9:11a 11:25p 4:37a 1:04p 11:58p 12:20p

Jly: A A T T T G G G C C C L L L V V V Li Li Li S
7:31p 9:13a 9:54a 11:02a 2:19a 9:06a 7:39p

Aug: T G G G C C C L L L V V V V Li Li Li S S S Sg Sg
4:28a 6:33a 8:36a 11:56a 6:03p 3:36a 3:59p

Sep: C L L L V V V V Li Li Li S S S S Sg Sg Sg Cp Cp Cp Aq
4:23p 8:37p 2:50a 12:01p 12:00a 12:49p 11:47p

Oct: L V V V Li Li Li S S S S Sg Sg Sg Cp Cp Cp Cp Aq Aq Aq P
3:30a 10:33a 7:58p 7:45a 8:45p 8:36a 4:57p

Nov: Li Li S S S Sg Sg Sg Sg Cp Cp Cp Aq Aq Aq P P P P A
2:49a 2:46p 3:35a 4:16p 2:03a 7:58a

Dec: S S Sg Sg Sg Cp Cp Cp Aq Aq Aq Aq P P P A A A T T T G
9:06p 10:07a 10:38p 9:20a 4:50p 8:43p 9:40p

```
 16   17   18   19   20   21   22   23   24   25   26   27   28   29   30   31
 G    G C C    C L L    L    L V V    V Li Li   Li    Li S S    S Sg Sg   S Sg Sg  Sg Cp Cp   Sg Cp
      1:37a    1:27p         2:20a    2:59p          1:46a               9:10a              12:48p
 L    L    L V V    V Li Li   Li    Li S S    S Sg Sg   Sg Cp Cp   Cp
      8:33a    9:02p         8:04a    4:40p              10:04p
 L    L V V    V Li Li   Li S S    S Sg Sg   Sg Cp Cp   Cp Aq Aq   Aq P
      2:51p    3:08a    1:46p    10:23p    4:48a    8:41a              10:14a
 V Li Li   Li S S    S Sg Sg   Sg Cp Cp   Cp Aq Aq   Aq P P    P A A
 10:01a    8:09p         4:06a    10:13a    2:43p    5:39a              7:26p
 Li S S    S Sg Sg   Sg Cp Cp   Cp Aq Aq   Aq P P    P    P A A    A T T    T G
 3:53a    11:12a    4:20p    8:08p    11:13p    1:59a    4:58a              9:11a
 Sg    Sg Cp Cp   Cp Aq Aq   Aq P P    P A A    A T T    T G G    G C C
 12:21a    2:56a    4:57a    7:21a    10:54a    4:06p              11:27p
 Cp Aq Aq   Aq P P    P A A    A T T    T G G    G G C C    C L L
 11:53a    12:31p    1:34p    4:21p    9:42p    5:43a              4:04p
 P A A    A T T    T    T G G    G C C    C L L    L    L V V    V Li Li
 9:55p    11:08p    3:25a    11:17a    10:00p              10:20a    11:08p
 T    T G G    G C C    C    C L L    L V V    V    V Li Li   Li S S
 10:48a    5:27p    3:50a    4:18p              5:06a    5:06p
 G    G C C    C L L    L V V    V    V Li Li   Li S S    S    S Sg Sg   Sg Cp
 1:21a    10:36a    10:44p    11:31a              11:14p    9:17a              5:31p
 L    L    L V V    V Li Li   Li    Li S S    S Sg Sg   Sg Cp Cp   Cp    Cp Aq
      6:10a    6:52p         6:36a    4:10p              11:28p    5:00a
 V    V    V Li Li   Li S S    S    S Sg Sg   Sg Cp Cp   Cp Aq Aq   Aq P P    P A
      2:58a    3:00p         12:44a    7:27a    11:46a              2:42p    5:16p
```

```
 16   17   18   19   20   21   22   23   24   25   26   27   28   29   30   31
 Li S S    S    S Sg Sg   Sg Cp Cp   Cp Aq Aq   Aq P P    P A A    A    A T
 11:38p    10:12a    5:18p    9:02p    10:35p    11:36p              1:37a
 Sg    Sg    Sg Cp Cp   Cp Aq Aq   Aq P P    P A A    A T T    T G G
 3:21a    7:46a    8:55a    8:35a    8:51a              11:30a
 Sg Cp Cp   Cp Aq Aq   Aq P P    P A A    A T T    T G G    G C C    C L L
 11:51a    5:52p    7:59p    7:31p    6:37p    7:31p    11:52p              8:04a
 Aq    Aq P P    P A A    A T T    T G G    G C C    C L L    L    L V
 5:37a    6:20a    5:37a    5:38a    8:23a    3:03p              1:22a
 P A A    A T T    T G G    G C C    C L L    L    L V V    V Li Li   Li
 3:14p    3:47p    4:12p    6:19p    11:42p    8:48a              8:38p
 T    T G G    G C C    C L L    L V V    V    V Li Li   Li S S    S
 1:30a    4:09a    9:06a    5:15p              4:24a    4:52p
 G C C    C L L    L    L V V    V Li Li   Li    Li S S    S Sg Sg   Sg Cp Cp
 12:28p    5:58p    1:54a    12:31p    12:54a    12:36p              10:23p
 L    L V V    V Li Li   Li S S    S    S Sg Sg   Sg Cp Cp   Cp Aq Aq   Aq P
 9:45a    8:17p    8:36a    9:09p              7:16a    2:12p              5:05p
 V Li Li   Li S S    S    S Sg Sg   Sg Cp Cp   Cp Aq Aq   Aq    Aq P P    P A
 3:12a    3:32p    4:24     3:52p    11:53p    3:38a              4:10a
 S    S    S Sg Sg   Sg Cp Cp   Cp    Cp Aq Aq   Aq P P    P A A    A T T    T G
      10:38a    10:37p         8:00a    1:28p    3:09p    2:34p              1:49p
 Sg    Sg Cp Cp   Cp Aq Aq   Aq P P    P    P A A    A T T    T G G    G C
 4:20a    2:11p    9:04p    12:37a    1:29a    1:11a              1:40a
 Cp Aq Aq   Aq    Aq P P    P A A    A T T    T G G    G C C    C L L    L V
 7:42p    2:43a    7:26a    10:05a    11:24a    12:20p    3:14p              8:50p
```

```
 16   17   18   19   20   21   22   23   24   25   26   27   28   29   30   31
 P    P A A    A T T    T G G    G C C    C    C L L    L V V    V Li Li
 12:48    4:07    6:53p    9:39p    1:10a    6:31a              2:53p
 T    T    T G G    G C C    C L L    L V V    V Li Li   Li
 12:23a    4:05a    8:51p    3:07p    11:30p
 G    G C C    C L L    V    V Li Li   Li    Li S S    S Sg Sg   Sg    Sg Cp
 6:19a    9:27a    9:43p    6:46a    5:53p
 L    L V V    V Li Li   Li S S    S    S Sg Sg   Sg Cp Cp   Cp    Cp Aq
 8:16p    3:38a    12:53p    12:21a    1:05p    1:56a
 V    V Li Li   Li S S    S    S Sg Sg   Sg Cp Cp   Cp    Cp Aq Aq   Aq P P    P
 9:21a    6:38p    6:18a    7:10a    7:54a    7:10p
 V Li Li   Li S S    S Sg Sg   Sg    Sg Cp Cp   Cp Aq Aq   Aq P P    P A
 1:06a    1:01p    10:35p    1:56p    12:52a    9:36a              3:46p
 S    S    S Sg Sg   Sg Cp Cp   Cp    Cp Aq Aq   Aq P P    P A A    A    A T T
      8:18a    8:48p         7:19a    3:18p    9:13p    1:29a
 Sg    Sg Cp Cp   Cp Aq Aq   Aq P P    P    P A A    A T T    T G G    G C C
 4:36a    3:02p    10:25p    3:22a    6:56a    10:02a              1:03p
 Aq    Aq    Aq P P    P A A    A T T    T G G    G C C    C L L    L
      7:19a    11:29a    1:49p    3:48p    6:26p              10:16p
 P    P A A    A T T    T G G    G C C    C L L    L V V    V Li Li
 9:28p    11:06p    11:40p    12:49a    3:44a    9:03a              4:50p
 A T T    T G G    G C C    C L L    L V V    V Li Li   Li    Li S S
 10:10a    10:10a    9:48a    10:57a    3:01p    10:26p              8:46a
 G    G C C    C L L    L V V    V    V Li Li   Li S S    S    S Sg Sg   Sg Cp
 9:03p    8:53p    11:02p    4:55a              2:47p    3:12a              4:16p
```

1938

```
         1      2      3      4      5      6      7      8      9     10     11     12     13     14     15
       Cp     Cp           Cp Aq  Aq           Aq P P      P A A      A            A T T      T  G G      G C C
Jan                       4:30a         3:04p        11:48p              5:04a         7:49a         8:21a
       Aq P P      P            P A A      A T T      T  G G      G C C      C  L L      L  V V
Feb   8:56p              4:53a         10:56a        3:05p         5:23p         6:34p         8:00p
       Aq P P      P A A      A T T      T  G G      G C C      C  L L      L  V V
Mar   4:12a              11:14a        4:28p         8:32p         11:45p        2:22a         5:06a
       A T T      T            T  G G      G C C      C  L L      L  V V      V  Li Li     Li  S
Apr   11:41p             2:33a         5:07a         5:51p         11:53a        5:05p                12:24a
       T  G G      G C C      C  L L      L  V V      V  Li Li     Li  S S      S  Sg Sg
May   10:44a             11:52a        1:44p         5:21p         11:08p        7:17a         5:43p
       C  L L      L  V            V  Li Li     Li  S S      S  Sg Sg     Sg           Sg Cp Cp     Cp
Jn    9:11p              11:25p        4:37a         1:04p         11:58p              12:20p
       L  V V      V  Li Li     Li  S S      S            S  Sg Sg     Sg Cp Cp     Cp           Cp Aq Aq     Aq  P
Jly   10:57a             11:12a        6:53p         5:46a         6:21p         7:06a         6:53p
       Li           Li  S S      S  Sg Sg     Sg Cp Cp     Cp Aq Aq     Aq           Aq P P      P  A A
Aug   1:53a              12:04p        12:34a        1:15p         12:43a        10:33a
       Sg           Sg           Sg Cp Cp     Cp Aq Aq     Aq           Aq P P      P  A A      A T T      T  G
Sep                      12:30a        7:09p         7:29a         4:38p         11:51p        5:23a
       Cp           Cp           Cp Aq Aq     Aq P P      P            P A A      A T T      T  G G      G C C
Oct                      3:56a         3:24p         12:20a        6:42a         1:09a         2:30p
       Aq           Ap P P      P A A      A T T      T  G G      G C C      C  L L      L            L  V
Nov   12:05a             9:33a         3:37p         7:01p         8:59p         10:51p        1:40a
       P A A      A            A T T      T  G G      G C C      C  L L      L  V V      V  Li Li
Dec   6:57p              1:57a         5:18a         6:07a         6:18a         7:37a         11:30p
```

1939

```
         1      2      3      4      5      6      7      8      9     10     11     12     13     14     15
       T            T  G G      G C C      C  L L      L  V V      V  Li Li     Li  S S      S  Sg
Jan   4:14p              5:17p         4:32p         4:28p         6:16p         11:58p        9:10a
       G C C      C  L L      L  V V      V  Li Li     Li  S S      S  Sg Sg     Sg           Sg Cp Cp
Feb   3:57a              4:05a         2:35a         3:33a         7:22a         3:28p         2:42a
       C            C  L L      L  V V      V  Li Li     Li  S S      S  Sg Sg     Sg           Sg Cp Cp     Cp Aq
Mar   2:28p              2:20p         2:35p         5:05p         11:28p        9:36a         10:01p
       V            V  Li Li     Li  S S      S  Sg Sg     Sg Cp Cp     Cp           Cp Aq Aq     Aq  P P
Apr                      12:51a        3:24a         8:48a         5:51p         5:34a         6:03p
       Li           Li  S S      S  Sg Sg     Sg Cp Cp     Cp Aq Aq     Aq           Aq P P      P  A A
May   12:39p             6:15p         2:36a         1:42p         2:01a         1:43p
       S  Sg Sg     Sg Cp Cp     Cp Aq Aq     Aq           Aq P P      P  A A      A            A T T      T  G
Jn    2:17a              10:52p        9:42p         10:04a        9:58p         7:42a         1:29p
       Cp           Cp           Cp Aq Aq     Aq P P      P            P A A      A T T      T  G G      G    G C
Jly                      4:55a         5:18p         5:50a         4:22p         11:14p        1:47a
       Aq P P      P            P A A      A            A T T      T  G G      G C C      C  L L      L  V
Aug   11:41p             12:21p        4:04a         8:04a         12:18a        1:07p         12:20p
       A            A            A T T      T  G G      G C C      C  L L      L  V V      V  Li Li     Li  S
Sep                      5:47a         2:58p         8:47p         11:07p        11:08p        10:41p        11:48p
       T            T  G G      G C C      C  L L      L  V V      V  Li Li     Li  S S      S  Sg
Oct   8:34p              3:16a         7:20a         8:45a         9:16a         10:44a        1:39p
       G C C      C  L L      L  V V      V  Li Li     Li  S S      S  Sg Sg     Sg           Sg Cp Cp
Nov   8:47a              2:00p         3:55p         6:03p         6:16p         11:44p        5:43a
       L            L  V V      V            V  Li Li     Li  S S      S  Sg Sg     Sg Cp Cp     Cp Aq Aq     Aq
Dec   9:23p              12:23a        3:57a         8:33a         2:55p         11:45p
```

1940

```
         1      2      3      4      5      6      7      8      9     10     11     12     13     14     15
       V  Li Li     Li  S S      S  Sg Sg     Sg Cp Cp     Cp           Cp Aq Aq     Aq P P      P    P A
Jan   5:44a              9:37a         3:14p         10:32p        7:43a         7:05p                7:55a
       S  Sg Sg     Sg Cp Cp     Cp           Cp Aq Aq     Aq           Aq P P      P  A A      A    A T T
Feb   8:39p              4:27a         2:24p         1:59a         2:49p         3:35a
       Sg           Sg Cp Cp     Cp           Cp Aq Aq     Aq P P      P  A A      A    A T T      T  G G
Mar   9:46a              8:09a         11:07p        9:00p         9:44a         8:48p
       Cp Aq Aq     Aq P P      P            P A A      A T T      T    T  G G      G C C      C  L
Apr   2:16a              2:12p         3:10a         3:37          2:31a         11:01a        4:39p
       P            P            P A A      A T T      T    T  G G      G C C      C  L L      L  V V
May                      9:50a         10:10p        8:33a         4:31p         10:19p        2:16a
       A            A T T      T  G G      G C C      C    C  L L      L  V V      V  Li Li     Li  S
Jn    5:42a              3:45p         10:59p        4:00a         7:41a         10:44a        1:32p
       T            T  G G      G C C      C  L L      L  V V      V  Li Li     Li  S S      S  Sg Sg
Jly   12:12a             7:11a         11:11a        1:44p         4:08p         7:08p         11:06p
       C            C  L L      L  V V      V  Li Li     Li           Li  S S      S  Sg Sg     Sg Cp Cp     Cp Aq
Aug   8:16p              9:49p         10:51p        12:48a        4:30a         10:17a        6:11p
       L  V V      V  Li Li     Li  S S      S  Sg Sg     Sg Cp Cp     Cp Aq Aq     Aq           Aq P P
Sep   7:56a              7:54a         8:18a         10:39a        3:50p         11:55p        10:25a
       Li           Li  S S      S  Sg Sg     Sg Cp Cp     Cp           Cp Aq Aq     Aq P P      P    P A A
Oct   6:15p              6:59p         10:34p        5:45a         4:19p         4:50a
       S  Sg Sg     Sg Cp Cp     Cp Aq Aq     Aq P P      P  A A      A    A T T      T  G
Nov   5:22a              7:23a         1:07p         10:49p        11:13a        12:11a        11:59a
       Cp           Cp Aq Aq     Aq           Aq P P      P  A A      A    A T T      T  G G      G C
Dec   10:18p             6:35a         6:28p         7:26a         7:05p         4:18a
```

Section 1

16 17 18 19 20 21 22 23 24 25 26 27 28 29 30 31

```
C  LL    L  VV    V  LiLi    Li  S  S    S    S  Sg Sg    Sg Cp Cp    Cp    Cp Aq Aq
8:09a     9:14a     1:32p    10:00p        9:51p       10:57p                 10:59a

V  LiLi    Li    Li  S  S    S  Sg Sg    Sg    Sg Cp Cp    Cp Aq Aq    Aq
11:32p     6:37a      5:36p      6:27a        6:32p

V  LiLi    Li  S  S    S    S  Sg Sg    Sg Cp Cp    Cp    Cp Aq Aq    Aq  P P    P  A A
9:06a      3:58p      2:03a      2:31p            2:55a          12:48p       7:29a

S    S  Sg Sg    Sg Cp Cp    Cp    Cp Aq Aq    Aq  P P    P    P  A A    A  T T
10:21a    10:32p         11:09a        9:49p         5:06a        9:00a

Sg    Sg Cp Cp    Cp Aq Aq    Aq    Aq  P P    P  A A    A  T T    T  G G    G  C C
5:51a     6:36p          6:07a          2:31p       7:21p      8:49p       7:52p

Cp Aq Aq    Aq  P P    P  A A    A    A  T T    T  G G    G  C C    C  L L
1:06a       1:01p       10:35p          11:02a      7:27a       6:46a

P    P    P  A A    A  T T    T  G G    G  C C    C  L L    L  V V    V  LiLi
5:01a      12:28p       4:42p      5:54a      5:25p      5:18o      7:42p

A  T T    T  G G    G    G  C C    C  L L    L  V V    V  LiLi    Li  S S    S  Sg
6:22p     11:47p       2:37a      3:26a      3:43a      5:28a     10:29a      7:32p

G  C C    C  L L    L  V V    V  LiLi    Li  S S    S    S  Sg Sg    Sg Cp
9:08a     11:25a      1:02p      3:22p      8:02p          4:04a       3:21p

C  L L    L  V V    V  LiLi    Li    Li  S S    S  Sg Sg    Sg Cp Cp    Cp    Cp Aq Aq
5:19p     8:10p      11:46p       5:01a      12:58p       11:40p      12:07p

V    V  LiLi    Li  S S    S  Sg Sg    Sg    Sg Cp Cp    Cp Aq Aq    Aq    Aq  P P
6:03a     12:28p      9:00p      7:38a          7:59p          8:29a

Li  S S    S    S  Sg Sg    Sg Cp Cp    Cp    Cp Aq Aq    Aq  P P    P  A A    A  T
6:16p      3:33a      2:39p          2:59p          3:40p       1:15a      11:43a
```

Section 2

16 17 18 19 20 21 22 23 24 25 26 27 28 29 30 31

```
Sg    Sg Cp Cp    Cp Aq Aq    Aq    Aq  P P    P  A A    A  T T    T    T  G G
8:44p     9:16p          9:50p          9:40a       7:24p      1:46a

Cp Aq Aq    Aq    Aq  P P    P  A A    A    A  T T  G G    G  G C
3:22p       3:52a       3:21p          1:17a  8:47p       1:03p

Aq    Aq    Aq  P P    P  A A    A    A  T T    T  G G    G  C C    C  L L    L  V
10:31a      9:38p       7:02a          2:12p      7:16p      10:12p     11:36p

P    P  A A    A  T T    T  G G    G  C C    C  L L    L  V V    V
5:13a     1:54p      8:13p      12:41a     3:54a      1:37a      9:03a

A  T T    T    T  G G    G  C C    C  L L    L  V V    V  LiLi    Li  S S    S
10:24p     6:04a      7:24a      10:14a     11:52a     3:09p      1:46p

G  G C C    C  L L    L  V V    V  LiLi    Li    Li  S S    S  Sg Sg    Sg Cp
4:04p       4:58p      5:57p      8:34p      1:54a      8:40a      5:56p

C    C  L L    L  V V    V  LiLi    Li  S S    S  Sg Sg    Sg Cp Cp    Cp    Cp Aq Aq
2:29a     2:08a      3:14a      7:04a      2:13p      11:53p      11:15a

V    V  LiLi    Li  S S    S  Sg Sg    Sg    Sg Cp Cp    Cp Aq Aq    Aq    Aq  P P    P  A
12:05p     2:25p      8:18p      5:35a          1:10p          5:43a       6:14p

S    S    S  Sg Sg    Sg Cp Cp    Cp    Cp Aq Aq    Aq    Aq  P P    P  A A    A  T
4:05a      12:13p      11:25p         11:59a          12:20a       11:28a

Sg    Sg Cp Cp    Cp    Cp Aq Aq    Aq  P P    P    P  A A    A  T T    T    T  G G
8:27p     6:40a          7:05p       7:28a      6:05p      2:30a

Cp Aq Aq    Aq    Aq  P P    P  A A    A    A  T T    T  G G    G  C C    C  L
3:03p       5:00a       3:33p          2:21a      10:07a     3:09p      6:33p

Aq  P P    P    P  A A    A  I I    T  G G    G    G  C C    C  L L    L  V V
11:19a      12:01a      11:28a     7:32a      12:00a     2:07a      3:31a
```

Section 3

16 17 18 19 20 21 22 23 24 25 26 27 28 29 30 31

```
A    A  T T    T  G G    G  C C    C  L L    L  V V    V  LiLi    Li  S S
8:11p     5:30a      10:32a     12:09p     12:12p     12:46p      3:22p

T  G G    G  C C    C  L L    L  V V    V  LiLi    Li  S S    S    S  Sg
2:05p     8:40p      11:15p     11:10p     10:31p     11:18p      2:57a

G  G C C    C  L L    L  V V    V  LiLi    Li  S S    S  Sg Sg    Sg Cp Cp    Cp
4:56a       9:13a      10:19a     9:48a      9:35a      11:34a      5:05p

L    L  V V    V  LiLi    Li  S S    S  Sg Sg    Sg Cp Cp    Cp Aq Aq    Aq  P
7:31p     8:21p      8:34p      9:52p      1:54a      9:41a       8:58p

V    V  LiLi    Li  S S    S  Sg Sg    Sg Cp Cp    Cp Aq Aq    Aq  P P    P  A A
4:40a     6:12a      8:01a      11:38a     6:23p      4:39a       5:17p

S    S  Sg Sg    Sg Cp Cp    Cp    Cp Aq Aq    Aq  P P    P  A A    A  T T
4:34p     8:48p          3:18a      12:57p      1:13a      1:50p

Sg    Sg Cp Cp    Cp Aq Aq    Aq  P P    P    P  A A    A  T T    T  G G    G  G C
4:19a     11:24a      9:02p      9:02a      9:53p      9:03a       4:27p

Aq    Aq    Aq  P P    P  A A    A  T T    T    T  G G    G  C C    C  L L
4:11a      4:16p       5:16a      5:08p      1:49a      6:31a

P  A A    A    A  T T    T  G G    G  C C    C  L L    L  V V    V  Li
10:44p     11:44a      10:03a     9:56a      4:03p      6:36p      6:45p

A  T T    T  G G    G  C C    C  L L    L    L  V V    V  LiLi    Li  S S
5:48p     5:58a      4:14p      11:46p     4:07a      5:36a      5:25a

G  G C C    C  L L    L    L  V V    V  LiLi    Li  S S    S  Sg Sg    Sg Cp
9:50p       5:37a      11:08a     8:22p      3:44p      4:20p      5:55p

C    C  L L    L  V V    V  LiLi    Li  S S    S    S  Sg Sg    Sg Cp Cp    Cp Aq Aq
11:15a     4:33p      8:35p      11:29p     1:37a      3:59a      8:09a
```

1941

	1	2	3	4	5	6	7	8	9	10	11	12	13	14	15

Jan Aq P P   P   A A   A   T T   T   T G G   G C C   C   L L   L   V
    3:40p 2:36p   3:27p   3:25p   12:31p 6:36p   10:45p

Feb A   A T T   T   T G G   G C C   C   C L L   L   V V   V Li Li
    11:41p 12:07p 9:53p   4:05a   7:22a   9:07a

Mar A   A T T   T G G   G   G C C   C L L   L   V V   V Li Li   Li S
    7:22a 8:09p   7:04a   2:14p   5:47p   6:50p   7:04p

Apr T G G   G C C   C L L   L   L   V V   V Li Li   S S   S Sg Sg
    3:05a 2:40p   11:21p   4:18a   5:53p   5:32a   5:08a

May C   C   C L L   L   V V   V Li Li   Li S S   S Sg Sg   Sg Cp Cp   Cp Aq
    6:33a 1:01p   4:06p   4:31p   3:52p   4:09p   7:21p

Jn L   V V   V   V Li Li   Li S S   S Sg Sg   Sg Cp Cp   Cp Aq Aq   Aq P P
    7:34p 12:13a   2:12a   2:24a   2:33a   4:44a   10:37a

Jly V Li Li   Li S S   S Sg Sg   Sg Cp Cp   Cp Aq Aq   Aq P P   P   P A A
    6:16a 9:32a   11:12a   12:22p   2:40p   7:47p   4:37a

Aug S Sg Sg   Sg Cp Cp   Cp Aq Aq   Aq   Aq P P   P A A   A   A T T   T G
    5:49p 9:27p   11:35p   4:52a   1:15p   12:33a   1:08p

Sep Cp Aq Aq   Aq P P   P A A   A   A T T   T G G   G   G C C
    6:39a 12:54p   9:31a   7:32a   9:05p   9:09a

Oct Aq P P   P   P A A   A T T   T   T G G   G C C   C   C L L
    7:30p 4:39a   3:53p   4:22a   4:50p   3:27a

Nov A   A T T   T   T G G   G C C   C   C L L   L   V V   V   V Li
    10:20p 10:53a   11:24p   10:47a   7:23p   12:16a

Dec T   T G G   G   G C C   C L L   L   L   V V   V Li Li   Li S
    5:00p 5:22a   4:41p   2:10a   8:44a   11:48a

1942

	1	2	3	4	5	6	7	8	9	10	11	12	13	14	15

Jan G C C   C L L   L   L   V V   V Li Li   Li S S   S Sg Sg   Sg Cp Cp
    11:41a 10:30p   7:41a   2:45p   7:20p   9:29p   10:07p

Feb L   L   V V   V Li Li   Li   Li S S   S Sg Sg   Sg Cp Cp   Cp Aq Aq   Aq P
    1:55p 8:15p   12:54   4:05a   6:18a   8:28a   11:53a

Mar L   V V   V Li Li   Li S S   S Sg Sg   Sg Cp Cp   Cp Aq Aq   Aq P P
    10:02p 3:21a   6:50a   9:28a   12:09p   3:33p   8:11p

Apr Li   Li S S   S Sg Sg   Sg Cp Cp   Cp Aq Aq   Aq   Aq P P   P A A   A T
    2:52p 4:05p   5:45p   9:00a   2:22a   9:51a   7:20p

May S   S Sg Sg   Sg Cp Cp   Cp Aq Aq   Aq P P   P A A   A   A T T   T G
    1:02a 1:05a   2:58a   7:44a   3:55p   1:39a   1:16p

Jn Cp   Cp Aq Aq   Aq P P   P A A   A   A T T   T G G   G   G C C
    11:02a 2:18p   9:15p   7:16a   7:13p   7:51a

Jly Aq P P   P A A   A   A T T   T   T G G   G C C   C   C L L
    10:51p 4:12a   1:26p   1:11a   1:51p   2:06a

Aug A   A   A T T   T G G   G C C   C   C L L   L   V V   V   V Li
    12:26a 7:55a   8:29p   8:39a   7:06p   3:29a

Sep T G G   G C C   C L L   L   L   V V   V Li Li   Li S S   S S
    3:43p 4:00a   4:12p   2:29a   10:03a   3:16p   6:57p

Oct G C C   C   C L L   L   V V   V Li Li   Li S S   S   S Sg Sg   Sg Cp
    12:03p 12:33a   11:11a   6:28p   10:43p   1:09a   3:14a

Nov L   L   V V   V Li Li   Li   Li S S   S Sg Sg   Sg Cp Cp   Cp Aq Aq   Aq P
    8:15p 4:19p   8:26a   9:46a   10:19a   11:51a   3:31a

Dec V   V Li Li   Li S S   S Sg Sg   Sg Cp Cp   Cp Aq Aq   Aq P P   P   P A
    1:50p 7:00p   8:30p   8:07p   9:38p   10:01p   3:07a

1943

	1	2	3	4	5	6	7	8	9	10	11	12	13	14	15

Jan Li S S   S Sg Sg   Sg Cp Cp   Cp Aq Aq   Aq P P   P A A   A T T   T
    4:37a 7:34a   7:35a   6:41a   7:03a   10:23a   5:26p

Feb Sg Cp Cp   Cp Aq Aq   Aq P P   P A A   A   A T T   T G G   G C C
    6:11p 6:10p   6:11p   8:06p   1:21a   10:27a   10:26p

Mar Sg Cp Cp   Cp Aq Aq   Aq P P   P A A   A T T   T   T G G   G   G C C
    2:17a 3:56   4:54a   6:42a   10:56a   6:44   5:52a

Apr Aq P P   P A A   A T T   T   T G G   G C C   C   C L L   L   V
    1:27p 4:20p   8:41p   3:43a   2:06p   2:40a   2:56p

May A   A   A T T   T G G   G C C   C   C L L.   L   V V   V   V Li
    4:58a 12:19a   10:19a   10:39a   11:19p   9:42a

Jn T G G   G C C   C L L   L   L   V V   V Li Li   Li   Li S
    7:32p 5:45a   6:04p   7:04a   6:17p   1:54a

Jly G C C   C   C L L   L   V V   V   V Li Li   Li S S   S Sg Sg   Sg Cp
    12:15p 12:40a   1:43p   1:15a   10:37a   3:31p   5:03p

Aug L   L   V V   V Li Li   Li S S   S   S Sg Sg   Sg Cp Cp   Cp Aq Aq
    7:44p 7:51a   5:35p   12:03a   3:06a   3:36a

Sep V Li Li   Li S S   S   S Sg Sg   Sg Cp Cp   Cp Aq Aq   Aq P P   P A A
    11:18p 11:18p   6:38a   11:11a   1:46p   1:46p   2:11p

Oct Li S S   S Sg Sg   Sg Cp Cp   Cp Aq Aq   Aq P P   P   P A A   A T T
    4:04a 12:01p   5:08p   8:37p   10:43p   12:12a   2:29a

Nov Sg Cp Cp   Cp   Cp Aq Aq   Aq P P   P A A   A T T   T   T G G   G   G C
    10:34p 2:09a   5:16a   8:10a   11:33a   4:35p   12:26a

Dec Cp Aq Aq   Aq P P   P A A   A T T   T   T G G   G C C   C L L
    8:01a 10:36a   2:01p   6:32p   12:34a   8:46a   7:39p

16 17 18 19 20 21 22 23 24 25 26 27 28 29 30 31

V V V LL L S S S Sg Sg Sg Cp Cp Cp Aq Aq Aq Aq P P P P A
2:00a   5:04a   8:17a   12:02p   5:03p   12:37a   11:03a

Li S S S Sg Sg Sg Cp Cp Cp Cp Aq Aq Aq Aq P P P P A A
10:36a   1:39p   5:56p   1:04a   8:19a   6:56p

S S Sg Sg Sg Cp Cp Cp Cp Aq Aq Aq Aq P P P P A A A T T T
8:12p   11:29p   5:36a   2:33p   1:41a   2:13p

Sg Cp Cp Cp Aq Aq Aq P P P P A A A T T T T G G G C
6:38a   11:34a   8:11p   7:34a   8:22p   9:11a   8:52p

Aq Aq Aq P P P A A A A T T T G G G G C C C L L
2:37a   1:35p   2:25a   3:09p   2:35a   12:14p

P A A A A T T T G G G G C C C L L L L V V
8:33p   9:02a   9:42a   8:50a   5:52   1:01a

A T T T T G G G C C C C L L L V V V Li Li Li S S
4:31p   5:09a   4:12p   12:46a   7:04a   11:40a   3:07p

G G G C C C L L L L V V V Li Li Li S S S Sg Sg Sg Cp
12:34a   9:14a   2:50p   6:19p   8:48p   11:14p   2:19a

C L L L L V V V Li Li Li S S S Sg Sg Sg Cp Cp Cp Aq Aq
6:30p   12:25a   3:15a   4:24a   6:25a   7:45a   12:19p

L V V V Li Li Li S S S Sg Sg Sg Cp Cp Cp Aq Aq Aq Aq P P P A
10:34a   1:50p   2:25p   2:02p   2:44p   6:08p   12:53a ·   10:39a

Li Li S S S Sg Sg Sg Cp Cp Cp Aq Aq Aq P P P A A A A T
1:37a   12:53a   12:14a   1:50a   7:09a   4:30p   4:19a

S Sg Sg Sg Cp Cp Cp Aq Aq Aq P P P A A A A T T T G G G
12:09p   11:27a   11:57a   3:36p   11:27p   10:44a   11:26p

---

16 17 18 19 20 21 22 23 24 25 26 27 28 29 30 31

Cp Aq Aq Aq Aq P P P A A A T T T T G G G C C C C L
10:55p   1:46a   8:09a   6:21p   6:44a   7:01p   5:37a

P P A A A A T T T G G G G C C C L L
5:50p   2:59a   2:49p   3:43a   2:02p

P P A A A T T T G G G G C C C C L L L L V V V Li
2:43a   11:41a   11:01p   11:32a   11:01p   7:29a   12:00a

T T T G G G C C C C L L L V V V Li Li Li Li S
6:36a   7:09p   7:22a   4:58p   10:45p   12:56a

G G G C C C L L L L V V V Li Li Li S S S Sg Sg Sg Cp
1:50a   2:19p   1:05a   8:20a   12:11p   11:38a   10:45a

C L L L L V V V Li Li Li S S S Sg Sg Sg Cp Cp Cp Aq Aq
8:18p   7:33a   3:59p   8:45a   10:06p   9:30p   9:05p

L V V V Li Li Li Li S S S Sg Sg Sg Cp Cp Cp Aq Aq Aq P P P A
1:06p   9:58p   4:00a   6:58a   7:38a   7:37a   8:51a   12:59p

Li Li S S S Sg Sg Sg Cp Cp Cp Aq Aq Aq P P P A A A A T T
9:36a   1:33a   3:45p   5:07p   6:58p   10:43p   5:30a

Sg Sg Cp Cp Cp Cp Aq Aq Aq P P P A A A T T T T G G
9:48p   12:28a   3:34a   7:57a   2:37p   12:07a

Cp Cp Aq Aq Aq P P P A A A T T T G G G C C C C L
6:02a   10:05a   3:39p   10:55p   8:19a   8:02p   8:48a

P P A A A A T T T G G G G C C C L L L L V
9:33p   5:39a   3:37p   3:17a   4:08p   4:28a

A A T T T G G G C C C C L L L L V V V Li Li Li
11:18a   9:48p   9:46a   10:35p   11:08a   9:40p

---

16 17 18 19 20 21 22 23 24 25 26 27 28 29 30 31

T G G G C C C C L L L V V V V Li Li Li S S S Sg Sg
3:40a   3:55p   4:44a   5:01p   3:45a   11:48a   4:29p

C C L L L V V V Li Li Li S S S Sg Sg Sg
11:18a   11:17p   9:29a   6:13p   10:56p

C L L L L V V V Li Li Li S S S Sg Sg Sg Cp Cp Cp Aq Aq
6:40p   6:42a   4:17p   11:20   4:22a   8:06a   10:57a

V V Li Li Li S S S Sg Sg Sg Cp Cp Cp Aq Aq Aq P P P A
2:37a   7:04a   10:56a   1:40p   4:26p   7:37a   11:41p

Li Li S S S Sg Sg Sg Cp Cp Cp Aq Aq Aq Aq P P P A A A T T
4:14p   7:29p   9:02p   10:25p   1:00a   5:18a   11:26a

S Sg Sg Sg Cp Cp Cp Aq Aq Aq P P P A A A T T T T G G
5:36a   6:29a   6:33a   7:37a   10:55a   4:55p   1:28a

Cp Cp Aq Aq Aq P P P A A A T T T T G G G C C C C L
4:46p   4:34p   6:13p   10:57p   7:04a   6:05p   6:43a

Aq P P P A A A T T T G G G C C C L L L L V V
3:07a   3:34a   6:39a   1:39p   12:10a   12:49p   1:46a

A T T T T G G G C C C C L L L V V V Li Li Li
4:19p   9:48p   7:10a   7:34a   8:30a   7:53p

T G G G C C C C L L L V V V Li Li Li S S S Sg Sg
7:07a   3:22p   3:14a   4:09p   3:35a   12:12p   6:11p

C C L L L L V V V Li Li Li S S S S Sg Sg Sg Cp Cp
11:29a   12:20a   12:16p   9:04p   2:33a   5:42a

L L V V V Li Li Li Li S S S Sg Sg Sg Cp Cp Cp Aq Aq Aq P P
8:21a   8:52p   6:45a   12:40p   3:21p   4:21p   5:19p

1944

```
        1    2    3    4    5    6    7    8    9    10   11   12   13   14   15
      P A A    A T T    T    T G G    G C C    C    C L L    L V V    V
Jan   7:37p      11:08p          6:45a    3:50p         2:59a        3:39p

      T    T G G    G C C    C    C L L    L V V    V    V Li Li    Li S S
Feb   12:22p      9:43p           9:19a         10:08p        10:53p     10:21p

      G    G G C C    C L L    L    L V V    V Li Li    Li    S S    S S
Mar   3:40a       3:20p         4:17a     4:54p          4:12a       1:27p

      C L L    L    L V V    V Li Li    Li    Li S S    S Sg Sg    Sg    Sg Cp Cp
Apr   9:56p        10:48a      11:20p          10:10a     6:58p              1:53a

      L V V    V    Li Li Li    Li S S    S    S Sg Sg    Sg Cp Cp    Cp Aq Aq    Aq P
May   6:04p        6:40a         5:15p        1:25a      7:33a       12:09p      3:33p

      Li    Li    Li S S    S Sg Sg    Sg Cp Cp    Cp Aq Aq    Aq P P    P A A    A
Jn    1:28a       9:26p        2:38p       6:11p        8:58p         11:41p

      S    S Sg Sg    Sg Cp Cp    Cp    Cp Aq Aq    Aq P P    P A A    A T T    T G
Jly   6:33p       11:38p        2:12a          3:40a      5:18a       8:17a      1:14p

      Sg Cp Cp    Cp Aq Aq    Aq P P    P A A    A T T    T G G    G C C
Aug   9:39a       12:09p       10:02a    12:45     2:23p      6:43p       2:06a

      Aq P P    P A A    A T T    T    T G G    G C C    C L L    L    L V
Sep   11:12p       10:28p       10:33p         1:18a      7:47a      5:54p          6:02a

      P A A    A T T    T G G    G C C    C    C L L    L V V    V    V Li
Oct   9:29a      8:46a       10:02a    3:02p          12:06a      12:04p         12:54a

      T G G    G    G C C    C L L    L V V    V    V Li Li    Li S S    S
Nov   8:33p       12:09a       7:45a      7:01p         7:44a        7:45p

      G C C    C L L    L V V    V    V Li Li    Li    Li S S    S Sg Sg    Sg Cp
Dec   10:19a      4:58p       3:05a      3:28p          3:41a       1:47p       9:19p
```

1945

```
        1    2    3    4    5    6    7    8    9    10   11   12   13   14   15
      L    L V V    V Li Li    Li    Li S S    S Sg Sg    Sg    Sg Cp Cp    Cp Aq Aq
Jan   11:52a      11:45p           12:11p        10:52p         6:27a       10:55a

      V Li Li    Li S S    S    S Sg Sg    Sg Cp Cp    Cp Aq Aq    Aq P P    P    A
Feb   7:46a      8:21p          7:58a      4:24p       9:07p       10:50p        11:13p

      Li    Li    Li S S    S Sg Sg    Sg    Sg Cp Cp    Cp Aq Aq    Aq P P    P A A
Mar   3:22a       3:41p        1:34a          7:39a       9:49a       9:32a

      S S Sg Sg    Sg    Sg Cp Cp    Cp Aq Aq    Aq P P    P A A    A T T    T G G
Apr   10:05p       8:50a          4:22a       8:04p      8:35p      7:41p      7:36p

      Sg Cp Cp    Cp Aq Aq    Aq    Aq P P    P A A    A T T    T G G    G C C
May   2:37p       11:02p         4:18a       6:24a      6:24a      6:12a      7:52a

      Aq    Aq P P    P A A    A T T    T G G    G C C    C L L    L    L V
Jn    10:23a      1:48p        3:22p      4:16p      6:07p      10:24p         6:07a

      P A A    A T T    T    T G G    G C C    C L L    L V V    V    V Li
Jly   7:27p      10:04p          12:20a     3:11a      7:43a      3:01p          1:14a

      T    T G G    G C C    C L L    L V V    V    V Li Li    Li S S    S
Aug   6:22a       10:23a     3:54p      11:26p         9:23a       9:26p

      C    C L L    L    L V V    V Li Li    Li    Li S S    S Sg Sg    Sg    Sg Cp
Sep   10:23p       6:37a        4:51p          4:49a      5:28p              5:11a

      L    L V V    V Li Li    Li    Li S S    S Sg Sg    Sg Cp Cp    Cp Aq Aq    Aq
Oct   12:35p      11:18p           11:25a        12:18a     12:30p      10:00p

      V Li Li    Li S S    S Sg Sg    Sg    Sg Cp Cp    Cp Aq Aq    Aq P P    P    A
Nov   5:09a      5:30p        6:18a          6:33p       4:57a       12:00p        3:19p

      S    S    S Sg Sg    Sg    Sg Cp Cp    Cp Aq Aq    Aq P P    P A A    A    A T
Dec   12:28p          12:22a          10:32a     6:16p       11:11p       1:27a
```

1946

```
        1    2    3    4    5    6    7    8    9    10   11   12   13   14   15
      Sg    Sg Cp Cp    Cp Aq Aq    Aq P P    P    P A A    A T T    T G G    G C
Jan   7:10a       4:32p       11:42p          4:52a      8:23a      10:43a     12:34p

      Cp Aq Aq    Aq P P    P A A    A T T    T G G    G C C    C L L    L
Feb   12:16a      6:30a       10:36a     1:48p      4:47p      8:01p      11:55p

      Aq    Aq P P    P A A    A T T    T G G    G    G C C    C L L    L V
Mar   3:17p       6:20p       8:10p      10:16p         1:34a       6:18a      12:38p

      P A A    A T T    T G G    G C C    C L L    L V V    V    V Li Li
Apr   4:10a      4:57a      5:29a      7:26a      11:44a     6:28p          3:17a

      T    T G G    G C C    C L L    L    L V V    V Li Li    Li S S    S
May   3:07p       3:31p      6:15p          12:04a     8:57a       8:12p

      G C C    C L L    L V V    V Li Li    Li    Li S S    S Sg Sg    Sg    Sg Cp
Jn    2:12a      2:48a      7:02a      3:05p          2:06a      2:51p              3:38a

      L    L V V    V Li Li    Li    Li S S    S Sg Sg    Sg Cp Cp    Cp Aq Aq
Jly   3:56p       10:31p          8:46a      9:21p       10:03a     9:12p

      V Li Li    Li S S    S    S Sg Sg    Sg Cp Cp    Cp Aq Aq    Aq P P    P A
Aug   7:09a      4:30p          4:38a      5:19p       4:19a       12:36p      6:33p

      S    S Sg Sg    Sg    Sg Cp Cp    Cp Aq Aq    Aq P P    P    P A A    A T T
Sep   1:19p       1:21a          12:35p     8:37p       1:41a          5:03a

      Sg Cp Cp    Cp Aq Aq    Aq    Aq P P    P A A    A T T    T G G    G C
Oct   9:28a       9:19p          6:03a      10:58a     1:18p      2:39p      4:29p

      Cp Aq Aq    Aq P P    P A A    A T T    T    T G G    G C C    C L L
Nov   5:32a      3:22p       9:18p      11:42p         12:07a     12:20a     2:01a

      P    P    P A A    A T T    T G G    G C C    C L L    L V V    V Li
Dec   6:44a          10:41a     12:26a     10:48a     10:54a     1:20p      7:18p
```

```
 16   17   18   19   20   21   22   23   24   25   26   27   28   29   30   31

 V  Li Li   Li    S S    S Sg Sg   Sg    Sg Cp Cp   Cp Aq Aq   Aq   P P    P A A    A  T
4:29a     3:23p      10:47p     2:23a      3:08a      2:48a      3:16a              6:08a

 S    S Sg Sg   Sg Cp Cp   Cp Aq Aq   Aq    P P    P A A    A T T    T  G
    7:15a      12:29p     2:23p      2:08p      1:33p      2:41p      7:12p

 Sg   Sg Cp Cp   Cp Aq Aq   Aq    Aq P P    P A A    A T T    T G G    G C C
    8:08p      11:50p     12:56a     12:42a     1:04a      4:01a      11:02a

 Cp Aq Aq   Aq P P    P A A    A T T    T G G    G C C    C    C L L
6:46a      9:27a      10:43a     11:30a     2:03p      7:54p           5:37a

 P    P A A    A T T    T G G    G    G C C    C L L    L    L V V    V  L
    6:02p      8:17p      11:30p     5:05a      2:08p      1:59a              2:35p

 A T T    T G G    G C C    C L L    L    L V V    V Li Li   Li   Li   ?
2:53a      7:11a      1:31p      10:28p     9:58a      10:30p          10:08a

 G    G C C    C    C L L    L V V    V    V Li Li   Li    S S    S    S Sg Sg
    8:24p      5:52       5:26p      6:07a      6:14p                 3:48a

 C L L    L    L V V    V Li Li   Li    Li S S    S Sg Sg   Sg Cp Cp   Cp Aq Aq
12:09p     12:01a     12:44p     1:12a      11:49a     7:06p      10:39p

 V    V Li Li   Li    Li S S    S Sg Sg   Sg    Sg Cp Cp   Cp Aq Aq   Aq P P
    5:52p      7:12a      6:14p      2:52a      8:09a      9:56a

 Li   Li S S    S Sg Sg   Sg Cp Cp   Cp    Cp Aq Aq   Aq P P    P A A    A T T
    1:02p      11:48p     8:47a      3:15p      6:48p      7:02p      7:47p

 S Sg Sg   Sg Cp Cp   Cp Aq Aq   Aq    Aq P P    P A A    A T T    T G G
6:00a      2:48p      8:44p      1:16a      3:56a      5:22a      6:55a

 Cp   Cp Aq Aq   Aq P P    P A A    A T T    T G G    G C C    C    C  L
    2:43a      6:39a      9:42a      12:25p     3:28p      7:47p              2:22a
```

```
 16   17   18   19   20   21   22   23   24   25   26   27   28   29   30   31

 Aq P P    P A A    A T T    T G G    G    G C C    C L L    L V V    V
1:26p      3:22p      5:50p      9:37p      3:07a      10:34a     8:11p

 A    A T T    T G G    G C C    C L L    L    L V V    V Li
    12:08a     3:03a      8:44a      5:01p      3:15a      2:57p

 A T T    T G G    G C C    C    C L L    L V V    V Li Li   Li    Li S S
8:56a      10:06a     2:00p      10:36a     9:11a      9:16p      9:50a

 G C C    C    C L L    L V V    V    V Li Li   Li S S    S    S Sg Sg
10:20p     4:53a      3:05p      3:14a      3:52p      3:55a

 C L L    L V V    V    V Li Li   Li S S    S Sg Sg   Sg Cp Cp   Cp    Cp Aq
1:01p      10:00p     9:44a      10:20p     10:10a     8:22p      4:34a

 V    V Li Li   Li    Li S S    S Sg Sg   Sg    Sg Cp Cp   Cp Aq Aq   Aq P P
    5:08p      5:35a      5:25p      3:12a      10:35a     3:49p

 Li   Li S S    S    S Sg Sg   Sg Cp Cp   Cp Aq Aq   Aq P P    P    P A A    A T
    1:28p      1:35a      11:26a     6:12p      10:25p     1:07a      3:30a

 S Sg Sg   Sg Cp Cp   Cp    Cp Aq Aq   Aq P P    P A A    A T T    T G G    G C
9:55a      8:25p      3:29a      7:05a      8:30a      9:34a      11:48a     4:03p

 Cp   Cp Aq Aq   Aq P P    P A A    A T T    T G G    G C C    C    C  L
    1:15p      5:14p      6:08p      5:55p      6:36p      9:42p              3:49a

 Aq   Aq P P    P A A    A T T    T G G    G C C    C L L    L V V    V
    3:30a      5:08a      4:29a      3:47a      5:13a      9:57a      6:15p

 A    A T T    T G G    G C C    C L L    L V V    V Li Li   Li S
    3:46p      3:04p      3:19p      6:18a      1:03a      11:20a     11:44p

 T    T G G    G C C    C L L    L V V    V Li Li   Li    S S    S Sg Sg
    2:02a      2:39a      4:33a      0:46a      0:49p      8:42a      7:30p
```

```
 16   17   18   19   20   21   22   23   24   25   26   27   28   29   30   31

 C    C L L    L V V    V    V Li Li   Li S S    S    S Sg Sg   Sg Cp Cp   Cp
    3:11p      7:50p      3:38a      2:43p      3:25a      3:11p

 L V V    V Li Li   Li S S    S    S Sg Sg   Sg Cp Cp   Cp    Cp Aq
5:07a      12:44p     11:11p     11:42a     11:54p     9:29a

 V    V Li Li   Li S S    S    S Sg Sg   Sg Cp Cp   Cp Aq Aq   Aq    Aq P P
    8:47p      7:08a      7:31p      8:15a      6:40p      1:17a

 Li S S    S    S Sg Sg   Sg Cp Cp   Cp    Cp Aq Aq   Aq P P    P A A    A T
2:07p      2:30a      3:26p      2:51a      10:45a     2:35p      3:27p

 S Sg Sg   Sg Cp Cp   Cp    Cp Aq Aq   Aq P P    P A A    A    A T T    T G G
8:48a      9:40p      9:27a      6:30p      11:55p     1:58a      1:54a

 Cp   Cp Aq Aq   Aq    Aq P P    P A A    A T T    T G G    G C C    C L
    3:11p      12:36a     7:16a      10:49a     12:04p     12:12p     12:55p

 Aq   Aq P P    P A A    A T T    T G G    G C C    C L L    L    L V V
    6:11a      12:54p     5:25p      8:15p      9:43p      11:01p     1:41a

 A    A T T    T    T G G    G C C    C L L    L V V    V Li Li   Li    Li S
    10:56p     2:20a      5:07       7:39a      11:00a     4:25p              12:57a

 T G G    G C C    C L L    L V V    V    V Li Li   Li S S    S Sg Sg
7:47a      10:44a     2:16p      7:36p      12:47a     9:16a      8:32p

 C    C L L    L    L V V    V Li Li   Li S S    S    S Sg Sg   Sg Cp Cp   Cp
    7:42p      12:42a     7:36a      4:47p      4:05a      4:59p

 L V V    V Li Li   Li S S    S    S Sg Sg   Sg Cp Cp   Cp Aq Aq   Aq P
8:10a      1:18p      11:03p     10:46a     11:40p     12:26p     11:22p

 Li   Li   Li S S    S Sg Sg   Sg Cp Cp   Cp    Cp Aq Aq   Aq    Aq P P    P A A
    4:47a      4:51p      5:51a      6:27p      5:40a      2:23p
```

1947

Days: 1 · 2 · 3 · 4 · 5 · 6 · 7 · 8 · 9 · 10 · 11 · 12 · 13 · 14 · 15

Jan — A T T T G G G C C C L L L V V V V Li Li Li S S
8:02p · 10:22p · 10:27p · 9:56p · 10:50p · 2:59a · 11:19a

Feb — G G C C C L L L V V V Li Li Li S S S S Sg Sg Sg Cp
8:39a · 9:02a · 9:45a · 12:44p · 7:36p · 6:16a · 7:12p

Mar — G C C C L L L V V V Li Li Li Li S S S Sg Sg Sg Sg Cp
12:36p · 6:00p · 7:49p · 10:55p · 4:53a · 2:37p · 3:02a

Apr — L L V V V Li Li Li S S S Sg Sg Sg Sg Cp Cp Cp Aq Aq Aq
3:31a · 7:41a · 10:46a · 11:16p · 11:09a · 11:50p

May — V Li Li Li S S S S Sg Sg Sg Cp Cp Cp Cp Aq Aq Aq P P P A
2:27p · 9:30p · 7:10a · 6:53p · 7:42a · 7:18p · 3:55a

Jn — S S Sg Sg Sg Sg Cp Cp Cp Aq Aq Aq Aq P P P A A A T T
1:57p · 1:52a · 2:37p · 2:46a · 12:30p · 6:40p

Jly — Sg Sg Cp Cp Cp Aq Aq Aq Aq P P P A A A A T T T G G
8:03a · 8:40p · 9:03a · 7:32p · 3:10a · 7:17a

Aug — Cp Aq Aq Aq P P P P A A A T T T G G G C C C L L
2:50a · 2:48p · 1:19a · 10:37a · 3:14p · 5:45p · 6:06p

Sep — P P A A A T T T G G G C C C L L L V V V Li
7:04a · 3:08p · 9:15p · 1:10a · 3:10 · 3:52a · 5:18a

Oct — A T T T T G G G C C C L L L V V V Li Li Li S S
9:13p · 2:43a · 6:48a · 6:41a · 11:58a · 3:26p · 6:50p

Nov — G G C C C L L L V V V Li Li Li Li S S S Sg Sg Sg Cp
12:32p · 3:04p · 5:58p · 9:45p · 3:06a · 10:35a · 8:41p

Dec — C L L L V V V V Li Li Li S S S Sg Sg Sg Cp Cp Cp Aq
9:32p · 11:26p · 3:17a · 9:27a · 5:53a · 4:16a · 4:17p

1948

Days: 1 · 2 · 3 · 4 · 5 · 6 · 7 · 8 · 9 · 10 · 11 · 12 · 13 · 14 · 15

Jan — V V Li Li Li S S Sg S Sg Sg Sg Sg Cp Cp Cp Aq Aq Aq Aq P P
10:12a · 2:54p · 11:44p · 10:42a · 10:54p · 11:39a

Feb — S S S Sg Sg Sg Cp Cp Cp Cp Aq Aq Aq Aq P P P P A A A T
5:26a · 4:31p · 4:50a · 5:36p · 5:36a · 4:05p

Mar — S Sg Sg Sg Cp Cp Cp Cp Aq Aq Aq P P P P A A A T T T
12:45 · 10:53p · 11:15a · 11:52p · 11:32a · 9:39p

Apr — Cp Cp Aq Aq Aq Aq P P P A A A A T T T G G G C C
6:20p · 6:56a · 6:10p · 3:57a · 11:18a · 4:39p

May — Aq Aq P P P P A A A T T T G G G C C C C L L
2:43p · 2:26a · 11:45 · 6:16p · 10:36p · 1:38a

Jn — P A A A T T T T G G G C C C L L L V V V Li Li
10:53a · 8:30p · 3:04a · 6:28a · 8:11p · 9:49a · 12:35p

Jly — A T T T G G G C C C L L L V V V Li Li Li S S S
5:39a · 12:44p · 4:02p · 4:52p · 5:06p · 6:35p · 10:32p

Aug — G G C C C L L L V V V Li Li Li S S S Sg Sg Sg Cp Cp
2:17a · 3:11a · 2:26a · 2:33a · 4:53a · 10:52a · 7:54p

Sep — L L V V V Li Li Li S S S Sg Sg Sg Sg Cp Cp Cp Aq Aq Aq
1:20a · 12:36p · 1:38p · 5:57p · 1:59a · 12:58p

Oct — V Li Li Li Li S S S Sg Sg Sg Cp Cp Cp Aq Aq Aq P P P P A
11:31p · 12:51a · 2:38a · 9:32a · 7:45p · 8:03a · 7:34p

Nov — S S Sg Sg Sg Cp Cp Cp Cp Aq Aq Aq P P P P A A A T T
1:50a · 6:45p · 2:10a · 3:34p · 4:11a · 3:21p

Dec — Sg Sg Cp Cp Cp Aq Aq Aq Aq P P P A A A A T T T G G
4:17a · 12:35p · 11:48p · 12:29p · 12:05a · 8:43

1949

Days: 1 · 2 · 3 · 4 · 5 · 6 · 7 · 8 · 9 · 10 · 11 · 12 · 13 · 14 · 15

Jan — Cp Aq Aq A P P P A A A A T T T G G G C C C C L
9:10p · 7:58a · 8:39p · 6:25p · 11:52p · 2:06a

Feb — P P A A A T T T T G G G C C C L L L V V V Li
4:05a · 4:56p · 3:37a · 10:19a · 12:58p · 1:06p · 12:46p

Mar — P A A A T T T T G G G C C C L L L L V V Li Li
10:35a · 11:31p · 11:02a · 7:15p · 11:28p · 12:21a · 11:40p

Apr — T T G G G C C C L L L V V V Li Li Li S S S Sg
5:00p · 7:58a · 10:30a · 10:55a · 10:29a · 11:27a

May — G C C C L L L V V V Li Li Li S S S S Sg Sg Sg Sg Cp
7:42a · 2:08p · 6:07p · 8:05p · 8:53p · 10:00p · 1:00a

Jn — L L V V V Li Li Li S S S Sg Sg Sg Cp Cp Cp Aq Aq Aq
11:52p · 2:58a · 5:14a · 7:24p · 10:42a · 4:31p

Jly — V V Li Li Li S S S Sg Sg Sg Cp Cp Cp Cp Aq Aq Aq P P P A
8:22a · 11:23a · 2:46a · 7:04p · 1:11a · 10:02a · 9:45p

Aug — S S Sg Sg Sg Sg Cp Cp Cp Aq Aq Aq P P P P A A A T T
8:26p · 1:37a · 8:34a · 5:49p · 5:20a · 6:18p

Sep — Sg Cp Cp Cp Aq Aq Aq Aq P P P A A A A T T T G G G C
7:06a · 2:39p · 12:29p · 12:13p · 1:11a · 1:44p · 11:47p

Oct — Aq Aq Aq P P P A A A A T T T G G G G C C C L
6:21a · 6:29p · 7:26a · 8:00p · 6:50a · 2:30p

Nov — P P A A A T T T T G G G C C C L L L L V V
12:34a · 1:36p · 1:53a · 12:33p · 8:56p · 2:40a

Dec — A A T T T G G G C C C C L L L V V V Li Li Li S
8:20p · 8:28a · 6:29p · 2:26a · 8:30a · 12:42p · 3:12p

```
 16   17   18   19   20   21   22   23   24   25   26   27   28   29   30   31

S  Sg Sg   Sg   Sg Cp Cp   Cp      Cp Aq Aq   Aq P P    P A A    A    A T T    T  G
   11:06p        12:11p          12:37a  11:23a     8:08p         2:44a        6:53a

Cp    Cp Aq Aq       Aq P P    P      P A A    A T T    T  G G
      7:39a          5:54p          1:56a    8:07a    12:47p

Cp    Cp Aq Aq   Aq   Aq P P    P A A    A T T    T  G G    G C C    C    C  L
      3:33p          1:56a   10:17a    3:21p    6:15p    9:26p         12:23a

Aq P P    P A A    A T T    T    T  G G    G C C    C L L    L V V
9:22a    6:21p    10:53p   1:28a    3:24a    5:46a    9:17a

A    A    A T T    T  G G    G C C    C L L    L V V    V Li Li    Li    Li S
     8:52a    10:49a   11:29a   12:21p   2:54p    7:58p              3:45a

T  G G    G C C    C L L    L V V    V    V Li Li    Li S S    S Sg Sg
9:19p    9:32p    9:09p    10:07p   1:31a    9:18a    7:40p

G C C    C L L    L V V    V Li Li    Li S S    S    S Sg Sg    Sg Cp Cp    Cp
8:14a    7:35a    7:20a    9:36a    3:46p    1:44a    2:02p

L V V    V Li Li    Li S S    S    S Sg Sg    Sg Cp Cp    Cp    Cp Aq Aq    Aq P P
5:53p    7:10p    11:40p   8:36a    8:32p    9:19a    9:02p

Li    Li S S    S Sg Sg    Sg    Sg Cp Cp    Cp Aq Aq    Aq    Aq P P    P A A
9:14a    4:55p    4:00a    4:37p    4:24a    1:57p

S    S Sg Sg    Sg Cp Cp    Cp    Cp Aq Aq    Aq P P    P A A    A T T    T  G
1:57a    12:16p   12:40a   12:44p   10:28p   5:18a    9:36a

Cp    Cp Aq Aq    Aq P P    P    P A A    A T T    T  G G    G C C
8:45a    9:15p    7:53a    3:02p    6:35p    7:31p

Aq    Aq    Aq P P    P A A    A    A T T    T  G G    G C C    C L L    L V
4:59a    4:34p    1:08a    5:46a    7:03p    6:43a    6:47a
```

```
 16   17   18   19   20   21   22   23   24   25   26   27   28   29   30   31

P A A    A T T    T  G G    G C C    C L L    L V V    V Li Li    Li S
11:41p   9:53a    3:55p    6:18p    5:58p    5:00p    5:35p

T    T  G G    G    G C C    C L L    L V V    V Li Li    Li S S
11:52p   4:08a    5:06a    4:21a    4:07a    6:24a

T  G G    G C C    C L L    L V V    V Li Li    Li S S    S Sg Sg    Sg    Sg Cp
5:44a    10:54a   1:55p    2:41p    3:04p    4:55p    9:50p         0:33a

C L L    L V V    V    V Li Li    Li S S    S Sg Sg    Sg Cp Cp    Cp    Cp Aq
8:14p    10:29p   12:17a   2:51a    7:31a    3:26p    2:17a

L V V    V Li Li    Li S S    S Sg Sg    Sg    Sg Cp Cp    Cp Aq Aq    Aq P P    P
4:15a    7:07a    10:57a   12:46p   12:10a   10:31a   10:46p

Li S S    S Sg Sg    Sg    Sg Cp Cp    Cp Aq Aq    Aq    Aq P P    P A A    A
5:07p    11:31p   7:52a    6:17p    6:24a    6:54p

S S S    S Sg Sg    Sg Cp Cp    Cp    Cp Aq Aq    Aq P P    P    P A A    A T T    T  G G
5:12a    2:15p    1:03a    1:14p    1:57a    1:30p    9:54a

Cp    Cp Aq Aq    Aq P P    P    P A A    A T T    T    T  G G    G C C    C L
7:02a    7:23p    8:04a    8:00p    5:38a    1:30a    1:11p

Aq P P    P A A    A    A T T    T  G G    G C C    C L L    L V V
1:26a    2:01p    1:44a    11:37a   6:40p    10:30p   11:38p

A    A    A T T    T  G G    G    G C C    C L L    L V V    V Li Li    Li S
7:54a    5:12p    1:13a    5:09a    7:53a    7:51a    10:33a

T  G G    G C C    C L L    L V V    V Li Li    Li S S    S Sg Sg
11:59p   6:10a    10:31a   1:47p    4:32p    7:03p    10:55p

G C C    C L L    L V V    V Li Li    Li    Li S S    S Sg Sg    Sg Cp Cp    Co
1:57p    5:02p    7:03p    10:00o   1:10a    6:28a    12:48p
```

```
 16   17   18   19   20   21   22   23   24   25   26   27   28   29   30   31

L  L V V    V Li Li    Li S S    S Sg Sg    Sg Cp Cp    Cp    Cp Aq Aq    Aq P P
2:52a    4:04a    7:00a    12:10p   7:24a    4:28a    3:28a

Li    Li S S    S Sg Sg    Sg Cp Cp    Cp Aq Aq    Aq P P    P
1:57a    5:54p    12:53a   10:26a   9:55p

Li S S    S    S Sg Sg    Sg Cp Cp    Cp Aq Aq    Aq    Aq P P    P A A    A    A T
11:29p   1:35a    7:37a    4:14p    3:51a    4:42p              5:29a

Sg Cp Cp    Cp Aq Aq    Aq    Aq P P    P A A    A T T    T  G G
2:46p    11:40p   10:06a   11:00p   11:39a   10:45p

Cp    Cp Aq Aq    Aq P P    P    P A A    A T T    T    T  G G    G C C    C L
7:19a    5:29p    6:01a    6:39p    5:25a    1:36p    7:34p

Aq P P    P A A    A T T    T  G G    G C C    C L L    L V
1:42a    1:45p    2:28a    1:16p    8:58p    1:50a    5:26a

A    A    A T T    T  G G    G    G C C    C L    L V V    V Li Li    Li S
10:35a   9:53p    5:51a    12:35p   2:21p    4:45p

T    T  G G    G C C    C L L    L V V    V Li Li    Li S S    S  S Sg Sg
6:22a    3:09p    8:02p    9:54p    10:25p   11:21p   2:03a

C  C    C L L    L V V    V Li Li    Li S S    S Sg Sg    Sg Cp Cp    Cp Aq
6:03a    8:32a    8:41a    8:21a    9:22a    1:11a    8:18p

L  L V V    V Li Li    Li S S    S Sg Sg    Sg Cp Cp    Cp    Cp Aq Aq    Aq P P
6:37p    7:44p    7:19p    7:11p    9:15p    2:54a    12:23p

V Li Li    Li S S    S Sg Sg    Sg Cp Cp    Cp Aq Aq    Aq P P    P A A
5:35a    6:18a    6:15a    7:20a    11:28a   7:40p    7:18a

S    S Sg Sg    Sg Cp Cp    Cp Aq Aq    Aq    Aq P P    P A A    A    A T T    T  G
4:32p    6:03p    9:30p    4:22a    3:07p    3:59a    4:13p
```

```
1950
          1     2     3     4     5     6     7     8     9     10    11    12    13    14    15
Jan    G   G   G C  C       C   L L       L   V V       Li V Li      Li S  S       S        S Sg Sg
          1:54a       8:56a         2:05p         6:07p         9:26p              12:16a
Feb    C   L L       L   V  V       V   Li Li      Li S  S       S  Sg Sg      Sg Cp Cp      Cp Aq Aq
Feb 5:30p     9:34p         12:18a        2:50p         5:52a         9:45a          2:59p
Mar    C   L L       L   V  V       V   Li Li      Li S  S       S  Sg Sg      SG Cp Cp      Cp Aq Aq    Aq
Mar 3:27a     7:23a         8:59a         8:17a         11:39a        3:11p          8:55p
Apr    V   Li Li      Li S  S       S  Sg Sg       Sg Cp Cp      Cp Aq Aq      Aq P  P       P   A  A
Apr 7:37p     7:35p         7:40p         9:34p         2:28p         10:39a         9:33p
May    Li S  S       S  Sg Sg       Sg Cp Cp      Cp Aq Aq      Aq P  P       P        P   A  A       A   T  T
May 6:36a     5:51a         6:08a         9:24a         4:39p                3:47a          3:59p
Jn     Sg Cp Cp      Cp Aq Aq      Aq       Aq P  P       P   A  A       A   T  T       T        T   G  G       G   C
Jn 4:30p      6:25p         12:02a        9:46a         10:13p               11:03a         10:43p
Jly    Cp Aq Aq      Aq P  P       P   A  A       A        A   T  T       T   G  G       G        G   C  C       C   L
Jly 4:21a     8:52a         5:28p         5:13a         6:01p                5:34a          2:50p
Aug    P        P   A  A       A   T  T       T        T   G  G       G   C  C       C   L  L       L        L   V  V
Aug 2:05a     1:07p         1:43a         11:28a        10:33p               5:02a
Sep    T        T   T  G  G       G   C  C       C        C   L  L       L   V  V       V   Li Li      Li S  S
Sep 9:47a     9:51p         7:33a         1:51p         5:25p                7:26p
Oct    G   G   G C  C       C   L  L       L   V  V       V        V   Li Li      Li S  S       S  Sg Sg
Oct 5:58a     4:36p         11:49p        3:26a         4:44a                4:45a
Nov    C   C   L L       L   V  V       V   Li Li      Li S  S       S  Sg Sg      Sg Cp Cp      Cp Aq Aq
Nov 12:34a    9:19a         2:05p         3:26p         2:52p         2:29p          4:20p
Dec    L        L   V  V       V   Li Li      Li       Li S  S       S  Sg Sg      Sg Cp Cp      Cp Aq Aq     Aq P  P
Dec 4:35p     11:36p        2:29a         2:15a         1:18a         1:38a          5:12a


1951
          1     2     3     4     5     6     7     8     9     10    11    12    13    14    15
Jan    Li S  S       S  Sg Sg       Sg Cp Cp      Cp Aq Aq      Aq P  P       P   A  A       A        A   T
Jan 11:00a    12:36p        12:32p        12:36p        3:02p         8:24p                  7:10a
Feb    Sg Sg       Sg Cp Cp      Cp Aq Aq      Aq       Aq P  P       P   A  A       A   T  T       T        T   G  G
Feb 12:13a 11:05p        1:32a         6:42a         3:36p                 3:19a
Mar    Sg Sg       Sg Cp Cp      Cp Aq Aq      Aq P  P       P   A  A       A        A   T  T       T   G  G       G
Mar 4:30a     7:10a         10:46a        4:20p         12:35a        11:37a
Apr    Aq       Aq P  P       P        P   A  A       A   T  T       T   G  G       G   C  C       C   L  L
Apr 5:47p     12:18a        8:53a         7:43p         8:05a         8:14p
May    P        P   A  A       A   T  T       T        T   G  G       G   C  C       C        C   L  L       L   V  V
May 6:27a     3:48p         2:51a         2:02p         3:49a         2:40p
Jn     T        T   T  G  G       G   C  C       C   L  L       L        L   V  V       V        V   Li Li      Li S
Jn 9:03a      9:31a         10:11a        9:43p         6:30a                  11:13a
Jly    G   G   G C  C       C   L  L       L        L   V  V       V   Li Li      Li S  S       S  Sg Sg
Jly 4:00p     3:35a         1:01p         7:12p         9:59p
Aug    C   L L       L        L   V  V       V   Li Li      Li S  S       S  Sg Sg      Sg Cp Cp      Cp Aq
Aug 10:06p    9:17a         6:30p         1:21a         5:29a         7:18a          7:54a
Sep    V        V   Li Li      Li S  S       S  Sg Sg       Sg Cp Cp      Cp Aq Aq      Aq P  P       P   A
Sep 12:29a    2:05p         11:10a        2:05p         4:12p         6:24p          9:50p
Oct    Li S  S       S  Sg Sg       Sg Cp Cp      Cp Aq Aq      Aq       Aq P  P       P   A  A       A   T
Oct 1:21p     4:47p         7:30p         10:20p               1:47a         6:19a          12:40p
Nov    S  Sg Sg      SG Cp Cp      Cp Aq Aq      Aq P  P       P   A  A       A   T  T       T   G  G
Nov 12:18a    1:40a         12:54p        7:23a         12:54p        8:09p          5:16a
Dec    Cp       Cp Aq Aq      Aq P  P       P   A  A       A        A   T  T       T   G  G       G   C  C       C
Dec 10:46a    1:21p         6:22p         2:05a         11:55a        11:23p


1952
          1     2     3     4     5     6     7     8     9     10    11    12    13    14    15
Jan    P        P   A  A       A   T  T       T   G  G       G   G  C  C       C  L L       L        L   V
Jan 12:47a    7:57a         6:13p         6:00a         6:42p                7:12p
Feb    A   T  T       T   G  G       G   C  C       C        C   L  L       L   V  V       V   Li Li      Li
Feb 3:06p     12:19a        12:18p        1:13a         1:10p         11:59p
Mar    G   G  G G      G   C  C       C        C   L  L       L   V  V       V   Li Li      Li S  S
Mar 7:36a     7:06p         8:57a         8:02p         6:27a         2:25p
Apr    G   C C       C   L  L       L        L   V  V       V   Li Li      Li S  S       S        S Sg Sg       Sg Cp
Apr 2:48a     3:45p         3:50a         1:53p         9:12p         2:16           6:29a
May    L        L   L  V  V       V   Li Li      Li S  S       S  Sg Sg      Sg Cp Cp      Cp Aq Aq
May 12:07p    10:27p        5:32a         9:45p         12:24p        2:44p
Jn     V        V   Li Li      Ii S  S       S  Sg Sg       Sg Cp Cp      Cp Aq Aq      Aq       Aq P  P       P   A
Jn 7:34a      3:15p         7:20p         8:53p         9:58p                11:17p         2:48p
Jly    Li       Li S  S       S  Sg Sg       Sg Cp Cp      Cp Aq Aq      Aq P  P       P   A  A       A   T  T
Jly 12:18a    5:38a         7:20a         7:10a         7:00a         9:05a          3:37p
Aug    Sg       Sg Cp Cp      Cp Aq Aq      Aq P  P       P   A  A       A   T  T       T        T   G  G       G   C
Aug 5:52p     6:20p         5:42p         6:08p         9:01p         3:36a          2:24p
Sep    Cp Aq Aq      Aq P  P       P   A  A       A   T  T       T        T   G  G       G   C  C       C   C. L
Sep 4:25a     4:10a         4:10a         6:10a         11:27a        8:42p          9:15a
Oct    P        P   A  A       A   T  T       T   G  G       G   G  C  C       C   L  L       L        L   V  V
Oct 2:45a     4:45p         8:42p         4:34a         4:10p                5:00a
Nov    A   T  T       T   G  G       G   C  C       C        C   L  L       L   V  V       V   Li Li      Li S
Nov 2:14a     6:39a         1:28p         12:24a        10:42a        10:53p         8:37a
Dec    G   G  G C C       C        C   L  L       L   V  V       V   Li Li      Li S  S       S        S Sg Sg
Dec 10:30p    8:36a         9:02p         9:36a         7:56p                2:30a
```

```
   16   17   18   19   20   21   22   23   24   25   26   27   28   29   30   31
Sg Cp Cp     Cp Aq Aq     Aq P P     P A A     A     A T T     T     T G G     G C C
3:07a        7:07a        1:45p      11:41p          12:07p          12:40a    10:47a

Aq P P     P     P A A     A T T     T     T G G     G C C     C
10:14p     8:02a          8:12p      9:02a           7:58p

Aq P P     P A A     A     A T T     T G G     G     G C C     C L L     L     V V
5:01a      3:23p          3:32a      4:26p           4:15a     1:00p           5:55p

A     A T T     T G G     G     G C C     C L L     L     L V V     V     Li Li
9:59a           10:54p          10:59a    8:52p           3:27a           6:25a

T     T G G     G C C     C     C L L     L V V     V Li Li     Li S S     S     Sg Sg
4:52a           4:48p          3:04a           10:47a     3:21p      4:58p           4:43p

C     C     C L L     L     V V     V Li Li     Li     Li S S     S     Sg Sg     Sg Cp Cp
8:36a              4:28p           10:06a          1:16a      2:25a           2:49a

L     L V V     V     V Li Li     Li S S     S     Sg Sg     Sg Cp Cp     Cp Aq Aq     Aq P P
10:03p     3:32a           7:27a      9:54a           11:39a    1:58p                       6:24p

V     Li Li     Li     Li S S     S     Sg Sg     Sg Cp Cp     Cp Aq Aq     Aq     Aq P P     P A A     A T
9:30a     12:48p          3:35p           6:23p          9:55p                  3:04a      10:47a          9:21p

S     Sg Sg     Sg Cp Cp     Cp     Cp Aq Aq     Aq P P     P A A     A     A T T     T G
9:13p          11:50p          4:01a            10:11a                5:09a           5:27p

Sg Cp Cp     Cp Aq Aq     Aq P P     P     P A A     A T T     T     T G G     G C C
5:55a        9:28a        3:56p      1:00a          12:04p          12:22a    1:02p

Aq P P     P     P A A     A T T     T     T G G     G C C     C     C L L
9:44p      6:39a           6:09p      6:38a           7:12p           7:02a

P A A     A     A T T     T G G     G     G C C     C L L     L V V     V     V Li
1:02p          12:11a          12:48p          1:17a     12:44p     10:38p          6:20a
```

```
   16   17   18   19   20   21   22   23   24   25   26   27   28   29   30   31
T     T G G     G C C     C     C L L     L V V     V Li Li     Li S S     S     Sg
7:36p           8:06a          10:17p          4:25a      11:45a     5:47p           8:13p

G C C     C     C L L     L V V     V Li Li     Li S S     S     Sg
3:49p     2:59a           11:41a     5:54p           10:29p          1:49a

G C C     C L L     L V V     V Li Li     Li S S     S     Sg Sg     Sg Cp Cp     Cp Aq
12:05a    11:43a          8:34p           2:18a      5:35a           7:40a        9:51a        1:04p

L     L V V     V Li Li     Li S S     S     Sg Sg     Sg Cp Cp     Cp Aq Aq     Aq P P
6:07a     12:09p          2:52p           3:40p           4:22p                6:36p        11:16p

V Li Li     Li     Li S S     S     Sg Sg     Sg Cp Cp     Cp Aq Aq     Aq P P     P A A     A T
9:59p              1:19a           1:42a           1:08a           1:45          5:10a      11:55a          9:35p

S     S Sg Sg     Sg Cp Cp     Cp Aq Aq     Aq P P     P A A     A     A T T     T G
12:24p       11:36a          11:07a           12:53p          6:17p           3:19a           2:53p

Sg Cp Cp     Cp Aq Aq     Aq P P     P     P A A     A T T     T G G     G     G C C
10:13p       9:43p        10:33p     2:24a          10:08a          9:09p           9:42a

Aq     Aq P P     P A A     A T T     T     T G G     G C C     C     C L L     L V
9:20a      12:01p          6:31p      4:28a           4:44p                5:10a           3:58p

A     A     A T T     T G G     G     G C C     C L L     L     L V V     V Li
3:44a              12:50p          12:35a          1:05p           12:01a          8:08a

T     T G G     G     G C C     C L L     L     L V V     V Li Li     Li S S     S
9:26p           8:43a          9:23p           8:59a           5:20p      10:06p

G C C     C     C L L     L V V     V     V Li Li     Li S S     S     Sg Sg     Sg Cp
4:30p     5:12a           5:32p           3:06a      7:31a           10:18a          10:23a

C L L     L     L V V     V Li Li     Li S S     S     Sg Sg     Sg Cp Cp     Cp Aq Aq     Aq P
12:05p    12:50a          11:37a          6:31p           9:22p          9:22p        8:36p        9:26p
```

```
   16   17   18   19   20   21   22   23   24   25   26   27   28   29   30   31
V     V Li Li     Li S S     S     Sg Sg     Sg Cp Cp     Cp Aq Aq     Aq P P     P A A
6:14p           2:28a           7:20a           8:38a           8:07a      7:59a           9:45a

Li S S     S     Sg Sg     Sg Cp Cp     Cp Aq Aq     Aq P P     P A A     A T T
9:50a      2:52p          5:57p           6:40p           6:51p      8:05p           11:54p

S     Sg Sg     Sg     Sg Cp Cp     Cp Aq Aq     Aq P P     P A A     A T T     T G G     G
8:30p      12:30a          3:20a           4:37a           6:21a      9:43a           4:22p

Cp     Cp Aq Aq     Aq P P     P A A     A T T     T     T G G     G C C     C L
9:21a      1:53a          3:12p      7:21p           1:40a           1:23a           11:24p

Aq P P     P A A     A     A T T     T G G     G G C     C     C L L     L V V
5:26p      9:20p          2:33a           9:51p     7:29p           7:12a           8:02p

A     A T T     T G G     G     G C C     C L L     L     L V V     V Li Li
8:18a           4:31p           2:41a     2:30p           3:09a           3:21p

T G G     G     G C C     C L L     L     L V V     V Li Li     Li     Li S S     S     Sg
10:03p    8:37a          8:37p           9:26a           9:36p      8:08a              2:57p

C     C     C L L     L V V     V     V Li Li     Li S S     S     Sg Sg     Sg Cp Cp
2:23a              3:04p           3:01a      1:21p           9:45p           2:41a

L V V     V     V Li Li     Li S S     S     S Sg Sg     Sg Cp Cp     Cp Aq Aq     Aq P
9:44p     9:11a           7:28p      3:28a            9:15a        12:48p                 1:48p

V Li Li     Li     Li S S     S Sg Sg     Sg Cp Cp     Cp Aq Aq     Aq P P     P A A     A
4:52p              2:02a      9:20a          2:41p           7:17p      9:12p           11:27p

S     S Sg Sg     Sg Cp Cp     Cp     Cp Aq Aq     Aq P P     P A A     A T T     T G
4:53p        3:55p          12:15a          2:57a      5:48a           9:49a           3:13p

Sg     Sg Cp Cp     Cp Aq Aq     Aq P P     P A A     A T T     T G G     G     G C C
5:41a        7:20a        9:00a      11:21a          3:53p           9:53p           6:15a
```

1953

	1	2	3	4	5	6	7	8	9	10	11	12	13	14	15
Jan	C LL	L	L	V V	V LiLi	Li	Li S S	S Sg Sg	Sg Cp Cp	Cp Aq					
	4:34p		4:36a		5:30p		4:53p	12:29p	4:11p	5:10p					
Feb	V	V	V LiLi	Li S S	S Sg Sg	Sg	Sg Cp Cp	Cp Aq Aq	Aq P P						
		12:24a	12:19p	9:35p		2:23a	4:08a	3:53a							
Mar	V	V LiLi	Li S S	S	S Sg Sg	Sg Cp Cp	Cp Aq Aq	Aq P P	A						
	6:24a	6:31p		4:53a	11:12a	2:38p	2:54p		2:14p						
Apr	Li S S	S Sg Sg	Sg Cp Cp	Cp Aq Aq	Aq	Aq P P	P A A	A T T							
	12:27a	10:33a	5:56p	10:46p	12:38a	1:00a	1:33a								
May	Sg	Sg Cp Cp	Cp	Cp Aq Aq	Aq P P	P A A	A T T	T G G	G C						
	11:11p	4:30a	7:51a	9:46a	11:18a	1:44p	6:36p								
Jn	Cp Aq Aq	Aq P P	P A A	A T T	T G G	G G C C	C L L								
	9:45a	1:25p	3:58p	5:43p	9:22p	2:30a	10:30a								
Jly	P	P A A	A	A T T	T G G	G C C	C L L	L	L V V						
	9:12p	1:29a	5:04a	11:25a	7:52a	6:14a									
Aug	A T T	T G G	G C C	C	C L L	L V V	V	V LiLi	Li S						
	5:50a	10:26a	5:14p	2:23a	1:19p	1:45a	2:33p								
Sep	G C C	C	C L L	L V V	V	V LiLi	Li S S	S	S Sg Sg						
	10:36p	8:11a	8:00p	8:00a	8:44p	8:22a									
Oct	C LL	L	L V V	V LiLi	Li	Li S S	S Sg Sg	Sg Cp Cp	Cp						
	2:02p	1:39a	2:20p	2:48a	2:24p	11:41p									
Nov	V	V LiLi	Li	Li S S	S Sg Sg	Sg	Sg Cp Cp	Cp Aq Aq	Aq P P						
	9:02p	9:22a	8:15p	5:29a	12:23p	2:53p									
Dec	Li	Li S S	S	S Sg Sg	Sg Cp Cp	Cp Aq Aq	Aq P P	P	P A A						
	4:53p	3:33a	12:06p	6:01p	10:36p	1:54a									

1954

	1	2	3	4	5	6	7	8	9	10	11	12	13	14	15
Jan	S Sg Sg	Sg Cp Cp	Cp	Cp Aq Aq	Aq P P	P A A	A T T	T G G							
	12:18p	8:06p	1:01a	4:59a	7:31a	10:15a	1:40p								
Feb	Cp	Cp Aq Aq	Aq P P	P A A	A T T	T G G	G C C	C L							
	10:26a	12:59p	2:25p	4:11p	7:21p	12:35a	7:30a								
Mar	Cp Aq Aq	Aq P P	P A A	A T T	T	T G G	G C C	C L L							
	8:44p	11:01a	11:26p	11:50p	1:30a	6:08a	1:25p								
Apr	P	P A A	A T T	T G G	G C C	C L L	L	L V V	V Li						
	10:13a	9:51a	9:59a	12:52p	7:22p	5:14a	5:23p								
May	A T T	T	T G G	G C C	C	C L L	L V V	V LiLi	Li	Li S						
	8:35p	8:15p	9:43p	2:28a	11:11a	11:20p	12:12p								
Jn	G	G C C	C L L	L V V	V	V LiLi	Li S S	S	S Sg Sg						
	7:51a	11:31a	6:55p	6:00a	7:06p	7:00a									
Jly	C LL	L	L V V	V LiLi	Li	Li S S	S Sg Sg	SG Cp Cp							
	9:20p	3:32a	1:45p	2:23a	2:30p	12:54a									
Aug	V	V LiLi	Li	Li S S	S Sg Sg	Sg	Sg Cp Cp	Cp Aq Aq	Aq P P						
	9:57p	10:01a	10:52p	9:27a	4:44p	9:10p									
Sep	Li S S	S	S Sg Sg	Sg Cp Cp	Cp	Cp Aq Aq	Aq P P	P A A	A T						
	5:41p	6:23a	6:08p	2:28a	7:00a	8:27a	9:17a								
Oct	S Sg Sg	Sg	Sg Cp Cp	Cp Aq Aq	Aq P P	P A A	A T T	T G G							
	1:31p	1:53a	11:25a	5:08p	7:01p	7:17p	6:51p								
Nov	Cp Aq Aq	Aq	Aq P P	P A A	A T T	T G G	G C C	C L							
	7:00p	2:24a	5:58a	6:04a	5:36a	5:36a	8:45a								
Dec	Aq	Aq P P	P A A	A T T	T G G	G C C	C L L	L V V							
	9:21a	2:25a	4:32p	4:29p	4:28p	6:20p	11:07p								

1955

	1	2	3	4	5	6	7	8	9	10	11	12	13	14	15
Jan	A	A	A T T	T G G	G C C	C L L	L V V	V LiLi	Li						
	12:29a	1:59a	3:06a	4:43a	8:49a	4:12p									
Feb	T G G	G C C	C L L	L V V	V	V LiLi	Li S S	S	S Sg						
	9:09a	11:34a	2:20p	6:31p	1:14a	11:48a	12:35a								
Mar	G	G C C	C L L	L V V	V	V LiLi	Li S S	S	S Sg Sg						
	5:47p	9:43p	3:02a	10:13a	8:17a	8:02a									
Apr	C LL	L V V	V LiLi	Li	Li S S	S Sg Sg	Sg	Sg Cp Cp	Cp Aq						
	3:29a	9:37a	5:47p	4:04a	3:57p	4:59a	4:30p								
May	V	V LiLi	Li	Li S S	S Sg Sg	Sg	Sg Cp Cp	Cp Aq Aq	Aq P						
	11:39p	10:21a	10:36p	11:17a	11:24p	9:11a									
Jn	Li S S	S	S Sg Sg	Sg Cp Cp	Cp	Cp Aq Aq	Aq P P	P A A	A						
	4:24p	4:49a	5:18p	5:13a	3:35p	10:35p									
Jly	S Sg Sg	Sg Cp Cp	Cp	Cp Aq Aq	Aq P P	P A A	A T T	T G						
	10:51a	11:24p	10:49a	8:55p	4:49a	9:53a	12:05p								
Aug	Cp	Cp Aq Aq	Aq	Aq P P	P A A	A T T	T G G	G C C	C L						
	5:19p	2:33a	10:03a	3:04p	6:51p	8:50p	10:44p								
Sep	Aq P P	P A A	A T T	T	T G G	G C C	C L L	L V V							
	10:09a	4:23p	8:49p	12:12a	2:50a	5:50a	9:38a								
Oct	P A A	A T T	T G G	G C C	C L L	L V V	V LiLi	Li							
	12:53a	4:18a	6:21a	8:21a	11:23a	4:04p	10:26p								
Nov	T G G	G C C	C L L	L V V	V	V LiLi	Li S S	S	S Sg						
	2:53p	3:39p	5:21p	9:39p	4:27a	1:28p	12:37a								
Dec	G C C	C L L	L V V	V LiLi	Li S S	S	S Sg Sg	Sg Cp Cp							
	1:10a	1:26a	4:05a	10:02a	7:24p	7:00a	7:19p								

Block 1

16	17	18	19	20	21	22	23	24	25	26	27	28	29	30	31
Aq	Aq P	P	P	A	A	A	T	T	T	T G	G	C	C C	C	L L
	5:19p	6:17p		9:27p			3:32a			12:15p		11:28p			11:27a

Signs row 1: Aq Aq P P P A A A T T T T G G C C C C L L L L V
Times row 1: 5:19p 6:17p 9:27p 3:32a 12:15p 11:28p 11:27a

P A A A T T T G G G C C C C L L L V V
3:32a 4:52a 9:47a 5:09p 5:37a 5:59p

A A T T T G G G C C C L L L L V V V Li Li Li
2:44p 5:51p 12:42a 11:59a 12:18a 12:51p

T G G G C C C L L L L V V V Li Li Li S S S Sg
3:47a 9:04a 6:53p 7:12a 8:00p 7:12a 4:08a

C C C L L L V V V V Li Li Li S S S Sg Sg Sg Sg Cp Cp
2:57a 2:36p 3:12a 2:36p 11:26p 5:32a

L V V V V Li Li Li S S S S Sg Sg Sg Cp Cp Cp Aq Aq Aq P
10:32p 11:06a 11:15p 8:17a 1:37p 5:03p 7:12p

V Li Li Li Li S S S S Sg Sg Sg Cp Cp Cp Cp Aq Aq Aq P P P A A
6:46p 7:12a 3:19p 11:28p 2:13a 3:15a 4:07a

S S S S Sg Sg Cp Cp Cp Aq Aq Aq Aq P P P A A A T T T G G
1:36a 9:16a 12:21p 1:22p 12:53p 1:18p 4:30a

Sg Cp Cp Cp Aq Aq Aq P P P P A A T T T T G G G C C
5:33p 10:10p 11:57p 3:31a 11:41p 12:35a 5:13a

Cp Aq Aq Aq P P P A A A T T T G G G C C C L L L L V
6:18a 9:39a 10:27a 10:04a 10:52a 1:55p 9:14p 8:01a

P A A A T T T G G G C C C C L L L V V V V Li
7:19p 8:25p 9:18p 11:59p 5:53a 3:48p 4:22a

A T T T G G G C C C L L L L V V V Li Li Li Li S S
4:25a 6:40a 10:00a 3:37p 12:15a 12:18p 1:07a

Block 2

16	17	18	19	20	21	22	23	24	25	26	27	28	29	30	31

G C C C C L L L V V V V Li Li Li Li S S S S Sg Sg Sg Sg Cp
6:22p 12:20a 8:57a 8:30p 9:03a 8:50p 5:33a

L L V V V V Li Li Li S S S S S Sg Sg Sg Cp Cp
4:50p 4:11a 4:34p 5:00a 2:49p

L V V V V Li Li Li S S S S Sg Sg Sg Cp Cp Cp Cp Aq Aq Aq P
11:31p 11:02a 11:29p 12:09p 11:01p 0:10a 9:50a

Li Li Li S S S Sg Sg Sg Sg Cp Cp Cp Aq Aq Aq P P P A A
5:59a 6:18p 5:36a 2:14p 7:21p 8:53p

S S S Sg Sg Sg Cp Cp Cp Aq Aq Aq Aq P P P A A A T T T G
12:12a 11:03a 7:55p 2:12a 5:31a 7:00a 6:50a

Sg Cp Cp Cp Cp Aq Aq Aq P P P A A A T T T G G G C C
5:19p 1:28a 7:43a 11:50a 2:46p 4:17p 6:10p

Cp Aq Aq Aq P P P A A A T T T G G G C C C L L L V
8:15a 1:16p 7:13p 11:53p 2:36a 5:48a 10:10a 3:09p

P A A A A T T T G G G C C C L L L V V V V Li
11:34p 1:33a 4:13a 8:04a 1:31p 8:41p 6:03a

T T G G G C C C L L L L V V V Li Li Li Li S S
10:21a 1:25p 7:05p 3:12a 1:07p 12:57a

G C C C C L L L V V V Li Li Li Li S S S S Sg Sg Sg Sg Cp
8:21p 12:44a 8:55a 7:13p 7:24a 7:55p 8:12a

L L V V V V Li Li Li S S S S S Sg Sg Sg Cp Cp Cp Cp Aq
2:50p 1:13a 1:40p 2:23a 2:04p 1:00a

V V Li Li Li S S S S Sg Sg Sg Cp Cp Cp Cp Aq Aq Aq P P P
8:11a 8:20p 8:48p 8:46p 6:49a 2:56p

Block 3

16	17	18	19	20	21	22	23	24	25	26	27	28	29	30	31

Li S S S S Sg Sg Sg Sg Cp Cp Cp Aq Aq Aq P P P P A A A T T
3:48a 4:24p 4:25a 1:41p 8:53p 2:32a

Sg Sg Cp Cp Cp Aq Aq Aq Aq P P P A A A T T T G
12:43p 1:23p 5:00a 9:04a 12:05p 2:52p

Sg Cp Cp Cp Cp Aq Aq Aq P P P A A A T T T G G G C C C
9:00p 7:34a 2:30p 5:48p 7:39p 9:04p 11:18p

Aq Aq Aq P P P A A A T T T G G G C C C L L L L V
12:19a 4:25a 5:23a 5:43a 6:22a 9:08a 3:03p

P A A A T T T G G G C C C L L L V V V V Li Li
2:16p 4:15p 3:59p 3:40p 4:53p 9:11p 5:07a

A T T T G G G C C C L L L V V V Li Li Li S S S
2:18a 2:43a 2:25a 2:38a 5:29a 10:32p

G G C C C L L L V V V Li Li Li Li S S S Sg Sg Sg Sg Cp
12:43p 1:06p 3:11p 8:18p 5:28a 5:41p 6:36a

L L V V V Li Li Li S S S S Sg Sg Sg Cp Cp Cp Cp Aq Aq
1:11a 5:32a 1:38p 1:19a 1:55p 1:23a

V Li Li Li S S S S Sg Sg Sg Cp Cp Cp Cp Aq Aq Aq P P P
2:49p 10:33p 9:01a 10:22p 10:06a 7:16p

Li S S S Sg Sg Sg Sg Cp Cp Cp Aq Aq Aq Aq P P P A A A T T
6:49a 5:07p 5:36a 6:18p 4:42a 11:07a 1:50p

Sg Sg Cp Cp Cp Cp Aq Aq Aq P P 'P A A A A T T T G G
12:48p 1:21a 12:54p 8:47p 12:36a 1:26a

Cp Cp Aq Aq Aq P P P P A A A T T T G G G C C C L L
8:00a 7:47p 5:08a 10:26a 12:27p 12:11p 11:41a

1956

	1	2	3	4	5	6	7	8	9	10	11	12	13	14	15
Jan	L	V V	V Li	Li	Li	Li S	S	S Sg	Sg	Sg	Sg Cp	Cp	Cp Aq	Aq	Aq
	1:00p		5:11p			1:36a		1:16p			1:55a		2:33p		
Feb	Li	Li S	S	S Sg	Sg	Sg	Sg Cp	Cp	Cp Aq	Aq	Aq	Aq P	P	P A	A
	9:06a		7:40p			8:38a		9:00p			8:09a		4:57p		
Mar	S	S	S Sg	Sg	Sg Cp	Cp	Cp	Cp Aq	Aq	Aq P	P	P A	A	A	T
	3:37a			3:49p			4:36a		3:23p		11:48p			5:57a	
Apr	Sg Cp	Cp	Cp	Cp Aq	Aq	Aq P	P	P	P A	A	A T	T	T G	G	G C
	11:44p		12:48p		11:59p			7:55a		1:28p		4:42p		7:31p	
May	Cp Aq	Aq	Aq	Aq P	P	P A	A	A T	T	T	T G	G	G C	C	C L
	8:19p		8:33a		5:14p		10:24p			1:01a		2:12a		3:38a	
Jn	P	P	P A	A	A T	T	T G	G	G C	C	C L	L	L V	V	V Li
	2:37a		8:33a		11:21a		11:38a		11:34a		1:13p		5:24p		
Jly	A	A T	T	T G	G	G C	C	C L	L	L V	V	V Li	Li	Li S	
	5:39p		9:24p		10:25p		9:45p		9:41p		12:10a		6:16a		
Aug	T G	G	G C	C	C L	L	L V	V	V Li	Li	Li S	S	S Sg	Sg	Sg
	6:29a		8:27a		8:25a		8:08a		9:13a		1:45p		9:54p		
Sep	C L	L	L V	V	V Li	Li	Li S	S	S	S Sg	Sg	Sg Cp	Cp	Cp	Cp Aq
	6:18p		6:41p		7:38p		11:01p		5:43a		4:48p		5:50a		
Oct	L V	V	V Li	Li	Li S	S	S Sg	Sg	Sg	Sg Cp	Cp	Cp Aq	Aq	Aq	Aq P
	3:41a		5:41a		8:46a		3:00p		12:46a		1:16p		1:55a		
Nov	Li S	S	S	S Sg	Sg	Sg Cp	Cp	Cp Aq	Aq	Aq	Aq P	P	P A	A	A
	5:56p		12:14a		9:33a		9:06p		10:11a		9:06p				
Dec	S Sg	Sg	Sg Cp	Cp	Cp	Cp Aq	Aq	Aq P	P	P	P A	A	A T	T	T G
	8:08a		5:44p		5:00a		5:53p		6:00a		2:27p		7:06p		

1957

	1	2	3	4	5	6	7	8	9	10	11	12	13	14	15
Jan	Cp	Cp Aq	Aq	Aq	Aq P	P	P A	A	A T	T	T	T G	G	G C	C
	12:18p		12:57a		1:01a		11:23p		5:27a			7:58a			
Feb	Aq P	P	P A	A	A	A T	T	T G	G	G C	C	C L	L	L V	V
	7:29a		7:49p		6:37a		2:25p		5:59p		6:58p		6:27p		
Mar	P	P	P A	A	A T	T	T G	G	G	G C	C	C L	L	L V	V
	1:51a			12:44a		9:06p		2:31a		5:02a		4:55a			
Apr	A T	T	T G	G	G C	C	C L	L	L V	V	V Li	Li	Li S	S	
	6:24p		2:44a		8:35a		12:26p		12:14p		3:17p		5:00p		
May	T G	G	G C	C	C L	L	L V	V	V Li	Li	Li	Li S	S	S Sg	Sg
	8:37a		2:00a		5:52p		8:45p		11:11p		2:17a		6:08a		
Jn	C L	L	L	L V	V	V Li	Li	Li S	S	S Sg	Sg	Sg Cp	Cp	Cp	Cp Aq
	11:37p		2:17a		5:10a		9:08a		2:18p		9:42p		7:24a		
Jly	L V	V	V Li	Li	Li S	S	S Sg	Sg	Sg	Sg Cp	Cp	Cp Aq	Aq	Aq	Aq P
	8:28a		10:35a		2:25p		8:29p		4:23a		2:53p		2:46a		
Aug	Li S	S	S	S Sg	Sg	Sg Cp	Cp	Cp Aq	Aq	Aq	Aq P	P	P A	A	A
	8:02p		1:44a		10:08a		9:10p		9:02a		9:46a				
Sep	Sg	Sg Cp	Cp	Cp	Cp Aq	Aq	Aq P	P	P	P A	A	A T	T	T	T G
	3:51p		2:59a		3:28p		3:46a		3:57p			2:22a			
Oct	Cp	Cp Aq	Aq	Aq P	P	P	P A	A	A T	T	T G	G	G C	C	C
	9:01a		9:44p		10:14a		9:45p		7:56a		3:37p				
Nov	Aq P	P	P A	A	A	A T	T	T G	G	G C	C	C	C L	L	L V
	4:45a		5:30p		4:44a		2:05p		9:23p		2:39a		6:40a		
Dec	P A	A	A T	T	T G	G	G	G C	C	C L	L	L V	V	V Li	Li
	1:25a		1:00p		10:06p		4:12a		8:44a		12:05p		2:32p		

1958

	1	2	3	4	5	6	7	8	9	10	11	12	13	14	15
Jan	T	T G	G	G C	C	C L	L	L V	V	V Li	Li	Li S	S	S	S Sg
	7:33a		1:16p		4:37p		6:35p		8:35p		11:28p			3:56a	
Feb	C	C	C L	L	L V	V	V Li	Li	Li S	S	S Sg	Sg	Sg Cp	Cp	Cp
	2:29a			3:32a		4:17a		5:31a		9:41a		4:17p			
Mar	C	C L	L	L V	V	V Li	Li	Li S	S	S Sg	Sg	Sg Cp	Cp	Cp	Cp Aq
	1:03p		2:14p		1:43p		1:56p		4:19p		9:51p			6:49a	
Apr	L V	V	V Li	Li	Li S	S	S Sg	Sg	Sg Cp	Cp	Cp Aq	Aq	Aq	Aq P	P
	12:49a		12:56a		12:20a		1:20a		4:55a		1:05p			12:27a	
May	Li	Li S	S	S Sg	Sg	Sg Cp	Cp	Cp Aq	Aq	Aq	Aq P	P	P	P A	A
	10:53a		11:34a		2:14p		8:29p		7:00a			7:37p			
Jn	Sg	Sg	Sg Cp	Cp	Cp Aq	Aq	Aq	Aq P	P	P	P A	A	A T	T	T
	2:54p		12:19a		5:33a		2:43p		2:46a		3:28p			2:33a	
Jly	Cp	Cp Aq	Aq	Aq P	P	P	PA	A	A T	T	T	T G	G	G C	C
	2:54p		11:06p		10:39a		11:25p		10:53a			7:11p			
Aug	Aq P	P	P A	A	A	A T	T	T G	G	G	G C	C	C L	L	L V
	7:24a		6:24p		6:48a		7:07p		4:45a		9:45a		12:27p		
Sep	A	A T	T	T	T G	G	G C	C	C L	L	L V	V	V Li	Li	Li S
	2:11p		2:51a		1:22p		7:57p		10:47p		11:14p			11:04p	
Oct	T	T G	G	G C	C	C	C L	L	L V	V	V Li	Li	Li S	S	S Sg
	9:36a		8:50p		5:10a		9:09a		10:18a		9:40a			9:37a	
Nov	G C	C	C L	L	L V	V	V Li	Li	Li S	S	S Sg	Sg	Sg Cp	Cp	Cp
	2:43a		12:19p		5:47p		8:33p		8:39p		8:22p		9:16p		
Dec	L	L	L V	V	V Li	Li	Li S	S	S Sg	Sg	Sg Cp	Cp	Cp Aq	Aq	Aq P
	12:30a			4:41a		6:22a		7:00a		8:00a		11:04a			5:35p

```
16   17   18   19   20   21   22   23   24   25   26   27   28   29   30   31

Aq   P P        P A A      A T T      T G G      G C C      C L L      L V V      V          V Li
     1:53a      11:19a     6:17p      9:50p      10:58p     10:58p     11:20p     2:14a

A    A T T      T G G      G C C      C L L      L V V      V Li Li    Li S
     12:12a     4:45a      7:47a      8:38a      9:50a      12:32p     6:11p

T    T G G      G C C      C L L      L V V      V Li Li    Li         Li S S     S Sg Sg
     10:37a     1:30p      4:21p      6:51p      10:08p     3:42a      12:04p

C    C L L      L          L V V      V Li Li    Li S S     S Sg Sg    Sg         Sg Cp Cp
     10:03p     1:28a      6:06a      12:24p     8:44p      8:00a

L    L V V      V Li Li    Li S S     S Sg Sg    Sg Cp Cp   Cp         Cp Aq Aq   Aq P
     6:39a      11:45a     7:00a      4:16a      3:17p      3:46a      4:15p

Li   Li         Li S S     S Sg Sg    Sg Cp Cp   Cp         Cp Aq Aq   Aq P P     P A
     12:27a     10:33a     9:50p      10:16a     11:12p     10:15a

S    S Sg Sg    Sg         Sg Cp Cp   Cp Aq Aq   Aq         Aq P P     P A A      A T T
     3:57p      3:48a      4:29p      4:49a      4:12p      1:09a

Sg   Cp Cp      Cp Aq Aq   Aq         Aq P P     P A A      A T T      T G G      G L L
     9:51a      10:44p     10:55a     9:38p      6:38a      1:08p      4:51p

Aq   Aq P P     P          P A A      A T T      T G G      G C C      C L L
     5:44p      4:17a      12:19p     6:27p      10:46p     1:50a

P    P A A      A T T      T          T G G      G C C      C L L      L V V      V Li Li
     12:14p     7:26p      12:31a     4:31a      7:21a      10:14a     1:26p

A T T          T G G      G C C      C L L      L V V      V Li Li    Li S S
     4:50a      9:02a      11:36a     1:11p      3:51p      7:33p      12:56

G    G C C      C L L      L V V      V          V Li Li    Li S S     S Sg Sg    Sg         SG Cp
     8:58p      9:21p      10:27p     1:16a      6:29a      2:30p      12:43a
```

```
16   17   18   19   20   21   22   23   24   25   26   27   28   29   30   31

C L L          L V V      V Li Li    Li S S     S Sg Sg    Sg         Sg Cp Cp   Cp Aq Aq   Aq
     7:48a      7:29a      8:22a      12:44p     8:20p      6:37a      6:48p

V Li Li        Li S S     S          S Sg Sg    Sg Cp Cp   Cp         Cp Aq Aq   Aq         P
     6:20p      8:46p      2:45a      12:48p     1:16a      1:43p

V Li Li        Li S S     S Sg Sg    Sg Cp Cp   Cp         Cp Aq Aq   Aq P P     P          P A A
     5:05a      6:31a      11:04a     7:4?       7:40a      8:30p      8:22a

S Sg Sg        Sg         Sg Cp Cp   Cp Aq Aq   Aq         Aq P P     P A A      A T T
     8:52p      4:00a      3:24p      3:59a      3:59p      1:42a

Sg   Cp Cp     Cp Aq Aq   Aq         Aq P P     P A A      A T T      T G G      G C C
     1:05p      11:03p     11:39a     12:08a     9:56a      4:47p      8:44p

Aq   Aq P P    P          P A A      A T T      T G G      G C C      C L L
     7:19p      8:23a      7:00p      2:24       5:41a      7:30a

P    P A A      A A T T    T G G      G C C      C L L      L V V      V Li Li
     3:28p      3:14a      11:50a     3:58p      5:24p      5:24p      5:54p

A T T          T G G      G C C      C L L      L V V      V Li Li    Li S S     S Sg
     10:08a     7:50p      1:45a      3:52a      3:51a      3:15a      4:24a      8:05a

G    G C C      C L L      L V V      V Li Li    Li S S     S Sg Sg    Sg Cp Cp
     9:40a      1:40p      2:22p      2:05p      2:14p      4:48p      10:56p

C L L          L V V      V Li Li    Li S S     S Sg Sg    Sg Cp Cp   Cp Aq Aq   Aq
     8:55p      11:34p     12:31a     12:56a     2:50a      7:34a      4:31p

V    V Li Li    Li S S     S Sg Sg    Sg Cp Cp   Cp         Cp Aq Aq   Aq P P     P
     8:31a      10:31      1:11p      5:29p      1:08a      12:30p

Li S S         S Sg Sg    Sg         Sg Cp Cp   Cp Aq Aq   Aq P P     P P A A    A Li
     5:46p      9:37p      2:42a      10:07a     8:50p      9:27a      9:38p
```

```
16   17   18   19   20   21   22   23   24   25   26   27   28   29   30   31

Sg   Sg Cp Cp   Cp Aq Aq   Aq         Aq P P     P A A      A          A T T      T G G      G C
     10:10a     6:18p      4:39a      5:05p      5:59a      4:27p      11:21p

Cp Aq Aq       Aq P P     P          P A A      A T T      T          T G G      G C
     1:05a      11:57a     12:09a     12:54p     12:43a     9:08a

Aq   Aq P P     P A A      A T T      T          T G G      G C C      C L L      L
     6:18p      6:48a      7:06p      7:12a      4:38p      10:40p

P A A          A A T T    T G G      G C C      C C L L    L V V      V Li
     1:04p      1:33a      12:54p     10:49p     6:05a      10:00a     11:24a

A T T          T G G      G          G C C      C L L      L V V      V Li Li    Li S S     S Sg
     8:00a      6:55p      4:11a      11:10a     4:20p      7:26p      8:33p      10:01p

G    G C C      C L L      L V V      V          V Li Li    Li S S     S Sg Sg    Sg Cp
     10:44a     5:02p      9:41p      1:11a      3:27a      6:31a      9:47a

C C L L        L V V      V Li Li    Li S S     S Sg Sg    Sg Cp Cp   Cp Aq Aq   Aq
     12:37a     3:56a      6:21a      8:45a      12:22p     5:02p      11:15p

V    V Li Li    Li S S     S Sg Sg    Sg Cp Cp   Cp Aq Aq   Aq P P     P          P A
     1:41p      2:44p      5:34p      10:30p     5:32a      2:50p      1:51a

S    S          S Sg Sg    Sg Cp Cp   Cp Aq Aq   Aq P P     P A A      A T T
     12:21a     4:04a      10:59a     8:57p      8:13a      8:44p

Sg   Sg Cp Cp   Cp Aq Aq   Aq P P     P A A      A T T      T G G      G
     11:31a     5:08p      2:22a      2:30p      3:09a      3:20p

Cp Aq Aq       Aq P P     P A A      A T T      T G G      G C C      C L
     1:18a      8:57a      8:49p      9:27a      9:53p      8:44a      5:53p

P    P A A      A T T      T          T G G      G C C      C L L      L          L V V
     4:02a      4:53p      5:12a      3:35p      11:47p     5:57a
```

1959

	1	2	3	4	5	6	7	8	9	10	11	12	13	14	15
Jan	V	Li	Li	Li	S	S	S	Sg	Sg	Sg	Cp	Cp	Cp	Aq	Aq

Jan: V Li Li / Li S S / S Sg Sg / Sg Cp Cp / Cp Aq Aq / Aq / Aq P P / P A A
10:39a 1:47p 3:41p 5:48p 9:07p 2:56a 12:21p

Feb: S Sg Sg / Sg / Sg Cp Cp / Cp Aq Aq / Aq P P / P / P A A / A / A T T / T G
10:10p 1:30a 5:48a 12:11p 9:14p 8:37a 9:32p

Mar: S Sg Sg / Sg Cp Cp / Cp Aq Aq / Aq P P / P / P A A / A T T / T / T G
3:40a 7:11a 12:36p 6:59p 5:14a 4:29p 5:12a

Apr: Cp Aq Aq / Aq / Aq P P / P A A / A T T / T / T G G / G / G C
6:11p 2:16a 12:09p 11:44p 12:27p 12:46a

May: Aq P P / P A A / A / A T T / T G G / G C C / C / C L L / L
7:12a 5:54p 6:00a 6:36p 7:00a 5:52p

Jn: A / A T T / T / T G G / G C C / C / C L L / L / L V V / V Li Li
11:56a 12:37a 12:45p 11:18p 8:06a 1:47p

Jly: T / T G G / G C C / C / C L L / L V V / V / Li Li / Li S S / S
7:12a 7:07a 5:17a 1:19p 7:21p 11:24p

Aug: G C C / C L L / L V V / V / V Li Li / Li S S / S Sg Sg / Sg Cp Cp
2:31a 12:21p 7:26p 12:53a 4:35p 7:41a 10:14a

Sep: L / L V V / V Li Li / Li S S / S Sg Sg / Sg Cp Cp / Cp Aq Aq / Aq P
3:44a 8:01a 10:42a 1:03p 4:07p 7:47p 1:17a

Oct: V Li Li / Li S S / S Sg Sg / Sg Cp Cp / Cp / Cp Aq Aq / Aq P P / P A A
5:03p 6:56p 9:03p 9:43p 1:14a 7:22a 3:21p

Nov: S Sg Sg / Sg Cp Cp / Cp Aq Aq / Aq P P / P A A / A / A T T / T G
5:05a 5:23a 7:32a 1:01p 9:18p 8:11a 8:07p

Dec: Sg Cp Cp / Cp Aq Aq / Aq P P / P / P A A / A / A T T / T G G / G C
3:37p 4:21p 7:49p 3:23a 2:06p 2:33a 3:04p

1960

Jan: Aq / Aq P P / P A A / A T T / T / T G G / G C C / C / C L L
5:00a 10:57a 8:42p 9:14a 9:52p 9:33a

Feb: A / A / A T T / T G G / G / G C C / C L L / L / L V V / V Li
4:28a 4:22p 5:12a 4:30p 1:55a 9:11a

Mar: A T T / T / T G G / G C C / C / C L L / L V V / V Li Li / Li S
1:10p 12:09a 12:54p 12:53a 10:07a 4:19p 9:35p

Apr: G / G C C / C L L / L / L V V / V / V Li Li / Li S S / S Sg
9:02p 9:22a 7:22p 1:27a 4:59a 6:41a

May: C / C L L / L / L V V / V Li Li / Li S S / S Sg Sg / Sg Cp Cp / Cp Aq
5:05p 4:17a 11:23a 2:36p 3:43p 3:59p 5:25p

Jn: L V V / V Li Li / Li / Li S S / S Sg Sg / Sg Cp Cp / Cp Aq Aq / Ag P P
12:00n 8:34p 12:53a 2:25a 1:57a 1:59a 3:47a

Jly: V / V Li Li / Li S S / S Sg Sg / Sg Cp Cp / Cp Aq Aq' / Aq P P / P A A / A T
3:49a 9:40a 12:31p 12:51p 12:06p 1:03p 4:27p 11:54p

Aug: S Sg Sg / Sg Cp Cp / Cp Aq Aq / Aq P P / P / P A A / A T T / T G G
8:52p 10:51p 10:42p 11:20p 1:30a 7:45a 5:41p

Sep: Cp / Cp Aq Aq / Aq P P / P A A / A T T / T / T G G / G C C / C
7:50a 9:21a 11:46a 4:40p 1:32a 1:31p

Oct: Aq P P / P A A / A / A T T / T G G C C / C / C L L / L V
5:34p 9:10p 2:17a 10:37a 9:34p 10:05a 10:01p

Nov: A / A T T / T G G / G / G C C / C L L / L / L V V / V Li Li
10:22a 6:50p 5:37a 6:05p 6:37a 4:17p

Dec: T / T G G / G C C / C / C L L / L V V / V / V Li Li / Li S S
2:02a 1:00p 1:31a 2:16p 1:05a 8:03a

1961

Jan: C / C / C L L / L V V / V / V Li Li / Li S S / S Sg Sg / Sg Cp Cp
8:24a 8:40p 8:22a 5:05p 9:32p 10:57p

Feb: L / L V V / V / Li Li / Li S S / S Sg Sg / Sg Cp Cp / Cp Aq Aq / Aq P
2:58a 2:32p 12:04a 5:58a 9:06a 9:14a 9:04a

Mar: L V V / V Li Li / Li S S / S Sg Sg / Sg Cp Cp / Cp Aq Aq / Aq P P
9:34a 8:26p 5:29a 12:13p 4:46p 6:41p 7:20p

Apr: Li / Li S S / S Sg Sg / Sg Cp Cp / Cp / Cp Aq Aq / Aq P P / P A A / A T
11:37a 5:56p 10:29p 2:08a 3:53a 6:00a 9:27a

May: S / S Sg Sg / Sg Cp Cp / Cp Aq Aq / Aq P P / P A A / A T T / T G G
12:15a 3:56a 7:00a 9:35a 1:05p 5:30p 11:58p

Jn: Cp / Cp Aq Aq / Aq P P / P A A / A T T / T / T G G / G C C / C
1:11p 3:11p 6:51p 11:58p 7:11a 4:22p

Jly: Aq P P / P / P A A / A T T / T G G / G C C / C / C L L / L V
10:02p 12:04a 5:00a 12:20p 10:25p 9:50a 11:04p

Aug: A / A T T / T G G / G / G C C / C L L / L / L V V / V Li Li
11:08a 5:53p 4:02a 4:17p 4:46a 5:05p

Sep: T G G / G C C / C L L / L / L V V / V Li Li / Li S S / S Sg
12:58a 10:01a 10:13p 11:00a 10:56p 9:41a 5:39p

Oct: C / C / C L L / L V V / V / V Li Li / Li S S / S Sg Sg / Sg Cp
4:40a 5:53 5:00a 3:54p 12:18a 6:18a

Nov: L / L V V / V li Li / Li S S / S / S Sg Sg / Sg Cp Cp / Cp Aq Aq / Aq P
1:33a 1:38p 11:37p 7:00a 12:15p 4:03p 2:11p

Dec: V Li Li / Li S S / S Sg Sg / Sg Cp Cp / Cp / Cp Aq Aq / Aq P P / P A
10:13p 8:41a 3:30p 9:32p 12:18a 2:52a 5:29a

16	17	18	19	20	21	22	23	24	25	26	27	28	29	30	31
A	A T 12:45a	T	T G 1:16p	G	G C 11:46p	C	C	C L 7:33a	L	L V 12:27p	V	V Li 4:23p	Li	Li S 7:06p	S
G	G	G C 8:54a	C	C L 4:42p	L	L V 9:04p	V	V Li 11:44p	Li	Li	Li S 1:22a	S			
G	G C 5:28p	C	C	C L 2:21a	L	L V 10:30a	V	V Li 9:25a	Li	Li S 9:36a	S	S Sg 10:39a	Sg	Sg Cp 12:54p	Cp
C L 11:08a	L	L V 5:20p	V	V Li 8:03p	Li	Li S 8:16p	S	S Sg 7:49p	Sg	Sg Cp 8:35p	Cp	Cp	Cp Aq 12:28a	Aq	
L V 1:47a	V	V Li 6:00a	Li	Li S 7:10a	S	S Sg 6:24a	Sg	Sg Cp 6:22a	Cp	Cp Aq 8:45a	Aq	Aq P 2:27p	P	P	P A 12:08a
Li S 4:32p	S	S Sg 4:59p	Sg	Sg Cp 5:37p	Cp	Cp Aq 6:20p	Aq	Aq P 10:42p	P	P	P A 6:37a	A	A T 6:36p	T	
S Sg 1:42a	Sg	Sg Cp 2:54a	Cp	Cp Aq 4:41a	Aq	Aq P 8:05a	P	P A 3:12p	A	A	A T 1:51a	T	T G 2:37p	G	G
Cp Aq 1:13p	Aq	Aq P 5:19p	P	P	P A 12:09a	A	A T 9:38a	T	T G 10:13p	G	G	G C 11:07a	C	C L 8:59p	L
P	P A 8:31a	A	A T 6:03p	T	T	T G 6:00a	G	G C 6:48p	C	C	C L 5:50a	L	L V 1:32p	V	
A	A T 1:42a	T	T G 1:28p	G	G	G C 2:10a	C	C L 2:10p	L	L V 10:57p	V	V	V Li 3:44a	Li	Li S 5:13a
G	G	G C 8:36a	C	C L 9:10p	L	L	L V 7:11a	V	V Li 1:26p	Li	Li S 4:04p	S	S Sg 4:06p	Sg	
C	C	C L 3:00a	L	L V 1:31p	V	V Li 9:13p	Li	Li	Li S 1:44a	S	S Sg 2:48a	Sg	Sg Cp 2:30a	Cp	Cp Aq 2:40a

16	17	18	19	20	21	22	23	24	25	26	27	28	29	30	31
L V 7:34p	V	V	V Li 3:32a	Li	Li S 9:05a	S	S Sg 11:47a	Sg	Sg Cp 12:53	Cp	Cp Aq 1:22p	Aq	Aq P 3:20p	P	P A 7:49p
Li	Li S 2:38p	S	S Sg 6:15p	Sg	Sg Cp 8:45p	Cp	Cp Aq 10:41p	Aq	Aq	Aq P 1:23a	P	P A 3:58a	A		
S	S Sg 11:07p	Sg	Sg Cp 11:30p	Cp	Cp	Cp Aq 12:58a	Aq	Aq P 5:13a	P	P A 12:16p	A	A T 9:38p	T	T	T G 8:35a
Sg Cp 8:31a	Cp	Cp Aq 11:17a	Aq	Aq P 3:48p	P	P A 9:45p	A	A	A T 5:53a	T	T G 4:25p	G	G	G C 4:36a	
Aq	Aq P 9:03p	P	P	P A 3:16a	A	A T 12:15p	T	T G 11:08p	G	G	G C 11:08a	C	C	C L 12:09p	L
P A 9:02a	A	A T 5:44p	T	T	T G 5:12a	G	G C 5:36p	C	C	C L 6:12a	L	L V 6:13p	V	V	
T	T	T G 11:00a	G	G C 11:41p	C	C	C L 12:03p	L	L V 11:44p	V	V	V Li 9:38a	Li	Li S 5:02p	S
G	G C 6:23a	C	C L 6:42p	L	L	L V 5:50a	V	V Li 3:10p	Li	Li S 9:59a	S	S	S Sg 3:29a	Sg	Sg Cp 6:31a
C L 2:12a	L	L V 1:28p	V	V Li 9:51p	Li	Li	Li S 3:58a	S	S Sg 8:53a	Sg	Sg Cp 12:15p	Cp	Cp Aq 2:36p	Aq	
V	V	V Li 6:30a	Li	Li S 12:03p	S	S Sg 3:17p	Sg	Sg Cp 5:52p	Cp	Cp Aq 8:06p	Aq	Aq P 11:31p	P	P	P A 4:04a
Li S 9:52p	S	S	S Sg 12:27a	Sg	Sg Cp 1:38a	Cp	Cp Aq 2:38a	Aq	Aq P 5:10a	P	P A 9:55a	A	A T 4:57p	T	
S Sg 11:07a	Sg	Sg Cp 11:30a	Cp	Cp Aq 11:35a	Aq	Aq P 12:21p	P	P A 4:00p	A	A T 10:36p	T	T	T G 6:11a	G	G c 7:49p

16	17	18	19	20	21	22	23	24	25	26	27	28	29	30	31
Cp Aq 10:20p	Aq	Aq P 9:59p	P	P A 11:53p	A	A	A T 4:49a	T	T G 1:54p	G	G	G C 2:02a	C	C L 2:30p	L
P	P A 9:43a	A	A T 1:22p	T	T G 8:55p	G	G	G C 8:26a	C	C L 9:00p	L	L			
P A 8:25p	A	A T 11:10p	T	T	T G 5:23a	G	G C 3:48p	C	C	C L 4:22a	L	L V 4:55p	V	V	V Li 3:09a
T	T G 2:40p	G	G	G C 12:16a	C	C L 12:08p	L	L	L V 12:57a	V	V Li 11:09a	Li	Li S 7:26p	S	
G	G C 8:34a	C	C L 8:08p	L	L	L V 8:38a	V	V Li 8:21p	Li	Li	Li S 4:30a	S	S Sg 9:30a	Sg	Sg Cp 11:36a
C L 3:36a	L	L V 4:17p	V	V	V Li 4:25a	Li	Li S 1:51p	S	S Sg 7:16p	Sg	Sg Cp 9:28p	Cp	Cp Aq 9:43p	Aq	
V	V	V Li 11:15a	Li	Li S 10:00p	S	S Sg 4:53a	Sg	Sg	Sg Cp 7:49a	Cp	Cp Aq 8:17a	Aq	Aq P 7:30a	P	P A 8:10a
Li	Li S 4:30a	S	S Sg 12:47p	Sg	Sg Cp 5:28p	Cp	Cp Aq 5:28p	Aq	Aq P 6:23p	P	P A 6:08p	A	A T 7:55p	T	T
Sg	Sg	Sg Cp 12:53a	Cp	Cp Aq 3:58a	Aq	Aq P 4:46a	P	P A 4:54a	A	A T 6:00a	T	T G 9:55a	G	G C 5:39p	
Cp	Cp Aq 10:42a	Aq	Aq P 1:01p	P	P A 2:34p	A	A T 4:23p	T	T G 7:43p	G	G	G C 2:21a	C	C L 12:48p	L
P	P A 10:03p	A	A	A T 12:58a	T	T G 5:05a	G	G C 11:43a	C	C L 9:07p	L	L	L V 9:27a	V	
A	A T 7:32a	T	T G 12:51p	G	G C 8:14p	C	C	c L 5:39a	L	L V 5:30p	V	V	V Li 6:24a	Li	Li S 5:39p

1962

	1	2	3	4	5	6	7	8	9	10	11	12	13	14	15
Jan	S	S	S Sg Sg	Sg Cp Cp	Cp Aq Aq	Aq P P	P A A	A T T	T G
			1:53a	5:38a	7:20a	8:00a	9:23a	12:50p	7:04p
Feb	Sg Cp Cp	Cp Aq Aq	Aq P P	P A A	A T T	T	T G G	G C C
	4:13p	6:02p	5:57p	5:24p	7:26p		12:30a	8:45a
Mar	Sg Cp Cp	Cp Aq Aq	Aq P P	P A A	A T T	T G G	G C C	C
	1:42a	4:52a	4:47a	4:07a	4:37a	7:54a	2:56p	
Apr	Aq P P	P A A	A T T	T G G	G C C	C	C L L	L V V
	3:27p	3:27p	3:00p	5:00p	10:23p		7:45a	8:20p
May	P A A	A T T	T G G C C	C	C L L	L	L V V	Li Li
	1:00a	1:40a	3:20a 7:22a		3:20p		3:10a	4:05p
Jn	T G G	G C C	C	C L L	L V V	V Li Li	Li	SS	S Sg
	1:00p	5:24p		12:27a	10:51a	11:40p		11:53a	9:21p
Jly	G C C	C L L	L V V	V	V Li Li	Li S S	S	S Sg Sg	Sg Cp
	1:50a	9:05a	7:54p		7:25a	8:00p		6:27s	12:40p
Aug	L	L V V	V Li Li	Li	Li S S	S S Sg	Sg Cp Cp	Cp	Cp Aq Aq
	2:43a	2:52p		3:33a	2:50p	10:24p		1:50a
Sep	Li	Li	Li S S	S Sg Sg	Sg	Sg Cp Cp	Cp Aq Aq	Aq P P	P A A
	10:37a	10:21p		7:33a	12:28p	2:02p	1:48p
Oct	S	S	S Sg Sg	Sg Cp Cp	Cp Aq Aq	Aq P P	P A A T T	T
	4:36a	2:40p	9:07p		12:00n	12:33a 11:55p	
Nov	Sg Cp Cp	Cp	Cp Aq Aq	Aq P P	P A A	A T T	T G G	G C C
	8:20p		4:02a	8:40a	10:27a	10:51a	11:00a	1:23p
Dec	Cp Aq Aq	Aq P P	P A A	A T T	T G G	G C C	C	C L L
	9:21a	2:52p	6:00p	7:54p	9:14p	11:47p		4:30a

1963

	1	2	3	4	5	6	7	8	9	10	11	12	13	14	15
Jan	P A A	A	A T T	T G G	G C C	C L L	L V V	V V Li
	11:41p		2:43a	5:19a	9:15a	2:07p	10:03p	8:37
Feb	T	T G G	G C C	C L L	L	L V V	V Li Li	Li	Li S S
	11:14a	4:04p	10:09p		6:38a	5:13p		5:24a
Mar	T G G	G C C	C	C L L	L V V	V	V Li Li	Li S S	S
	5:08p	9:42p		4:27a	1:35p		12:30a	12:51p	
Apr	C	C L L	L V V	V	V Li Li	Li S S	S S Sg Sg	Sg Cp Cp
	9:54a	7:35p		7:00a	7:25a		8:12a	7:53p
May	L	L V V	V Li Li	Li	Li S S	S S Sg	Sg	Sg Cp Cp	Cp Aq Aq
	1:12a	12:51p		1:33a	1:57p		1:18a	1:030a
Jn	Li	Li	Li S S	S Sg Sg	Sg	Sg Cp Cp	Cp Aq Aq	Aq P P	P A
	8:12a	8:13p		7:24a	4:22p	11:26p		4:03a
Jly	S	S	S Sg Sg	Sg Cp Cp	Cp Aq Aq	Aq	Aq P P	P A A	A T T
	4:00a	2:03p	10:34p		4:40a	9:15a	12:28p
Aug	Sg Cp Cp	Cp	Cp Aq Aq	Aq P P	P A A	A T T	T G G	G C C
	10:25p	6:18a	11:23a	3:04p	5:41p	8:31p	11:58p
Sep	Aq	Aq P P	P A A	A	A T T	T G G	G C C	C L L	L V
	8:23p	10:54p		12:23p	2:03a	5:08a	10:38a	5:53p
Oct	P	P A A	A T T	T G G	G C C	C L L	L V V	V	V Li
	8:40a	9:33a	9:29a	11:29a	3:55p	11:37a		9:23p
Nov	T	T G G	G C C	C L L	L	L V V	V Li Li	Li	Li S S
	7:43p	7:58p	10:46p		5:10a	3:13p		3:23a
Dec	G	G C C	C L L	L V V	V Li Li	Li	Li S S	S S Sg Sg	Sg
	6:31a	7:52a	12:36p	9:24p		9:26a	10:07p	

1964

	1	2	3	4	5	6	7	8	9	10	11	12	13	14	15
Jan	L	L V V	V	V Li Li	Li S S	S	S Sg Sg	Sg Cp Cp	Cp Aq
	9:50p		5:19a	4:29p		5:24a	5:34p		3:35a
Feb	V Li Li	Li	Li S S	S S Sg Sg	Sg	Sg Cp Cp	Cp Aq Aq	Aq P P	P
	2:21p		12:24a	12:54p		1:30a	11:41a	6:54p	
Mar	Li	Li S S	S Sg Sg	Sg	Sg Cp Cp	Cp Aq Aq	Aq	Aq P P	P A A
	8:48a	8:56p		9:58a	8:20p		3:47a	8:12a
Apr	S Sg Sg	Sg Cp Cp	Cp	Cp Aq Aq	Aq P P	P A A	A T T	T G G
	4:59a	5:47p		5:26a	1:38p	5:59p	7:34p	8:33p
May	Sg Cp Cp	Cp Aq Aq	Aq P P	P	P A A	A T T	T G G	G C C
	12:37a	1:04p	10:34p		4:05a	6:10a	6:16a	5:43a
Jn	Aq	Aq P P	P A A	A T T	T G G	G C C	C L L	L V V
	5:52a	1:20p	4:17p	4:59p	4:22p	4:36p	7:14p
Jly	P A A	A	A T T	T G G	G C C	C L L	L V V	V Li Li
	8:00p	1:06a	2:55a	3:02a	2:58a	4:43a	9:36a
Aug	T	T G G	G C C	C L L	L V V	V Li Li	Li S S	S S Sg
	10:42a	12:14p	1:06p	2:51p	6:50p		2:24a	1:52p
Sep	C	C L L	L	L V V	V Li Li	Li S S	S S Sg Sg	Sg	Sg Cp Cp
	8:50p	12:15a		4:33a	11:14a	9:50p		10:17a
Oct	L	L V V	V Li Li	Li S S	S	S Sg Sg	Sg Cp Cp	Cp	Cp Aq Aq
	7:22a	12:51p	8:08p		6:14a	6:18p		7:12a
Nov	Li	Li	Li S S	S Sg Sg	Sg	Sg Cp Cp	Cp Aq Aq	Aq	Aq P P	P A
	3:46a	1:54p		2:02a	2:47p		2:18a	10:24a
Dec	S	S Sg Sg	Sg	Sg Cp Cp	Cp Aq Aq	Aq	Aq P P	P A A	A A T
	9:13p		8:49a	9:39p		9:46a	7:10p		12:34a

Section 1

16	17	18	19	20	21	22	23	24	25	26	27	28	29	30	31
G	G	G C C		C L L	L	L V V	V Li Li		Li	Li S S		Li S S		S Sg Sg	
		2:53a		1:10p		12:55a	1:31p			2:01a				11:00a	
C L L		L		L V V		V Li Li	Li		Li S S	S	S Sg Sg	Sg			
7:42p		7:37a		8:02p		8:48a			6:54p						
C L L L			L V V		V Li Li	Li	S S		S Sg Sg		Sg Cp Cp		Cp Aq Aq		
1:30a	1:42p		2:33a		2:27p		12:54a		9:18a				1:45p		
V	V Li Li	Li		Li S S		S Sg Sg		Sg Cp Cp		Cp Aq Aq		Aq P P		P	
9:13a			8:40p		5:40a		2:56p		8:40p		11:52p				
Li	Li S S		S Sg Sg		Sg Cp Cp		Cp	Cp Aq Aq		Aq P P		P A A		A T T	
3:53a	1:12p		8:32p		1:50a		5:38a		8:35a		12:07p				
Sg	Sg	Sg Cp Cp		Cp Aq Aq		Aq P P		P A A		A T T		T G G	G		
	3:47a		8:02a	11:03a		2:03p		4:53p		8:45p					
Cp	Cp Aq Aq		Aq P P		R A A		A T T		T	T G G	G C C		C : L		
4:00p		6:06p		7:20p		10:13p		2:24a		8:40a	4:43p				
Aq P P		P A A		A T T		T G G		G C C		C L L		L V V		V Li	
3:15a	3:16a		4:43a	7:434a		2:01p		10:53p		9:35a	9:38p				
A T T		T G G		G C C		C	C L L		L V V	V	V Li Li		Li S		
1:22p	2:55p		7:55p		4:17a		3:32p		4:10a	4:34p					
T G G		G C C		C L L		L V V	V		V Li Li		Li S S	S		S Sg Sg
12:36a	3:39a		10:50a	9:44p		10:28a		10:52p			10:10a				
C L L		L		L V V		V Li Li	Li		Li S S	S Sg Sg		Sg	Sg Cp Cp		
7:10p		4p40a		5:11p		5:48a		4:57p			2:16a				
L V V		V		V Li Li		Li	Li S S		S Sg Sg	Sg Cp Cp		Cp Aq Aq		Aq P P	
12:57p		12:45a		1:40p		1:03a		9:34a		3:53p		8:29p			

Section 2

16	17	18	19	20	21	22	23	24	25	26	27	28	29	30	31
Li	Li S S		S	S Sg Sg		Sg Cp Cp		Cp Aq Aq	Aq		Aq P P		P A A		A T
	9:27p		9:21a		6:11p		11:48p			3:05a		5:18a		7:52a	
S Sg Sg		Sg	Sg Cp Cp		Cp aq Aq		Aq P P		P A A		A T T				
6:08p		3:59a		10:24a		12:50p		1:52p		2:57p					
S Sg Sg		Sg Cp Cp		Cp Aq Aq		Aq P P		P A A T T		T	T G G		G C		
6:45a	12:44p		8:03p	11:27p		12:16a 1157p			1:36a			3:32a			
Cp	Cp Aq Aq		Aq P P		P A A		A T T		T G G	G C C		C L L			
4:57a		9:32a		11:12a		10:40a		10:31a		11:50a	4:38a				
Aq P P		P A A		A T T		T G G		G C C	C		C L L		L V V		V Li
5:25p		8:40p		9:26a		9:04p		9:44p		1:03a		8:21a	7:13p		
A	A T T		T G G		G C C		C L L		L V V	V		V Li Li		Li S	
	6:22a		7:10a		8:11a		11:00a		4:54p		2:48a		3:04p		
T G G		G C C		C L L		L V V		V Li Li		Li S S	S		S Sg Sg		
2:48p	5:13p		8:35p		2:07a		10:56a		10:44p			11:38a			
C	C L L		L V V		V Li Li		Li	Li S S		S Sg Sg	Sg		Sg Cp Cp		Cp Aq
	4:21a		10:44a		7:18p		6:24a		7:19p			7:12a	3:33p		
V	V Li Li		Li S S		S	S Sg Sg		Sg Cp Cp		Cp	Cp Aq Aq		Aq P		
	2:57a		2:13p		2:45a		3:08p		12:57a		6:29a				
Li	Li S S		S	S Sg Sg		Sg Cp Cp		Cp	Cp Aq Aq		Aq P P		P A A		A T
	8:56p		9:38a		9:53p		9:05a		4:19p		7:38p		7:57p		
S Sg Sg		Sg	Sg Cp Cp		Cp Aq Aq		Aq	Aq P P		P A A		A T T		T G G	
3:48p		4:11a		3:37p		12:09a		12:09a		5:17a		7:00a		8:32a	
Sg Cp Cp		Cp Aq Aq		Aq	Aq P P		P A A		A T T		T G G	G C C		C L
10:43a		9:18p		6:16a		12:29p		3:50p		4:58p		5:16p		6:20p	

Section 3

16	17	18	19	20	21	22	23	24	25	26	27	28	29	30	31
Aq	Aq P P		P A A		A T T		T G G		G C C		C L L		L V V		
	11:54a		6:08p		10:26p		12:52p		2:45a		4:32a		7:43a		
P A A		A T T		T G G		G C C		C L L		L V V		V Li Li		
12:11a		3:56a		7:00a		0:53a		12:48p		5:14p		11:35p			
A T T		T G G		G C C		C L L		L	L V V		V Li Li		Li S S	S
10:41a		12:50p		3:20p		7:08p		12:33a		7:46a	5:17p				
G C C		C L L		L	L V V		V Li Li		Li	Li S S		S Sg Sg		Sg	
9:34p		12:30p		6:29a		2:25p		12:27a		12:18p					
C L L		L V V		V Li Li		Li	Li S S		S Sg Sg		Sg Cp Cp Aq Aq		Aq	
7:21a		11:50a		7:58p		6:36a		6:30p		7:00a 7:30p					
V	V Li Li		Li S S		S	S Sg Sg		Sg Cp Cp		Cp	Cp Aq Aq		Aq P P	
	1:57a		12:12p		12:31a		1:14p		1:15a		10:47a				
Li S S		S	S Sg Sg		Sg Cp Cp		Cp	Cp Aq Aq		Aq P P	P		P A A		A T
6:41p		6:46a		7:43p		7:24a		5:18p			1:31a		7:31a		
Sg	Sg	Sg Cp Cp		Cp Aq Aq		Aq P P		P	P A A		A T T		T G G		G C
	2:46a		2:46a		11:53p		7:22a		12:29p		4:23p		7:06p		
Cp Aq Aq		Aq	Aq P P		P A A		A T T		T G G		G C C		C L		
10:44p		8:18a		2:56p		6:55p		10:03p		12:45a		3:44a			
Aq P P		P		P A A		A T T		T G G		G C C		C L L		L V V	V Li
5:43p		12:19a		3:40a		5:29a		6:41a		9:04a		1:16p			
A	A T T		T G G		G C C		C L L		L V V		V Li Li		Li S	
	2:14p		3:27p		3:21p		4:15p		7:05p		1:02a		9:45a		
T	T G G		G C C		C L L		L V V		V Li Li		Li S S		S	S Sg Sg
	2:26a		2:06a		1:46a		2:54a		7:22a		3:37p			2:51a	

1965

	1	2	3	4	5	6	7	8	9	10	11	12	13	14	15
Jan	Sg Cp 3:21p	Cp	Cp	Cp Aq 3:59a	Aq	Aq P 4:02p	P	P	P A 2:23a	A	A T 9:18a	T	T G 12:43p	G	G C 1:32p
Feb	Aq	Aq P 9:53p	P	P	P A 7:53a	A	A T 3:51p	T	T G 8:44p	G	G C 11:04p	C	C L 11:32p	L	L V 11:55p
Mar	Aq	Aq P 4:34a	P	P	P A 2:08p	A	A T 9:15p	T	T	T G 2:39a	G	G C 5:41a	C	C L 8:00a	L V 9:50a
Apr	A	A	A T 3:55a	T	T G 8:14a	G	G C 11:53a	C	C L 2:25p	L	L V 5:26p	V	V Li 9:07p	Li	Li
May	T	T G 4:33p	G	G C 5:27p	C	C	C L 7:49p	L	L V 10:54p	V	V	V Li 3:55a	Li	Li S 9:37a	S Sg 6:03p
Jn	G C 1:47a	C	C L 2:47a	L	L V 4:41a	V	V Li 8:58a	Li	Li S 3:31p	S	S	S Sg 12:40a	Sg	Sg Cp 11:37a	Cp
Jly	L	L V 12:10p	V	V Li 2:59p	Li	Li S 3:53p	S	S	S Sg 6:03a	Sg	Sg Cp 5:54p	Cp	Cp Aq 5:48a	Aq	Aq P
Aug	Li	Li	Li S 3:35a	S	S Sg 11:44a	Sg	Sg Cp 11:24p	Cp	Cp Aq 12:06p	Aq	Aq	Aq P 12:04p	P	P A 12:04p	A
Sep	S Sg 7:11p	Sg	Sg	Sg Cp 5:49a	Cp	Cp Aq 6:42p	Aq	Aq	Aq P 7:00a	P	P A 9:46a	A	A	A T 3:02a	T
Oct	Sg Cp 1:33p	Cp	Cp	Cp Aq 1:55a	Aq	Aq P 2:33p	P	P	P A 1:23a	A	A T 9:46a	T	T G 3:48p	G	G C 8:22p
Nov	Aq	Aq P 10:48p	P	P	P A 9:51a	A	A T 5:59p	T	T G 11:10p	G	G	G C 2:43a	C	C L 5:29a	L
Dec	P	P A 6:41p	A	A	A T 3:32a	T	T G 8:52a	G	G C 11:07a	C	C L 12:33	L	L V 2:03p	V	V Li 5:13p

1966

	1	2	3	4	5	6	7	8	9	10	11	12	13	14	15
Jan	A T 1:15p	T	T G 7:05p	G	G C 9:28p	C	C L 10:03p	L	L V 10:03p	V	V Li 11:37p	Li	Li	Li S 3:38a	S
Feb	G	G C 8:11a	C	C L 8:55a	L	L V 8:25a	V	V Li 8:29a	Li	Li S 10:55a	S	S Sg 5:06p	Sg	Sg	Sg Cp 2:41a
Mar	G C 5:26p	C	C L 7:24p	L	L V 7:24p	V	V Li 6:56p	Li	Li S 8:26p	S	S	S Sg 12:33a	Sg	Sg Cp 9:00a	Cp
Apr	L	L V 5:31a	V	V Li 5:52a	Li	Li S 6:30a	S	S Sg 10:04a	Sg	Sg Cp 5:13p	Cp	Cp Aq 4:02a	Aq	Aq P 4:58p	P
May	V Li 2:40p	Li	Li S 4:48p	S	S Sg 7:57p	Sg	Sg Cp 2:04a	Cp	Cp Aq 11:46a	Aq	Aq P 12:18a	P	P A 12:54p	A	A
Jn	S	S	S Sg 4:55a	Sg	Sg Cp 11:06a	Cp	Cp Aq 8:17p	Aq	Aq	Aq P 8:01a	P	P A 9:02p	A	A	A T 7:57a
Jly	Sg Cp 6:48p	Cp	Cp	Cp Aq 4:28a	Aq	Aq P 3:45p	P	P	P A 4:23a	A	A T 4:27p	T	T	T G 1:06a	G
Aug	Aq	Aq P 10:40p	P	P	P A 11:17a	A	A T 11:50p	T	T G 9:37a	G	G C 3:38p	C	C L 5:51p	L	L
Sep	P A 5:23p	A	A	A T 6:00a	T	T G 4:48p	G	G C 12:23a	C	C L 4:07a	L	L V 4:46a	V	V Li 4:16a	Li
Oct	A T 11:46a	T	T G 10:33p	G	G C 7:00a	C	C L 12:20p	L	L V 2:40p	V	V Li 3:03p	Li	Li S 2:59p	S	S
Nov	G	G C 12:41p	C	C L 6:30p	L	L V 10:26p	V	V Li 12:12a	Li	Li S 1:22a	S	S Sg 2:52a	Sg	Sg Cp 6:49a	
Dec	C	C L 12:11a	L	L V 4:04a	V	V Li 7:10a	Li	Li S 9:31a	S	S Sg 12:30p	Sg	Sg Cp 4:36p	Cp	Cp Aq 11:19p	Aq

1967

	1	2	3	4	5	6	7	8	9	10	11	12	13	14	15
Jan	C	C L 12:42p	L	L V 3:35p	V	V Li 7:37p	Li	Li S 12:51a	S	S Sg 8:08a	Sg	Sg Cp 5:40p	Cp	Cp	Cp
Feb	L	L	L V 1:18a	V	V Li 7:11a	Li	Li S 3:29p	S	S Sg 1:30a	Sg	Sg Cp 1:28p	Cp	Cp	Cp Aq 2:29a	
Mar	L V 7:11a	V	V	V Li 12:54p	Li	Li S 10:36p	S	S	S Sg 8:12a	Sg	Sg Cp 8:19p	Cp	Cp Aq 9:02a	Aq	Aq P
Apr	Li	Li	Li S 3:12a	S	S Sg 2:24p	Sg	Sg Cp 2:46a	Cp	Cp Aq 3:17p	Aq	Aq	Aq P 3:23a	P	P A 1:49p	
May	S	S Sg 8:19p	Sg	Sg Cp 8:49a	Cp	Cp Aq 9:24p	Aq	Aq	Aq P 8:58a	P	P A 6:54p	A	A	A T 2:59a	
Jn	Sg Cp 3:39p	Cp	Cp	Cp Aq 4:14a	Aq	Aq P 3:42p	P	P	P A 1:20a	A	A T 8:48a	T	T G 2:15p	G	G C 5:48p
Jly	Cp Aq 12:00n	Aq	Aq P 11:34p	P	P	P A 8:39a	A	A T 2:56p	T	T G 7:14p	G	G C 10:40p	C	C L 1:25a	
Aug	P	P A 5:29p	A	A T 11:21p	T	T	T G 2:52a	G	G C 4:43a	C	C L 6:41a	L	L V 9:46a	V	V Li 2:17p
Sep	A T 9:25a	T	T G 12:33p	G	G C 1:19p	C	C L 2:08p	L	L V 3:34p	V	V	V Li 7:37p	Li	Li S 2:09a	S
Oct	G	G	G C 12:02a	C	C L 11:31p	L	L V 11:47p	V	V Li 2:10a	Li	Li S 7:45a	S	S Sg 4:02	Sg	Sg
Nov	C L 10:40a	L	L V 10:14a	V	V Li 11:04a	Li	Li S 4:15p	S	S Sg 10:56p	Sg	Sg Cp 10:25a	Cp	Cp Aq 11:04p	Aq	Aq
Dec	V	V Li 9:44p	Li	Li	Li S 12:22a	S	S Sg 6:49a	Sg	Sg Cp 5:15p	Cp	Cp Aq 5:59a	Aq	Aq P 6:18p	P	

```
   16    17    18    19    20    21    22    23    24    25    26    27    28    29    30    31

C    C L   L    V V   Li Li  S S   S Sg Sg  Sg Cp Cp  Cp   Cp Aq
     12:25p 1:03p 3:56p 10:40p       9:13a    9:52p          10:16a

V    V    V Li Li  Li S S   S Sg Sg  Sg   Sg Cp Cp  Cp Aq Aq
          1:56a   7:11a    4:27p         4:45a       5:30p

V    V Li Li  Li S S   S   S Sg Sg  Sg Cp Cp  Cp   Cp Aq Aq  Aq P P   P A
     12:10p   4:40p        12:52a    12:30p         1:01a    12:37p   9:31p

Li S S   S Sg Sg  Sg Cp Cp  Cp   Cp Aq Aq  Aq P P   P   P A A   A T
2:10a    9:54a    8:24p         9:15a      9:25p        6:28a    12:20p

Sg   Sg  Sg Cp Cp  Cp Aq Aq  Aq   Aq P P   P A A   A T T   T   T G G
4:17a    4:46p         5:24a      3:47p        10:11p      1:06a

Cp Aq Aq  Aq   Aq P P   P A A   A   A T T   T G G   G C C   C L
11:53p    12:40p        11:58p       8:03a   11:28a     12:27p     12:05

Aq P P   P   P A A   A T T   T G G   G C C   C L L   L V V   V Li
6:36p        6:37a    3:48p        9:10p       10:58p     10:55p     10:16p   11:14p

A    A T T   T G G   G   G C C   C L L   L V V   V Li Li  Li S S
9:44p    4:30p         8:10a      9:13a    8:47a        9:30a    12:29p

T G G   G C C   C L L   L V V   V Li Li  Li S S   S   S Sg Sg  Sg
10:13a   3:01p       5:43p     6:45p     7:54p        10:20p       4:00a

C    C L L   L V V   V Li Li  Li S S   S Sg Sg  Sg Cp Cp  Cp   Cp Aq
     11:41p  2:17a    4:52a     8:14a    1:34p         10:07p       9:40a

L V V   V Li Li  Li S S   S Sg Sg  Sg Cp Cp  Cp   Cp Aq Aq  Aq   Aq P
8:02a    11:21a   4:04p     10:10p    6:38a         5:47p            6:36a

Li Li  Li S S   S   S Sg Sg  Sg Cp Cp  Cp   Cp Aq Aq  Aq P P   P   P A A
10:21p    5:19a        2:24p         1:37a        1:50p          2:46a
```

```
   16    17    18    19    20    21    22    23    24    25    26    27    28    29    30    31

S Sg Sg  Sg Cp Cp  Cp   Cp Aq Aq  Aq P P   P   P A A   A T T   T   T G
11:03a   8:50p         8:36a      8:51p        9:25a        8:44p          4:19a

Cp   Cp Aq Aq  Aq   Aq P P   P A A   A   A T T   T G G
2:41p    3:20a        3:20a        3:06a   11:57a

Cp Aq Aq  Aq   Aq P P   P A A   A   A T T   T G G   G C C   C L
9:12p    9:30a        9:53p        8:44a   5:48p       12:25a     3:58a

P    P   P A A   A T T   T G G   G C C   C L L   L V V
5:02a        3:29p       11:38p     5:57p     10:07a     1:13p

A    A T T   T   T G G   G C C   C L L   L V V   V Li Li  Li Li  Li S
11:01p   5:39a        11:42a   3:35p     6:40p       9:22p        12:29a

T G G   G C C   C L L   L V V   V Li Li  Li S S   S Sg Sg  Sg
3:40p    7:47p       10:24p     12:21a   2:43a      6:29a    11:33a

G C C   C L L   L V V   V Li Li  Li S S   S Sg Sg  Sg   Sg Cp Cp  Cp Aq
5:38a    7:20a      8:09a      9:00a    11:44a   5:18p         1:08a       11:05a

L V V   V Li Li  Li S S   S Sg Sg  Sg Cp Cp  Cp   Cp Aq Aq  Aq   Aq P P
6:02p    5:36p      6:51p      10:54p   6:38a         5:05p            5:12a

Li Li  S S   S   S Sg Sg  Sg Cp Cp  Cp   Cp Aq Aq  Aq P P   P A A   A   A
4:18a    6:31a        12:41p        10:48p        11:04a     11:57p

S Sg Sg  Sg Cp Cp  Cp   Cp Aq Aq  Aq   Aq P P   P A A   A T T   T   T G
4:34p    9:01p         5:39a        5:28p        6:36a        6:13p          4:23a

Cp   Cp Aq Aq  Aq   Aq P P   P A A   A   A T T   T G G   G C C
1:59a    1:13p        2:00p        1:53a   11:30a     6:45p

Aq   Aq P P   P A A   A   A T T   T G G   G   G C C   C L L   L V
9:23a    10:04p        10:21a   8:19p        2:52a      7:00a       10:03a
```

```
   16    17    18    19    20    21    22    23    24    25    26    27    28    29    30    31

Cp Aq Aq  Aq P P   P   P A A   A T T   T G G   G C C   C L L   L
6:00a    6:36p        5:39a    12:40p     4:11p      6:01p      7:04p

Aq   Aq P P   P A A   A   A T T   T G G   G C C   C L L
2:02p    10:18p        2:52a    4:07a      4:10a      4:43a

Aq P P   P A A   A T T   T G G   G C C   C L L   L V V   V   V Li
9:05p    6:49a      12:40p     2:56p     2:47p     2:25p     3:13p       7:20p

A    A T T   T   T G G   G C C   C L L   L V V   V Li Li  Li S S
8:52p    12:54a       1:47a    1:18a      1:18a     4:05a        10:20a

T T   G G   G C C   C L L   L V V   V Li Li  Li S S   S   S Sg Sg
8:12a   10:47a     11:32a     11:50a   1:51p      6:48p        3:40a

C    C L L   L V V   V Li Li  Li S S   S Sg Sg  Sg Cp Cp  Cp
7:35p    9:20p      12:02a     4:21a    12:04p     11:20p

L L   V V   V Li Li  Li S S   S Sg Sg  Sg Cp Cp  Cp   Cp Aq Aq  Aq P
4:15a   8:04a      1:11p      9:01p    7:12a         7:55p            8:11a

Li Li  Li S S   S   S Sg Sg  Sg Cp Cp  Cp   Cp Aq Aq  Aq P P   P A A   A
8:29p    4:33a        2:56p         3:33a        4:00p          2:39a

S Sg Sg  Sg Cp Cp  Cp   Cp Aq Aq  Aq   Aq P P   P A A   A T T   T G
11:07a   9:53p         10:26a       11:04p       7:00p        11:04p

Sg Cp Cp  Cp   Cp Aq Aq  Aq P P   P A A   A   A T T   T G G   G C C
4:24a    4:29p        5:24a      5:15p        2:41a   8:33a      10:44a

Aq   Aq P P   P A A   A   A T T   T G G   G C C   C L L   L V
11:37a   11:00p        8:52a    4:33p      7:50p      9:10p      9:04p

P    P A A   A T T   T G G   G   G C C   C L L   L V V   V Li Li
5:26a    2:25p      9:42p         2:39a    5:41a      6:50a      8:00a
```

1968

	1	2	3	4	5	6	7	8	9	10	11	12	13	14	15
Jan	Li	S S	S Sg Sg	Sg Cp Cp	Aq Aq	Aq	Aq P P	P A A	A	T					
	10:47a	5:55p		1:15a		3:22p	3:51a		12:03p	9:21p					
Feb	Sg	Sg Cp Cp	Cp Aq Aq	Aq	Aq P P	P A A	A A T T	T G G							
	9:46a		9:15p		10:14a	9:31p	5:54a	11:29							
Mar	Aq Aq	Aq P P	P A A	A	A T T	T G G	G C C	C L L							
	5:24a		5:53p		6:24a	3:30p	8:53p	11:24p							
Apr	P	P A A	A T T	T	T G G	G C C	C L L	L V V	V Li						
	1:21a		2:00p		12:40a	7:11a	9:06a	8:14a	10:16a						
May	A T T	T G G	G C C	C L L	L V V	V Li Li	Li S S								
	8:37p	8:09a	3:57p	8:06p	9:10p	8:34p	8:28p								
Jn	G	G C C	C	C L L	L V V	V Li Li	Li S S	S Sg Sg	Sg Cp						
	10:08p	4:53a		8:29a	8:19a	8:19a	9:12a		12:08p						
Jly	C	C L L	L V V	V Li Li	Li S S	S Sg Sg	Sg Cp Cp	Cp	Cp Aq						
	10:56a	3:13p	4:52p	5:31p	6:35p	10:26p			4:11a						
Aug	V	V Li Li	Li	Li S S	S Sg Sg	Sg Cp Cp	Cp Aq Aq	Aq P P	P						
	11:52p	2:02a		3:53a	7:21a		1:07p		10:25p						
Sep	Li S S	S Sg Sg	Sg Cp Cp	Cp Aq Aq	Aq	Aq P P	P A A	A	A T						
	7:02a	11:21a	4:00p	10:07p		7:00a	6:36p		7:25a						
Oct	Sg	Sg Cp Cp	Cp	Cp Aq Aq	Aq P P	P	P A A	A T T	T	T G					
	10:30p	5:52a		3:12p	2:25a		3:09p			3:35a					
Nov	Cp Aq Aq	Aq P P	P A A	A	A T T	T	T G G	G C C	C L						
	11:58a	10:05p	9:36a		10:07p		10:40a	9:04p	3:22p						
Dec	Aq P P	P A A	A	A T T	T G G	G	G C C	C L L	L V						
	4:02a	4:05p		4:36a	5:00p		4:06a	12:01p	4:15p						

1969

	1	2	3	4	5	6	7	8	9	10	11	12	13	14	15
Jan	A T T	T G G	G C C	C	C L L	L	L V V	V Li Li							
	11:04p	11:01p	10:06p		6:32p		12:32a	2:52a							
Feb	T G G	G C C	C	C L L	L V V	V Li Li	Li S S	S Sg Sg							
	5:37a	3:04p		2:09a	6:18a	10:06a	12:31p	1:25p							
Mar	G	G C C	C	C L L	L V V	V Li Li	Li S S	S Sg Sg	Sg						
	11:19p	6:38a		11:57p	3:56p	6:51p	9:16p								
Apr	C V V	V Li Li	Li S S	S Sg Sg	Sg Cp Cp	Cp Aq Aq	Aq P P								
	2:59p	7:16p	9:56p	12:24a	3:16a	7:21a	12:31p								
May	V Li Li	Li S S	S Sg Sg	Sg Cp Cp	Cp Aq Aq	Aq	Aq P P	P	P A A						
	3:10a	6:00a	7:00a	8:43a	12:29p		6:36p		2:26a						
Jn	S Sg Sg	Sg Cp Cp	Cp Aq Aq	Aq P P	P	P A A	A T T	T	T G						
	4:04p	4:22p	6:34p	11:55p		8:10a	7:07p		7:12a						
Jly	Sg Cp Cp	Cp Aq Aq	Aq P P	P A A	A	A T T	T G G	G	G C						
	2:06a	2:45a	5:19a	2:53p		12:37a	1:16p		1:43a						
Aug	Aq P P	P A A	A	A T T	T G G	G C C	C L L	L							
	3:01p	8:57p		5:37a	7:19p	8:00a	7:24p								
Sep	A	A T T	T	T G G	G C C	C	C L L	L V V	V Li Li						
	2:21a	2:10a		3:04p	3:31a		1:18p	~ 7:04p							
Oct	T	T G G	G C C	C L L	L V V	V	V Li Li	Li S S							
	11:41a	12:24a	11:58a	8:00p			1:37a	5:27a							
Nov	G C C	C V V	V	V Li Li	Li S S	S Sg Sg	Sg Cp Cp	Cp Aq Aq							
	6:38a	7:13p		5:08a	11:18a	2:33p	4:26p	6:12p							
Dec	L V V	V Li Li	Li S S	S	S Sg Sg	Sg Cp Cp	Cp Aq Aq	Aq P P							
	3:10a	2:11p	9:25p		12:48a	1:47a	2:04a	3:20a							

1970

	1	2	3	4	5	6	7	8	9	10	11	12	13	14	15
Jan	S S S	Sg Sg	Cp Cp	Aq Aq	P P	A A	T T								
	11:34a	12:33	11:48a	11:37a	1:48p	7:21p									
Feb	Sg Cp Cp	Aq Aq	Aq	A A A	T T	G G	C								
	11:22p	11:20p	10:38p	11:18p	3:00a	10:30a	9:17p								
Mar	Sg Cp Cp	A	A P P	A A T	T G G	G C	C								
	7:55a	9:35a	9:49a	10:17a	12:44p	6:37p	4:19a								
Apr	Aq P P	A A	T T T	T G	G C C	C L L	L								
	7:01p	8:32p	11:02p	4:02a	12:34p	12:16a									
May	P A A	T T	G G	C C C	L L	V V	V								
	4:33a	8:05a	1:18p	9:17p	8:22a	9:11p									
Jn	T G G	G	C C	L L	L V V	V	Li Li Li	S							
	9:10p		5:16a	4:17p	5:02a	5:28p		3:02a							
Jly	L L	C C	L L	L V V	V	Li Li	S Sg Sg	Sg							
	12:21p	11:26p	12:12p	1:03		11:41a	6:26p								
Aug	L L	V V	Li Li	S S S	Sg	Sg Cp Cp	Cp								
	6:45	6:35p	7:33a	6:57p	3:08a	7:25a	8:32a								
Sep	V Li	Li Li	S S	Sg Sg	Cp Cp	Aq Aq	P P	A							
	1:26p	12:55a	9:59a	3:52p	6:34p	6:58p	6:36p								
Oct	Li S S	Sg Sg	Cp Cp	Cp	P P	A A	T								
	6:36a	3:32p	10:11p	2:26a	4:31a	5:13a	6:00a								
Nov	Sg Sg Cp	Aq Aq	P P	A A	T T	G G									
	3:33a	8:11a	11:33a	1:52p	3:51p	6:49p									
Dec	Cp Aq Aq	P P	A A	T T	G G	C C	L								
	1:45p	4:56p	8:04p	11:25p	3:34a	9:33a	6:22p								

16	17	18	19	20	21	22	23	24	25	26	27	28	29	30	31
T	T	T G 3:29a	G	G C 8:13a	C	C L 11:32a	L	L V 2:06p	V	V Li 4:42p	Li	Li S 8:06p	S	S	S Sg 1:32a
G C 12:39p	C	C Li 10:17p	Li	Li S 7:47p	S	S Sg 11:14p	Sg	Sg	Sg	Sg Cp 3:47p	Cp	Cp	Cp Aq 6:24p		
L	L V 12:38a	V	V Li 1:54a	Li	Li S 4:47a	S	S Sg 9:35a	Sg	Sg Cp 4:42p	Cp	Cp	Cp Aq 1:55a	Aq	Aq P 1:00p	P
Li	Li S 11:34a	S	S Sg 3:19p	Sg	Sg Cp 10:23p	Cp	Cp	Cp Aq 8:23a	Aq	Aq P 7:42p	P	P	P A 8:00a	A	
S Sg 10:40p	Sg	Sg	Sg Cp 3:02a	Cp	Cp Aq 1:33p	Aq	Aq	Aq P 1:33a	P	P A 2:13p	A	A	A T 2:36a	T	T G 1:51p
Cp	Cp Aq 8:04p	Aq	Aq	Aq P 8:49a	P	P A 8:30p	A	A	A T 8:47a	T	T G 7:41p	G	G	G C 4:45a	
Aq	Aq P 2:37p	P	P	P A 3:10a	A	A T 3:41p	T	T	T G 2:11a	G	G C 10:20a	C	C L 4:34p	L	L V 8:53p
P A 10:52a	A	A T 11:24p	T	T	T G 10:02a	G	G C 7:19p	C	C L 10:35p	L	L	L V 2:32a	V	V Li 5:18a	Li
T	T G 6:49p	G	G	G C 2:44a	C	C L 7:00a	L	L V 9:46a	V	V Li 11:20a	Li	Li S 1:39p	S	S S 5:16p	
G	G C 12:17p	C	C L 5:12p	L	L V 7:09p	V	V Li 7:34p	Li	Li S 8:25p	S	S Sg 10:46p	Sg	Sg	Sg Cp 3:56a	Cp
L	L	L V 6:01a	V	V Li 6:12a	Li	Li S 5:43a	S	S Sg 6:22a	Sg	Sg Cp 10:15a	Cp	Cp Aq 5:30p	Aq	Aq	
V	V Li 5:09p	Li	Li S 4:33p	S	S Sg 4:32p	Sg	Sg Cp 6:34p	Cp	Cp	Cp Aq 12:14a	Aq	Aq P 10:01a	P	P A 10:11p	A

16	17	18	19	20	21	22	23	24	25	26	27	28	29	30	31
Li S 5:32a	S	S Sg 5:11a	Sg	Sg Cp 4:50a	Cp	Cp Aq 8:50a	Aq	Aq P 5:23p	P	P	P A 4:49a	A	A T 5:48p	T	T
Sg Cp 3:20p	Cp	Cp Aq 6:50p	Aq	Aq	Aq P 1:40a	P	P A 12:42p	A	A	A T 1:28a	T	T G 1:36p			
Sg Cp 12:00a	Cp	Cp Aq 3:22a	Aq	Aq P 10:59a	P	P A 8:57p	A	A	A T 9:16a	T	T G 9:58p	G	G	G C 8:07a	C
P A 7:46p	A	A	A T 5:40a	T	T G 5:13p	G	G	G C 6:12a	C	C L 5:07p	L	L	L V 12:40a	V	
A T 12:43p	T	T	T G 12:24a	G	G C 1:18p	C	C	C L 1:18a	L	L V 9:54a	V	V Li 2:44p	Li	Li S 4:13p	S
G	G C 7:37p	C	C	C L 8:00	L	L V 6:04p	V	V	V Li 12:14p	Li	Li S 2:47a	S	S Sg 3:02a	Sg	
C	C L 1:33p	L	L	L V 12:15a	V	V Li 7:54a	Li	Li S 12:12p	S	S Sg 1:22p	Sg	Sg Cp 1:05p	Cp	Cp Aq 1:03p	Aq
L V 5:39a	V	V Li 1:14p	Li	Li S 6:50p	S	S Sg 9:54p	Sg	Sg Cp 10:58p	Cp	Cp Aq 11:23p	Aq	Aq	Aq P 1:25a	P	P A 5:41a
Li	Li S 12:23a	S	S Sg 3:04a	Sg	Sg Cp 6:31a	Cp	Cp Aq 8:41a	Aq	Aq P 11:09a	P	P A 3:30p	A	A T 10:52p	T	
S Sg 8:31a	Sg	Sg Cp 10:55a	Cp	Cp Aq 2:15p	Aq	Aq P 6:39p	P	P	P A 12:28a	A	A T 8:23a	T	T G 7:43p	G	G
Aq P 8:58p	P	P A 1:22a	A	A	A T 11:34a	T	T G 3:42p	G	G	G C 2:02a	C	C L 2:23p	L	L	
P A 7:11a	A	A T 9:49a	T	T G 6:43p	G	G	G C 5:37a	C	C L 9:32p	L	L	L V 10:12a	V	V Li 10:01p	Li

16	17	18	19	20	21	22	23	24	25	26	27	28	29	30	31
T	G 4:08a	G	C 3:14p	C	L 3:41a	L	V	V	V	Li 4:43a	Li	Li	S 2:35p	S	Sg 8:50p
C	C	L 9:54a	L	V 1:42p	V	V	Li 10:30a	Li	S 8: 4p	S	S	Sg 3:39a			
C	L 4:40p	L	L	V 5:38a	V	Li 4:57p	Li	Li	S 2:16a	S	Sg 9:07a	Sg	C 2:01p	C	Aq 5:09p
V 1:08p	V	V	Li 12:36a	Li	S 9:16a	S	Sg 3:15p	Sg	Cp 7:27p	Cp	Aq 10:44p	Aq	Aq	P 1:38a	P
Li 9.03a	Li	S 5:50p	S	Sg 1:12p	Sg	Sg	Cp 2:14p	Cp	Aq 4:26a	Aq	P 6:59a	P	A 10:27a	A	T 3:04p
S	Sg 8:40a	Sg	Cp 1:05p	Cp	Aq 2:01p	Aq	P 3:12p	P	A 5:53p	A	T 8:35p	T	T	G 3:25a	G
Cp 9:20p	Cp	Aq 8:45a	Aq	P 9:37a	P	A 10:43a	A	A	T 2:19a	T	G 8:53a	G	C 6:14p	C	C
Aq	P 8:02a	P	A 7:51	A	T 9:46a	T	G 3:04p	G	C 11:59p	C	C	L 11:39a	L	L	V 12:36a
A	A	T 7:21a	G 11:02p	G	G	C 6:41a	C	L 5:55p	L	L	C 6:54a	C	Li 7:34p	Li	Li
T	G 8:44a	G	C 2:59p	C	C	L 1:13a	L	V 1:58p	V	V	Li 2:38a	Li	S 1:15p	S	Sg 9:25p
C 12:24a	C	L 9:36a	L	V 9:50p	V	V	Li 10.40a	Li	S 9:25p	S	S	Sg 5:03a	Sg	Cp 10.06a	Cp
L	L	V 6:05a	V	Li 7:02p	Li	Li	S 6:28a	S	Sg 2:28p	Sg	Cp 7:02p	Cp	Aq 9:24p	Aq	P 11:08p

1971

	1	2	3	4	5	6	7	8	9	10	11	12	13	14	15
Jan	P	P 1:27a	A	A 5:01a	T	T 10:09a	G	G 5:09p	C	C	C	L 2:25a	L	V 1:58p	V
Feb	T 10:49a	T	G 3:35p	G	C 11:07p	C	C	L 9:07a	L	V 8:58p	V	V	Li 9:51a	Li	S 10:22p
Mar	T 10:02p	G	G	G	C 4:48a	C	L 2:56a	L	L	C 3:11a	Li 4:06p	Li	Li	S 4:32a	
Apr	C 11:51a	C	L 9:06p	L	V 9:17a	V	V	Li 10:17p	Li	Li 10:28a	S	S 9:04p	Sg	Sg	
May	L 4:35a	L	V 4:04p	V	V 5:00a	Li	Li 5:04p	S	S	S 3:08a	Sg	Sg 11:10a	Cp	Cp 5:20p	Aq
Jn	V 12:27p	Li	Li	Li 12:37p	S	S 10:29a	Sg	Sg 5:46p	Cp	Cp 11:03p	Aq	Aq	Aq 3:02a	P	P
Jly	Li 8:47a	S	S 6:59p	Sg	Sg	Sg 2:04a	Cp	Cp 6:27a	Aq	Aq 9:15a	P	P 11:33a	A	A	T 2:11p
Aug	Sg 3:50a	Sg	Cp 11:33a	Cp	Aq 3:47p	Aq	P 5:35p	P	A 6:17p	AT	G 7:56p	G	G	G 11:11p	
Sep	Cp 2:05a	Aq	Aq 3:51a	P	P 3:44a	A	A 3:38a	T	T 5:25a	G	G 10:21a	C	C 6:38p	L	L
Oct	P 2:37p	P	A 2:41p	A	T 1:42p	T	G 1:54p	G	C 5:11p	CC	C	L 12:31a	L	V 11:17a	V
Nov	A 12:56a	A	T 12:28a	T	G 2:15a	G	C 7:57a	C	L 5:45p	L	V	V 6:06a	V	Li 6:50p	Li
Dec	G 1:26p	G	C 12:51p	C	L 5:17p	L	L	V 1:41a	V	Li 1:20p	Li	Li 2:02a	S	S 1:38p	Sg

1972

	1	2	3	4	5	6	7	8	9	10	11	12	13	14	15
Jan	P 3:22a	L	L 10:51a	V	V 9:34p	Li	Li	Li	S 10:04a	S	Sg 9:58p	Sg	Sg	Cp 7:27a	Cp
Feb	V	V	Li 6:07a	Li	S 6:18p	S	S	Sg 11:38a	Sg	Cp 4:51p	Cp	Aq 11:37p	Aq	Aq	P 3:12a
Mar	Li 2:01p	Li	Li	S 2:01a	S	Sg 2:37a	Sg	Sg	Cp 1:50a	Cp	Aq 9:43a	Aq	P 1:40p	P	A 2:38p
Apr	S 9:28a	Sg	Sg	Sg	Cp 9:21a	Cp	Aq 6:38p	Aq	P 11:58p	P	P	A 1:33a	A	T	T 12:55a
May	Sg 3:29p	Cp	Cp	Cp	Aq 1:36a	Aq	P 8:28a	P	A 11:35a	A	T 11:48p	T	G 10:58a	G	C 11:17p
Jn	Aq 7:16a	Aq	P 2:53p	P	A 7:28p	A	T 9:15p	T	G 9:25p	G	C 9:45a	C	C	L 12:10a	L
Jly	P	P	A 1:23a	A	T 4:25a	T	G 6:05a	G	C 8:30a	C	L 10:06a	L	V 3:17p	V	Li 11:49p
Aug	T 9:58a	T	G 12:34p	G	C 3:18p	C	L 5:57p	L	V	V 12:23a	Li 8:26a	Li	S 7:29p	S	
Sep	G 9:12a	C	C	L 1:54a	L	V 8:16a	V	Li 4:37p	Li	Li	S 3:16a	S	Sg 3:43p	Sg	Sg
Oct	L 7:36a	L	V 2:31p	V	Li 11:35p	Li	Li	S 10:28a	S	Sg 10:53p	Sg	Cp 11:45a	Cp	Aq 10:52a	
Nov	V	Li 5:28a	Li	S 4:17p	S	S	Sg 5:17p	Sg	Cp 6:12p	Cp	Cp	Aq 6:03a	Aq	P 2:57p	P
Dec	S 10:43p	S	S	Sg 11:23a	Sg	Sg	Cp 12:07a	Cp	Aq 11:54a	Aq	P	P 9:33p	P	A	A 4:00a

1973

	1	2	3	4	5	6	7	8	9	10	11	12	13	14	15
Jan	Sg	Sg	Cp 6:31a	Cp	Aq 5:48p	Aq	Aq	P 3:03a	P	A 9:58a	A	T 2:25a	T	G 4:42p	G
Feb	Cp 12:56a	Aq	Aq 9:23a	P	P 3:29p	A	A 7:54p	T	T 11:11p	G	G	G 1:45a	C	C 4:13a	L
Mar	Aq 9:23a	Aq	P 5:32p	P	A 10:38p	A	A	T 1:51a	T	G 4:31a	G	C 7:30a	C	L 11:08a	L
Apr	P	A 7:49a	A	T 9:59a	T	G 11:12a	G	C 1:05p	C	L 4:32p	L	V 9:47p	V	V	Li 4:51a
May	T 8:02p	T	G 8:16p	G	C 8:36p	C	L 10:37p	L	L	V 3:13a	V	Li 10:31a	Li	S 8:10p	S
Jn	G	C 6:21a	C	L 6:50a	L	V 9:52a	V	Li 4:16p	Li	Li	S 1:52a	S	Sg 1:43p	Sg	Sg
Jly	L 4:56p	L	V 6:31p	V	Li 11:24p	Li	Li	S 8:06a	S	Sg 7:48p	Sg	Sg	Cp 8:46a	Cp	Aq 9:15p
Aug	V	Li 8:13a	Li	S 3:36p	S	S	Sg 2:37a	Sg	Cp 3:30p	Cp	Cp	Aq 3:53a	Aq	P 2:15p	P
Sep	S 12:18a	S	Sg 10:25a	Sg	Cp 11:02p	Cp	Cp	Aq 11:31a	Aq	P 9:41p	P	P	A 4:57a	A	T 10:00a
Oct	Sg	Sg	Cp 7:03a	Cp	Aq 7:49p	Aq	Aq	P 6:24p	P	A 1:29p	A	T 5:37p	T	G 8:09a	G
Nov	Cp 3:59a	Aq	Aq 3:27p	P	P 11:20p	A	A	A 3:26a	T	T 5:00a	G	G 5:47a	C	C 7:20a	L
Dec	P 11:33p	P	P	A 8:51a	A	T 2:09p	T	G 3:58a	G	G	C 3:52p	C	L 3:45p	L	V 5:21p

Block 1

16	17	18	19	20	21	22	23	24	25	26	27	28	29	30	31
V	Li 2:54a	Li	S 3:04p	S	S	Sg 12:16a	Sg	Cp 5:33	Cp	Aq 7:37a	Aq	P 8:02a	P	A 8:37a	A
S	S	Sg 8:46a	Sg	Cp 3:37p	Cp	Aq 6:44p	Aq	P 7:06p	P	A 6:30p	A	T 6:55p			
S	Sg 3:24p	Sg	Cp 11:38p	Cp	Cp	Aq 4:29a	Aq	P 6:08a	P	A 5:46a	A	T 5:16	T	G 6:44a	G
Cp 5:39a	Cp	Aq 11:46a	Aq	P 3:08p	P	A 4:09p	A	T 4:07p	T	G 4:59p	G	C 8:44p	C	C	C
Aq 9:40p	P	P	P	A 12:12a	A	T 1:32a	T	G 3:20a	G	C 6:27a	C	L 1:17p	L	V 11:49p	V
A 6:06a	A	T 8:39a	T	G 11:24a	G	C 3:31p	C	L 10:13p	L	L	V 8:07a	V	Li 8:23p	Li
T	G 5:47a	G	C 10:57p	C	C	L 6:17a	L	V 4:10p	V	V	Li 4:12a	Li	S 4:51p	S	S
C 4:50a	C	L 12:58p	L	V 11:19p	V	V	Li 11:23a	Li	Li	S 12:09a	S	Sg 11:57a	Sg	Cp 8:55p
V 5:29a	V	V	Li 5:48p	Li	Li	S 6:34a	S	Sg 6:44p	Sg	Sg	Cp 4:53a	Cp	Aq 11:39a	Aq
Li 1148p	Li	Li	S 12:31p	S	S	Sg 12:32a	Sg	Cp 11:06a	Cp	Aq 7:12p	Aq	P 11:57p	P	P	A 1:27a
S	S	Sg 6:30a	Sg	Cp 4:37p	Cp	Aq 12:53a	Aq	P 6:48a	P	A 10:04a	A	T 11:09a	T		
Sg 11:08p	Cp	Cp	Cp	Aq 6:33a	Aq	P 12:10p	P	A 4:10p	A	T 6:46p	T	G 8:39p	G	C 11:02p	C

Block 2

16	17	18	19	20	21	22	23	24	25	26	27	28	29	30	31
Aq 2:04p	Aq	P 6:24p	P	A 9:36p	A	A	T 12:18a	T	G 3:14a	G	C 7:22a	C	L 12:22p	L	V 7:56a
P 4:51a	A	A 6:12a	T	T 8:36a	G	G	C 12:53p	C	C 7:15p	L	L	L 3:40a	V		
A 2:28p	T	T	G 3:31p	G	C 6:27p	C	C	L 12:47a	L	V 8:48a	V	Li 8:42p	Li	Li	S 8:49a
G 12:17a	G	C 1:47a	C	L 6:47a	L	V 3:25p	V	V	Li 2:35a	Li	S 2:56p	S	S	Sg 3:31a	Sg
C 2:38p	L	L	V 9:57p	V	V	Li 8:37a	Li	S 9:01p	S	S	Sg 9:34a	Sg	Cp 9:13p	Cp	
V 6:04a	V	Li 3:39p	Li	Li	S 3:43a	S	Sg 4:15p	Sg	Sg	Cp 3:37a	Cp	Aq 1:03p	Aq	P 8:19p	
Li	Li	S 11:16a	S	Sg 11:47p	Sg	Sg	Cp 11:14a	Cp	Aq 8:08p	Aq	Aq	P 2:30a	P	A 6:51a	A
S 7:50a	Sg	Sg 7:38p	Cp	Cp	Cp	Aq 4:44a	Aq	P 10:29a	P	A 1:41p	A	T 3:43p	T	G 5:56p	G
Cp 4:08p	Cp	Aq 2:05p	Aq	P 8:10p	P	A 10:45p	A	T 11:28p	T	T	G 12:15a	G	C 2:39a	C	
Aq	Aq	P 6:13a	P	A 9:23a	A	T 9:38a	T	G 9:03a	G	C 9:45a	C	L 1:15p	L	V 8:00p	V
A 7:45p	A	T 8:53p	T	G 8:05p	G	C 7:31p	C	L 9:12p	L	L	V 2:25a	V	Li 11:16a	Li	
T 7:00p	T	G 7:25a	G	C 6:57a	C	L 7:35a	L	V	V 11:03a	Li 5:22p	Li	Li	S 5:11a	S	Sg 4:52p

Block 3

16	17	18	19	20	21	22	23	24	25	26	27	28	29	30	31
C 5:41p	C	L 6:41p	L	V 9:24p	V	V	Li 3:17a	Li	S 12:25p	S	S	Sg 1:11a	Sg	Cp 1:55p	
L	V 7:32a	V	Li 12:59p	Li	S 9:36p	S	S	Sg 9:15a	Sg	Cp 10:04p	Cp	Cp			
V 3:43p	V	Li 9:49p	Li	Li	S 6:16a	S	Sg 5:27p	Sg	Sg	Cp 6:16a	Cp	Aq 6:13p	Aq	Aq	P 12:56a
Li 1:52p	S	S	S	Sg 1:02a	Sg	Cp 1:50p	Cp	Cp	Aq 2:22a	Aq	P 12:10p	P	A 5:54p	A	
S	Sg 7:42a	Sg	Cp 8:31p	Cp	Cp	Aq 9:18a	Aq	P 8:06p	P	P	A 3:15a	A	T 6:28a	T	G 6:53a
Cp 2:37a	Cp	Aq 3:20p	Aq	Aq	P 2:29a	P	A 10:49a	A	T 3:38p	T	G 5:18p	G	C 5:09p	C	
Aq	Aq	P 8:08a	P	A 4:44	A	T 10:41p	T	T	G 1:59p	G	C 3:11p	C	L 3:30a	L	V 4:35a
A 10:16a	A	A	T 4:14a	T	G 8:27a	G	C 11:08a	C	L 12:50p	L	V 2:34p	V	Li 5:53p	Li	Li
T 1:48p	G	G 5:02p	C	C 7:57p	L	L	V 10:59p	V	V	Li 3:01a	Li	S 9:19a	S	Sg 5:48p	
C 10:29p	C	C	L 1:25a	L	V 5:19a	V	Li 10:29a	Li	S 5:28p	S	S	Sg 2:58a	Sg	Cp 2:50p	Cp
L 10:42a	V	V 4:16p	Li	Li	Li	S 12:07a	S	SG 10:11a	Sg	Cp 10:13p	Cp	Aq	Aq 11:18a		
Li 9:54p	Li	Li	S 5:44a	S	Sg 4:20p	Sg	Sg	Cp 4:42a	Cp	Aq 5:43p	Aq	Aq	P 6:10a	P	A 4:35p

1974

	1	2	3	4	5	6	7	8	9	10	11	12	13	14	15
Jan	A 11:38p	T	T	T 3:00a	G	G	C 3:29a	C	L 2:43a	L	V 2:42a	V	Li 5:22a	Li	S 11:55a
Feb	G 11:54a	G	C 2:06p	C	L 2:12p	L	V 1:52p	V	Li 3:11p	Li	S 7:58a	S	S	Sg 5:02a	Sg
Mar	G 10:00p	C	C 11:49p	L	L	L 12:34a	V 1:52a	V	Li 1:52a	Li	S 5:40a	S	Sg 1:20p	Sg	Sg
Apr	L 6:41a	L	V 8:57a	V	Li 11:23a	Li	S 3:25p	S	Sg 10:28p	Sg	Sg	Cp 8:57a	Cp	Aq 9:35p	Aq
May	V 6:40p	V	Li 11:44p	Li	S	S	S 7:06a	Sg	Sg 5:16p	Sg	Cp	Aq 5:35a	Aq	P 6:04p	P
Jn	S 6:11a	S	SG 2:22p	Sg	Sg	Cp 12:49a	Aq 1:03p	Aq	Aq	P	P 1:44p	A	A 12:53p	A	T 8:47p
Jly	Sg	Sg	Cp 7:20a	Cp	Aq 7:42a	Aq	Aq	P 8:26a	P	A	A 8:11p	A	T 5:22a	T	G 10:55a
Aug	Cp 1:47a	Aq	Aq	P 2:27p	P	P	A 1:16a	A	T 12:13p	T	G 7:16p	G	C 10:49p	C	11:27p
Sep	P	P 7:59a	A	A 5:51p	T	T	T 1:37a	G	G 6:40a	C	C 8:55a	L	L	V 9:13a	V
Oct	A 11:40p	T	T	T 7:01a	G	G 12:31p	C	C	L 4:03p	L	V 5:57p	V	Li 7:11p	Li	S 9:24p
Nov	G 1:24p	G	C 6:02p	C	L 9:31p	L	L	V 12:19p	V	Li 2:59p	Li	S 6:24p	S	Sg 11:39a	Sg
Dec	C 1:22a	C	L 3:32a	L	V 5:41a	V	Li 8:43a	Li	S 1:14a	S	Sg 7:35p	Sg	Sg	Cp 4:04a	Cp

1975

	1	2	3	4	5	6	7	8	9	10	11	12	13	14	15
Jan	V 12:33p	V	Li 2:22p	Li	S 6:39p	S	S	Sg 1:40a	Sg	Cp 10:59a	Cp	Aq 10:04p	Aq	Aq	P 10:24a
Feb	L 12:54a	S	S	Sg 7:11a	Sg	Cp 4:43p	Cp	Cp	Aq 4:17a	Aq	P 4:46p	P	P	A 5:23a	A
Mar	S 9:34a	S	Sg 2:06p	Sg	Cp 10:40p	Cp	Cp	Aq 10:10a	Aq	P 10:50p	P	P	A 11:19a	A	T 10:53p
Apr	Sg	Cp 6:09a	Cp	Aq 4:46p	Aq	Aq	P 5:17a	P	A 5:45p	A	A	T 4:54a	T	G 2:15p	G
May	Cp 12:34a	Aq	Aq 12:35p	P	P	P 1:03a	A	A	T 12:04a	T	G 8:45p	G	G	C 3:08a	C
Jn	P	P	A 9:02a	A	T 8:19p	T	T	G 4:50a	G	C 10:22a	C	L 1:46p	L	V 4:11p	V
Jly	A	A	T 4:55a	T	G 1:59p	G	C 7:24p	C	L 9:51p	L	V 10:56p	V	V	Li 12:22a	Li
Aug	G 11:03p	G	G	C 5:18a	C	L 7:44a	L	V 7:54a	V	Li 7:51a	Li	S 9:31a	S	Sg 2:00p	Sg
Sep	C 6:09p	L	L 6:30p	V	V 5:38p	Li	Li 5:46p	S	S 8:41p	Sg	Sg	Sg	Cp 3:12a	Cp	Aq 12:52p
Oct	L 5:04a	V	V 4:39a	Li	Li 4:09a	S	S 5:36a	Sg	Sg 10:29a	Cp	Cp 7:10p	Aq	Aq	Aq	P 6:41a
Nov	Li 3:08p	S	S 4:11p	Sg	Sg 7:46p	Cp	Cp	Cp 3:00a	Aq	Aq 1:42p	P	P	A 2:18a	A	A
Dec	S 2:34a	Sg	Sg 5:59a	Cp	Cp 12:13p	Aq	Aq 9:52p	P	P	P	A 10:07a	A	T 10:40p	T	T

1976

	1	2	3	4	5	6	7	8	9	10	11	12	13	14	15
Jan	Cp 9:33p	Aq	Aq	Aq	P 6:36a	P	A 6:22p	A	A	T 7:10a	T	G 6:20p	G	G	C 2:01a
Feb	P 2:47p	P	P	A 2:18a	A	T 3:14p	T	T	G 3:17p	G	C 11:59a	C	C 4:33p	L	V 6:00p
Mar	P 9:23a	A	A	T 10:19p	T	T	G 10:56a	G	C 8:59p	C	C	L 2:56a	L	V 4:59a	V
Apr	T 4:35a	T	G 5:16p	G	G	C 4:07a	C	L 11:37a	L	V 3:17p	V	Li 3:55p	Li	S 3:15p	S
May	G	G	C 9:54a	C	L 5:10p	L	V 11:22p	V	V	Li 1:40a	Li	S 2:03a	S	Sg 2:05a	Sg
Jn	L 11:38p	L	V 5:22a	V	Li 9:00a	Li	S	S 10:59a	S	Sg 12:07p	Sg	Cp 1:46p	Cp	Aq 5:32p	Aq
Jly	V 10:47a	V	Li 2:35p	Li	S 5:34p	S	Sg 8:06p	Sg	Cp 10:50p	Cp	Aq	Aq 2:54a	P	P 9:37a	P
Aug	S 10:56p	S	S	Sg 2:04a	Sg	Cp 5:55a	Cp	Aq 10:58a	Aq	P 6:01p	P	P	A 3:50a	A	T 4:06p
Sep	Sg	Cp 11:30a	Cp	Aq 5:21p	Aq	Aq	P 1:12a	P	A 11:19a	A	T 11:31p	T	T	G 12:33p	G
Oct	Aq 10:50p	Aq	Aq	P 7:10a	P	A 5:50p	A	A	T 6:12a	T	G 7:15p	G	G	C 7:25a	C
Nov	P 11:46p	A	A	A 12:24p	T	T	T 1:22a	G	G 1:29p	C	C 11:37p	C	L	L	V 6:47a
Dec	A 6:42p	T	T	T	G 7:39a	G	G 7:22p	C	C	C 5:13a	L	L 12:56p	V	V 6:14p	Li

16	17	18	19	20	21	22	23	24	25	26	27	28	29	30	31
S	Sg 10:13p	Sg	Sg	Cp 10:48a	Cp	Aq 11:50p	Aq	Aq	P 12:01p	P	A 10:32p	A	A	T 6:42a	T
Cp 5:16p	Cp	Cp	Aq 6:21a	Aq	P 6:16p	P	P	A 4:13a	A	T 12:12p	T	G 6:11p			
Cp 12:42a	Cp	A 1:39p	A	A	P 1:34a	P	A 11:03a	A	A	T 6:10p	T	G 11:34p	G	G	C 3:40a
Aq 9:45a	P	P 7:21p	A	A	A	T 1:54a	T	G 6:11a	G	C 9:18a	C	L 12:04p	L	V 3:01p	
P	A 4:20a	A	T 11:11a	T	G 2:55p	G	C 4:46p	C	L 6:13p	L	V 8:26p	V	V	Li 12:17p	Li
T	T	G 1:00a	G	C 2:22a	C	L 2:30a	L	V 3:12a	V	Li 5:58a	Li	S 11:41a	S	Sg 8:21p	
G	C 12:57p	C	L 12:54p	L	V 12:10p	V	Li 1:19p	Li	S 5:46p	S	S	Sg 2:00a	Sg	Cp 1:11p	Cp
L 10:43p	V	V 10:45p	Li	Li	Li	S 1:38a	S	SG 8:35a	Sg	Cp 7:16p	Cp	Cp	Aq 7:53a	Aq	P 8:30p
Li 9:17a	Li	S 11:14a	S	SG 4:47p	Sg	Sg	Cp 2:22a	Cp	Aq 2:39p	Aq	Aq	P 3:15a	P	A 2:26p	
S	S	Sg 2:15a	Sg	Cp 10:44a	Cp	Aq 10:21p	Aq	Aq	P 10:57a	P	A 10:14p	A	A	T 7:01a	T
Cp 7:42p	Cp	Cp	Aq 6:39a	Aq	P 7:12p	P	P	A 7:00a	A	T 4:05p	T	G 9:59a	G	G	
Aq 2:49p	Aq	Aq	P 3:12a	P	A 3:36p	A	A	T 1:45a	T	G 8:16a	G	C 11:16a	C	L 12:05	

16	17	18	19	20	21	22	23	24	25	26	27	28	29	30	31
P	A 11:04p	A	A	T 10:22a	T	G 6:23p	G	C	C 10:21p	C	L 11:01p	L	V 10:14p	V	L 10:14p
T 5:10p	T	T	G 2:35a	G	C 8:19a	C	L 10:14a	L	V 9:38a	V	Li 8:39a	Li			
T	T	G 8:44a	G	C 3:49p	C	L 7:32p	L	V 8:22p	V	Li 7:52p	Li	S 8:08	S	Sg 11:10p	Sg
C 9:28p	C	C	L 2:15a	L	V 4:43a	V	Li 5:42a	Li	S 6:40a	S	Sg 9:20a	Sg	Cp 3:09p	Cp	
L 7:39a	L	V 10:46a	V	Li 1:06p	Li	Li 3:26p	S	S 6:52p	Sg	Sg	Cp 12:31a	Cp	Aq 9:10a	Aq	P 10:33p
Li 6:41p	Li	S 10:00p	S	S	Sg 2:35a	Sg	Cp 8:57a	Cp	Aq 5:34p	Aq	Aq	P 4:34a	P	A 5:03p	
S 3:24a	S	Sg 8:33a	Sg	Cp 3:46p	Cp	Cp	Aq 12:56a	Aq	P 11:59a	P	P	A 12:28a	A	T 12:54p	T
Cp 9:26p	Cp	Cp	Aq 7:10a	Aq	P 6:33p	P	P	A 7:03a	A	T 7:45p	T	T	G 6:54a	G	C 2:36p
Aq	Aq	P 12:32a	P	A 1:08p	A	A	T 1:44a	T	G 1:14p	G	C 10:08p	C	C	L 3:21a	
P	A 7:21p	A	A	T 7:44a	T	G 6:52p	G	G	C 3:58a	C	L 10:20a	L	V 1:47p	V	Li 2:56p
T 2:38p	T	T	G 1:16a	G	C 9:37a	C	L 3:49p	L	V 8:05p	V	Li 10:48p	Li	Li	S 12:37a	
G 9:13a	G	C 4:50p	C	L 9:54p	L	L	V 1:28a	V	Li 4:28a	Li	S 7:29a	S	Sg 10:54a	Sg	Cp 3:17p

16	17	18	19	20	21	22	23	24	25	26	27	28	29	30	31
C	L 6:16a	L	V 8:26a	V	Li 10:11a	Li	S 12:49p	S	Sg 4:52p	Sg	Cp 10:25p	Cp	Cp	Aq 5:35a	Aq
V	Li 6:15p	Li	S 7:14p	S	Sg 10:19p	Sg	Sg	Cp 3:55a	Cp	Aq 11:49a	Aq	P 9:42p	P		
Li 4:45a	Li	S 4:18a	S	Sg 5:34a	Sg	Cp 9:49a	Cp	Aq 5:20p	Aq	Aq	P 3:34a	P	A 3:38p	A	A
Sg 3:16p	SG	Cp 5:44p	Cp	Aq 11:48p	Aq	Aq	P 9:28a	P	A 9:37p	A	A	T 10:38p	T	G 11:06p	
Cp 3:32a	Cp	Aq 8:03a	Aq	P 4:27p	P	P	A 4:08a	A	T 5:08p	T	T	G 5:23a	G	C 3:40p	C
Aq	P 12:44a	P	A 11:33a	A	A	T 12:22a	T	G 12:37p	G	C 10:30p	C	C	L 5:40a	L	
A 7:40p	A	A	T 8:12a	T	G 8:41p	G	G	C 6:40a	C	L 1:19p	L	V 5:24p	V	Li 8:14p	Li
T	T	G 4:55a	G	C 3:35p	C	L 10:31p	L	L	V 2:04a	V	Li 3:42a	Li	S 5:06a	S	Sg 7:29a
G 12:07a	C	C 8:11a	L	L	V 12:17p	V	Li 1:28p	Li	S 1:34p	S	Sg 2:22p	Sg	Cp 5:14p	Cp	
L 4:50p	L	V 10:25p	V	Li 12:27a	Li	S 12:18a	S	Sg 11:49p	SG	SG	Cp 12:56a	Cp	Aq 5:06a	Aq	P 12:54p
V	Li 10:35a	Li	S 11:32a	S	SG 11:04a	Sg	Cp 11:04a	Cp	Aq 1:30p	Aq	P 7:48p	P	P	A 6:02a	
S 9:02p	S	Sg 9:55p	Sg	Cp 10:12p	Cp	Aq 10:49p	Aq	Aq	P 4:37a	P	A 1:32p	A	A	T 1:44a	

1977

Month	1	2	3	4	5	6	7	8	9	10	11	12	13	14	15
Jan	G 2:43p	G	G	C 2:13a	C	L 11:21a	L	V 5:24p	V	Li 11:48a	Li	Li	S 3:45a	S	Sg 6:19a
Feb	C 7:12p	C	L 1:18a	L	V 5:37a	V	V	Li 9:05a	Li	S 12:12p	S	Sg 3:14p	Sg	Cp	Aq 6:46p
Mar	C 4:26a	L	L	V 10:19a	V	Li 1:35p	Li	S 3:38p	S	Sg 5:42p	Sg	Cp 8:40p	Cp	Cp	Aq 1:01a
Apr	V 11:40p	Li 12:40a	Li	Li	S 1:09a	S	Sg 2:41a	Sg	Cp 6:24a	Cp	Aq 12:50p	Aq	P	P	A 9:53p
May	Li 11:24a	S	S	Sg 10:59a	Sg	Cp 10:55a	Cp	Aq 1:00p	Aq	P 6:30p	P	P	A 3:30a	A	T 3:05p
Jn	Sg 9:08p	Cp	Cp	Aq 9:44p	Aq	Aq 1:36a	P	P 9:35a	A	A 8:57p	T	T 9:50a	G	G	G
Jly	Cp 7:57a	Aq	Aq 10:32a	P	P 5:04p	A	A 3:34a	A	T 4:16p	T	G	G 4:50a	G	C	C
Aug	P 1:55a	P	A 11:19a	A	T 11:30p	T	T	G 12:05p	G	C 2:05p	C	V 10:57p	L	L	L 7:26a
Sep	T 7:52p	T	T	G 7:28a	G	C 8:04p	C	C	L 7:14a	L	V 3:35p	V	Li 9:08p	Li	Li
Oct	G 3:34p	G	G	C 4:10a	C	L 3:58p	L	L	V 12:59a	V	Li 6:30a	Li	S 9:12a	S	Sg 10:28p
Nov	C 12:04a	C	L 10:17a	V	V 4:52p	Li	Li 7:43p	S	S 8:04p	Sg	Sg 7:51p	Cp	Cp 9:01p	Aq	—
Dec	L 6:06a	V	V	V 2:18a	Li	Li 6:34a	S	S 7:22a	Sg	Sg 6:27a	Cp	Cp 6:00a	Aq	Aq 8:10a	P

1978

Month	1	2	3	4	5	6	7	8	9	10	11	12	13	14	15
Jan	Li 9:32a	Li	S 3:36p	S	Sg 6:04p	Sg	Cp 5:55p	Cp	Aq 5:06p	Aq	P 5:51p	P	P 10:06p	A	A
Feb	S 2:14a	Sg	Sg 3:51a	Cp	Cp 4:05a	Aq	Aq 4:48a	P	P 7:57a	A	A 2:51p	T	T	T 1:25a	G
Mar	Sg 8:03a	Sg	Cp 10:59a	Cp	Aq 12:51p	Aq	P 2:46p	P	A 6:09p	A	A 12:19a	T	G 9:49a	G	—
Apr	Aq 7:06p	Aq	P 10:21p	P	P 2:52a	A	A 9:22a	T	T 6:28p	G	G 6:00a	C	C 6:31p	L	—
May	P 4:00a	P	A 9:28a	A	T 4:53p	T	T 2:19a	G	G 1:42p	C	C 2:17a	L	L 2:16p	V	—
Jn	T 10:51p	T	T	G 8:54a	G	C 8:31p	C	C	L 9:08a	L	V 9:35p	V	V 7:56a	Li	Li
Jly	G 2:38p	G	G	C 2:34a	C	L 3:14p	L	L	V 3:45a	V	Li 2:49p	Li	Li 10:48p	S	S
Aug	C 9:11p	L	L	L 9:30a	V	V 8:30p	Li	Li 5:12a	Li	S 10:44a	S	Sg 1:04p	Sg	Cp	Cp
Sep	V 3:47p	V	V	Li 2:16a	Li	S 10:39a	S	Sg 4:40p	Sg	Cp 8:20p	Cp	Aq 10:09p	Aq	P 11:10p	P
Oct	Li 9:17a	Li	S 4:49p	S	Sg 10:07p	Sg	Cp 1:53a	Cp	Aq 4:43a	Aq	P 7:13a	P	A 10:07a	A	—
Nov	S 5:04a	Sg	Sg 7:41a	Cp	Cp 10:04a	Aq	Aq 1:07p	P	P 5:12p	A	A 10:36p	T	T	T 5:45a	G
Dec	Cp 3:45p	Cp	Aq 4:36p	Aq	P 7:37p	P	A 10:40p	A	A	T 4:51a	T	G 12:55p	G	C 10:50p	C

1979

Month	1	2	3	4	5	6	7	8	9	10	11	12	13	14	15
Jan	Aq	P	P	A 4:42a	A	T 10:18a	T	G 6:43p	G	G	C 5:15a	C	L 5:17p	L	L
Feb	A 5:04p	T	T	G 12:34a	G	C 11:06a	C	L 11:26a	L	L	V 12:18p	V	V 12:38a	Li	—
Mar	A 2:10a	T	T 7:59a	G	C 5:35p	C	C	L 5:48a	L	V 6:43p	V	V 6:42a	Li	Li	—
Apr	G	G 1:24a	C	L 12:58p	L	L	V 1:53a	V	Li 1:46p	Li	S 11:16p	S	S	Sg 6:19a	—
May	C 8:57p	L	L	L 9:42a	V	V 9:48p	Li	Li	Li 7:11a	S	S 1:25p	Sg	Sg 5:26p	Cp	Cp
Jn	V 5:41p	V	V	Li 6:12a	Li	S 4:06p	S	Sg 10:15p	Sg	Sg 1:24a	Cp	Aq 3:07a	Aq	P 4:57p	—
Jly	Li 2:09p	Li	Li	S 12:58a	Sg 7:56a	Sg	Cp 11:08a	Cp	Aq 12:00	Aq	P 12:23p	P	A 1:58p	A	—
Aug	S 5:06p	Sg	Sg	Cp 9:24p	Aq 10:29p	Aq	P 10:06p	P	A 10:11p	A	A 12:22a	T	T 5:42a	—	—
Sep	Cp 6:34p	Cp	Aq 9:00a	Aq	P 9:04a	P	A 8:30a	A	T 9:13a	T	T 12:55p	G	G 8:28p	C	C
Oct	A 7:24p	P	P 7:29a	A	A 7:34p	T	T 10:08p	G	G 4:10a	G	C 2:12p	C	—	—	—
Nov	A 5:10a	A	T 6:17a	T	G 8:26a	G	C 1:24p	C	L 10:15p	L	L	V 10:21a	V	Li 11:17p	Li
Dec	T	G 6:03p	G	C 11:02p	C	C	L 7:10a	L	V 6:33p	V	V	Li 7:30a	Li	S 7:09p	S

16	17	18	19	20	21	22	23	24	25	26	27	28	29	30	31
Sg	Cp 8:03a	Cp 10:13a	Aq	Aq 2:31p	P	P	A 10:20p	A	A	T 9:42a	T	G 10:38a	G	G	C 10:21a
Aq	P 11:45p	P	P 7:23a	A	A 6:07p	T	T	T 6:51a	G	G 7:03p	C	C			
Aq	P 7:06a	P	P 3:24p	A	A 2:06a	T	T 2:39p	G	G	C 3:17a	C	C	L 1:41p	L	V 8:26p
A	A 9:03a	T	T 9:38p	G	G	G 10:26a	C	C 9:44p	L	L	L 5:53a	V	V	Li 10:13a	
T	T 3:51a	G	G 4:36p	C	C	C	L 4:14a	L	V 1:32p	V	V 7:29p	Li	Li 9:57p	S	S 9:55p
C 10:29p	C	C	L 9:54a	L	V 7:30p	V	V	Li 2:36a	Li	S 6:43a	S	SG 8:03a	Sg	Cp 7:49a	
L 3:52p	L	L	V 12:59a	V	Li 8:10a	Li	S 1:14p	S	Sg 4:50p	Sg	Cp 5:16p	Cp	Aq 6:05p	Aq	P 8:24p
V	Li 1:50p	Li	S 6:36p	S	Sg 10:03p	Sg	Sg	Cp 12:31a	Cp	Aq 2:41a	Aq	P 5:47a	P	A	A 11:12a
S	S 12:46a	Sg	Sg 3:29a	Cp	Cp 6:05a	Aq	Aq 9:13a	P	P 1:30p	A	A	A 7:41p	T	T 4:22a	T
Sg	Cp 11:51a	Cp	Aq 2:37p	Aq	P 7:27p	P	P	A 2:35p	A	T 11:54a	T	G 11:09p	G	G	C 11:41a
Aq	Aq 12:59a	P	P 8:14a	A	A 6:10p	T	T	T	G	G 5:49a	C	C 6:21p	C	C	L 6:54a
P 2:12p	A	A 11:55p	T	T	T	G	G 11:52a	G	C	C 12:30a	L	L 12:52p	L	V	V 12:14a

16	17	18	19	20	21	22	23	24	25	26	27	28	29	30	31
T 6:31a	T	G 6:07p	G	G	C 6:51a	C	L 7:03p	L	L	V 5:57a	V	Li 3:08p	Li	S	S 10:04p
G 1:56p	C	C	C	L 2:10a	L	V 12:40p	V	Li 9:04p	Li	Li	S 3:29a	S			
C 9:50p	C	C	L 10:13a	L	V 8:50p	V	V	Li 4:42a	Li	S 10:02a	S	Sg 1:38p	Sg	Cp 4:24p	Cp
L	L 5:45a	V	V 1:54p	Li	Li 6:40p	S	S	Sg 9:01p	Sg	Cp 10:28p	Cp	Cp	Aq 12:29a	Aq	
V	Li 11:25p	Li	Li	S 4:40a	S	Sg 6:32a	Sg	Cp 6:42a	Cp	Aq 7:10a	Aq 9:37a	P 9:37a	P	A 2:59p	A
S 2:29p	S	Sg 5:02p	Sg	Cp 4:53p	Cp	Aq 4:08p	Aq	P 4:57p	p	A 8:54p	A	A	T 4:22a	T	
Sg 2:51a	Sg	Cp 3:34a	Cp	Aq 2:42a	Aq	P 2:27a	P	A 4:46a	A	T 10:51a	T	G 8:31p	G	G	C 8:29p
Aq 1:16p	Aq	P 1:05p	P	A 2:30p	A	T 7:06p	T	T	G 3:32a	G	C 3:00p	C	C	L 3:40a	L
P	A 12:51a	A	T 4:44a	T	G 11:57a	G	C 10:32a	C	C	L 11:02a	L	V 11:12p	V	V	
T 2:23p	T	G 9:06p	G	G	C 6:53a	C	L 7:05p	L	L	V 7:33a	V	Li 5:52p	Li	Li	S 12:53a
G 5:17p	C	C	C	L 3:10a	L	V 3:58p	V	V	Li 3:08a	Li	S 10:39a	S	Sg 2:24p	Sg	
G 10:38a	L 11:35p	L	V	V	V	Li 11:41a	Li	S 8:33a	S	S	Sg 1:08a	Sg	Cp 2:16a	Cp	Aq 1:54a

16	17	18	19	20	21	22	23	24	25	26	27	28	29	30	31
V 6:11a	V	Li 6:41p	Li	Li	S 4:52p	S	Sg 11:09a	Sg	Cp 1:28p	Cp	Aq 1:13p	Aq	P 12:26p	P	A 1:12p
Li	S 11:13a	S	Sg 6:52p	Sg	Cp 11:01p	Cp	Cp	Aq 12:13a	Aq	P 11:53p	P	A 11:55p	A	A	
S 4:50p	S	S	SG 12:39a	Sg	Cp 5:57a	Cp	Aq 8:53a	Aq	P 10:05a	P	A 10:48a	A	T 12:37p	T	G 5:09p
Sg	Cp 11:24a	Cp	Aq 3:03p	Aq	P 5:42p	P	A 7:52p	A	T 10:28p	T	T	G 2:49a	G	C 10:12a	
Aq 8:26p	Aq	P 11:19p	P	P	A 2:31a	A	T 6:21a	T	G 11:29a	G	C 6:51p	C	C	L 5:09a	L
P 7:53a	A	A 12:19p	T	T 6:23p	G	G	G	C 2:25a	C	L 12:48p	L	L	V 1:15a	V	
T 5:44p	T	T	G 12:00a	G	C 8:41a	C	L 7:31p	L	L	V 8:02a	V	Li 9:07p	Li	Li	S 8:47a
G 2:18p	C	C	C	L 1:29a	L	V 2:12p	V	V	Li 3:14a	Li	S 3:13p	S	S	Sg 12:40a	Sg
L 7:26a	L	V 8:16p	V	V	Li 9:11a	Li	S 8:55p	S	S	SG 6:36a	Sg	Cp 1:41p	Cp	Aq 5:50p	
V 2:52a	V	Li 3:45p	Li	Li	S 3:03a	S	Sg 12:10p	Sg	Cp 7:12p	Cp	Aq	Aq 12:17a	Aq	P 3:30a	P
Li 10:30a	S	S 6:57p	Sg	Sg	Sg	Cp 1:02a	Cp	Aq 5:37a	Aq	P 9:18a	P	A 12:17p	A	T 2:55p	
S 3:37a	Sg	Sg 8:55a	Cp	Cp	Aq 12:13p	Aq	P 2:51p	P	A 5:41p	A	T 9:08p	T	T	G 1:33a	G

1980

	1	2	3	4	5	6	7	8	9	10	11	12	13	14	15
Jan	G	C	C	C	L L	L	L	V V	V Li	Li	Li	Li S	S	S Sg	Sg / Sg Cp
	7:30a			3:48p			2:49a		3:39p		3:56a		1:18p		6:52p
Feb	L	L	V V	V Li	Li	Li	Li S	S	S Sg	Sg	Sg	Sg Cp	Cp	Cp Aq	Aq
	10:22a		11:05p			11:47a		10:20p			5:13a		8:20a		
Mar	V	V	V Li	Li	Li S	S	S	S Sg	Sg	Sg Cp	Cp	Cp Aq	Aq	Aq P	P
	5:41a		6:23p		5:39a			2:03p		6:46p			8:11p		
Apr	Li	Li S	S	S Sg	Sg	Sg Cp	Cp	Cp	Cp Aq	Aq	Aq P	P	P A	A	A / T
	12:22a		11:35a		8:43p			3:00a		6:08a		6:41a		6:11a	
May	S Sg	Sg	Sg	Sg Cp	Cp	Cp Aq	Aq	Aq P	P	P	P A	A	A T	T	T G
	6:22p			2:15a		9:04a		1:34p		3:45p		4:25p		5:08p	
Jn	Cp	Cp Aq	Aq	Aq P	P	P A	A	A	A T	T	T G	G	G C	C	C L
	2:30p		7:11p		11:24p			12:30a		2:23a		5:30a		11:23a	
Jly	Aq	Aq P	P	P A	A	A T	T	T	T G	G	G C	C	C L	L	L V
	12:49a		3:47a		6:31a			9:34a		1:45p		8:03p		5:12a	
Aug	A	A T	T	T G	G	G C	C	C	C L	L	L V V	V	V Li
	11:56a		3:10p		8:13p			3:24a		12:55p		12:33a		
Sep	G	G	G C	C	C L	L	L V	V	V	V Li Li	Li	Li S	S	S	S Sg
	1:40a		9:23a		7:32p		7:23a			8:07		8:29a		
Oct	C	C L	L	L V	V	V Li	Li	Li	Li S	S	S Sg	Sg	Sg	Sg Cp
	2:58p		1:20a		1:30p		2:16a		2:38p		1:37a		
Nov	L V	V	V Li	Li	Li	Li S	S	S Sg	Sg	Sg	Sg Cp	Cp	Cp Aq	Aq	Aq P
	7:19a		7:32p			8:20a		8:26p			7:16a		4:11p		10:22p
Dec	V	Li Li	Li	Li S	S	S Sg	Sg	Sg Cp	Cp	Cp Aq	Aq	Aq	Aq P	P	P A
	2:14a		3:01p			2:58a		1:13p		9:37p			2:04a		8:22a

1981

	1	2	3	4	5	6	7	8	9	10	11	12	13	14	15
Jan	S	S Sg	Sg	Sg Cp	Cp	Cp	Cp Aq	Aq	Aq P	P	P A	A	A T	T	T G
	10:43a		8:42p			2:13a		9:43a		1:44p		4:46p		7:18p
Feb	Sg Cp	Cp	Cp Aq	Aq	Aq P	P	A A	A	A T	T	T	T G	G	G C
	5:33a		12:56p		5:22p		8:02p		10:11p			12:52a		4:13a
Mar	Cp	Cp Aq	Aq	Aq P	P	P A	A	A T	T	T G	G	G C	C	C L
	10:52p			3:13a		4:49a		5:23a		6:43a		10:06a		4:03p
Apr	Ap P	P	P A	A	A T	T	T G	G	G C	C	C L	L	L V
	1:42p		3:26p		3:05p		2:49p		4:34p		9:37p		5:37a
May	P A	A	A T	T	T G	G	G C	C	C L	L	L	L V	V	V Li	Li
	1:58a		2:00a		1:02a		1:18a		4:41a		11:56a		10:25p	
Jn	T G	G	G C	C	C L	L	L V	V	V Li	Li	Li S	S	S	S Sg
	11:49a		11:39a		1:43p		7:26p		4:56a		4:55p		5:32a
Jly	C	C L	L	L V	V	V Li	Li	Li	Li S	S	S Sg	Sg	Sg	Sg Cp
	11:43p		4:27a		12:43p		12:03a		12:36p		12:20a
Aug	L V	V	V Li	Li	Li	Li S	S	S Sg	Sg	Sg Cp	Cp	Cp Aq	Aq	Aq
	1:55p		9:25p			7:59a		8:23p		8:21a		5:57p		
Sep	Li	Li S	S	S Sg	Sg	Sg Cp	Cp	Cp	Cp Aq	Aq	Aq P	P	P A A
	4:11p		4:24a		4:49p			2:59a		9:35a		12:57p	
Oct	S	S Sg	Sg	Sg	Sg Cp	Cp	Cp Aq	Aq	Aq P	P	P A	A	A T	T	T G
	12:00p			12:50a		12:02a		7:33p		11:02p		11:44p		11:42p
Nov	Sg Cp	Cp	Cp Aq	Aq	Aq	Aq P	P	P A	A	A T	T	T G	G	G C
	5:47a		7:52p			4:53a		9:37a		10:45a		10:00a		9:37a
Dec	Cp Aq	Aq	Aq P	P	P A	A	A T	T	T G	G	G C	C	C L L
	2:10a		12:17p		6:50p		9:32p		9:31p		8:41p		9:02p

1982

	1	2	3	4	5	6	7	8	9	10	11	12	13	14	15
Jan	P	P A	A	A T	T	T G	G	G C	C	C L	L	L V	V	V Li	Li
	1:34a		6:03a		7:49a		8:02a		8:33a		10:38a		4:18p	
Feb	T	T G	G	G C	C	C L	L	L V	V	V	V Li	Li	Li S	S	S Sg
	3:21p		5:19p		6:51p		9:16			2:03a		10:17a		9:46p
Mar	T G	G	G C	C	C	C L	L	L V	V	V Li	Li	Li S	S	S Sg
	8:51p		11:49p			2:51a		6:28a		11:35a		7:17p		6:04a
Apr	C	C L	L	L V	V	V Li	Li	Li	Li S	S	S Sg	Sg	Sg	Sg Cp	Cp
	8:37a		1:19p		7:27p		3:34a		2:07p			2:42a	
May	L V	V	V	V Li	Li	Li S	S	S Sg	Sg	Sg	Sg Cp	Cp	Cp Aq	Aq	Aq
	6:46p		1:33a		1:25a		9:17p		9:50a		10:45p			
Jn	Li	Li S	S	S Sg	Sg	Sg Cp	Cp	Cp	Cp Aq	Aq	Aq P	P	P	P A
	4:13p		3:32a		4:13p			5:09a		4:45p			1:21a
Jly	S	S Sg	Sg	Sg Cp	Cp	Cp	Cp Aq	Aq	Aq P	P	P	P A	A	A T	T
	9:26a		10:16p			10:04a		10:36a			7:50a		2:01p
Aug	Sg Cp	Cp	Cp Aq	Aq	Aq P	P	P	P A	A	A T	T	T	T G	G	G C
	7:37a		5:18p		5:24a			1:21p		8:01p			12:23a		2:41a
Sep	Aq	Ap P	P	P A	A	A	A T	T	T G	G	G C	C	C L	L	L V
	11:12a		7:15p		1:29a			5:50a		9:19a		11:47a		1:58p
Oct	P	P A	A	A T	T	T G	G	G C	C	C L	L	L V	V	V Li
	3:07a		8:10a		11:40a		2:40p		5:45p		9:10p			1:23a
Nov	T	T G	G	G C	C	C L	L	L	L V	V	V	V Li	Li	Li S	S
	7:23p		9:00p		11:11p			2:41a			7:48a		2:43p		11:52p
Dec	G	G C	C	C L	L	L V	V	V Li	Li	Li	Li S	S	S	S Sg	Sg / Sg Cp
	5:58a		6:27a		8:33a		1:11p		8:35p			6:28a		6:16p	

```
   16     17      18      19      20      21      22      23      24      25     26      27      28      29      30      31

Cp     Cp Aq Aq    Aq P P     P A A     A T T     T        T G G     G C C     C L L
       9:26p       10:34p     11:52p    2:32a              7:12a     2:03p     11:09p

Aq P P    P A A     A T T     T G G     G C C     C        C L L     L V
8:55a     8:43a     9:36a     12:59p    7:35p              5:11a     4:54p

P A A     A T T G G    G       G        G C C     C L L     L V V     V        V Li Li
7:42p     7:14p 8:48p          1:56a              10:59a    11:53p             11:50a

T        T G G     G C C     C L L     L        L V V     V Li Li    Li       Li S S
6:42a    10:12a    5:53p     5:13a              6:10p                         6:36a

G C C    C        C L L     L V V     V        V Li Li    Li S S     S        S Sg Sg    Sg Cp
7:53p    2:15a              12:33p             1:12a              1:37p       12:05a     8:15a

L        L V V     V        V Li Li    Li S S     S        S Sg Sg    Sg Cp Cp   Cp Aq Aq
8:43p              8:56a              9:27p               10:02a     3:47p      9:04p

V        V Li Li    Li       Li S S     S Sg Sg    Sg       Sg Cp Cp   Cp Aq Aq   Aq P P    P A
4:56p              5:34a              4:43p               12:45a     5:35a      8:11a     9:54a

Li S S    S        S Sg Sg    Sg Cp Cp   Cp Aq Aq   Aq P P    P A A     A T T     T G
1:16p     1:08a              10:12a     3:32p      5:44p     6:12p     6:42p     8:51p

Sg       Sg Cp Cp   Cp       Cp Aq Aq   Aq P P    P A A     A T T     T G G     G C
6:46p    1:31a              4:28a      4:38a      3:54a     4:22a     5:44a

Cp       Cp Aq Aq   Aq P P     P A A     A T T     T G G     G C C     C L L     L
9:54a    2:32p      1:44p     2:56p     2:17p     4:01p     4:39p

P        P        P A A     A T T     T G G     G C C     C L L     L V V
         1:22a    1:52a     1:28a     2:19a              5:24a     2:38p

A        A T T     T G G     G C C     C L L     L V V     V        V Li Li    Li S S
10:37a   11:40a    1:04p     4:34p     11:33p             10:06a    10:27p
```

```
   16     17      18      19      20      21      22      23      24      25     26      27      28      29      30      31

G        G C C     C        C L L     L V V     V Li Li    Li       Li S S     S Sg Sg    Sg       Sg
10:08p             2:22a              9:03a     6:46p               6:49a      7:12p

C L L     L V V     V        V Li Li    Li S S     S        S Sg Sg    Sg Cp Cp
10:11a    5:35p              5:13a              2:55p               3:30a      2:47p

L        L        L V V     V        V Li Li    Li S S     S        S Sg Sg    Sg Cp Cp   Cp       Cp Aq Aq
12:20a             10:31a             10:16p             10:52a    10:53p               8:16a

V Li Li    Li       Li S S     S Sg Sg    Sg       Sg Cp Cp   Cp Aq Aq   Aq P P    P
4:39p     4:40a              5:16p      5:32a      3:58p      10:57p

Li S S     S Sg Sg    Sg       Sg Cp Cp   Cp Aq Aq   Aq       Aq P P    P A A     A T T
10:38a    11:15p             11:21a     10:01p              6:00a     10:45a     12:11p

Sg       Sg Cp Cp   Cp       Cp Aq Aq   Aq P P    P A A     A T T     T G G     G C
5:22p    3:37a              11:45a     5:19p      8:17p     9:22p     9:58p

Cp       Cp Aq Aq   Aq P P     P A A     A        A T T     T G G     G C C     C L L
10:03a   5:26p      10:44p    2:19a     4:42a     6:42a     9:21a

Ap P P    P A A     A T T     T G G     G C C     C L L     L V V     V        V Li
12:35a    4:50a     7:44a     10:19a    1:17p     5:11p     10:32p             6:03a

A T T     T G G     G C C     C L L     L        L V V     V Li Li    Li S S
2:31p     4:00p     6:40p     11:09p             5:29p     1:41p     11:53p

G        G C C     C L L     L V V     V Li Li    Li       Li S S     S Sg Sg    Sg
         12:53a    4:53a     11:06a    7:57p               6:39a      5:49p

C L L     L V V     V        V Li Li    Li S S     S        S Sg Sg    Sg Cp Cp   Cp
11:53a    4:59p              1:34a     12:37p             1:01a      1:53p

L V V     V Li Li    Li S S     S        S Sg Sg    Sg C C     G        G Aq Aq    Aq P P
12:09a    7:58a     5:40p              7:12a     8:00a              7:54a      6:02p
```

```
   16     17      18      19      20      21      22      23      24      25     26      27      28      29      30      31

Li       Li S S     S Sg Sg    Sg       Sg Cp Cp   Cp Aq Aq   Aq P P    P        P A A     A T
1:47a    2:01p              2:52p      2:26p      11:50p              6:59a     12:04p

Sg       Sg       Sg Cp Cp   Cp Aq Aq   Aq       Aq P P    P A A     A T T
         10:37a    10:16p             7:10a      1:18p     5:33p

Sg       Sg Cp Cp   Cp       Cp Aq Aq   Aq P P    P A A     A        A T T     T G G     G C
6:48p    6:54a              4:02p      9:02p              12:40a    2:45a     5:10a

Cp Aq Aq    Aq       Aq P P    P A A     A T T     T G G     G C C     C L Li
3:19p       1:20a    7:24a     9:59a     10:49a    11:44a    2:10p

Aq P P    P A A     A T T     T G G     G C C     C L L     L        L V V     V Li
9:47a     5:05p     8:23p     8:55p     8:39p     9:08p              12:44a    7:03a

A        A T T     T G G     G C C     C L L     L V V     V Li Li    Li S S
5:08a    7:35a     7:13a     6:57a     8:57a     1:31p     10:02p

T G G     G C C     C L L     L V V     V Li Li    Li       Li S S     S Sg Sg    Sg
5:04p     5:47p     5:36p     6:21p     9:46p               4:59a      3:48p

C        C L L     L V V     V Li Li    Li S S     S        S Sg Sg    Sg Cp Cp   Cp       Cp Aq
3:41a    4:40a     7:23a     1:22p     11:12p              11:42a               12:24a

V        V Li Li    Li S S     S        S Sg Sg    Sg Cp Cp   Cp       Cp Aq Aq   Aq P P
5:04p    10:33p             7:31a      7:32p      8:22a              7:19p

Li       Li S S     S Sg Sg    Sg Cp Cp   Cp       Cp Aq Aq   Aq       Aq P P    P A A     A T
7:21a    4:03p              3:39a      4:37p              4:13p     12:26p     5:04p

Sg       Sg       Sg Cp Cp   Cp       Cp Aq Aq   Aq P P    P A A     A        A T T     T G G
         11:22a    12:21a             12:43a     10:02p             3:32a     5:37a

Cp       Cp       Cp Aq Aq   Aq P P    P        P A A     A T T     T G G     T C C     C L
         7:13a     7:57p              6:35a     1:32p     4:49p     5:13p     4:34p
```

1983

	1	2	3	4	5	6	7	8	9	10	11	12	13	14	15
Jan	L	L V V		V Li Li		Li		Li s S		S S Sg		Sg	Sg Cp		Cp Aq Aq
		4:50p		7:45p				2:17a		12:14p			12:27a		1:27p
Feb	L Li Li		Li S S		S Sg Sg		Sg		Sg Cp Cp		Cp Aq Aq		Aq	Aq P P	P A
	4:48a		9:33a		6:29p				5:34a		7:41p			8:03a	6:47p
Mar	Li	Li S S		S Sg Sg		Sg		Sg Cp Cp		Cp		Cp Aq Aq	Aq P P	P	P A
	6:52p		2:16a				1:30p		2:31a			2:42p			1:01a
Apr	S Sg Sg		Sg Cp Cp		Cp		Cp Aq Aq		Aq P P		P	P A A		A T T	T G
	11:20a		9:30p		10:07a				10:31p			8:58a	4:00p		9:16p
May	Sg Cp Cp		Cp Aq Aq		Aq		Aq P P		P A A		A	A T T		T G G	G C
	5:02a		6:10p		5:44a				5:17p			12:37a	5:04a		7:49a
Jn	Aq	Aq P P		P		P A A		A T T		T G G		G C C		C L L	L V
	2:43p			2:00a		10:06a		2:38p		4:33p		5:22p		6:39p	
Jly	P	P A A		A T T		T		T G G		G C C		C L L		L V V	V Li
	9:48a		7:06p				12:42a		2:51p		2:54p		2:44p		4:11a
Aug	A T T		T G G		G C C		C L L		L V V		V Li Li		Li S S		S Sg
	2:38a		9:44a		1:10p		1:38p		12:50p		12:52p		3:45p		12:34p
Sep	G C C		C L L		L V V		V Li Li		Li		Li S S		S Sg Sg		Sg Cp Cp
	9:54p		11:48p		11:37p		11:14p				12:50a		6:09a		3:43p
Oct	C L L		L V V		V Li Li		Li S S		S Sg Sg		Sg Cp Cp		Cp	Cp Aq Aq	
	7:55a		9:16a		9:46		11:07a		3:21p		11:31p			11:01a	
Nov	V Li Li		Li S S		S		S Sg Sg		Sg Cp Cp		Cp Aq Aq		Aq	Aq P P	P A
	6:31p		8:54p		1:10a		10:32a		7:11p					7:42a	7:37p
Dec	Li S S		S Sg Sg		Sg Cp Cp		Cp		Cp Aq Aq		Aq P P		P	P A A	A T
	4:41a		9:57a		5:29p				3:40a		3:54p			4:17a	2:34p

1984

	1	2	3	4	5	6	7	8	9	10	11	12	13	14	15
Jan	Sg	Sg Cp Cp		Cp Aq Aq		Aq P P		P		P A A		A T T		T	T G G
	1:08a		11:31a		11:35p				12:16p		11:37p				7:41a
Feb	Aq	Aq P P		P A A		A		A T T		T G G		G		G C C	C L L
	7:34a		4:43p		4:42a				5:32p			4:29a			11:59a
Mar	P	Aq P P		P A A		A T T		T G G		G		G C C		C L L	L V
	12:30p		1:08a		1:10p		11:30p				6:49a		10:22a		10:49a
Apr	A	A T T		T		T G G		G C C		C L L		L V V		V Li Li	Li S
	6:58p		5:05a		1:00p		6:02p		8:12p		8:30p		8:42p		
May	T	T G G		G C C		C L L		L		L V V		V Li Li		Li S S	S Sg
	11:03a		6:27p		11:44p				3:03a		4:55a		6:23a		8:51p
Jn	G C C		C L L		L V V		V Li Li		Li S S		S Sg Sg		Sg Cp Cp		Cp
	12:54a		5:10a		8:28a		11:04a		1:49p		5:27p		10:49p		
Jly	L	L V V		V Li Li		Li S S		S		S Sg Sg		Sg Cp Cp		Cp Aq Aq	Aq
	2:28p		4:27p		7:29p				12:04a		6:24a		2:52p		
Aug	Li	Li S S		S Sg Sg		Sg Cp Cp		Cp Aq Aq		Aq		Aq P P		P A A	
	1:05a		5:30a		12:25p		9:26p				8:14a		8:29p		
Sep	S Sg Sg		Sg Cp Cp		Cp		Cp Aq Aq		Aq P P		P		P A A		A T T	T
	11:30a		5:56p		3:12a				2:25p		2:47a		3:34p		
Oct	Sg Cp Cp		Cp Aq Aq		Aq P P		P		P A A		A T T		T		T G G	G C
	12:29a		9:04a		2:20p				8:52a		9:29p			9:15a	7:01p
Nov	Aq	Aq P P		P A A		A		A T T		T G G		G		G C C	C L L
	9:50a		3:21p		3:54p				3:11p			12:32a		5:34a
Dec	P A A		A		A T T		T G G		G		G C C		C L L		L V V	V Li
	10:43p			11:21a		10:25p				6:57a		1:09p		5:36p	8:53p

1985

	1	2	3	4	5	6	7	8	9	10	11	12	13	14	15
Jan	T	T		T G G		G C C		C L L		L V V		V		V Li Li	Li S S
	7:01a		3:18p		8:29p		11:40p		2:14p			5:08a		
Feb	G	G C C		C L L		L V V		V Li Li		Li S S		S Sg Sg		Sg Cp Cp
	1:00a		6:03a		8:10a		9:11a		10:50a		2:10p		7:28p	
Mar	G C C		C L L		L V V		V Li Li		Li S S		S Sg Sg		Sg Cp Cp	
	10:24a		4:29p		6:43p		6:48p		6:48p		8:30p		12:55a	
Apr	L	L V V		V Li Li		Li S S		S Sg Sg		Sg Cp Cp		Cp Aq Aq		Aq P P
	5:26a		5:55a		5:11a		5:18a		7:58a		2:05p		11:31p	
May	V Li Li		Li S S		S Sg Sg		Sg Cp Cp		Cp Aq Aq		Aq		Aq P P		P A A
	4:23p		4:18p		3:57p		5:12p		9:39p			5:57a		5:26p
Jn	S	S Sg Sg		Sg Cp Cp		Cp Aq Aq		Aq P P		P		P A A		A T T	T
	8:34a		3:35a		6:53a		1:47p		12:25a		1:12p		
Jly	Sg Cp Cp		Cp Aq Aq		Aq P P		P		P A A		A T T		T		T G G	G C
	1:23p		4:37p		10:41p				8:21a		8:45p			8:24a	7:55p
Aug	Aq	Aq P P		P A A		A		A T T		T G G		G		G C C	C L L
	7:34a		4:43p		4:42a				5:32p			4:29a		11:58a
Sep	P A A		A T T		T		T G G		G C C		C L L		L		L V V	V Li
	12:43a		12:28p		1:28p		1:11p		9:28p			1:53a		3:35a
Oct	T	T		T G G		G C C		C		C L L		L V V		V Li Li	Li S S
	8:37a		9:00p		6:34a		12:10p		2:13p			2:14p		
Nov	G	G C C		C L L		L V V		V		V Li Li		Li S S		S Sg Sg	Sg Cp
	3:32		2:04p		9:19p		12:53a		1:32a		12:53a		12:54a	
Dec	C L L		L		L V V		V Li Li		Li S S		S Sg Sg		Sg Cp Cp		Cp Aq Aq
	8:00p		4:15a		9:34a		11:57a		12:14p		12:00p		1:16p	

Section 1

16	17	18	19	20	21	22	23	24	25	26	27	28	29	30	31
Aq	Aq P P		P A A		A T T		T		T G G		G C C		C L L		L V V
2:03a		1:09p		9:37p			2:41a		4:29a		4:11a			3:35a	
A	A		A T T		T G G		G C C		C L L		L		L V V		V Li
	3:31a		9:53a		1:32p		2:47p		2:50p			3:31p			
A	A T T		T G G		G C C		C L L		L		L V V		V Li Li		Li S S
	9:05a		3:21p		7:53p		10:44p			12:19a		1:49a			4:57a
G	G		G C C		C L L		L V V		V Li Li		Li S S		S Sg Sg		Sg
		1:15a		4:27a		7:12a		10:05a		2:05p			8:29p		
C	C L L		L V V		V Li Li		Li S S		S		S Sg Sg		Sg Cp Cp	Cp	Cp Aq
10:02a		12:37p		4:12p		9:18p			4:28a		2:06p				2:00a
V	V Li Li		Li		Li S S		S Sg Sg		Sg Cp Cp		Cp		Cp Aq Aq		Aq P P
9:37p			3:00a		10:56a		10:09p			9:07a			9:53p		
Li	Li S S		S Sg Sg		Sg		Sg Cp Cp		Cp Aq Aq		Aq		Aq P P		P A A	A
8:39a		4:32a		3:12a		3:27p			4:12a		6:22p				
Sg	SG		Sg Cp Cp		Cp Aq Aq		Aq		Aq P P		P A A		A		A T T	T G G
	9:00a		9:26p			10:11a		10:09a			8:39a		3:50p .		
Cp	Cp Aq Aq		Aq P P		P		P A A		A T T		T G G		G C C		
	9:46a		4:31p			9:11a		2:13a		10:25p			4:24a		
Ap	P		P		P A A		A T T		T		T G G		G C C		C L L	L V V
11:42p		11:19a		8:48p			4:11a		9:48a		3:51p			4:34p	
A	A		A T T		T G G		G C C		C L L		L V V		V		V Li Li
	5:07a		11:46a		4:11p		7:20p		10:03p			12:52a			
T	T G G		G		G C C		C L L		L V V		V Li Li		Li S S		S Sg Sg
9:24p		1:03a		2:44a		4:02a		6:19a		10:17a			4:45p		

Section 2

16	17	18	19	20	21	22	23	24	25	26	27	28	29	30	31
G C C		C L L		L V V		V Li Li		Li S S		S Sg Sg		Sg		Sg Cp Cp	Cp Aq
11:48a		12:50p		12:36p		1:08p		4:05p		10:13p		7:13a			6:12p
L	V V		V Li Li		Li S S		S		S Sg Sg		Sg Cp Cp		Cp		Cp Aq Aq
7:16p		6:45p		8:52p		4:23a		12:50p						
V	V Li Li		Li S S		S Sg Sg		Sg Cp Co		Co		Cn An An		Aq P P	P	P A
9:52a		9:49a		12:42p		7:37p			6:10a		6:38p				7:15a
S	S Sg Sg		Sg		Sg Cp Cp		Cp Aq Aq		Aq		Aq P P		P A A		A	A T T
	10:44p		4:11a		1:29p			1:27a		2:03p			1:31a		
Sg	Sg Cp Cp		Cp Aq Aq		Aq		Aq P P		P A A		A T T		T G G		G
	1:44p		9:56p			9:09a		9:40p			9:14a		6:24p		
Sg Aq Aq		Aq P P		P		P A A		A T T		T		T G G		G C C	C L
6:42a		5:19p			5:41a		5:39p			3:05a		9:10a			12:31p
Aq P P		P A A		A		A T T		T G G		G C C		C L L		L V V	V Li
1:11a		1:27p			1:53a		12:11p		6:45p		9:42p		10:30p		11:04p
A	A T T		T G G		G		G C C		C L L		L V V		V Li Li		Li S S
	9:14a		8:32p		4:21a		8:01a		8:32a		7:58a			8:24a	
T G G		G C C		C L L		L V V		V Li Li		Li S S		S Sg Sg		Sg	
3:26a		12:37p		5:50p		7:20p		6:42p		6:05p		7:33p			
C	C		C L L		L V V		V Li Li		Li S S		S Sg Sg		Sg Cp Cp		Cp Aq Aq
	1:42a		4:57a		5:32a		5:08a		5:44a		9:09a			4:14p
L V V		V Li Li		Li		S S Sg		Sg Cp Cp		Cp		Cp Aq Aq		Aq P P	
12:00p		2:30p		3:31p		4:35p		7:18p		1:07a		10:34a			
Li	Li S S		S		S Sg Sg		Sg Cp Cp		Cp Aq Aq		Aq P P		P		P A A	A T
11:20p		1:59a		5:21a		10:48a		7:19p		6:50a			7:37p		

Section 3

16	17	18	19	20	21	22	23	24	25	26	27	28	29	30	31
S Sg Sg		Sg Cp Cp		Cp Aq Aq		Aq		Aq P P		P A A		A		A T T	T G G
8:49a		1:30p		7:39p		4:03a		3:06p			3:54a		4:01p		
Cp	Cp Aq Aq		Aq P P		P A A		A		A T T		T		T G G		
2:37a		11:39a		10:43p		11:28a			12:12a						
Cp Aq Aq		Aq P P		P		P A A		A T T		T		T G G		G C C	C	C L
8:12a		5:21p			5:21a		6:07p			7:03a		6:14p			1:52a
P	P A A		A		A T T		T G G		G		G C C		C L L		L V V	
11:19a			12:13a		1:01p		12:27a		9:11a			2:25p			
A	A T T		T G G		G		G C C		C L L		L V V		V		V Li Li	Li S
6:24a		7:02p		5:06a		2:55p		9:07p			12:41a			2:08a	
T G G		G C C		C L L		L		L V V		V Li Li		Li S S		S Sg Sg	
1:46a		12:23p		8:33p		2:33a		8:48p		9:38a			11:31a		
C	C		C L L		L V V		V Li Li		Li S S		S Sg Sg		Sg Cp Cp	Cp	Cp Aq
	1:26a		8:30a		12:11p		3:17a		6:13p		9:22p				1:26a
L V V		V Li Li		Li S S		S Sg Sg		Sg		Sg Cp Cp		Cp Aq Aq		Aq P P	P
4:16p		6:45p		8:52p		11:37p			3:25a		8:32a			3:26p	
Li	Li S S		S		S Sg Sg		Sg Cp Cp		Cp Aq Aq		Aq P P		P		P A A	A T
4:18a		5:41a		8:50a		2:12p		9:51p			7:43a		7:36p		
S Sg Sg		Sg Cp Cp		Cp Aq Aq		Aq		Aq P P		P A A		A T T		T G G	
2:06p		3:36p		7:55p		3:28a		1:48p			2:00p		3:00p		
Cp	Cp Aq Aq		Aq P P		P A A		A		A T T		T G G		G C C		
3:26a		9:43a		7:34p			8:08a		9:09a			9:24a			
Aq P P		P		P A A		A T T		T		T G G		G C C		C		C L L	L V
5:51p		2:37a		2:41p		3:46a		3:45p			1:45a			9:44a	

1986

	1	2	3	4	5	6	7	8	9	10	11	12	13	14	15
Jan	V	V Li Li 3:46p		Li S S 7:45p		S Sg Sg 9:48p		Sg	Cp 10:43p	Cp	Cp	Cp Aq 12:02a		Aq P P 3:40p	P A 11:04a
Feb	Li S S 1:20a		S Sg Sg 4:32a	Sg	Sg Cp Cp 7:02a	Cp	Cp Aq Aq 9:36a	Aq	Aq P P 1:33p		P A A 8:21p		A	A 6:39a	A T T
Mar	S 9:52a		S Sg Sg 12:57p	Sg	Sg Cp Cp 4:43p	Cp	Cp Aq Aq 9:49p	Aq	Aq P P	P	P A A 5:04a		A T T 3:05p		T
Apr	Cp 10:12p		Cp Aq Aq	Aq	Aq 4:04a		Aq P P 12:13p		P A A 10:37p		A T T 10:52a		T	T G G 11:43p	G C C
May	Aq 9:31a		Aq P P 6:02p		P S S	S 5:00a		S T T 5:22p		T G G 6:19a	G	G 6:16p	C C		C L L
Jn	A 10:46a		A A T T 11:27p		T G G 12:17p		G	G C C 12:12a		C	C L L 10:19a		L V V 5:19p		V Li
Jly	T 5:33a		T T G G 6:10p		G C C 5:57a		C	C L L 3:51p		L V V 11:41p		V Li Li 4:59a		Li	Li
Aug	G 1:05a		G C C 12:27p		C L L 9:45p		L V V 5:05a		V	V Li Li 10:37a		Li S S 2:18p		S Sg Sg 9:23p	Sg C
Sep	L 5:07a		L L V V 11:34a		V Li Li 4:13p		Li S S 7:41p		S Sg Sg 10:29p		Sg Cp Cp 1:08a		Cp	Cp Aq Aq	
Oct	V 8:04p		V Li Li 11:36p		Li S S 1:49a		S Sg Sg 3:53p		Sg Cp Cp 6:46a		Cp Aq Aq 11:04a		Aq P P 5:14p		P A
Nov	Li S S 9:20a		S Sg Sg 10:20a		Sg Cp Cp 10:49a		Cp Aq Aq 12:29p		Aq P P 4:30p		P A A 11:15p		A	A T T 8:25a	
Dec	Sg 8:29p		Sg Cp Cp 8:24p		Cp Aq Aq 10:41p		Aq P P	P	P A A 4:50a		A T T 12:11p		T	T G G 1:42a	

1987

	1	2	3	4	5	6	7	8	9	10	11	12	13	14	15
Jan	Aq 6:54a	Aq	Aq P P 7:37a		P A A 11:52a		A T T 8:14p		T	T G G 7:40a		G C C 8:19p		C	C L 8:46a
Feb	P A A 9:10p		A	A T T 3:54a		T G G 2:24p		G	G C C 2:56a		C L L 3:22p		L	L V V 2:27a	
Mar	P A A 7:38a		A T T 1:12p		T G G 10:27p		G	G C C 12:15a		C L L 10:55p		L	L V V 9:56a		V Li 6:35p
Apr	T 7:17a		T G G 6:34p		G C C 7:05a		C	C L L 6:29p		L V V 3:06a		V	V Li Li 8:42a		Li S S
May	G 2:40a		G C C 3:07p		C L L 3:08a		L V V 12:30p		V Li Li 6:10p		Li S S 8:42p		S Sg Sg 9:37p	Sg Cp
Jn	L 10:57a		L L V V 9:25p		V Li Li 4:07a		Li	Li S S 8:54a		S Sg Sg 7:06a		Sg Cp Cp 6:46a		Cp Aq Aq
Jly	V 4:56a		V V Li Li 1:04p		Li S S 5:06p		S Sg Sg 5:44p		Sg Cp Cp 4:50p		Cp Aq Aq 4:37p		Aq P P 7:01p		P A
Aug	Li S S 8:10p		S 1:48a		S Sg Sg 3:52a		Sg Cp Cp 3:38a		Cp Aq Aq 3:02a		Aq P P 4:10a		P A A 8:39a		A T T
Sep	Sg 12:05p		Sg Cp Cp 1:23p		Cp Aq Aq 1:38p		Aq P P 8:35p		P A A 5:58p		A T T 12:55a		T	T G G 11:23a	G C
Oct	Cp Aq Aq 8:52p		Aq P P 10:40p		P	P A A 12:36a		A T T 3:58a		T G G 10:04a		G C C 7:32p		C	C L 7:35a
Nov	P 8:41a		P A A 1:03p		A T T 7:17p		T G G 4:11a		G	G C C 3:46p		C L L	L	L V V 4:30a	
Dec	A T T 8:06p		T	T G G 3:14a		G C C 12:21p		C L L 11:41p		L	L V V 10:31p		V	V Li Li 12:41a	

1988

	1	2	3	4	5	6	7	8	9	10	11	12	13	14	15
Jan	G 7:17p		G C C 6:48a		C	C L L 7:36p		L V V 8:18a		V	V Li Li 6:40p		Li S S 12:59a		S	S Sg
Feb	C L L 1:07p		L	L V V 1:55a		V Li Li 2:37p		Li	Li S S 1:43a		S Sg Sg 9:37a		Sg Cp Cp 1:37p		Cp Aq 2:26p
Mar	L 8:07a		L V V 8:33p		V Li Li 7:28a		Li	Li S S 4:00p		S Sg Sg 9:32p		Sg Cp Cp 12:09a		Cp	Cp Aq
Apr	V Li Li 3:06a		Li S S 1:27p		S Sg Sg 9:30p		Sg	Sg Cp Cp 3:20a		Cp Aq Aq 7:11a		Aq P P 9:25a		P A A 10:48a	
May	S 3:53a		S	S Sg Sg 8:55a		Sg Cp Cp 12:38p		Cp Aq Aq 3:40p		Aq P P 6:24p		P A A 9:23p		A T T	T
Jn	Sg Cp Cp 3:59p		Cp Aq Aq 6:35p		Aq P P 9:01p		P A A 12:05a		A	A T T 4:03a		T G G 9:15a		G C C 4:20p	
Jly	Cp Aq Aq 2:30a		Aq P P 3:34a		P A A 5:38a		A T T 9:28a		T	T G G C C 3:17p 11:09p			C 9:12a		C L L	
Aug	P A A 12:54p		A T T 3:25p		T G G 8:44p		G	G C C 4:53a		C L L 3:27p		L	L V V 3:46a		V Li 4:53p
Sep	T 3:12a		T G G 10:38a		G C C 9:15p		C L L 9:49a		L	L V V 9:52p		V Li Li 11:08a		Li	Li S S
Oct	G C C 5:39p		C	C L L 5:32a		L V V 4:02p		V 5:04a		V Li Li 4:59p		Li S S 2:59a		S	S Sg Sg
Nov	L 11:03p		L V V 12:05p		V	V Li Li 11:47p		Li S S 9:07p		S	S Sg Sg 4:13p		Sg Cp Cp 9:37p		Cp Aq Aq
Dec	V Li Li 7:57p		Li	Li S S 7:52p		S Sg Sg 4:56p		Sg	Sg Cp Cp 12:08a		Cp Aq Aq 3:26a		Aq P P 6:54a		

Table 1

16	17	18	19	20	21	22	23	24	25	26	27	28	29	30	31

```
A    A T T   T    G G    G C C   C    C L L   L V V   V    V Li Li   Li
     10:14p        11:13a       11:15p        8:48a       3:52p         9:11p

T G G   G    G C C    C L L   L V V   V    V Li Li   Li S
7:18p   7:40a        5:26p   11:59p       4:08a            7:07a

T G G   G C C   C    C L L   L V V   V Li Li   Li S S   S Sg Sg   Sg Cp
3:24a   4:05p        2:39a       9:40a   1:23p     3:06p      4:21p       6:26p

C    C L L   L V V   V Li Li   Li S S   S Sg Sg   Sg Cp Cp   Cp Aq
     11:11a  7:25p   11:51p            1:16a     1:17a       1:42a        4:07a

L    L V V   V Li Li   Li S S   S Sg Sg   Sg C C   C Aq Aq   Aq P P   P A
     3:46a   9:42a     12:03p   11:58a    11:16a   12:01p    3:55p          11:44p

Li   Li S S   S Sg Sg   Sg Cp Cp   Cp Aq Aq   Aq   Aq P P   P A A   A T
     9:37p    10:37p    10:01p     9:41p           12:13a   6:35a      4:55p

S    S Sg Sg   Sg Cp Cp   Cp Aq Aq   Aq P P   P A A   A T T   T G G
     7:35a     8:11a      8:18a      10:00a   3:03p        12:12a    12:20p

Cp   Cp Aq Aq   Aq P P   P    P A A   A T T   T G G   G    G C C   C L
     5:45p      7:53p         12:28a  8:37a   8:01p       8:41a        8:09p

Aq P P   P A A   A T T   T    T G G   G C C   C    C L L   L V
4:28a    9:34a   5:26p        4:14a   4:45p        4:40a   1:58p

A    A T T   T G G   G C C   C L L   L V V   V    V Li Li
     1:36a   12:16p  12:38a  1:03p   11:21p       6:05a

T G G   G    G C C   C L L   L    L V V   V Li Li   Li S S   S Sg
7:27p   7:47a        8:26p        7:47a   4:00p     8:44p    9:09p

G C C   C    C L L   L V V   V    V Li Li   Li S S   S Sg Sg   Sg C C
2:10p   2:45a        2:31p        12:06a   6:07a    8:21a     7:55a
```

Table 2

16	17	18	19	20	21	22	23	24	25	26	27	28	29	30	31

```
L    L V V   V    V Li Li   Li S S   S Sg Sg   Sg Cp Cp   Cp Aq Aq   Aq P P
     8:16p        6:10a     1:31p    5:36p     6:43p      6:18p           6:25p

V Li Li   Li S S   S    S Sg Sg   Sg Cp Cp   Cp Aq Aq   Aq P P
11:45a    7:05p        12:10a     2:58a      4:09a      5:08a

Li   Li   Li S S   S Sg Sg   Sg Cp Cp   Cp Aq Aq   Aq P P   P A A   A T T
     12:50a 2:22p   5:33a     8:49a      11:19a     1:46a    5:13p       10:47p

S Sg Sg   Sg Cp Cp   Cp Aq Aq   Aq P P   P    P A A   A T T   T G G
12:02p    2:22p      4:46p      8:03p        12:42a  7:07a   3:07p

Cp   Cp Aq Aq   Aq   Aq P P   P A A   A T T   T G G   G    G C C   C L
     10:43p         1:25a     6:24a   1:40p   10:56p       10:00a       10:26p

Aq P P   P A A   A T T   T    T G G   G C C   C    C L L   L V
7:55a    11:57a  7:10p        4:55a   4:23p        4:53a   5:53p

A    A    A T T   T G G   G C C   C    C L L   L V V   V    V Li Li
     1:05a  10:33a  10:14p        10:51a       11:26p       11:00a

T G G   G    G C C   C L L   L    L V V   V Li Li   Li   Li S S   S Sg
5:00p   4:20a        4:59p        5:24a   4:36p          1:50a        8:25a

C    C L L   L V V   V Li Li   Li S S   S Sg Sg   Sg Cp Cp
     11:51a  12:14p  10:59p    7:31a    1:50p     6:09p

L    L V V   V    V Li Li   Li S S   S Sg Sg   Sg Cp Cp   Cp Aq Aq   Aq P
     8:07p        6:51a     2:42p    7:58p     11:34p     2:28a          5:20a

V Li Li   Li S S   S    S Sg Sg   Sg Cp Cp   Cp Aq Aq   Aq P P   P A A
3:49p     11:48p       4:17a      6:30a      8:13a      10:41a   2:37p

Li S S   S Sg Sg   Sg Cp Cp   Cp Aq Aq   Aq P P   P A A   A    A T T   T G
9:42a    2:34p     4:08p      4:21p      5:11p    8:06p        1:37a       9:30a
```

Table 3

16	17	18	19	20	21	22	23	24	25	26	27	28	29	30	31

```
Sg   Sg Cp Cp   Cp Aq Aq   Aq P P   P A A   A T T   T G G   G    G C C
     3:16a      3:03a      2:27a    3:32a   7:37a   3:03p        1:12a

Aq   Aq P P   P A A   A T T   T G G   G C C   C L L
     1:45p    1:36p   3:51p   9:43p   7:13a   7:13p

Aq P P   P A A   A T T   T G G   G C C   C    C L L   L V V   V
12:43a   12:46a  2:06a   6:22a   2:28p        1:55a   2:50a

A T T   T G G   G C C   C    C L L   L V V   V    V Li Li   Li S
12:32p  4:11p   11:05p       9:35a   10:17p       10:38a     8:40p

T G G   G C C   C L L   L    L V V   V Li Li   Li   Li S S   S Sg Sg
1:32a   8:06a   5:52p        6:13a   6:50p          5:07a    11:58a

C    C L L   L V V   V    V Li Li   Li S S   S Sg Sg   Sg   Sg Cp Cp
     1:58a   2:04p        2:58a     1:59a    9:19p          1:01a

L V V   V    V Li Li   Li S S   S    S Sg Sg   Sg Cp Cp   Cp Aq Aq   Aq P P
9:18p        10:23a    10:14p       6:43a     11:08a     12:26p          12:24p

Li   Li   Li S S   S Sg Sg   Sg Cp Cp   Cp Aq Aq   Aq P P   P A A   A T T
     5:13a  2:56a   8:40p     11:06p     11:02p     10:30p   11:23p

S Sg Sg   Sg   Sg Cp Cp   Cp Aq Aq   Aq P P   P A A   A T T   T G G
9:26p     4:46a  8:44a     9:52a      9:30a    9:30a        11:44a

Sg Cp Cp   Cp Aq Aq   Aq P P   P A A   A T T   T G G   G C C   C L
10:45a     4:06p      6:59p    7:00p   7:23p   8:56p   2:29a      11:04p

Aq   Aq P P   P A A   A T T   T G G   G C C   C L L   L V
     1:35a    4:13a   6:03a   8:12a   12:20p  7:53p   7:00a

P A A   A T T   T G G   G C C   C    C L L   L V V   V    V Li Li
10:04a  1:12p   4:44p   9:36p        4:58a   3:28p        4:10a
```

```
1989
        1    2    3    4    5    6    7    8    9    10   11   12   13   14   15
Jan    Li   S    S         S  Sg Sg   Sg  Cp  Cp   Cp  Aq  Aq   Aq  P   P    P   A   A    A   T   T
       4:35p              2:13a        8:15a        11:21a       1:32p        3:22p        6:37p
Feb    Sg   Sg  Cp Cp    Cp  Aq Aq   Aq  P   P    P   A   A    A        A   T   T    T   G   G    G   C
       6:31p              9:52p        10:53p       11:19p  12:46a       4:23a        10:41a
Mar    Sg   Sg  Cp Cp    Cp  Aq Aq   Aq  P   P    P   A   A    A   T   T    T   G   G    G   C   C
       3:59a              8:37a        10:00a       9:57a        9:26a        11:17a       4:28p
Apr    Aq   Aq  P   P    P   A   A    A   T   T    T   G   G    G   C   C    C        C   L   L    L   V
       8:38p              8:52p        8:08p        8:32p        11:59p            7:32a        6:40p
May    P    P   A   A    A   T   T    T   G   G    G   C   C    C   L   L    L        L   V   V    V  Li
       6:51a              8:56a        7:04a        9:20a        3:24p        1:31a        2:08p
Jn     T    T   G   G    G   C   C    C   L   L    L        L   V   V    V  Li  Li   Li       Li  S   S
       5:03p              7:18p        12:29a       9:30a             9:32p             10:12a
Jly    G    G   C   C    C   L   L    L   V   V    V        V  Li  Li   Li  S   S    S        S  Sg  Sg
       4:20a              9:38a        6:05p        5:31a        8:10p             5:32a
Aug    L    L        L   V   V    V  Li  Li   Li       Li  S   S    S  Sg  Sg   Sg  Cp  Cp   Cp       Cp Aq
       2:20a        1:29p             8:06a        2:30p        11:17p            5:00a
Sep    V   Li  Li   Li       Li  S   S    S  Sg  Sg   Sg       Sg  Cp  Cp   Cp  Aq  Aq   Aq  P   P    P   A
       8:48p             9:24a        9:52p        8:14a        3:03p        6:08p        6:39p
Oct    Li   S   S    S        S  Sg  Sg   Sg  Cp  Cp   Cp       Cp  Aq  Aq   Aq  P   P    P   A   A    A   T
       3:54p              4:30a        3:46p        12:07a       4:38a        5:42a        4:53a
Nov    Sg   Sg  Cp  Cp   Cp  Aq  Aq   Aq       Aq  P   P    P   A   A    A   T   T    T   G   G    G   C
       9:47p              7:10a        1:20p        4:09p        4:10p        3:19p        3:52p
Dec    Cp   Cp  Aq  Aq   Aq  P   P    P        P   A   A    A   T   T    T   G   G    G   C   C    C   L
       12:43p             7:49p        12:12a       8:00a        8:16a        2:50a        5:42a
```

```
1990
        1    2    3    4    5    6    7    8    9    10   11   12   13   14   15
Jan    Aq   P   P    P   A   A    A   T   T    T   G   G    G   C   C    C   L   L    L   V   V    V
       1:11a              5:57a        9:05a        11:03a       12:53p       4:03p        9:58p
Feb    A    T   T    T   G   G    G   C   C    C        C   L   L    L   V   V    V  Li  Li   Li      Li  S
       2:28p              5:13p        8:26p             12:52a       7:14a        4:10p             3:35a
Mar    T    T   G   G    G   C   C    C   L   L    L   V   V    V        V  Li  Li   Li  S   S
       10:38p             2:03a        7:25a        2:48p             12:10a       11:26a
Apr    G    C   C    C   L   L    L   V   V    V  Li  Li   Li       Li  S   S    S  Sg  Sg   Sg
       7:50a              12:51p       8:43p        6:45a        6:19p        6:49a        7:16p
May    L    L        L   V   V    V  Li  Li   Li       Li  S   S    S  Sg  Sg   Sg       Sg  Cp  Cp   Cp  Aq
       2:19a              12:29p            12:23a       12:57p       1:22a        12:31p
Jn     V   Li  Li   Li       Li  S   S    S  Sg  Sg   Sg       Sg  Cp  Cp   Cp  Aq  Aq   Aq       Aq  P   P
       6:32p             5:22a        7:00p        7:13a        6:10p        3:01a
Jly    Li   S   S    S        S  Sg  Sg   Sg  Cp  Cp   Cp       Cp  Aq  Aq   Aq  P   P    P   A   A    A   T
       1:02p              1:36a        1:40p        12:07a       8:30a        2:37a        6:30p
Aug    Sg   Sg  Cp  Cp   Cp       Cp  Aq  Aq   Aq  P   P    P   A   A    A   T   T    T        T   G   G
       9:09p              7:20a        7:55a        8:14p        11:56p            2:42a
Sep    Cp  Aq  Aq   Aq  P   P    P        P   A   A    A   T   T    T   G   G    G   C   C    C   L   L
       3:52p              11:07p       3:24p        5:56a        8:05a        10:54a       2:53p
Oct    Aq   P   P    P   A   A    A   T   T    T   G   G    G   C   C    C   L   L    L        L   V   V
       8:43a              12:43p       2:07p        2:48p        4:30p        8:17p             2:22a
Nov    A    A   T   T    T   G   G    G   C   C    C   L   L    L   V   V    V  Li  Li   Li      Li  S
       12:32a             12:07a       12:06a       2:25a        7:59a        4:09p             2:40a
Dec    T    G   G    G   C   C    C   L   L    L   V   V    V  Li  Li   Li       Li  S   S    S  Sg  Sg   Sg
       11:23a             10:26a       11:01a       2:40p        10:01p            10:29a       8:45p
```

```
1991
        1    2    3    4    5    6    7    8    9    10   11   12   13   14   15
Jan    C    L   L    L   V   V    V        V  Li  Li   Li  S   S    S        S  Sg  Sg   Sg  Cp  Cp   Cp
       9:55p              11:58p            5:34a        3:00p             3:07a        4:01p
Feb    V    V  Li  Li   Li  S   S    S        S  Sg  Sg   Sg  Cp  Cp   Cp       Cp  Aq  Aq   Aq  P   P
       3:03p              11:02p            10:24a       11:17p       11:17a       9:00p
Mar    V    V  Li  Li   Li  S   S    S  Sg  Sg   Sg       Sg  Cp  Cp   Cp  Aq  Aq   Aq       Aq  P   P
       1:04a              8:09a        6:36p        7:15a        7:32p        5:12a
Apr    S    S        S  Sg  Sg   Sg  Cp  Cp   Cp       Cp  Aq  Aq   Aq  P   P    P   A   A    A        A   T
       3:00a              3:20p        4:01a        2:19p        8:50p             12:06a
May    Sg   Sg  Cp  Cp   Cp  Aq  Aq   Aq       Aq  P   P    P   A   A    A   T   T    T   G   G
       10:55p             11:52a       11:05p       6:36a        10:08a       11:03a
Jn     Cp  Aq  Aq   Aq       Aq  P   P    P   A   A    A   T   T    T   G   G    G   C   C    C   L   L
       6:42p              6:37a        3:26a        8:14p        9:37p        9:17p        9:11p
Jly    Aq   P   P    P   A   A    A        A   T   T    T   G   G    G   C   C    C   L   L    L   V   V
       12:52p             10:34p            4:53a        7:43a        8:04a        8:26a        9:12a
Aug    A    A   T   T    T   G   G    G   C   C    C   L   L    L   V   V    V  Li  Li   Li      Li  S
       11:33a             3:55p        5:48p        6:10p        6:36p        8:53p             2:34a
Sep    G    G   C   C    C   L   L    L   V   V    V  Li  Li   Li  S   S    S  Sg  Sg   Sg
       1:20a              3:14a        4:36a        6:52a        11:43a       8:15p
Oct    C    C   L   L    L   V   V    V  Li  Li   Li  S   S    S        S  Sg  Sg   Sg  Cp  Cp   Cp
       9:54a              12:46p       4:01p        9:01p        4:59a             4:11p
Nov    V    V  Li  Li   Li  S   S    S  Sg  Sg   Sg       Sg  Cp  Cp   Cp  Aq  Aq   Aq       Aq  P
       11:13p             5:10a        1:22p        12:17a       1:07p        1:34a
Dec    Li   Li  S   S    S  Sg  Sg   Sg  Cp  Cp   Cp       Cp  Aq  Aq   Aq  P   P    P   A   A
       11:34a             8:33p        7:42a        8:28p        9:20a        8:07a
```

16	17	18	19	20	21	22	23	24	25	26	27	28	29	30	31
T	G 10:50p	G	C 4:58a	C	L 1:03p	L	V 11:33p	V	Li 12:02p	Li	Li	S 12:50a	S	Sg 11:31a	Sg
C	C	L 7:34p	L	L	V 6:35a	V	V	Li 7:06p	Li	Li	S 7:58a	S	S	Sg 7:58a	Sg
C	C	L 1:14a	L	V 12:40p	V	Li 1:25a	Li	S 2:11p	S	Sg 1:55a	Sg	Cp 11:26a	Cp	Aq 5:46p	Aq
V	V	Li 7:32a	Li	Li	S 8:14p	S	S	Sg 7:39p	Sg	Cp 5:16p	Cp	Aq 12:34a	Aq	P 5:04a	P
Li	Li	S 2:49a	S	Sg 1:53p	Sg	Cp 10:55p	Cp	Aq 6:02a	Aq	P 11:14a	P	A 2:26p	A	T 4:00p	T
S	S	Sg 9:13p	Sg	Cp 5:42a	Cp	Aq 11:58a	Aq	P 4:37p	P	A 8:07p	A	T 10:46p	T	G 1:09a	G
Sg	Cp 2:02p	Cp	Aq 7:36p	Aq	P 11:08p	P	A 1:41a	A	T 4:11a	T	G 7:16a	G	C 11:33a	C	L 5:42p
Aq	Aq	P 7:46a	P	A 9:00a	A	T 10:11a	T	G 12:40p	G	C 5:14p	C	L 12:12a	L	V 9:30a	V
A	A	T 6:23p	T	G 7:17p	G	C 10:05p	C	L 5:45a	L	V 3:33p	V	Li 3:16a	Li	Li	
T	T	G 4:20a	G	C 6:10a	C	L 11:48a	L	V 9:16p	V	Li 9:12a	Li	S 9:57p	S	Sg 10:24a	Sg
C	C	L 7:46p	L	V 3:55a	V	Li 3:26p	Li	S 4:14a	S	Sg 4:31p	Sg	Cp 3:27a	Cp	Cp	
L	L	V 12:20p	V	Li 10:46p	Li	S 11:19a	S	Sg 11:38p	Sg	Cp 10:11a	Cp	Aq 6:39p	Aq	Aq	

16	17	18	19	20	21	22	23	24	25	26	27	28	29	30	31
V	Li 7:58a	Li	S 7:17p	S	Sg 5:45a	Sg	Cp 6:28p	Cp	Aq 2:26p	Aq	P 7:52a	P	A 11:35a	A	A
S	S	Sg 4:08p	Sg	Cp 3:31a	Cp	Aq 11:53a	Aq	P 4:50p	P	A 7:17p	A	T 8:44p	T	T	
S	Sg 1:57p	Sg	Cp 12:02p	Cp	Aq 9:32p	Aq	P 9:00a	P	A 3:16a	A	T 5:17a	T	G 5:43a	G	
Cp	Cp	Aq 5:54a	Aq	P 12:58p	P	A 3:59p	A	T 4:04p	T	G 3:13p	G	C 3:40p	C	L 7:09a	L
Aq	Aq	P 2:55p	P	A 1:32a	A	T 2:43a	T	G 2:01a	G	C 1:35a	C	L 3:30a	L	V 9:09a	V
P	A 8:56a	A	T 11:44a	T	G 12:15p	G	C 12:10p	C	L 1:26p	L	V 5:43p	V	Li 1:48a	Li	
T	T	G 8:33p	G	C 9:45p	C	L 11:30p	L	V 3:18a	V	Li 10:19a	Li	S 8:40p	S	Sg 9:01a	Sg
G	C 5:13a	C	L 8:12a	L	V 12:34p	V	Li 7:17p	Li	S 4:57a	S	Sg 4:58p	Sg	Cp 5:24a	Cp	
L	V 8:19p	V	Li 3:35a	Li	S 1:07a	S	Sg 12:53a	Sg	Cp 1:37p	Cp	Aq 12:55a	Aq	Aq		
V	Li 10:27a	Li	S 8:25p	S	Sg 8:10a	Sg	Cp 9:04p	Cp	Aq 9:15a	Aq	P 6:23p	P	A 11:15p	A	
S	S	Sg 2:40p	Sg	Cp 3:32a	Cp	Aq 4:08p	Aq	P 2:33a	P	A 9:07a	A	T 11:38a	T	T	
Sg	Cp 9:30a	Cp	Aq 10:00p	Aq	P 8:49a	P	A 4:46p	A	T 9:10p	T	G 10:27p	G	C 10:03p	C	

16	17	18	19	20	21	22	23	24	25	26	27	28	29	30	31
Cp	Aq 4:05a	Aq	P 2:24p	P	A 10:28p	A	T 4:02a	T	G 7:07a	G	C 8:24a	C	L 9:04a	L	V 10:45a
P	P	A 4:12a	A	T 9:25a	T	G 1:11p	G	C 3:37p	C	L 6:13p	L	V 8:51p	V	V	
P	A 11:38a	A	T 3:41p	T	G 6:38p	G	C 9:38p	C	L 12:44a	L	V 4:42a	V	Li 9:50a	Li	S 5:02p
T	T	G 1:42a	G	C 3:18a	C	L 6:05a	L	V 10:30a	V	Li 4:37p	Li	S 12:35a	S	Sg 10:43a	Sg
G	C 11:15a	C	L 12:31p	L	V 4:01p	V	Li 10:09p	Li	S 6:42a	S	Sg 5:22p	Sg	Cp 5:41a	Cp	
L	V 11:04p	V	Li 4:02a	Li	S 12:19p	S	Sg 11:17p	Sg	Cp 11:50a	Cp	Aq 12:48a	Aq	Aq		
V	Li 11:35a	Li	S 6:42p	S	Sg 5:17a	Sg	Cp 5:56p	Cp	Aq 6:50a	Aq	P 6:36p	P	A 4:21a		
S	Sg 12:12p	Sg	Cp 12:35a	Cp	Aq 1:28p	Aq	P 12:52a	P	A 10:02a	A	T 5:01p	T	G 10:03p		
Sg	Cp 8:05a	Cp	Aq 8:59p	Aq	P 8:21a	P	A 4:57p	A	T 11:00p	T	G 3:26a	G	C 6:59a		
Cp	Aq 5:05a	Aq	P 4:54p	P	A 1:34a	A	T 4:57p	T	G 10:10a	G	C 12:38p	C	L 3:21p	L	V 6:48p
P	P	A 11:09a	A	T 4:50p	T	G 7:23p	G	C 8:23p	C	L 9:38p	L	V 12:13a	V	Li 4:48a	
A	A	T 3:11a	T	G 6:22a	G	C 6:55a	C	L 6:39a	L	V 7:24a	V	Li 10:38a	Li	S 5:04p	S

1992

	1	2	3	4	5	6	7	8	9	10	11	12	13	14	15
Jan	S Sg Sg		Sg Cp Cp	Cp	Cp	Cp Aq Aq		Aq P P		P	P A A		A T T		T G
	2:31a		2:10p			3:00a		3:53p			3:23a		12:01a		4:56p
Feb	Cp	Cp Aq Aq		Aq P P		P	P A A		A T T		T	T G G		G C C	
	9:10a			9:52p			9:16a		6:37p			1:09a		4:32a	
Mar	Aq	Aq	Aq P P		P	P A A		A	A T T		T G G		G C C		C L L
	4:12a			5:08p			12:06a		7:04a		1:51p		2:21p		
Apr	P A A		A	A T T		T G G		G C C		C L L		L V V		V	V Li
	10:05p			6:19a		12:34p		5:19p		8:47p		11:10p			1:11a
May	A T T		T G G		G C C		C	C L L		L V V		V Li Li		Li S S	
	2:10p		7:29p		11:10p			2:08a		4:57a		8:06a		12:16p	
Jn	G	G C C		C L L		L V V		V Li Li		Li S S		S	S Sg Sg		Sg
	6:59a		8:36a		10:29a		1:34p		6:28p			1:30a		10:51a	
Jly	C L L		L V V		V Li Li		Li S S		S	S Sg Sg		Sg	Sg Cp Cp		Cp	Cp Aq
	5:16p		5:38p		7:28p		11:59p			7:10a			5:17p		5:04a
Aug	V	V Li Li		Li S S		S Sg Sg		Sg Cp Cp		Cp	Cp Aq Aq		Aq P P		P
	3:18a		6:17a		12:58p		11:01p			11:07a		11:52p			
Sep	S	S Sg Sg		Sg	Sg Cp Cp		Cp	Cp Aq Aq		Aq P P		P	P A A		A	A T
	7:51p		5:07a		5:09p		5:57a		6:03p		4:48a			
Oct	Sg	Sg Cp Cp		Cp	Cp Aq Aq		Aq	Aq P P		P A A		A T T		T G G	
	12:30p		11:54p		12:39p		12:37a		10:49a		7:09p			
Nov	Cp Aq Aq		Aq P P		P	P A A		A T T		T	T G G		G C C		C L
	7:33a		8:14a		8:20a		6:20p			1:50a		7:20a		11:24a	
Dec	Aq P P		P A A		A	A T T		T G G		G C C		C L L		L V V	
	4:24a		4:50p			3:17a		10:38a		3:06p		5:48p		7:57p	

1993

	1	2	3	4	5	6	7	8	9	10	11	12	13	14	15
Jan	A	A T T		T G G		G C C		C	C L L		L V V		V Li Li		Li S
	12:31p		8:43p		1:11a			2:50a		3:21a		4:31a		7:43a	
Feb	T G G		G V V		V L L		L V V		V Li Li		Li S S		S Sg Sg		Sg
	6:16a		11:57a		1:52p		1:30p		12:59p		12:24p		7:09p		
Mar	G	G C C		C	C L L		L V V		V Li Li		Li S S		S	S Sg Sg		Sg
	9:17p		12:41p		12:53p	11:47p		11:40p			2:34a		9:29a	
Apr	C L L		L V V		V Li Li		Li S S		S Sg Sg		Sg Cp Cp		Cp	Cp	Cp Aq Aq	Aq
	9:22a		11:11a		10:55a		10:33a		12:11p		5:25p			2:37a
May	V	V Li Li		Li S S		S Sg Sg		Sg Cp Cp		Cp	Cp Aq Aq		Aq P P		P
	8:21p		8:58p		10:35p		2:52a		10:45a		9:51p			
Jn	Li S S		S Sg Sg		Sg Cp Cp		Cp	Cp Aq Aq		Aq	Aq P P		P A A		A	A T
	5:23a		8:02a		12:27p		7:40p			5:58a		6:15p		6:20a
Jly	Sg	Sg Cp Cp		Cp	Cp Aq Aq		Aq P P		P	P A A		A T T		T	T G
	8:49p		4:15a		4:10a		2:12a			2:38p		1:08a	
Aug	Cp Aq Aq		Aq P P		P	P A A		A T T		T	T G G		G C C		C L
	11:37a		9:44p		9:40a		10:23a			9:48a		5:47p		9:44p	
Sep	P	P A A		A	A T T		T G G		G	G C C		C L L		L V V	
	4:22p		5:10a		5:17p		2:38a		7:52a		9:21a			
Oct	A	A T T		T G G		G	G C C		C L L		L V V		V Li Li		Li S
	11:14a		11:28p		9:43a		4:35p		7:37p		7:48p		7:02p	
Nov	T G G		G C C		C L L		L	L V V		V Li Li		Li S S		S Sg Sg		Sg
	5:14a		3:27p		11:07p		3:48a		5:43a		6:01a		6:21a	
Dec	C	C C L L		L V V		V Li Li		Li S S		S Sg Sg		Sg Cp Cp		Cp	Cp Aq
		4:34a		9:44a		1:04p		3:05p		4:20p		7:07p		11:52p

1994

	1	2	3	4	5	6	7	8	9	10	11	12	13	14	15
Jan	L V V		V L L		L S S		S	S Sg Sg		Sg Cp Cp		Cp Aq Aq		Aq P P	
	3:16p		6:32p		9:30p		12:35a		4:17a		9:26a		5:05p		
Feb	Li	Li S S		S Sg Sg		Sg Cp Cp		Cp	Cp Aq Aq		Aq P P		P A A		A
	2:50a		6:15a		11:03a		5:17p		1:24a		11:50a			
Mar	Li S S		S Sg Sg		Sg Cp Cp		Cp	Cp Aq Aq		Aq	Aq P P		P A A		A	A T
	9:44a		11:55a		4:25p		11:16p			8:10a		7:00p		7:28a
Apr	Sg Cp Cp		Cp	Cp Aq Aq		Aq	Aq P P		P	P A A		A T T		T G G	
	10:38p		4:46a		1:52p		1:10p		1:49p		2:49p			
May	Cp Aq Aq		Aq P P		P	P A A		A T T		T	T G G		G C C		C
	11:35a		7:48p		7:02a		7:51p			8:44a		8:48p		
Jn	P	P A A		A	A T T		T G G		G	G C C		C L L		L V V	
	1:32p		2:15a		3:04p		2:23a		11:30a		6:17p			
Jly	A	A T T		T G G		G	G C C		C L L		L V V		V Li Li	
	9:24a		10:13p		9:18a		5:44p		11:49p		4:16a			
Aug	T G G		G C C		C	C L L		L V V		V Li Li		Li S S		S Sg Sg	
	6:06a		5:23p		1:32a		6:43a		10:08a		12:57p		3:34p		
Sep	C	C L L		L V V		V Li Li		Li S S		S Sg Sg		Sg	Sg Cp Cp		Cp Aq
	10:38a		3:54p		5:58p		7:27p		9:26p		12:45a		5:43a	
Oct	L	L V V		V Li Li		Li S S		S Sg Sg		Sg Cp Cp		Cp	Cp Aq Aq		Aq P P
	1:40a		3:57a		4:23a		4:48a		6:45a		11:10a		6:19p	
Nov	Li	Li S S		S Sg Sg		Sg Cp Cp		Cp Aq Aq		Aq	Aq P P		P A A		A T
	3:20p		2:47p		3:03p		5:49p			12:05a		9:45a		9:45p
Dec	S	S Sg Sg		Sg Cp Cp		Cp Aq Aq		Aq P P		P A A		A	A T T		T G
	2:14a		1:43a		2:52a		7:25a		4:04p			3:57a		5:01p

```
     16    17    18    19    20    21    22    23    24    25    26    27    28    29    30    31

G     G C C   C L L   L V V   V Li Li  Li S S   S S Sg Sg   S  S Sg Sg  Sg Cp Cp
6:27p        5:58p        5:23p       6:43p        11:55p         8:21a          8:08p

C L L   L  V V   V Li Li  Li  S S   S Sg Sg   Sg Cp Cp   Cp Aq
5:16a       4:48a        5:05a       8:12a        3:27p         2:34a         3:35p

L  V V   V Li Li  Li  S S   S   S Sg Sg   Sg Cp Cp   Cp Aq Aq   Aq   Aq P P
3:14p       3:56p        6:21p       12:14a       10:09a        10:45p             11:24a

Li   Li S S   S Sg Sg   Sg Cp Cp   Cp   Cp Aq Aq   Aq  P P   P    P A A
4:11a        9:41a        6:41p       6:39a        7:21p         6:14a

S Sg Sg   Sg   Sg Cp Cp   Cp Aq Aq   Aq   Aq P P   P A A   A T T   T G
6:23p        3:14a        2:44p       3:26a        2:53p         11:17p        4:20a

Cp   Cp Aq Aq   Aq   Aq P P   P A A   A   A T T   T G G   G C C
10:20a       11:01a       11:04p      8:29a        2:15p         4:43p

Aq   Aq P P   P   P A A   A T T   T G G   G   G C C   C L L   L V
5:45p        6:08a        4:37p       11:45p       3:09a         3:40a        3:02a

P A A   A T T   T   T G G   G C C   C L L   L V V   V Li Li  Li S
12:12p       11:11p       7:37a       12:37p       2:16p         1:47p        1:11p       2:39p

T   T G G   G C C   C L L   L   L V V   V Li Li  Li S S   S Sg
1:41p        8:00p        11:20p      12:09a       12:56a        12:45a       4:34a

T   T C C   C L L   L V V   V Li Li  Li S S   S Sg Sg   Sg Cp Cp   Cp
1:37a        6:02a        8:28a       9:40a        11:05a        2:30p        9:19p

L   L V V   V Li Li  Li S S   S   S Sg Sg   Sg Cp Cp   Cp Aq Aq   Aq
2:29p        5:04p        7:53a       12:02a       6:39a         4:20p

V Li Li  Li   Li S S   S Sg Sg   Sg Cp Cp   Cp   Cp Aq Aq   Aq P P   P   P A
10:34p       2:21a        7:43a       3:05p        12:44a        12:29p        1:08a
```

```
     16    17    18    19    20    21    22    23    24    25    26    27    28    29    30    31

S   S Sg Sg   Sg Cp Cp   Cp   Cp Aq Aq   Aq P P   P    P A A   A T T   T
1:31p        9:47p        8:01a       7:48p        8:29a         8:38p

Sg Cp Cp   Cp Aq Aq   Aq   Aq P P   P A A   A   A T T   T G
3:21a        2:06p        2:13a       2:51p        3:12a         1:53p

Co   Cn An An   An   An P P   P A A   A   A T T   T G G   G C C
7:53p        8:12a        8:52p       9:00a        7:49p         4:15a

Aq P P   P   P A A   A T T   T   T G G   G C C   C L L   L V
2:33        3:15a        3:09p       1:28a        9:46a         3:40p        7:01p

P A A   A T T   T   T G G   G C C   C L L   L   L V V   V Li Li
10:25a       10:17a       8:08a       3:39p        9:04p         12:47a       3:19a

T   T G G   G C C   C   C L L   L V V   V Li Li  Li S S   S Sg
4:13p        11:00p       3:27a       6:19a        8:46a         11:38a       3:29p

G   G C C   C L L   L V V   V Li Li  Li S S   S Sg Sg   Sg   Sg Cp Cp
8:09a        11:48a       1:25p       2:40p        5:01p         9:14p        3:28p

L   L V V   V Li Li  Li S S   S   S Sg Sg   Sg Cp Cp   Cp Aq Aq   Aq   Aq P
10:42p       10:36p       11:28p      2:46a        8:59a         5:43p        4:19a

V Li Li  Li S S   S Sg Sg   Sg Cp Cp   Cp Aq Aq   Aq   Aq P P   P A A
8:45a        8:15a        9:54a       2:55p        11:20p        10:14a       10:30p

S   S Sg Sg   Sg Cp Cp   Cp   Cp Aq Aq   Aq P P   P   P A A   A   A T T
7:24p        10:43p       5:50a       4:18p        4:40a         4:21p

Sg Cp Cp   Cp Aq Aq   Aq   Aq P P   P   P A A   A   A T T   G G   G C
8:35a        2:09p        11:28p      11:31a       12:15a        11:49a       9:18p

Aq   Aq   Aq P P   P A A   A   A T T   T G G   G   G C C   C L L
8:00a        7:20p        8:06a       7:47p        4:47a         11:00a
```

```
     16    17    18    19    20    21    22    23    24    25    26    27    28    29    30    31

P   P A A   A T T   T   T G G   G C C   C L L   L V V   V   V Li
3:43a        4:23p        4:36a       1:56p        7:39p         10:40p               12:35a

A T T   T G G   G C C   C   C L L   L V V   V Li Li
12:21a       1:06p        11:28p      5:49a        8:28a         9:07a

T   T   T G G   G C C   C L L   L V V   V Li Li  Li S S   S Sg Sg
8:30p        7:55a        3:40p       7:15p        7:47p         7:16p        7:42p

G C C   C L L   L   L V V   V Li Li  Li S S   S Sg Sg   Sg Cp Cp
2:42p        11:46p       4:59a       6:41a        6:19a         5:49a        7:06a

C L L   L V V   V Li Li  Li S S   S Sg Sg   Sg Cp Cp   Cp Aq Aq   Aq   Aq P
5:59a        12:32p       3:55p       4:52p        4:44p         4:18p        8:20p              3:04a

V Li Li  Li S S   S   S Sg Sg   Sg Cp Cp   Cp Aq Aq   Aq P P   P A A
10:49p       1:21a        2:33a       3:38a        6:11a         11:45a       9:08p

Li S S   S Sg Sg   Sg Cp Cp   Cp Aq Aq   Aq P P   P    P A A   A T T   T
7:36a        10:10a       12:31p      3:29p        8:57p         5:32a        5:14p

Sg Cp Cp   Cp Aq Aq   Aq   Aq P P   P A A   A   A T T   T G G   G   G C
7:19p        11:35p       5:28a       1:56p        1:14a         2:08p        2:01a

Aq   Aq P P   P A A   A   A T T   T G G   G   G C C   C L L
12:32p       9:31p        8:48p       9:42p        10:13a        7:56p

P   P A A   A T T   T   T G G   G C C   C   C L L   L V V   V Li
3:57a        3:35p        4:29a       5:16p        4:06a         11:22a       2:47p

T   T G G   G C C   C   C L L   L V V   V Li Li  Li S
10:42a       10:22p       10:34a      7:10p        12:23a        2:22a

G   G   G C C   C L L   L   L V V   V Li Li  Li S S   S Sg Sg   Sg Cp
5:26a        4:14p        1:02a       7:28a        11:18a        12:47p       12:58p
```

1995

	1	2	3	4	5	6	7	8	9	10	11	12	13	14	15
Jan	Cp	Cp Aq 1:40p	Aq	Aq P P 4:50p	P	P A A 11:57p	A	A T T 10:59a	T	T G G 11:58p	G	G	G	G C C 12:21p	C
Feb	Aq P P 3:06a	P	P A A 9:13a	A	A T T 7:10p	T	T	T G G 7:45a	G	G C C 8:18p	C	C	C L L 6:32a	L	L V 1:53p
Mar	P	P A A 6:31p	A	A T T 3:51a	T	T G G 3:29p	G	G	G C C 4:41a	C	C L L 3:29p	L	L V V 10:55p	V	
Apr	A T T 12:00p	T	T G G 11:50p	G	G	G C C 12:41p	C	C	C L L 12:17p	L	L V V 8:40a	V	V Li Li 1:21p	Li S 3:14p	
May	T G G 6:54a	G	G C C 7:46p	C	C	C L L 7:56a	L	L V V 5:34p	V	V Li Li 11:31p	Li	Li S S 1:54a	S	S Sg 1:59a	
Jn	C	C L L 2:18p	L	L	L V V 12:47a	V	V Li Li 8:14a	Li	Li S S 12:04p	S	S Sg Sg 12:51p	Sg	Sg Cp Cp 12:06p	Cp	Cp Aq 11:53a
Jly	L	L V V 6:36a	V	V Li Li 2:56p	Li	Li S S 8:20p	S	S Sg Sg 10:39p	Sg	Sg Cp Cp 10:44p	Cp	Cp Aq 10:22p	Aq	Aq P P 11:38p	
Aug	Li	Li	Li S S 2:30a	S S Sg 6:15a	Sg	Sg Cp Cp 7:53a	Cp	Cp Aq 8:29a	Aq	Aq P P 9:47a	P	P A A 1:42p	A	A T 9:26p	
Sep	S Sg Sg 11:58a	Sg	Sg Cp Cp 2:46p	Cp	Cp Aq 4:48p	Aq	Aq P P 7:09p	P	P A A 11:15p	A	A	A 6:22a		4:49p	T G G
Oct	Cp	Cp Aq 11:00p	Aq	Aq	Aq P P 2:36a	P	P A A 5:42a	A	A T T 3:06p	T	T	T G G 1:11a	G	G C C 1:21p	
Nov	Aq P P 8:18a	P	P A A 2:22p	A	A T T 10:36p	T	T	T G G 8:56a	G	G C C 8:58p	C	C	C L L 9:38a	L	L V 9:03p
Dec	A	A	A T T 7:41a	T	T G G 3:36p	G	G C C 3:45a	C	C	C L L 4:25p	L	L	L V V 4:27a	V	V Li 2:10p

16	17	18	19	20	21	22	23	24	25	26	27	28	29	30	31
C L 10:27p	L	L	L V 6:40a	V	V Li 12:55p	Li	Li S 5:23p	S	S Sg 8:38p	Sg	Sg Cp 10:27p	Cp	Cp	Cp Aq 12:04a	Aq
V	V Li 7:01p	Li	Li S 10:56p	S	S	S Sg 2:14a	Sg	Sg Cp 5:12a	Cp	Cp Aq 8:15a	Aq	Aq P 12:17p			
V	V Li 3:19a	Li	Li S 5:53a	S	S Sg 7:58a	Sg	Sg Cp 10:32a	Cp	Cp Aq 2:11p	Aq	Aq P 7:19p	P	P	P A 2:27a	A
S	S Sg 3:52a	Sg	Sg Cp 4:55p	Cp	Cp Aq 7:39p	Aq	Aq	Aq P 12:52a	P	P A 8:42a	A	A T 6:54p	T	T	
Sg	Sg Cp 1:37a	Cp	Cp Aq 2:40a	Aq	Aq P 6:41a	P	P A 12:14p	A	A T 12:47a	T	T G 1:08p	G	G	G C 2:00a	C
Aq	Aq P 2:14p	P	P A 8:30p	A	A	A T 6:36a	T	T G 4:03p	G	G	G C 7:57a	C	C	C L 8:03a	
P	P A 4:24a	A	A T 1:21p	T	T	T G 1:24a	G	G C 2:17p	C	C	C L 2:08a	L	L V 12:13p	V	V Li 8:24p
T	T	T G 8:41a	G	G C 9:25p	C	C	C L 9:14a	L	L V 6:51p	V	V Li 2:16a	Li	Li	Li S 7:52a	S
G	G C 5:17a	C	C L 5:20p	L	L	L V 3:02a	V	V Li 9:51a	Li	Li S 2:21p	S	S Sg 5:31p	Sg	Sg Cp 8:11p	
C	C L 1:47a	L	L V 5:19a	V	V Li 7:16p	Li	Li S 11:08p	S	S	S Sg 12:57a	Sg	Sg Cp 2:16a	Cp	Cp Aq 4:24a	Aq
V	V	V Li 5:19a	Li	Li S 9:41a	S	S Sg 10:57a	Sg	Sg Cp 10:49a	Cp	Cp Aq 11:16a	Aq	Aq P 2:00p	P	P A 7:52p	
Li	Li S 8:08p	S	S Sg 10:14p	Sg	Sg Cp 9:47p	Cp	Cp Aq 8:53p	Aq	Aq P 9:46p	P	P	P A 2:07a	A	A T 10:22a	T

FASCINATING BOOKS
OF SPIRITUALITY
AND PSYCHIC DIVINATION

THE DICTIONARY OF MIND AND SPIRIT
compiled by Donald Watson
71792-1/$12.50 US

SECRETS OF SHAMANISM:
TAPPING THE SPIRIT POWER
WITHIN YOU
by Jose Stevens, Ph.D. and Lena S. Stevens
75607-2/$4.50 US/$5.50 Can

TAROT IN TEN MINUTES
by R.T. Kaser
76689-2/$10.00 US/$12.00 Can

Coming Soon

THE LOVERS' TAROT
by Robert Mueller, Ph.D., and Signe E. Echols, M.S.,
with Sandra A. Thomson
76886-0/$11.00 US/$13.00 Can